I0754230

THE HUNTER-NATURALIST.

ROMANCE OF SPORTING;

OR,

WILD SCENES AND WILD HUNTERS.

BY C. W. WEBBER,

AUTHOR OF

"SHOT IN THE EYE," "OLD HICKS THE GUIDE," "CHARLES WINTERFIELD PAPERS,"
"GOLD MINES OF THE GILA," ETC. ETC.

PHILADELPHIA:
J. B. LIPPINCOTT & CO.
1856.

INTRODUCTION.

THE first volume of the HUNTER-NATURALIST is merely introductory to what I propose to make, in every sense, a "progressive" series of seven volumes.

My cherished object in this undertaking is, to introduce within the general scope of Polite Literature, a popular Natural History: upon the production of which I have so brought to bear the latest discoveries of Science, in the application of mechanical forces to pictorial illustration, as to cheapen all their cost without any deterioration of artistic value; and bring the essential spirit of what have been heretofore as sealed books, from their excessive costliness, within the reach of the People.

Then, again, what I mean by "popular" is to be found in a regard of the highest sense of this vulgarized and misused term in contrast with that of the scholastic use of "technical"—a work belonging rather to the general literature than technical science of Natural History—treating of its facts as well as cognate associations. A work, indeed, aiming to be as gay as it is grave—as fanciful as it is profound—as theoretical as accurate—as full of flesh and blood as of philosophy—as human as it is transcendental—as rhapsodically intoxicate as the hale air and blithe sunshine out-of-doors can make it—and just sufficiently spiced with "learning" not to make one "mad." A work in which the Animal Kingdom shall illustrate the Spiritual, and the Spiritual the Animal, as well. A work in which Bird and Beast shall be humanized to Man through Nature, and Man shown to have been inhumanized to Beast and Bird through Society—which shall rebuke fanaticism for its ignorance of natural laws, while it shall plead against wantonness with our race for reconciliation and for mercy to the humblest of God's creatures;—in a word, which shall endeavor always, and in every country, to present the Human Actor with the natural scene—the hunter with the hunted—and the Hunter-Naturalist, placed amidst his chosen accessories, however remote, whether of climate, individual action and adventure, or the living and characteristic objects of his pursuit.

And who is this Hunter-Naturalist? I answer, something of the Primitive Hunter and modern Field-Naturalist combined. The name best defines itself—since *Hunter*-Naturalist implies at once a rugged and freebooter intrusion into the realms of Nature, in which the nice mail of Science has exchanged its glitter and its polish for the greasy, powder-blackened, blood-stained buckskins of the rough, earnest wilderness.

While pretending to no dainty refinements of technical accuracy, if his clear eye, aided by his stout limbs, explores, discovers and assists to glorify, through art and thought, the wide fields of Natural Science, I see no good reason why his pale Brother of the Closet should sneer at him if he forgets his Latin in a "stampede," or spells the jaw-cracking name of a genus wrong, when his notes are often written, as much by the flashes of the covering storm, or the smouldering light of a half-drowned fire, as by honest sun light.

Familiar with Nature in all her modes and moods, the Hunter-Naturalist is he who being accustomed to know her through the medium of his own senses rather than books, should only be held responsible, in a scientific sense, for what he himself has felt, seen, tasted, smelt, heard, and thought, out in unchallenged communion with the secrets of his great Mother. His observations then are essentially his own.

They but constitute one man's impressions of Nature, and convey an individual method of expressing them, which may be as reliable in the facts presented,—to say the least of it,—as if they had been drained, diluted, altered and amended through the musty pages of an hundred folios.

Not that I would presume by any means to arrogate for

the Hunter-Naturalist, even under my own comprehensive definition of his mission, any independence of his pale Brother, so far as his relations to absolute science are concerned. His individual observations would soon become, to the stern accuracy of practical classification, more crude than savage myths; and his deductions vaguer than the shadows of a day-dream—but that when submitted to this colder, more learned, and deliberate analysis, his "facts" and his "discoveries" have been inexorably technicalized.

Yet from my earliest childhood I have felt individually wronged when constantly compelled to turn from the dry, inert and formal methods of "*the Books*," to the gay, suggestive or subtile treatment of the Goldsmiths, Huberts and St. Pierres, who have spoken so successfully for the People, the charmed "sesame" of Science—or else in hopeless sense of the comparatively narrowed artificialities of each, have thrown myself back, with a calmed and steadied enthusiasm, upon the devouter study of those green and living pages of the Natural World, which have never yet failed me in their truth.

Thus in assuming my position with regard to the method of treating the subjects of Natural History, to be observed in this work, the whole matter has resolved itself with me into the simple question whether "lion-heart" and "eagle-eye" shall be banished from heroic poetry, because they lack the learned prefixes of *Aquillæ* and *Leonis*—or sentimental rhymes resign all images of "plaintive Philomels," "cooing Doves," and "Gazelle eyes," because they are not defined to the people according to the "dead letter" of Museum catalogues?—or, indeed, whether it be vitally essential to the general purposes of human enlightenment, that "all the world" should become strictly technical Naturalists, in the scientific sense, before the many who possess an eye for the Beautiful, an ear for its language, a spiritual recognition of its unities, and heart for the joy it brings, can be admitted to its presence?

It is thus the feeling has continued to grow with my growth, and strengthen with my strength, that the Literature of Natural History has been too much circumscribed within the mere formulas of Scientific utility to meet the mental requisitions of the period in its text, or the practical demand for cheapness in its illustration, which the rapid progress of discovery in this department clearly demands! I have, therefore, in bringing this enterprise to a head, consistently acted with an early conceived purpose, that so far as the devotion of individual energies could go, the General Mind should no longer be thus rudely shut off from the contemplation of themes which, in their free and legitimate presentation, are the most healthful, refreshing and ennobling! I speak this in no arrogance, for of such I have no sense—but of a collected purpose.

I have remarked that this first Volume is put forward as merely an introductory to the Series. My object has been to present my Reader at once to the Hunter-Naturalist in that broad and comprehensive meaning of the character which it implies to me. The Narrative and Sketchy form into which I have moulded this Volume, is to continue a distinctive feature of the Series. The wild creature and its Human peer must go together in our treatment—the one re-acts upon and modifies the other; let us exhibit the passions and the life of both. Therefore, in each successive volume, whether it be the Wild Indian and his Buffalo—the Trapper and his Beaver—the buck-skinned Nomad of Art and Science, with Specimen-box and precious Port-folio of Drawings—or the amateur Adventurer with his insatiable appetite for novelty—however foreign, strange, or distant such may be, they shall appear amidst their separate accessories of the Animal World.

Each Volume shall contain at least five such Plates as those we give in this, devoted to the illustration of the Wild Scenes of our own Indian Border Life, which will be furnished from the noble and unequalled pencil of Alfred J. Miller, of Baltimore, who accompanied Sir William Drummond Stuart, on his noted expedition among the Indian Tribes of the Plains, as Artist. How splendidly he has accomplished his mission those who may not be familiar with his former works will at once comprehend, in looking over the five first Lithographs in this volume. I say with perfect confidence that it remains yet for Art in this country, to approach the amazing fidelity and spirit of these Drawings—and his glorious Portfolio is but yet just opened! I shall give in addition—as in this volume—five other Lithographs of Foreign Scenes quite as elaborately drawn, but of less costly finish. And I hope so far to perfect, through the skill of my Lithographer, Mr. Rosenthall, the processes by which he has produced these unparalleled specimens of the art of Printing in colors upon stone, as to be able to present all the figures of animal life in color and at a cost which will come within the limit of that of the present volume. This I shall regard as indeed a triumph. But the Reader will perceive, that in the singular skill with which the colorist and lithographer, have produced the pictures for this volume, I and he have much to anticipate. I hope through such able seconding to demonstrate, that the art of printing in colors, which is yet in embryo in Europe, has been left for us to develope in this country, as we have that of Daguerreotyping.

I scarcely think that any specimens of that mysterious art can be produced in England, where it has been longest a subject of emulation, that will compare with my first five lithographs by Rosenthall and Kramer, from Miller—at least I am very well content to abide the issue of public sentiment with regard to this first experiment in a novel field!

Here I would introduce to the Reader a new ally—such an one as certainly is not often presented in such enterprises. This is no less a personage than my "little Wife," Mrs. E. M. Webber, whose portrait you see associated with my own on the title page of this volume. She is an Artist; and to her hand I am indebted for much of the fine work in illustration of this volume. But this is not her peculiar field—the delicate accuracy of the Woman artist will be more prominently and characteristically displayed in our second volume, the title of which will be "Wild Scenes and Song Birds of the World."

The drawings of birds and flowers for this and all succeeding volumes, will be by her; and I rest most proud and happy with such a "help-mete" in my labors!

In presenting this first volume to the Public, I have felt a proper diffidence in regard to the whole subject of scientific classification, and have therefore solicited and fortunately obtained aid in the highest legitimate quarter known amongst us.

Mr. John Cassin, the Secretary of the Academy of Natural Sciences in Philadelphia, has consented to edit, with me, the future volumes of the series; so that my subscribers and readers may not only rely upon the scientific accuracy of the work through his learned supervision of this department, but may as well look for a ripe, quaint and scholastic vein of humor, such as has seldom been brought to bear upon such themes, and which will form a pleasing contrast with my own headlong methods. I thus hope to offer a work which shall be complete in itself, as a Salmagundi of the facts, thoughts and suggestions of the natural world, with enough of technical accuracy to constitute it a reliable authority to the Student of Science, and a sufficiency of genial reverence, gaiety and kindliness, to render it always a safe, welcome and valued companion of the fireside, into the chaste penetralia of which I so much desire to win my way. We should not be permitted to rest unconscious of the sacred serenities of Nature; all the harmonies rest therein and they bring peace with them! Though men may grow callous and dumb in listening forever to the clink of dollars, shall not the sense of their fair children be attuned to voices more soft, more mellowed, more divine!

In conclusion, I would remark, that for my wood-cuts I am indebted to Mr. Joseph T. Brightly, who has not only performed his part as an engraver ably, but has with an unexpected skill, thrown himself into the department of design, and furnished me with the rough draughts of many of my finest wood-cuts. To Mr. A. Woodside, artist of this city, I am also much indebted for a number of highly artistic drawings on wood.

CONTENTS.

CHAPTER I. PAGE.
Bird, Beast, and Hunter........ 17

CHAPTER II.
The Boy Hunter........ 34

CHAPTER III.
The Naturalist Developing........ 54

CHAPTER IV.
The Night Hunt in Recess........ 75

CHAPTER V.
Audubon—the Hunter-Naturalist—Audubon and Wilson........ 87

CHAPTER VI.
Audubon and Boone........ 123

CHAPTER VII.
The Grave of the Silent Hunter........ 191

CHAPTER VIII.
Old Bill Smith—the Silent Hunter........ 211

CHAPTER IX.
The Hunters of Kentucky—James Harrod of Harrodsburg........ 231

CHAPTER X.
The Fox and Fox Hunting in America........ 248

CHAPTER XI.
The Texan Huntress........ 274

CHAPTER XII.
Metaphysics of Bear Hunting........ 343

CHAPTER XIII.
Hunting Peccaries in Texas—a Bear-Hunt without the Metaphysics........ 381

PAGE

CHAPTER XIV.
The Buffalo 394

CHAPTER XV.
Panthers, and our other Felines 403

CHAPTER XVI.
Captain Dan Henrie; his Adventure with Wolves 425

CHAPTER XVII.
The Darkie Fiddler and the Wolves 446

CHAPTER XVIII.
Skater Chased by Wolves 454

CHAPTER XIX.
The Mustang, or Wild Horse 460

CHAPTER XX.
A Bird's-eye View of the Speclater 472

CHAPTER XXI.
Trolling in June 482

CHAPTER XXII.
A Night-hunt up the Cungamunck 492

CHAPTER XXIII.
Trouting on Jessup's River 503

CHAPTER XXIV.
Anecdotes of Moose and Deer Hunting among the Northern Lakes. 515

CHAPTER XXV.
Hunting Elephants in South Africa 536

CHAPTER XXVI.
The Giraffe 561

CHAPTER XXVII.
South African Lions 572

CHAPTER XXVIII.
The Rhinoceros and Hippopotamus 594

CHAPTER XXIX.
Buffalo and Antelopes of South Africa 604

THE WILD HUNTSMAN.

THE ROMANCE OF SPORTING.

CHAPTER I.

BIRD, BEAST AND HUNTER.

THE air is filled with birds that fly, and are pursued by bird and beast. The earth, with beasts that run, and are pursued by beast and bird; while man, in a world of pursuers and pursued, is chief hunter of them all!

Whatever may have been the case in primeval times, it certainly seems very natural now that our relations to the living creatures by which we are surrounded should be mainly those of hunter and the hunted; and that these relations should be most immediate to bird and beast seems equally of course, since they more nearly approach us on the ascending scale of being. But these most intimate relations to the life below us express far more than is conveyed in mere consanguinity, for they are each separate and living types of our compounded selves.

Thus we see in the bird the type of our intellect—of the soul. We feel that they address the imagination, appeal to what is exulting and exalting in us—to "the aspiration in our heels!"

The beast, on the other hand, is the type of our sensuous life—it appeals to our material and lower impulses. It prefigures and embodies individually those purely physical attributes which we find expressed in man the Microcosm. In a word, quadrupeds are the indices of our passions which belong to sense; and birds, of our passions which belong to soul. The bird has wings, and like thought, triumphs over time and space. It lives in the pure ether, and all its modes and associations are apparently those of the soul's life.

> "As birds within the wind
> As fish within the wave,
> As the thought of man's own mind
> Floats through all above the grave."

Even the impulses of the bird are those of cold and clear intellection. When it strikes it kills—the quick, fierce, promptitude of appetite knows no pause. It never dallies with the prey, to gloat upon its agonies and heat a hunger on the struggles of fear in the efforts to escape, as do the felines and many others of the quadrupeds. With it to feel is to do, and to do quickly. *Veni, vidi, vici!* is the accepted motto of fiery, keen, victorious thought. They are the vicious and ignoble sluggards of action that creep to conquer. The beast is crushed by its grossness, and in its highest moods is a crawler, with its belly in the dust. Even in the exultings of its passion, in the murderous bound upon its prey, it must shake the earth from its claws. It is indeed, "of the earth, earthy," and associated with the baseness and lowliness of filth and dirt. However nice it may be, however intact of the habitual soil it may keep its pelage, yet are its appetites thirsty for blood like the absorbing earth; its passions lingering, deadly, but sure as the revolving seasons. Birds do not linger so. When they strike, it is for the death; and then, with no pause between, they swallow. Sometimes, as with many of the fishers, they do not even tarry that they may tear their prey, but deglutate alive.

As with the higher intellection, alimentation seems with the bird rather a means than an end. Life has higher blisses for them, and they eat to live; while the animal but lives to eat. The joy of wings, of sunshine and of singing, of battle with the wind and storms, of rocking on the wave of forest-tops, or swinging with the bound of waters, is with the bird the nobler purpose; while the beast must lick its thirsty chops forever, and with baleful eye glare always the insatiate lust of ravin through the smiles of peaceful nature!

With all this we have to confess that as yet the beast more closely approximates our sympathies, appeals to us through more numerous traits of consanguinity than the bird. This, though honest, and sufficiently honorable to us, is nevertheless most humiliating to a transcendental pride.

They who would have the human all spiritualized, with wings, forget that such conditions belong to a remote development, or the other life; that, linked as we are here with the material, it is as brave of us, and as necessary, that we should be true animals, as that we should be true angels. Our mingled being can, as yet, be neither one nor the other wholly, but must wisely compound between the extremes, and be simply what we are—*men!* As *men*, then, all the venerable past is sacred to our memory, as the cheerful future is to our hope. The youth of humanity, in which the material or passionate life predominated so much over the spiritual, was just as excellent and as noble as its present condition.

Our past is as illustrious in its facts as our future can ever be in its hopes. We should as much venerate that antediluvian era in which our giant progenitors wrestled hand to claw with their brute antagonists, as this latter one, in which our science, through chemistry and mechanics, has so entirely quelled and fully restrained them.

Although fanatics may regard this proposition as crude and profane, it is, nevertheless, absolutely true, that beginning with germination, every stage of development to its highest point, is equally honorable and to be honored. Is the flower with the sun-light on it more to be regarded than the first pale leaf which struggles to the air from out the gloomy foldings of the earth? Is the great tree, bending beneath the ruddy weight of fruitage, more respectable in God's economy of progress, than the small dark seed from the entombment of which its proud show is the resurrection?

Struggle, throughout all life, so far as it has been revealed to us, is the law of ascension, as well as of fixed grades; and hence we justify all those rude antagonisms between man and man, which a namby-pamby sentimentalism would convert into the "piping times of peace." War is a legitimate consequence of the conditions of our race, and all the concomitants of war, martial games, hunting, &c., are equally legitimate. It is astonishing that the lymphatic "peace" men should leave out of view the fact, that when battle and death shall cease, the whole animal world must be annihilated. In the first place, even the graminivorous animals live upon the destruction of some forms of animal life. There is no blade of grass or leaf plucked by them, upon which myriads of animalculæ and hundreds of insects are not destroyed—they cannot move upon the surface of the earth without destroying such creatures—every lifting of a hoof leaves crushed and writhing victims in its track, and when the foot comes down, it is like Behemoth raging through the thronged cities of men. The law is, that animal life must be perpetuated through death and decay. The carnivorous animals confessedly live by mutual destruction. How ridiculous is the effort to institute a scale of sympathy, at the head of which the red-blooded animals are to be placed as more nearly appealing to our mercy. They are, to be sure, nearest in fact, for the reason that we too are red-blooded animals.

What right have we to suppose that the animalculæ or a caterpillar does not experience the same pangs from sudden dissolution, that are felt by ourselves, or a stag or a boar? What difference, in this respect, does it make whether the blood of the slain creature be red, green or white? Is not every vegetable devoured, even by your *Grahamite*, a microcosm of the world, and like it populous with living things? If then the destruction of animal life be a crime, does He who marks the fall of every sparrow, regard with less complacency this wholesale annihilation of a little world, with all its joys and passions, by the remorseless jaws of that soft-hearted vegetable eater? Four-fifths of the creatures which are visible to the naked eye live in our sight upon mutual destruction—while the remaining fifth live by the destruction of those creatures of the existence of which the microscope has taught us! Where will our sickly benevolence stop? All things that live in the grades below man are the fungi of decay, and all that is material of him is alike so! Death is indeed so entirely the law of life, that though fed on air you must do murder with every breath; it is the fuel of all life, except, perhaps, that of baby ethics, *alias*, transcendentalism!

Why, then, give to the red-blooded animals so disproportionate an amount of sympathy? The monadic, vegetable and insect lives, are as necessary to the economy of God's World, as he has been pleased to institute it, as our own, or the lives of any other of the higher animals.

Indeed, it is a curious fact, entirely left out of view in modern theories, that even the lustful battles of the animal tribes among themselves, are necessary to their own integrity and perpetuation. In these battles, which always result in mutilation and death to many, the *strong*, of course, conquer, and the weak being killed or driven off, are prevented from perpetuating their own imbecility, and thus degenerating the race. All are familiar with the savage contests of the canines, felines, &c. At such periods, even among the graminivorous tribes, old Spencer tells of

> "As greet a noyse as when in Cymbrian plain
> An heard of bulles whome kindly rage doth sting,
> Doe for the milky mother's want complain,
> And fill the fields with troublous bellowing."

It is a fact, with regard to the habits of the Mustangs, or wild horses of our great prairies, which we have frequently observed personally, that the weaker stallions are invariably, after desperate contests, either killed or driven into solitary banishment, from which they never return to the herd, until their strength and prowess have been so far developed in the solitude, as to give them some hopes of being able to triumph in a renewed struggle with their conquerors. The mares, in the mean time, are passive observers, and surrender without hesitation, to whichever of the opponents may have demonstrated the right to approach them legitimately. There is a still more curious instance, which we have learned from books, of this stern recognition of the utilitarian principle amongst the lower animals. The stork, which belongs to the old world, and is a migrating bird, furnishes this illustration. It is said, that when the period for their annual journey arrives, all those storks who neighbor in the district assemble, as do our martins and swallows, at a given place, for the purpose of practising their wings, and thoroughly testing their powers of flight, before they set off on their long pilgrimage towards the Orient. After several weeks, spent in ærial circlings and evolutions, the stronger storks suddenly fall upon those which have shown, in this probation, such deficient energy of wing, as to make it unsafe for them to undertake the projected flight, without embarrassment to their comrades, and dispatch them with their long sharp beaks, sending them as quickly thumping to the earth, as if a rifle-ball had struck them to the heart. Here is a necessitarian justice, coming out of the code God himself has instituted for the government of his natural world, which will no doubt greatly horrify the sickly word-heroes of the anti-capital punishment and non-resistant creeds. Although God himself has established these severe ultimatums, there are those wiser than he, who would substitute their own pale shadows of thought for the nervous substance of his will!

I do not deny progress, even in the fanatics' sense of it; but I assert that war has been one of its greatest physical agents; that it has convulsed and broken up those stagnations of the moral sense which would have been fatal to it. Though the necessity for war is gradually giving way to the higher and more defined development of the spiritual life, yet it must, for a long time yet, continue to be an important agent of civilization.

Do not let us, in the meantime, forget that the vocation of the soldier and laborer is as honorable in God's sight, and as necessary to the real progress of humanity, as that of the intellectualist. And do not let us forget, either, that all those associations of the past, which link our race more immediately with these under types of passional life, are equally glorious with that primeval time, when Ham, with the hirsute strength, and passion for the chase, which gave birth from him to the stalwart progeny of "mighty hunters before the Lord," perpetuated those fierce instincts of combat and destruction, which have made the gloom as well as the glory of our progress. Brave times, certainly, were those of

——"Nimrod, the founder
Of empire and chase,
Who made the woods wonder,
And quake for their race;

When the lion was young,
In the pride of his might,
Then 'twas sport for the strong
To embrace him in fight:
To go forth with a pine
For a spear 'gainst the mammoth,
Or strike through the ravine
At the foaming behemoth;
While man was in stature
As towers in our time—
The first-born of nature,
And like her. sublime."

And something of the same rough stupendous cast from nature's mould, must have been an old Briton of that young time, when the first Roman came across, as the earliest navigator to civilize—for it is certain, that if the Romans came as conquerors, they came equally as civilizers. And though they found the man savagely rude, yet, also, they found that he had taken one step, at least, towards the investment of civilization. From him Spencer took his famous picture—

"About his shoulders broad he threw
An harie hide of some wild beast, whom hee
In salvage forest by adventure slew,
And reft the spoyle his ornament to bee,
Which spreading all his back with dreadful view,
Made all that him so horrible did see,
Think him Alcides with the lyon's skin,
When the Neamean conquest he did win."

And now with the knotted club in hand, the round bull's-hide shield advanced, with the long matted locks, hairy limbs, and savage eyes, we have a pretty clear outline of the fierce wild figures which met "with dreadful view" the Roman gallies in the surf on their descent.

They were strange times, too—those of the acorn-eating Druids. The Man was, in fact, but a few degrees removed above the brute, from which he

"——Reft the spoyle his ornament to bee,"

so far as habits went. But habits are not all the man, and they were most sublime rites, the incense of which went up from beneath those truest temples—the sacred forests! At such a period the strong contrasts are exhibited. The brute-man literally wrestles with his brute prototype for glory, "spoyle," and food; while the higher man sits with grey venerable poll beneath the leafy shadows of his sacred place, musing beside a rude stone altar; or on the plain, upturns the white calm of his time-beleagured front towards the stars, in still communion with their mysteries.

Then comes that finer union of the animal and spiritual lives, when the science of Eld Egypt—the God-revealed legislation of the Hebrew—the magic of the far wondrous East—the Ionian polish, and the Roman sternness, had, in their gradual progress towards the West, so greatly modified human development, that, out of such combinations, chivalry sprung forth. This is that most generous balance of the two natures, which even at the present day more nearly appeals to our nobler instincts; and

"In rough magnificence arrayed,
When ancient chivalry displayed

The pomp of her heroic games,
And crested chiefs and tissued dames
Assembled at the clarion's call,
In some proud castle's high arched hall"

;—we have the most illustrious period of our race, in which, through the expansion of the higher virtues, woman emerged to her true place, and stood forth in light—the angel of the fireside! Though the feudal age was partial in its immediate effects, and the masses were still held in rude vassalage, yet such developments as came to and for the few, were large and grand. Then came the accession, though it was much confined to the privileged classes, of that bold individuality which dared to question any despotism, or hoary precedent for truth, and out of which emancipation, sprung those liberal opinions which have so far through blood and "terror" worked out the modern ideas of liberty and equality. Thence came, too, those regal impulses—those mild and liberal sentiments, which in their open-handed dispensations fell like the benediction of blessed dews from heaven, upon the feverish embittered struggle of man with man; and which cooled down their heat, restoring that calm, mutual faith, that is the basis of any attempt at self-government. Thence came as well "the pomp and circumstance" of tournaments and hunts, in which "the civil courteseys" of polished intercourse was most delicately defined, even amidst the stern collisions of opposing forces, and from which all those beautiful amenities, named politeness by modern civilization, had their truest source.

Then the human chased the brute, surrounded by all the regalia of a more exalted state, and the physical was cultivated through magnificence. Then "crested chiefs, and tissued dames," were not above being thoroughly developed men and women. Animals now arose to a more correct estimation, and under the proper culture, soon became rather the companions and subjects of our hilarious sports, than abject slaves and enemies, or objects of alimentive lust. Then the fleet and fire-eyed barbs were transported from their desert homes, with all the appointments of a ducal progress, to lend their game and tireless speed to the ambition of our rural sports. Then the boar was left to whet his tusks and strength together in his native and inviolated solitudes, until his savage energies came to him, and he was fitted to add that hardy attraction to the chase which danger gives. So was the stag nourished in those solemn forest haunts where its antlered pride grew and was matured for the noble struggle of its chase. Even the falcon, with its steel-hinged wings, and indomitable wildness, was brought down from its crag-eyrie to serve our pastimes; and falconry became the most graceful of all the sports in which the two sexes elegantly united. Then came the manly fox hunt, in which sly Reynard's cunning was made to increase the joviality and excitement of the pursuit, and from which this creature has made itself associate with the lusty habitudes and ruddy cheeks of the English gentry.

But the free and courteous indications thus nourished, soon opened for the race a new field, as well as novel surroundings, in which their legitimate results would be wrought out fairly. The New World was discovered by a bold inquisition of science, which the newly released thought—exulting in its freedom—could only have attempted; and was conquered by the proud daring of a chivalry, which was first sublime to undertake and strong enough to accomplish, all that its fiery dreams had conceived. Then the Matador knights of Southern Europe, possessed themselves of gold-bearing, gorgeous Mexico; and the cut-and-thrust agility—the ferocious cowardice of their national show, "the bull-fight"—has been well perpetuated in the assassin's skill with the assassin's blade; and the brutal thirst for blood, wreaking itself the more mercilessly as the victim is more helpless—which has distinguished the modern Mexico of that conquest!

But another people—from the hardy North of the Old World, which has always preserved the physical integrity of its races—went across to possess the, to them, congenial North of the New.

The elemental war—the thundering of wind-driven waves upon "the rock-bound coast"—the white desolation of snows crowning the cliffs and bowing the gnarled tangles of scrubby forests, had no formidable terrors to them—whose manhood had been cultivated amidst the out-door hardships of those gallant feudal sports to which we have alluded. They had been cradled by the tempestuous North, and knew how to match all its moods in self-defence. They could wrench the fire from dead trees by friction, and even when this resource failed, knew how to strip the warm skin from the newly slain beast to wrap around them in their slumbers, and defy the winter. They were not appalled by the savage red man with his scalp lock, for they had conquered brutes as savage in the wild fastnesses of their mutual home. Though certainly there is a wide difference between the rough boar hunts, through which some of our pilgrim fathers may be supposed to have been habituated to "imminent perils by flood and field"—to which the knights went forth with their peers around them, with hundreds of retainers at their heels—and those stern conflicts in the wide wilderness of our forests to which the single hunter went forth with his rifle and knife; and in which he had not only to meet in awful solitudes the bear, the bison, the panther and the moose, but as well, the still creeping, deadly subtlety of an Indian foe!

The latter had all the aid of numbers, and a common purpose, which, even under imperfect discipline, may convert a physical coward into the hero. The former, shorn of all these associations, was compelled to push his way *alone* into the grim surrounding of the "howling waste," and single-handed cope with all its dangers. He came with nerves of steel and heart of rock, to subdue the bleak wilderness, and he accomplished it—though "dark and bloody grounds" may have marked each arena of his stern and struggling progress! His own quick senses, and his prompt right arm were his only dependences for the preservation of "dear life!" It is not at all astonishing, then, that from the nurturings of such scenes and habitudes, that bold and strong individuality, that untamable self-reliance, which constitutes the basis of self-government and a free republic, should have come forth *cap-a-pie*, to assert its claim to national character, in the eight, or even had it been necessary, the eighteen years' war of a revolution. The war of the Revolution, and every one that has occurred since, proves, that however deficient in discipline, the North Americans are the best individual soldiers that the world has ever known. The remarkable skill in rifle shooting, and the constant familiarity with sudden exigencies of the ruder sports of hunting, which the every-day habitudes of their wild life has given them, has fitted almost every common soldier for the station of an officer, so far as skill, coolness, promptness and self-dependence can go.

All the impulsion of our national character—all of the hardy, stern, resolute and generous that may be native, we take through the noble blood of our hunter ancestors. That terrible soldiery which devastated Mexico, was composed of hunters almost to a man; the eagle they carried before them was a hunting bird—the fierce-eyed king of the winged hunters!

To me, the wild and peculiar sports of our country, are as noble and ennobling subjects of curiosity, as I feel our science should be of jealous accuracy, and philosophy of liberal breadth. Our physical character has been quite as much developed by the first, as our intellectual or moral by the second, and our spiritual by the last.

Here, the civilized man, the savage and the brute have been brought into extraordinary relations. Nor is this all. It is through this remarkable collision, that a more intimate knowledge of the habits of all the forms of animal life has been obtained in the New World than has come through any other source. The savage was the earliest and most accurate student of their habits, from the necessities of his condition, which compelled him to familiarize himself with all their moods, in view of the facilities for capture, which the want of food and raiment entailed. His familiarity with such themes was then purely compulsory, while that of our American pioneers has been nearly quite as much so. They, too, were bound to be naturalists. They came to the unbroken solitudes to cope with the savage in the conditions of his own life. Though they had more science, and a better architecture, yet were they equally dependant for subsistence upon personal prowess. They were compelled to learn from their savage antagonist—as they could, through their manner of taking them—the nature and habits of the new animal races amongst which they found themselves. What they could not acquire from such sources, their own intelligent observation furnished them; so that, in reality, the first American Naturalists were our pioneer hunters, who learned through starvation, and all the perils of savage warfare, and the inconstant seasons, to know more accurately the habits, passions, transitions and localities of our animals, than whole fleets of navigators and scientific pedants in silk stockings, could attain to in half a century.

It is only those who have dared to live such lives as they did, and through familiar associations with them, have been enabled to unite scientific accuracy with the gleanings of their rude lore, who are to be depended upon as true delineators. Such men have our great naturalists been. Such men were Wilson, Godman and Audubon. With the eye, step, and frame of an Indian—the astuteness, nerve and intrepid skill of the pioneer hunter, and the learning of the savan united in himself, the Hunter Naturalist of America has pushed his way, rifle in hand, into the secret places and confidences of nature. He has carried her jealous defences by storm, and may almost be said to have "wooed her as the lion wooes his bride," *will ye, nill ye!* There have been few such ardent investigators among the Old World Naturalists until of late. Though many of them have been great travellers, and have professed to examine the subjects of their favorite science, amidst native surroundings—yet in method and spirit they have been entirely unlike the American. While the American, in the confidence of practice and self-reliance, has been content to trust in his own good right arm for provision and defence, they have been sent out by Royal Institutes, with all the unwieldy appointments of a scientific progress, to explore the "sands and shores and desert wildernesses." While he, with habits as hardy and simple as those of the wild creatures themselves, has moved among them without their being aware—has plucked the same berries, drank from the same spring, and rested beneath the same shades, with his calm, bright eye, like that of an invisible presence, forever upon their unconscious lives, has read them in their freedom like an unsealed book—the Europeans, with their lumbering trains, have brought dismay and terror into the startled solitudes, and at best have obtained nothing but unsatisfactory glimpses of retreating forms, or the clumsily slain "specimens." While he, with the experience of a boyhood and manhood spent in hunting and among hunters, can subject the wild legends and the vague tales he may hear to a sure test within himself, and skilfully sift them of whatever truth they may contain, for his own use—the Europeans, whose years have been spent amidst the musty folios of a library, or the faded specimens of museums, must take whatever they may hear for granted—since it would puzzle a quizzing "native" to romance more sillily than the venerated dullards of those folios, and it would equally puzzle their astuteness to recognize the living animals when they had only seen the dried skins thereof! The consequence has been, that the efforts of Europeans in Ornithology and Mammalogy have been comparatively "lame and impotent conclusions," especially when they have undertaken to delineate American birds and animals. As laborious systematizers and technicalists, they of course have preceded and far surpassed us. We will not dispute the husks of honor with them—but must insist that as to all wherein consists the proper vitality and purpose of such themes, our own—the American—treatment has been the most original, vigorous and true.

To such causes as we have traced, the fact is owing that in European treatment, the subject of Natural History has been technicalised into what may be almost called a perfect whalebone state of sapless system. The subject, of all others possessing the greatest amount of inherent vitality, it has been so heavily overlaid by the dry bones of the Linnæan nomenclature as to have become a veritable Golgotha of Science. Among us the people, with whom it is necessarily a favorite theme, are repulsed, in dismay of its formidable hieroglyphics, from what is to them as a sealed book. Thrown back upon individual resources solely, they become as we have seen, of necessity, close observers, and so far as opportunity goes, much better naturalists than your pur-blind Professors of the Science, who see only a learned name in its proper "class" and "order," not a living creature on the green earth and under the sun, and therefore it has been that only such heathful and hardy treatment as our naturalists have given to Natural History, has found favor among us. Our glorious Audubon, who is just now dead, lived and wrote like one of the people, and therefore we love and venerate him passed away. The people everywhere will have the familiar objects and subjects of their every-day life treated in a familiar way, and all the stilted terminology of an over-done wisdom is, and must continue to be, gibberish to them. One such fanciful and eloquent romancer as Buffon, will continue through all time more dear to the popular heart in the Old World, than fifty rude stolid compilers as Gesner or Pennant, or even than the venerated Linnæus himself; and Goldsmith, too, has made "A Fairy Tale" (as Sam Johnson called it,) of Natural History, that must live as a substantial reality in the memories of mankind more enduring than the heavy monuments of learning.

It is therefore entirely from the stand-point of the Hunter Naturalist,—the indigenous growth of our New World,—that I propose to regard the Romance of Sporting, and the relations of Bird, Beast and Hunter.

CHAPTER II.

THE BOY-HUNTER.

I MUST surely have been intended for a hunter, as the first thing I can remember was an animal.

I have often tried to trace as far back as possible into the days of my childhood, the period when consciousness first became linked with external things;—or, in other words,—my memory of life began. Curiously enough, I have never been able to get farther back than to a time when I was kicking and screaming in my nurse's arms, in extacied and uncontrollable eagerness to get my hands upon a beautiful little white rabbit which had been sent home by my father in a basket.

The picture of that snowy creature, with its "pink eyne," and long ears laid back, couched and trembling amidst the tow on which it had been placed, in its rough wicker cage, is to this hour as distinct as a scene of yesterday. It was the sweet surprise of that soft vision that startled my new life into full awakening. I have no memory of the dull dawn before; it is here my actual being commenced.

They tell me I had already vegetated a few months, but it must have been as a sprawling negation, dim-eyed and dreamless, clutching feebly the untenanted air; for now was my first amazed recognition of separate being; now was that vague Infinite first made palpable to me through sense in form.

Ah! the miracle of that mysterious outer world, where such shapes of wondrous beauty grew! I now felt the sunshine, and saw all things glitter. How strange and vivid familiar things around me seemed; the rough fence, the old trees and house wore golden halos on them; the green earth was glorified in splendors that entered to possess me in warm thrills; and a creeping joy, mingled of I know not what delicious pains, glowed through my life, until it swooned in love! Ah, the ecstatic influx of that sensuous birth! would it might hold my heart to nature in that sacred glow forever!

There is a philosophy which takes man for the highest and purest exhibition of the divisible, for that type of being in which all organism is perfected; it recognizes him also as linking this being with the indivisible, as the penultimate of forms—a part of heaven and a part of earth.

This being accepted, his relations towards inferior creatures become beautifully dignified, and constitute a sort of arch-archangelship under the sun, drawn by the common ties of common sympathy towards all things that breathe and move, yet holding an awful throne by right of its spiritual lineage. Then doth he become, to their material nature, a "God made visible,"—the palpable, immediate expression of that mystery and power which are the elements of all supreme rule, whether it be human or divine.

These earth-mated creatures are his subjects; and here, at least, his lust of despotism can be gratified, for he is ruler and lord above them all, for evil as well as for good. When it is for evil, how terrible he must be to them with his dread engines and his fierce subtlety! When for good, what moving of strange thoughts, what yearnings for a better and gentler being must visit them! Was it not so, even with ourselves, when there were giants in those days, and angels sought the daughters of Adam on our earth?

If creation be an unresting tendency, eternally ascending towards the perfect, then is our supposition less a fancy than a truth, and our dominion over the beast of the earth and the fowl of the air becomes a heritage of fearful responsibilities, embracing wide extremes of pleasure and of pain. Duties, then, of startling significancy, open to us, and we feel the presence of self-derived majesty expand throughout our principality, and in beneficence above immortal subjects. We are no longer their tyrants, but right royal masters. We know them not as the insensate objects of a rude caprice, dumb foot-balls to our blind and heady passions, to be chased and torn and worried in our savage glee,—but as the creatures of our dedicated love, to be guarded gently, nurtured well, and led by easy ways up, through serener airs, to happier fields.

This is the Apocalyptic Vision of an elder race—man, THE ASCENDER, beckoning the flocks and herds, the live ocean-tide of his inheritance, up the steep; the calm radiance of his merciful brow drawing its flood towards the stars! It is a healthful philosophy, full of noble teachings, and we should hold it to our hearts, though the reality of such a vision may be so remote—though, alas! fallen ourselves, we have cursed them.

It is sad enough that all these creatures have scented

murder on our red right hands, and fly from our darkened brows,—that the archangel of our birth has been dethroned, and that shining Presence, once upturned over them in blessings, as a God, become terrible in wrath! Yet are we monarchs still, and yearn towards our ancient subjects, though it be in empty mockery of state. In our domesticated creatures we call them around us once again to feed from our hands, though they be rather as the captives of our will, the slaves of our necessities, than as loyal subjects in the bonds of love.

What wonder that the man seeks savage compensation for the loss of empire? What wonder if, in the shadow where he walketh now, those mighty memories turn his heart to gall, when he looketh out upon his subjects, shining sleek, in beauty and in strength, amidst their sun-lit plains; and they regard not his voice, lifted up as of old, to call them to his feet? Is it strange that, in the bitterness of quickened wrath, his fierce pride turn upon them, glorying in the strife of will with will, and strength with strength, to overtake them in their vaulting freedom, and grimly laugh amidst their slaughter?

Yet are they co-mates and sharers of the sun with us, and dark, unnatural passions cannot always shut them out from the full circle of our sympathies. Childhood has yet a birthright of innocent illusion; and while its ethereal haze lingereth over all things in enchantment, we may at least believe and love!

We become curst and harsh with dwelling forever amidst false hopes and care-weighed aspirations, and therefore is it sad, indeed, when we outgrow that charming Faith of innocence, since by it do we hold eternal youth. In its deathless happiness it takes us forth into this marvellous outer world to grow strong again in wondering, to freshen on the loveliness, and grow mirthful with its gay and careless lives. Here are beings infinitely numerous, who breathe and move by the same laws with ourselves, and yet, who in their apparelling their modes and humors, answer mere nature; and just as we love the matron-smiling front of her eternal freshness, must we love these, and continue to shed upon them out of our hearts, a wide beneficence.

How can we fail to love a keen-eyed wild-bird, coming from the solitude, burnished and many-hued, as if the air, where its surpassing beauty grew, held stores of gold, of amethyst and glittering gems within its depths, and had sifted them in gradual splendors down upon the plumy thing that sat within its stillness! What a pleasant mystery its gay, eccentric being is! How we delight to watch its tameless heart pulsing through every gesture, and to wonder what it thinks and feels, and how its moods go!

Who has not noted the joyful amazement lighting up an infant's eye when you hold a bird before it, or a sleek-furred squirrel just from its leaf-cradle. How it screams with the novel joy as its shrinking fingers feel the strange, soft touch. Its first impulse—the royal patron roused already!—is to fondle and caress the little prisoner, and, though the chubby, awkward fist of the young Hercules may strangle his delicate vassal at the first grasp, yet is it not from cruelty, but from the eagerness of the new delight.

All children are enthusiastic naturalists so long as the happy time of innocent free impulse lasts, and well do I remember all that mellow time with me! Then was my faith in the beautiful most mighty; then gave it a charmed life to me; then was it my dintless shield,—the Sigil of my necromance;—by it did I "strange deeds upon the clouds," and fairy fantasies of earth, and air, and sea, came in my dreams obedient to its spell;—it made to me a world of God's free nature, wherein its creatures wore his glories for a garment, the light of his own eternity in their clear eyes, and syllabled in most sweet voices the language of his own harmonious tongue!

I knew these for my twin-born brothers, for, with the common forms about me, I grew weary: they did not fill my longings for—I knew not what!—but when the wild-bird, gleaming past, told me of the beautiful, the vivid, and the free, I no longer tarried with dull sense! I wore no wings, but yet I followed it, beating the air with visionary plumes, to fling the sunshine off; mine were no mellow pipes, but yet I felt a carol in the blossoming tree, and sung by shady streamlets a low, rippling trill—wild among flowers and vines, darting through shadows in tameless shine, I went, with the swift thing, in riot through our joy! Ah, it filled me with the freshness of untamable delight, and set my spirit free on its gem-dusted wings!

As for that young squirrel, out from deep woods where some old oak had nursed it, rocking the soft sprite in his rigid arms, it won my very soul, with its dark glistening eyes and feathery brush! I felt the frosty patriarch of shades embrace it gently and warm within his knotted bosom, when the battle-wind of winter had come forth; and saw its airy boundings lend a frolic grace to his grey poll, when gay spring breezes wooed him. Enchanted now, and eager of sweet mysteries, I entered where its leafy bed was rolled, and where the garnered stores lay fragrant in dim chambers of that oaken heart.

And then I smiled in dreaming, for I saw it here with strange surroundings! It had troops of little friends, the leaf-winged elves, that came into its chambers when the moon went down, and were all a-shiver with the cold, raw morning; and with puffy cheeks, straining at the load, they brought it round, fat nuts, an armful each, and threw them on the little heaps within its garner;—some, rare acorns, too, and some, triangled beech-nuts, or purple wild grape, or a bursting bud —this was for love and—breakfast! Then they would creep in bed with folded wings, and I could plainly see them pulling its soft brush aside to get beneath the cover, and it would stir a bit as if in vision it saw the dainties they had brought, and

snuff drowsily at the perfume. Now they all lay so warm and cozey, rolled delicately snug in that furry ball—and when daylight came and it went forth to play, they would keep the bed warm for it through the glaring time of sunshine!

There's no use saying I could not, for I could see those little fellows just as plain as the squirrel itself;—and when night came, I could see them, too, at their airy antics, plainly against the moon as it rose up, and, at playing bo-peep, I have caught them kissing the sleeping flowers, sure enough!

They used to fight with the old owls, too, and thrust sharp spear grass in their moony eyes, that would stare murder at gay, heedless chip munck, or pretty little panting wood-mouse pattering on the withered leaves below! Indeed, I saw them often gathering from afar in arms—troop after troop, in snail-shell helms, to drive such monsters bodily away when they had ventured near that squirrel's house; and then, the battle over, they would throw aside their arms, and take Æolian instruments they frame, and, with stealthy footing round the oriole's hanging nest, make creeping music, steal into her happy dreams, until she twitters in her sleep, of the dim sweetness, fitfully!

All this I saw with that young squirrel!—aye, and much more, too! I have not told you yet about its friends that live in the cold shade of little mossy grottos down the deep glen, where it must go to drink! They are grotesque little fellows, with fin-like wings, and you might any time see squirrels play with them—whether you could see them or not—jumping from rock to rock, darting under dark old mossy roots, to hide in gurgling water underneath; diving in still pools, where it will fear to follow, or shooting a swift rapid to some island pebble in the midst, where master bushy-tail, with all his long bounds, cannot reach!—if I should go on to tell you of all these doings, and of ever so much more, you would know him just as well as I did; but I don't tell every thing!—we had our secrets between us, and I am bound over about some of the daintiest of them!

Whether you believe all this or not, its just the same to me, for I did, and that even before I was big enough to go into the woods alone to see for myself! When I did go, I found it was all the same, except that I couldn't see the little friends very plain, though I could see squirrel plain enough!

Then, when I went out by myself into the deep wood, I sat down on the moss at the root of an old tree, to watch for him. When every thing was still again, I would see him after awhile poking his nose slily out of the hole, snuff! snuff! Then out his head would pop to rest his chin upon his fore-paws, and he would look all around, above and below, very cunning, to see if it was all right. Then out, like a thought, he would glide, and I could see his lovely brush quickly curled and spread all so grand above his head as he sat upon a limb, still, for the moment. Lo! there is another snuffing nose, and then great shining eyes filling the round black knot-hole, and out another pops—and then another and another—three of them—his brother and sisters!

Hark!—listen,—qua! qua! quagh! That is another one over on another tree! He answers it, and then such a time! such whisking of tails, darting along limbs and bounding from swinging twig to rustling tree-tops, until they all meet, —two families of them!

Now the frolic begins in earnest, and round and round the rough trunks, rattling the bark down as they chase each other! Their tails are spread now as wide as they can, as if they were badly scared, and that young lady he makes love to, you may be sure, for now he has chased her out to the very end of a great high limb, and hard pushed, here she comes right off into the air!—down almost into my face —the white of her arms underneath, spread wide like her stiffened tail!—into the leaves head foremost, and then up and away, patter! patter! patter! Here he comes, too, sailing down after her, plump! and rattles off along the old logs and swinging vines in hot chase!

So they all would frolic, chasing one another, and one would see me, and stop and stamp his tiny feet and bark hoarsely at me, jerking his tail in comic wrath. Sometimes another would dart away suddenly, as if possessed, scurrying round and round the tree after nothing; and then I knew well enough that it was not its tail that it was chasing, but one of its little airy friends, only it was of too transpraent substance for me to see it by the day-light.

Nor were these all the sights I saw out there in those quaintly peopled woods. There was saucy chip-munck, with black and white stripes down his brown back; he was a spry fellow, too, upon the ground, and lived in the prettiest house under an old stump. He would show his striped nose pushing through the long moss hanging over his little hole under the decaying root. How bright his soft, vivid eyes, and how

his long black whiskers tremble as he pricks his short ears to listen! Then, quick as lightning, he mounts the stump, frisking his pert tail at a great rate; you can see his little white bosom beating fast, like a toy watch in a flurry, as he glances sharply round; then away he darts, pit-a-pat! leaping on another stump to look again; now he is satisfied the coast is clear, and with a soft chirping squeak dives down into the leaves, scratching them aside and pushing under them his inquisitive nose. Ha! another soft chirp, and he darts back upon the stump again, and you can see his small cheeks are all puffed out. In a moment one of the acorns he has found is in his paws, and sitting up straight as a little goblin man, you can soon hear his sharp teeth creak! creak! against the hull.

He, too, has friends that live with him; that are kin to

the gnomes; they are a very funny sort of people. They cannot see at all after day, and they are so fond of their antics, that sometimes light overtakes them, and then they have to crawl under shelter of the first stone they can find, until night comes again. Whenever you happen to turn over the stone and see a blind, sluggish creature under it, looking like a brick-dusted lizard, don't hurt the wee, helpless thing, for when dark comes it will dart about and sparkle in the most beautiful manner, like a living carbuncle, among the strange night-flowering fungi that droop like it in the morning. You often see them at play, and if you do not notice, will think they are nothing but fire-flies.

There were many more creatures that these gnome-people loved very well, and which lived under the earth, too. They lighted the long galleries of the tiny shrews, and when the star-nozed moles held their root festivals in domed chambers, they were there to blaze amidst the velvet-coated throng, right merrily at midnight. And the soft mice ! they had some games with them, too, and loved mightily their warm round nests beneath the stubble, or in leafy hollows of dead trees. As for the gaunt and bloody weasels, they fright them with a sudden glare in those dark passages where they dig, nosing for murder; and blind, too, the sullen mink with splendor in his earthy prowls !

So at first I went forth among the creatures of earth, in peace, and saw them in my simple faith; and all my pleasantest memories of calm, unmixed delight, are associated with that time of innocent wonder and loving familiarity with these fresh articulations of God's thought in forms.

But as my passions grew, this harmless wonder changed into curiosity, that became insatiable for a more intimate knowledge. I yearned to know them better, to see them more closely, to feel them, to possess ! I became jealous of that graceful freedom I had at first admired so much, because it took them away from me just when my heart was overflowing towards them; I reached forth my arms to clasp them to my bosom, the empty air I folded chilled me at first, and then anger rose. The pride of a despotic will, the rights of the natural lord, were wounded from the tender side, and thus became aroused to an embittered consciousness of strength, and a willful purpose to use it against my gentle playfellows.

It was not that I grew cruel suddenly, and sought them with the dark curse of Cain in my heart, at once; but that I was impatient of this liberty that could take them from me when they willed, and desired to restrain them to come to me when I willed.

I had no thought of murder at first, when I learned to ensnare them. It would have broken my heart then to have slain one; and so full was I of love for them, that I could not fully realize how much they suffered in being deprived of freedom. Though they did struggle desperately, and cry aloud in fear and sorrow, I comforted myself in thinking that it was because they did not understand what I desired; that, when they came to know of the good I intended, what a nice little house I should build for them, what delicate food I would bring, and above all, how dearly I should love them, that then they would learn to love me, and become reconciled to everything, and happy as I was in having them.

So, in my simplicity, I tried to believe, until the whole thing became as real as if it were true; and the sunny attic, I proudly called my room, soon became a sort of caravansary, filled with these captive travellers of air and earth. What a happiness it was to me to familiarize each new prisoner with my presence, and sit and watch in low-breathed quiet all their ways, as I used to in the woods, and laugh out suddenly, until the old house rang, at some odd whimsicality of passionate gesture. How I loved to have them on my person, to caress me, to feed from my hands and mouth, to peck at me in feigned wrath, or seize my hands with harmless teeth in fierce dissembled savagery. Aye, I was lordly proud then,—even happy as a king.

When the snow came, too, what a joyful time that was to be,—for now I was to capture many more lovely friends.

When the grey heavy cloud gathered over night, and a few broad flakes came scattering slowly down through the twilight, then I knew there would be a heavy snow in the morning. What a restless, fidgety fever I was in! I went to bed early that night, that I might get up early, and meanwhile sleep away the suspense.

I forgot to say my prayers—for I did say them nightly in those sinless times—and lay tossed in restless visions of traps, and snares, and dead-falls; of monstrous hares, as big as my dog Milo, swung up by the neck at the end of a pole; of great flocks of quails, with strange beautiful birds among them, fluttering and peering their heads through the sticks of my traps; of white foxes and black foxes, or of a great opossum, lying with crushed heads beneath my dead-falls; or of tracking some creature that left the foot-mark of an elephant on the fresh snow for miles and miles through the bowed and foreign-looking woods, until I had tree'd it at last; when, after toiling and tugging, with sweaty brows, I had drawn it forth from the hollow, and held it in my hand, I saw, without the least surprise, that it was a soft little wood-mouse! Ah! delicious fantasies were they!

When at cock-crow I bounded out of bed and ran to the window, the first thing—how I clapped my hands and danced for joy, and waked every body with my shoutings—"The snow! the snow! a deep snow!"

Then what a fussing time!—making new traps, stealing clap-boards, and every other kind of boards that were available, to be split into trap pieces! What a teasing my father for triggers, to make me triggers for spring-falls, nooses, partridge traps, traps for little birds, and all! How I wondered I could not get the old gentleman to understand that I should be ruined! dead-ruined! if I did not get my traps ready to be set early—even by breakfast-time—for the other boys would be setting their's, too, and take all the best places.

Little did I care for the hot coffee and cakes that morning, but snatching a sup and a bite, was off, whistling for Milo, and shouting for Pomp the negro boy, to accompany and help me. Eagerly did we discuss, by the way, as we lugged our heavy traps through the deep snow, whether the sink-hole in the pasture, the thicket in the corn-field fence row, the blackberry patch in the corner, or on the edge of the woods, were the surest places for "Bob Whites," (partridges), or "Molly Cotton-tails," (hares). There was no deciding between them, so, to settle the matter, a trap was set at each place, and one in addition for larks, doves, red-birds, and sparrows, by the old wheat-stack behind the barn.

Pompey, who carried the spade, dug away the snow from

each sagaciously chosen place, and exposed the black earth beneath, so that our tempting bait might show from afar. Then was the trap placed over it on the bare spot, and set with such careful nicety! Now with many a wistful look behind to see if the birds were not at it already, we went on to set the next.

When this first and most important business was got through with, then came hare hunting under the snow.

Ah, that was the sport! Molly Cotton would sit still wherever the storm overtook her, and when the snow began to cover her over, she would keep crowding, and pushing gently back and forth, pressing it to one side until she had formed a roomy little chamber all about her. The snow would go on heaping and heaping until a domed arch grew over all with just one little round hole, kept open through its top by the warm air of her breathing—and there she would sit, snug as a Russian Princess, in her palace of ice, and dreaming of luscious cabbage leaves and tender apple-shoots in the neighboring garden. But Molly's golden visions were as subject to be rudely dispelled as those of other people!

See! Milo's keen nose has scented one of those very breathing-holes on the smooth, glistening surface of the snow—he has stopped suddenly on the plunge, with his foot raised! "Steady! steady, boy!" We are up with him in long leaps! Now for it! "Hie on, boy!" and helter, skelter, here we come! I, Milo, Pompey, all together, tumbling heels over head upon the snowy roof of Mistress Molly's palace! There she is—I feel the soft, warm fur! Squeak! quai! quai! quai!—her plaintive cry sings out; we have her! "Hold hard, Pompey; she kicks so with her strong hind-legs that she will surely get away!—Down, you Milo!—There now!—we have her tied—she is secure!"

Every hour or two the traps near at hand are visited, and those at a distance twice a day. We start upon our round. From afar we can see that one is down! My heart jumps!

I long sorely to run!—Pompey starts off, I call him back! It is necessary I should be dignified—should prove to him and all the world, by my unhurried calmness,—

> "———— that my demerits
> May speak unbonneted to as proud a fortune
> As this that has befallen."

I walk slow and stately, feeling exalted by my self-denial—speculating after what manner the fates are about to reward me—thinking of a whole dozen of partridges, a splendid male red-bird—or, it may be, a large fat pheasant, or some entirely new and wondrous creature, as best befitting my just claims.

We are close at hand—we can see the little tenement shake—hear the heavy beat of struggling wings. Too much for my stoicism is that sound! With fluttering pulse I spring eagerly forward—bah!—it is nothing but a common thieving jay!

I almost stagger with the revulsion of my soaring aspirations—while Pompey proceeds to get out the poor bird with sundry abusive epithets and gabbled threats of neck-wringing. "Yah! yah! ole feller!—cotch at last! Carry sticks to de debbil, to make fire, burn dis child wid, will you! Da! now you carry sticks to debbil!" and away flutters the obnoxious jay's headless body over the bloodied snow.

I have said I was not cruel, and it was a perfect agony to me to witness the death of any of my prisoners—but the shock of the fall of my high-flown hopes was too much for me, and in this case I did not recover in time to save the unlucky victim of a superstition universal among our negroes, and to which, if I were not ashamed of the confession, I might admit having been more than half inclined myself!

But this was not all our sport on the snow, either! If it grew damp towards evening, then the cold night-winds would freeze its untrampled surface, and, by the time morning came again, there would be a hard crust over all—hard enough to bear Molly Cotton's weight at any rate.

Now, such grand chases as we would have after her upon the crust! Milo's nose was to find her in the old stubble-field, by the little breathing-holes through the top of her palace under the snow; then we had all the little dogs from the Quarter, who were not much heavier than she, to chase her on the crust.

Ah! this was the greatest affair of all!—greater than catching her at once in her house, for here we gave Molly a fair start, and could see the whole chase to the end.

Before sunrise, Pomp had assembled from the quarter the other young darkies, Dick, Sambo, and the rest, with their cur-dogs, fices, terriers, and all other kinds of light dogs, each one lead by a tow-string around its neck—for it would spoil the fun and interfere with Milo, to have them loose until the time came. Such a gabbling and a yelping as they made, the darkies and their dogs between them, when Milo and I came running out, and took the lead through the deep crackling snow towards the great field.

Sometimes the snow would bear us for a moment, and then up somebody's heels would fly, and such a shrieking and tumbling about with the laughter as there would be; then the eager mongrels, when they saw Milo run ahead with long high plunges through the snow, would yell with anger at being tied, and leap against their tow-leashes, or darting between the holder's legs, would trip him up, and break away. Then there was no catching the little wretch, for he would be cunning enough not to come when his master called, just to be caught again, so I would have to order a halt, and call in my obedient Milo, and then the runaway would be decoyed in reach of some one who would snatch the trailing tow-string, and make him prisoner once more.

So, at last, with all our stoppages in this way, and in climbing the half-buried fences, where the negroes' dogs would be sure to get nearly hung to death in jumping through the wrong places, we would come to the old stubble just about when the sunrise scattered the purple dawning, and everything was a-glitter with the yellow blaze. We veiled our eyes from the dazzle with our coat-sleeves and caps when the white glare of the wide, unbroken surface was thrown into our faces.

But my eyes would soon bear it when I caught a glimpse of Milo's flying ears almost disappearing in his deep plunges through the snow, then rising again with his high leaps. He knew the time for action had come in earnest, and the little dogs, straining on their leashes, would whine and shift their feet, and yelp to get away, while they watched him, with great white eyes, almost popping out of their heads with their choked eagerness.

We all stand still, in breathless watching, as he covers his ground right and left, scientifically, as if there were no snow to hinder. But standing still, over the knees in the snow, is very hard for boys, and I begin to stamp with the cold and impatience, and rub my hands, while Pomp and his darkies gradually draw their breaths and commence gabbling away as noisy as ever.

"Yah! yah! Massa Charles,—see dat Milo jump! He long ear down dat sink-hole dar look jes like de big pheasant fly 'long de snow! He hab dat molly-cotton soon, now!"

"Keigh! hush you nigger, dar! d' 'aint no cotton tail down dat briar-patch, 't all!"

"Sambo, what you know? Milo knows more 'n ten sich nigger! He find him!"

"There! he stops! that's a point!"

"Whoop! yah! yah! told you nigger! dar dat cotton—!"

"Hush your noise! Steady boy! steady! Silence! Hold

on to your dogs. come on quietly! Steady, boy! steady. steady!"

Bursting almost with impatience, I have great trouble to hold back my rabble, for we must get close before Milo is hied on, so as to have a fair run of it.

"Steady, boy! steady! Hold back there Dick, you rascal! hold the dogs! Steady, old boy!"

I can see the point of his tail shaking, and his ears quiver with restrained excitement. We are in ten steps, now for it!

"Hie on, boy!" One long bound—he plunges beneath the snow amidst the briars!—one breathless moment! there she is!

From beneath his very feet she bursts through the powdered snow, and shaking it from her fur, at one leap she is clear upon the firm crust, and after slipping up once or twice, makes steadily off.

Such a burst of yells, yelps and screeches! Such a jumble-together, helter, skelter, heels-in-the-air start as we make of it. I, little dogs, negroes and all! such falls, and such tripping up! such crackling and crashing! Now the little dogs, that have at first slipped up and rolled over each other, all in a yelling heap, gather their legs together and stretch away with fierce cries after poor molly-cotton, who is going off like a bird, with her black shadow on the snow.

We are wild, frantic with the excitement, and whoop and screech as if tearing out our very lungs, as we follow, throwing each other down in the jostle, and leaving soon the smallest ones far behind.

"They are closing on her! she slips up! Whoop! hurrah!"

"Golly! dat's Snap! yah! yah! he de dog!"

"You Pomp, dat's my Sanch! O you nigger, dat's no Snap! Da, now! he got her!"

"You Sanch! you Snap! get out, you dogs! get out! begone!" I shriek, but it is too late now to save poor molly-cotton from being torn.

"Hoo-ey! dat my Snap! yah! yah!"

"You nigger, dat Sanch, fust! Mass Charles dat Sanch? yah! yah! dis nigger's dog! Hoo-ray! hoo-ray!"

CHAPTER III.

THE NATURALIST DEVELOPING.

WHEN the crust had melted, then came tracking hares on the snow, and here Pompey and I were better than Milo's nose—for we could see the beautiful little triangles Molly left behind with her feet at each bound, laid as plain along the snow as three ink-marks on white paper.

Out from the cabbage-patch or the nursery we would follow it, winding round and round, through the fences and by the briar-patch—across the fields and away towards the wood we would trail, bending down to look as we went, and keeping Milo back behind us. Now the edge of the wood is reached, and here the track gets all mixed up with others, and twisted back upon itself, so that for a long time we cannot make it out—but Pompey strikes a circuit round in the wood, and after awhile he shouts—

"Here he am, Massa Chas.! Got her agin!—soon find dat hollow, now!"

Away we tramp again—Pompey as eager on the new trail as any hound—crashing through hazel thickets—falling over buried logs and grape vines—to be up and scramble on again until—"Ha!—that great old oak tree! That's the place—see, the tracks go right into the hollow at its root."

"We've got her! we've got her!"

Matches were not known in those days, but we had a little steel and flint, with some "punk" between us, and now soon we had scraped away the snow to get at the dry leaves, and broken off all the dead boughs and twigs we could find around for a heap—a great heap at the mouth of the hole.

It was very hard to keep Milo's nose out, for snuff and snuff he would in spite of us, when we turned our backs. Now the punk burns—the pile is fired, and then we throw on damp leaves to make a great smoke to rise up the hollow. Milo stands by, looking on now with a very wise expectation—but Pompey kneels by his side, and holds him round the neck tight. A little while! we hear snuff! snuff! and scrambling inside the hollow! Now she comes! thump! sneeze! There she bursts through the smoking pile stifling and helpless. I seize her quickly.

"Down, Milo! down! Hold him, Pomp!" as I wheel round and round to escape him, swinging poor Molly above my head. Now she has got her breath again. Quai! quai! quai! How sad her wail is! But, after a desperate struggle, Milo is beat off, and she is saved!

By the time the snow was gone, my attic had become populous enough; but when the busy, gay and glowing spring had come, and the carolling out of doors, and the warm, deepening green, and the faint odors of the youngest flowers came stealing on the air, the prisoners there grew so restless and looked so out of place in their bare wooden cages, that day by day compunctious visitings grew upon me, until one after one, with many a yearning sigh as I looked after them, all were turned loose upon the sunny earth again. I would be saddened for days to think of their ingratitude, for no one of them would ever come back to me again.

Sorrows could not last long in those days. The sap run vigorously, and new pleasures soon grew over the old scars. My pets were all gone, but with the same spring that wooed their freedom came nesting time.

Ah, what an eye I had for localities most apt to be selected by my wild favorites to build their homes in then! I was seldom taken by surprise in finding any nest. I could almost tell beforehand the very fork, thick clustered round with veiling leaves, in which Master Dandy Jay would wisely hide his clumsy house.

I knew the very limb out near the end of which the Robin meant to build. I could tell the very stump or hollow which yonder twittering pair of Blue Birds would select—that is, if they didn't choose a hole in the great gate-posts of the meadow.

The blackberry thicket in the corner of the "worm fence" where the Brown Thrasher would build amidst sharp briars, I knew well of old; and the very pear tree top, or swinging locust in the yard, from which the Oriole, with black and golden coat, would hang its woven cradle, was prophetically foreshadowed.

I knew the apple-tree in the orchard, too, that sober-coated reverend of jollity, the Parson Oriole, would be sure to select to preach his garrulous sermons of glee on, while his tender mate rocked pendent, listening from the same breezy bough.

I could tell before I reached yonder dead young mulberry, whether it was a Tom-Tit's populous nursery that had filled that sap-sucker's deserted chamber, or whether I might expect,

when I tapped its sounding sides, to see the great soft black eyes and trembling whiskers of the velvety Flying Squirrel fill the round little hole before she darted out to sail down on the creamy spread of her furred drapery;—as for the red-crested Flicker with his spotted breast, who loved this kind of house, too, I knew his droll ways better than his better-half herself, and many a sunshiny morning have I sat beneath and mocked his noisy laugh and hammering rattle.

I knew the Screech Owl stood to blink and stare on sleepy watch the livelong day, out from his door in that old hollow beech that held his little family of horned goblins warm within; and where the robber Hawk circled on moveless wing with plaintive cries at noonday, I knew his savage heart was yearning towards that huge oak's clustering top below—and if eagle's eyried on the cliff, I told it when I saw them stealing quickly in.

It was no mystery to me where the shy Flame Bird hid its eggs—nor could the artist Hummer, with all its matchless skill, deceive me—for the moss-cloaked bulb that seemed so like the gradual swelling of a natural knot upon the twig, revealed its delicate secret to my sharpened eye.

The cunning, noisy crow, with all its loud-mouthed gammon, never could mislead me, and even the subtle mocking-bird had to give in to my untiring watchfulness. As for Bob White, I heard him daily call "wife-e! wife-e!" to nest in the deep clover; and the meek, simple dove, I patronized, especially, and visited her each day, to watch, lest some rude boy or prowling cat had marked the low and exposed nest where the silly thing had placed it on an apple-tree limb, right across the orchard path; and respecting the wren,—Miss Kitty, the jade! I believe she would have built in my coat sleeve, had I given her half a chance!

The blue martin and I knew each other's faces, Spring in, and Autumn out; for many a friendly and familiar gossip did we hold together from my attic window, that overlooked the little painted palace on a pole I had set up for it outside.

Ah, that fatal structure, with its red walls of painted brick! its mimic turrets, saw my first foul deed of wanton murder!

These purple martins I most dearly loved, because they brought me from the farthest south the first news of Spring in their glad, low twitterings, and I placed this gorgeous house there in lofty state for them to occupy in welcome to their weary wings; but then, the little warlike blue bird would take possession first, and cruelly buffet the tired wanderer when it came to claim its own; then my blood boiled to witness the inhospitable deed, for the blue bird was no stranger, and lived here through the winter.

I plead now with my father for a gun, and by one tremendous effort, learned to say my multiplication table backwards, to win it as a reward, and then grasping the bright new weapon, in truculent rage, slew, with my first shot, the audacious intruder, as it fluttered in triumph above the house it had usurped.

What a strange sensation it was as I lifted that first gasping victim of my prowess, and saw the blood upon my hands.

I believe that blood, warm, dropping blood, maddens our race, and makes fiends of us,—for any devil of them all might have envied my ferocious exultation! It was my first taste of blood, shed by my own act, and the red, infernal nectar fired through my veins the raging ecstacies of a new lust that all incarnadined the blue, holy sky, and dimmed, angrily, the green, cheerful earth! From that moment the fiercer impulse of the hunter was aroused, to grow apace towards its stern joys!

The tyrant king bird knew me for a foe, and would ruffle his vermilion crest at the very sight of me, and dip at my head with waspish, querulous twitterings, for now there was mortal feud between us; and when I saw the quarrelsome braggart persecute, with cruel buffetings, such blithe embodyments of musical mirth as the little Parson Oriole, and wagging Wren, my heart would be moved to deadly indignation on behalf of my gentle playmates; but when the warrior-bird screamed its game defiance as it fell before my aim, and pecked and clawed at me to the last gasp, then my respect was aroused, and I stood over it, sorrowing for my hasty wrath.

But such compunctious visitings would become less and less frequent with each new deed of bloody retribution!—as I fain would call it now. In my puisance I assumed to be the champion of weakness and the oppressed, out in this free world of nature; and going forth slaying, and to slay, its tyrants, I loved to call by self-approving names this lust for slaughter that grew upon me.

How my cheek paled when a warning cry from some watchful singer would hush all the timid choir around, and with a sudden swoop of overcoming wings, the dark hawk hurled its fearful form down amidst the scattering throng; and then, the flushing hot blood, how it tingled through me, as I grasped my gun!

My very soul on fire, I shivered with the eagerness of vengeful wrath, when that sharp wail broke upon the breathless silence, and upward, with shrill, triumphing screams, the robber mounted, in heavy flappings, with the stricken victim struggling in his claws.

One concentrated instant, with my nerves all steel, and his strong flight swerves to the report!—a shriek of baffled fierceness, and he is whirling prone to earth!

No errant knight, careering earth intent on deeds of "high emprise," did ever press his mailed foot, at last, on slain dragon's scaly neck, with more exulting consciousness of loftiest mede, than I in that proud moment of stern victory.

It was the madness of a glorious exultation when I thus slew the prowlers of earth, or air, or water! I was exalted by the act, and felt happy in their pangs, as it seemed to me, because they chased and tore the gentle creatures that I loved! I could not realize in this foolish illusion, the mere "savagery of unreclaimed blood," therefore did I rejoice in it with unutterable delight! It was not that I was cruel, either,—I was drunk!—drunk with blood in the bewildering riot of youthful energies and unaccustomed power!

Ah, and I was a daring climber, too, in those days! a clean shaft, thirty feet to the limbs, was a mere irritation to me, especially if I had espied a grey squirrel's summer pavilion swinging to the breeze upon its lofty top.

When I had mounted, what a joy it was, rocking with undizzied brain from topmost fork, to look out over the upheaving, restless ocean of green leaves, and hear their low, solemn murmurings go by! They filled me with a strange exulting, those wild symphonies, with their deep, mellow, muffled roar, and I would rock my perilous perch in reckless sweepings, to and fro, until it swung me in delicious vaultings through the resonant tumult, like a sea-bird lifted on the storm-tossed waves.

Many a ferruling has climbing for such a swing, or for a bird's nest, cost me, savagely laid on by a brutal and captious pedagogue; and I hate the mean oppressor to this day! I was a scape-grace truant, to be sure; but God had made the glad sun and beautiful earth that wooed my lagging steps, and I should not have been bruised and scarred by a base, thick-blooded wretch, because I yielded an hour to their holy spell, and could forget, amid scenes of such enchantment, even the terrors of his gloomy reign.

Verily, that "Old Field Schoolmaster" will have many grievous sins to answer for in his day of account. May the justice that shall be measured unto him be more lenient than any he meted out to me!

I fought him at last, tooth and finger nails, with the scornful but futile spite of the little warrior King Bird, caught napping by the claws of a carrion crow.

I ran away to my friends, and was protected from his vengeance. Dread was the ire that shook his mighty soul when he saw that the victim was beyond the reach of his tyranny! It rose and expanded into prophecy, and he registered the vow before the Fates, that he would live to see me—the worst boy in the county—"hanged!"

Ha! ha! It might certainly have befallen me, as with Absalom, to have been hung by the hair in a vine or tree-top, for daily I ran the risk in my predacious climbing, but, as yet, the neck of "the worst boy in the county" claims to be innocent of any unpleasant familiarity with hemp! May the shadow of that prophecy never be less! Ah, boys who loved the green-wood better than the horn-book, saw hard times in my young days.

But now came the first great revolution to my young life. I must be sent from home to school! The rebel-boy is to be tamed by stern and wholesome lessons—by the necessity of self-sustained struggle with the rough actualities of being.

The soft delicious haze of home—the warm thrill of nestling love beneath a gentle mother's wing, must even be chilled away in the bare, unaided conflict, for place and recognition among my fellows in the strange dreary world outside. The tender soothings of that sweet seclusion, where my heart had grown all fenced about by charms, must now give place to wanton gibes; and ruffian buffettings dispel my dream-born delicate visions, in the bare melee of vulgar license!

It was a fearful trial, but I endured it; for it was a wild country house they sent me to, and I sought for compensation amidst my old surroundings of the natural world. Those loved associations of the shady wood gave me new calm with the mild presence of their familiar graces, and strengthened, with music of the songs they sung at home, my sinking heart to bear the sharp bereavement. Here, from my first cheering refuge, they became my almost sole companions in rough solitary sports, until every secret place they made their haunts, for miles and miles around, was known to me in loving visitation, wild foray, or vengeful raid.

For a long time I shrank from the coarse companionship of the rude boys of my own age, who were my school-fellows—for, fresh from my sacred home, where bird voices had mingled most with the gentle tones of playmate sisters, their brutal recklessness of speech could but sound repulsive and disgusting to my dainty sense. I scorned them with fastidious haughtiness; and they of course taunted me until, my pride aroused, I stood at bay with sullen desperation, and in many a fierce battle pounded a full respect into their thick skulls for these same "womanish ways" of mine, as they had dared to name them!

Now the ice was fairly broken—shocked by these rude collisions, out of Dream-land into the Real, I waked into a lusty sympathy with its stern and boisterous elements. The hardy spirit that had joyed before to wrestle in isolation with the unhoused wild conditions of mere nature, learned now to cope with turbulent passions amidst lawless peers—to feel new exultings in an emulous strife with my own race!

Ah, then came the glorious time of most ambitious feats! The spirit of rivalry once aroused, to what superb extreme would not the extravagant energies be hurled in their fierce lust of eminence! What feats of incredible audacity and hysterical endurance!

The pale and rigid wrestler, writhing with a stouter foe—the desperate runner straining at a distant goal, with teeth clenched, lest he should pant and fall—the climber, taunted to a perilous feat, swinging some fearful gap, with flying bound, from limb to limb at dizziest height—the swimmer, breasting swollen torrents with blue limbs, beating vainly to advance—these were my playmates now in reckless emulation! When Saturday came, and in trembling eagerness we girded up our loins to meet our freedom, and scattered in hurrying troops over the rough hills and away to seek adventure for this happy time, how dauntless and how strong were we! Dangers we loved for danger's sake, and shouted for the joy to meet them.

Those holiday hours were indeed precious fragments from the Nomad's Dream of Paradise, we had time to snatch, fresh with the sparkle of dew and sunshine on them, during those cloudy times of irksome servitude—and how we reveled in them when they came! A year of enjoyment was crowded through those fast minutes into the day.

Away with the rising sun to the "Bottomless Spring" Mill Pond, six miles off!—in bare feet—with jackets slung over arms, and fishing lines in pockets, we pattered along the bridle-path at the long swinging gait of an Indian runner—never pausing, in our merry chattering, for breath, since such time was too precious! We must be there in an hour, for the greatest fish bite early!

The dark hills are past, and we have reached the level on the other side, and through the great trees can see the sobered glisten of the vexed tumbling stream we have leaped across so often in the highlands, now creeping in slow crystal spread beneath the overhanging shadows toward its neared bourne. There they go in splendid shoals, the great white trout, darting like wild pigeons through a fluid air, as we are seen; and now, too, we can slacken our swift pace to gaze in panting ecstacy for awhile. The green pike, lithe and swift, glances its white belly, like a sword flash, up at us as he darts past—the active succors scattering from its dreaded path! We cannot take them here—they hold their way towards the deep water that now shows like a great fog-bank through the thick towering forest stems ahead.

Here we are at last! as the wide burst of water, blazing in the morning sun, dazzles our eyes accustomed to the shades! One shout of joyous greeting and then to work! Quickly the long tapering poles are cut from the bordering thickets—bait for our small hooks produced, and in hurried eagerness the favored spot secured. They are thrown in. Hey! hey! Hurrah!—a fluttering splash!—and the first fish is landed amidst laughing congratulations, altogether at war with the favorite precepts of legitimate angling! But what care we for the shades of Cotton and Walton?—the fish are too abounding and too eager to be frightened easily, and the noisy sport goes on.

Yonder, away across the lake-like Pond, is the Bottomless Spring. There the greatest fish are taken, and very soon, with a sufficiency of minnows secured, we hire the boat from the mill below to cross. At last comes the real time for sport. The excitement is too great now, and the stakes too important, for unseemly mirth or noise. With rapid silent oars we urge across the broad sheet, avoiding here and there the formidable snags that protrude their dry rugged arms from some buried trunk imploringly towards the sunshine. Now we stem with laboring oars the polished glide with which the dark pool throws up its green waters from unsounded depths.

We strain our eyes downwards through that dim yawning gulf in wondering awe, for here the legends say the earth-crust has been rent by the Evil One, who came one dark night of storm and horror to carry off a noted Infidel, who lived not far from hence, on a great plantation, years ago! Just beyond a great cave yawns, too, and we can push the boat upon the lapsing transparency up beneath the dripping roof, until we shudder, of the rayless gloom, and dare not venture to go farther; though it is said to bring us at last beneath a vast and vaulted roof, far under the hills. Here we let go our long lines over the side of the boat, in the Bottomless Spring, a hundred feet or so, and now for the trout or greedy pike. Ah, what a strange thrill it is, when we drag up with many a wary strain of hissing lines, the sparkling prey from that mysterious abyss.

When the noon comes with its sultry heats, we leave our finny sport for new refreshing in those cool depths. Delicious plunges! down! deep down, with eager eyes opened on the wave, we strive to pierce its secrets—but in vain. Many an hour we struggled and plashed through the freshening waters, until the hot sun would scorch our exposed backs, and the blistered skin peel from the writhing flesh. Evening, and the return through lengthening shadows with our burdens of fish carried between us, found our flagging steps drag heavily on the hilly way, and the late moon rose behind the tall chimneys as the "Big House" came in welcome view!

Then there came, too, the long excursions in search for young squirrels through the deep trackless heart of the wild forest—or in the autumn to gather nuts; when, for either, we must climb the loftiest of the hoary trees, and that with a lithe daring that would have curdled soberer blood.

With the winter came new sports, more hardy still—the long night hunts by stealth with the younger darkies and their little cur dogs, for the sulky "'Possum." That was great sport to begin with—for we seldom ventured far from the skirts of the plantation for fear of getting lost, and we were not yet old enough to be promoted to sharing the dangerous honors of the Coon hunt with the grown negroes, because we could not keep up with their weary tramps.

But the 'Possum hunt was our own affair, and well we knew to manage it among ourselves. It all had to be done very quietly; and if a dog barked before we got clear out of ear-shot of the "Big House," he got well kicked for it by all in reach—black or white. We dreaded betrayal in the least sound; and even the chunk of fire carried by the biggest darkie, was carefully sheltered by our hats and bodies, lest its tell-tale gleam might be seen. Once round the turn and fairly in the woods, we breathed freely, and might venture to raise our voices from the eager whispers of consultation to the more decided tones of decision and command—encouraging each other and the dogs: for "outer-darkness" is a great damper upon both boys and dogs!

Now we may cheer, and even whoop, as we are beginning to enter the old field, where the persimmons grow, and wild grapes mat, with their strong tendrils, the scrubby thickets. Here the "'possums" resort to feast upon the fruits, and the "old har" keeps his form, too, in the long grass and briar patches; and every now and then, with a sudden burst of screeching yelps, the little curs break away after a bounding fellow, which they soon lose in the thickets. We do not care for these interruptions, for the little dogs cannot trail them far, and soon lose them in doubling through the briars. We have no fear that the noise they make will spoil our sport a great deal, for the sluggish 'possum does not care to trust its heels much on the ground to run away, and we shall be apt to find it where it has come to feed on the persimmons, or overtake it on the way. With many a shrill whoop and yell we cheer the dogs on to greater activity, now that the forage-grounds are gained, and the game must be at hand.

Hark, a low, wary yelp, quick, short, half-smothered with hesitation and eagerness! There it goes, the gathering cry! yelp, screech, quaver, whine! They are bursting to let go their voices. Hurrah! the shrill yell rises from every throat at once, curs, boys, darkies screeching all together in one sharp, sudden cry of savage exultation; then all is silent.

"Tree'd!" "tree'd!" Yes, a short, sullen bark is followed by another and another, as each dog comes up, and smelling at the tree, satisfies himself that all is right; now we plunge, tearing through the brush, regardless of briars and thorns, in the direction of these sounds, and soon we hear the eager whining of the dogs, through all the noise of their barking. We are very close now; and bursting through the thicket, come upon them, all leaping up against a fence-corner of the plantation; there, showing plain against the moon, and hanging by the tail from a limb of that bare persimmon over the fence, we see the great grey 'possum savagely grinning at the scene below, with his long, white teeth full bared!

Hah! hah! hah! what yells of merry laughter greet the grotesque sight! Some point their fingers at his shame-faced grins, some pelt him with rotten boughs caught up from the dry leaves at our feet; while the dogs yell louder still, and leaping against the tree and fence fall back in scrambles between our legs.

"Ha, yah! ole boy! what do dar, grinnin' at dat moon? steal more ole hen, suck more eggs, 'nudder night, will yer?"

"Come out dat! dat curl-tail no hold whar dis child climb!" and up starts a young darkie to shake him out.

"Yah! yah! see dat 'possum laugh! grin nudder side you's mout 'fore long, ole chicken thief!"

"Shake he, Josh! shake hard, nigger! he hold on good wid he curl-tail!"

"Ha! yah! whoop! hear he growl! now dat 'possum laugh! dar he come!"

A simultaneous rush,—screams, shrieks, growls, all mingled for an instant, while we beat off the dogs, and then he is swung in triumph above their heads by the tallest of the party. Now the well known trick of the opossum, in feigning to be dead, affords new amusement; and he is surrounded by his merry torturers, who, amidst noisy clamors, tease him in a thousand ingenious ways to make him show signs of life, though all but the greener ones take good care not to give him *too* good a chance to bite, which he sometimes does with severity while thus "playing 'possum."

Sometimes he is tree'd in a large tree, and then the fire must be built, and a serious job we have of it to get at him; but the attempt is seldom relinquished until success has attended it. The negroes take charge of the game on our return, and the next night there is a grand 'possum roast at the Quarter, in which we participate only on the sly as have been with the hunt.

But to digress about our teacher. He was an eccentric person, who having been poor in his young days, had acquired a fondness for teaching, which he had adopted then from a necessity, but which continued to cling to him through his life, although his marriage had brought him a handsome fortune. He therefore kept up his school as an amateur, rather than from the necessities of the case. His plantation was a very extensive one, situated on the edge of a wild country, and his admirable school the favored and noted resort of the sons of the southern gentry, from far and wide.

He was a good old man, that father Hinton, and loved us all as his own children. We were allowed much more license, on parole of honor, than was usual at such places; the old gentleman even took a grotesque sort of pleasure, which he awkwardly attempted to conceal, in examining and commenting upon, and particularly in weighing and noting down the weight of our game, the legitimate produce of any and all our wild sports, except the night-hunts, which were strictly interdicted.

I shall remember his appearance to my dying day, on one occasion of this sort.

We had made an unusually successful excursion to the distant Bottomless Spring Mill Pond on one Saturday, and the next morning, which was Sunday, we were very eager to exhibit to him our trophies, of which we were very proud.

He was a very zealous Presbyterian, of the Old School doctrine, and of course very strict in regard to his and our demeanor on the Sabbath. We were therefore a little afraid to parade our fish before him this morning; but there was one among the rest, a great white perch, or trout, as it was incorrectly called in that locality, of such extraordinary size, and with the capture of which, too, there was such a ridiculous story of mishaps, to me connected, that all my comrades were bursting with eagerness to tell it before Mr. Hinton.

They would not venture, however, to take the fish to him before breakfast, because there was no opportunity, as we were always marched out in solemn procession from morning prayers to the breakfast table, which was placed in a long and wide passage of the large house. The fish, however, were hung in a grand cluster against a pillar which stood near the head of the table, in such a position that his eye must necessarily fall upon them as he took his accustomed position to pronounce the grace standing.

Now Mr. Hinton was a person of genuine dignity of character, and we stood in great awe of the earnest solemnity of manner with which he always addressed himself to the observances of his religion; but the story with regard to the capture of the great trout had got all among the boys, and the sight of it, paraded so ostentatiously, now caused a general disposition to titter, which was even ill suppressed, as our teacher assumed his place. He had not chanced to notice it, and raised his hands reverently, and the habit of respect for his tall and thin, but commanding presence in these solemn functions, for the instant hushed every one breathlessly. It was his well known habit to hold his eyes reverently closed during the pronunciation of the somewhat lengthy benediction; and I am sorry to say that it had been a general habit, too, among the worst of us, to seize irreverently this occasion to snatch in wanton mischief, sundry articles of food from the dishes before us, which could be transferred to our pockets; or else to throw a crust of bread across the table and hit a neighbor on the nose, or pull the ears of the servant girls in waiting, or indeed perform any other ingenious antics which did not require too much time, or cause too great a noise!

No sooner did the good man close his eyes than there was so general a movement of heads and hands, such loud whispering and noisy attempts to choke down laughter, that with all his Sunday morning solemnity he could not help hearing, and accordingly cut short the grace in time to open his eyes upon the most vivid, interesting tableaux conceivable of grins, grimaces, hob-nobbing heads and pointing fingers; following the direction of which, involuntarily his eye rested first upon my unlucky self, and then upon the monster trout against the pillar, as the cause of this ill-timed hubbub. He started somewhat as his eye took in its size, and the severe frown gathering upon his brow was contradicted by a slight nervous twitch of relaxation at the corner of his mouth; our watchful eyes detected instantly this favorable sign, and there was one general burst of the smothered laughter from all sides, above which rose the stern command,—

"Silence! what does this mean, young gentlemen?"

But it was too late now for authority to be regained at once, and peal after peal of unrestrainable laughter set order at defiance. But, fortunately for the delinquents, the good man's eyes seemed to wander abstractedly, drawn by some irresistible attraction towards the trout. Suddenly he muttered, as if to himself,—

"Why, as I live, that fish must weigh more than ten pounds!" and forgetting all our outrageous conduct for the moment, he strode across the passage, took down his little spring balance, which he always used for such purposes, and, to our increased amusement and delight, proceeded immediately to satisfy himself as to the weight.

"Twelve pounds!" he exclaimed, drawing a long breath

"Whew, pro-di-gious! Greatest trout ever taken at the Spring Pond since my memory!" Then replacing fish and scales, he turned and looked sharply along the table, while the hubbub was silenced in an instant. "You Charles, Henry, Tom, you will all three remain after school, to-morrow morning!"

This was said with a severity that chilled the hearts of those of us named, for remaining "after school" was well known to portend punishment of some sort.

However, by the time the terrible hour of judgment came, the whole story of the capture having reached his ears, he was evidently more disposed, at that awful moment, when all the other boys had vanished, and we left alone with him to receive sentence, to laugh at the affair himself, than to be severe with us, so we got off with a slight reproof.

The incident which had caused so much fun was this:— During the whole day of Saturday there had been a match going on among us all, as to who should catch the most and largest fish. It so happened that I had either not been in the mood for fishing, or had been in poor luck, for I had caught little or nothing.

As evening closed the party embarked in the boat to return across the Pond, and were quizzing me most unmercifully for my poor success; and I in return was making empty boasts, which I had no dream of realizing, as I stood in the bow idly lashing the water with my line, that I would surely catch a larger fish than all their's put together, before we reached the other shore. There was no bait on my hook, and there seemed surely no great probability of my performing any such miracle. Our boat was slowly winding among the buried logs, of which I have spoken, when suddenly, as my line dropped in our wake, the gleam of the leaden sinkers caught the eye of a huge fish which made its lair under the logs, and in a twinkling I was jerked head-foremost over the bow into the water, amidst the laughing shouts of my companions, who understood the thing in an instant. Some one shouted comfortingly in my ear, as I rose spluttering from the sudden plunge, "Ha! ha! I think the fish has caught you instead! Hold on to him! hold on!"

The fish was secured, after a desperate struggle, with our united force; and as I was yet quite a little fellow, the joke of my having been "caught by the fish," was too good a one not to tell for a long time among such boys!

We had skating, too, in the winter, and many a wild scene there was when we were flying, like squads of swallows, hither and yon upon the ice. There were some winters when extraordinary floods came in the early part of the season, and then the whole forest on the lowest side of the plantation would be flooded, and its trunks stand several feet deep in the clear water. The change of a night or two would freeze this over suddenly—and then such a time!

The earliest dawn of Saturday found us afoot with preparation, for we had scarcely slept for eagerness through that long dull night of Friday! Such clanking of skates as we set off in a run, with a cold bite for breakfast in our hands, and some more stuffed into our pockets for dinner! This was too great a time to think much of eating.

Away across the wide bare fields, scrambling over the rough, hard frozen ploughed ground in our thick boots, which made great clamor on the crisp clear morning air, we hurried with smoking nostrils and thick gloved hands. Our bodies just from the warm bed, are almost cut in two at first by the cold scythe of that winter's breath in its wide keen sweep across the open fields—but soon we reach the shelter of the heavy wood, and then our blood comes glowing warm again back to the tingling surface, and with eager shouts we greet the strange scene.

Sunrise is streaming now down through the dark trunks in many a line of rosy light that is reflected in sharp broken blazes far and wide, from the aerial mirror underneath, that holds that mighty forest, all glory-tipped, reversed, in its hard clear bosom. The fire is soon built to warm our freezing fingers while the skates are fitted; but it seems a fearful thing to trust ourself out on mid-air thus—for so to our awed sense, that dark translucent depth appears—as we shoot above its mysteries, almost of our own volition,

"And yet no footing seen."

Motion soon dispels the chill of strangeness, and now with hardy eagerness we spring away in facile glide among the great trees, and soon we dart, and wind, and fly, as in that marvelous sense of motion without wings, in overcoming space, that sometimes visits us in dreams. How rapturous that wild ecstacy of speed! We flew past walls of trunks, run into each other—we circled like thoughts, whirling as mountain winds are eddied—into the light, and out, like glittering shadows dimmed, while the ringing clangors of our steel-shod heels receded in soft moanings from our swift way!

So sped our lives, winter and summer, as a vision goes, until the time came at last when we must leave that old place, some of us for wider fields of busy strife, out in the great world of men, and others for college. With what fond regrets my memory revisits those rude and pleasant scenes. They are near the last of those still-life pictures, where the soul rests calmly in the past.

Now the action thickens as the opening turmoil hourly includes new scenes, new experiences, with diversified excitements rousing deeper passions. The boy is yet not all a boy, and the consciousness of strange yearnings and new ambitions begin to move his breast with undefined wonder.

CHAPTER IV.

THE NIGHT HUNT IN RECESS.

But still the old leaven leaveneth the whole lump, and with the advent of Commencement, earlier passions soon displaced the new ambitions. Ah! do I not remember well those turbulent times—when, having got somewhat up in my "teens," I began to "feel myself," and think of a truant independence in college recess?

The "old folks," as I and sundry other "young gentlemen sophomores" of the neighborhood, were disposed to believe unanimously,—were entirely too close and particular; or, in a word, since our college experience, apron-strings were beginning to be manacles! A declaration of independence had become necessary! not an open one, but a declaration of "*expediency!*" such an one as we could make without involving serious consequences.

For instance, *item*, our right to creep out of our windows when the "sleepless Gryphons" were a-bed—for once "caught napping"—to keep "tryst" with our "peers" in view of a descent upon some old snarler's watermelon patch, which lay odd miles away. *Item*, our right by the same mode of exit, or other strategy, at a given hour of the night, to meet at the said given place, with the intention of enjoying the moon in a "coon" or "'possum" hunt with the "Darkies" and their dogs, down at the "Quarter,"* &c., &c., &c.

As the time had come when we felt it necessary to make such doughty demonstrations, our measures were of course taken with due and necessary forecast.

Old Sambo, down at the Quarter, the dingy Nimrod of darkness and the "Dárkies," was first to be propitiated. He is somewhat coy at first, for his grizzly poll has been penetrated with a veneration most profound for the dictum of the constituted authorities at the "Big House!" Sundry presents of "baccar" pipes, and odd shillings, assisted by a most condescending and confidential manner on our part, gradually bring him around to a reciprocation. In vague hints, and through telegraphic nods and gestures of most profound signification, the time, place, probable force, and accompaniments of his next great turn-out from the Quarter, for a "coon" hunt, are all imparted to the "young massa." We of course instantly convey the momentous news through somewhat less mysterious mediums to sundry young companions, living near at hand, who are eagerly awaiting it.

The important night has arrived. The "old folks" have

---

* On the plantations there are usually several villages, or settlements of the negroes, which are called "Quarters."

barely time to commence their first snooze, having taken it for granted that we are where dutiful and obedient sons should be at such an hour—in the land of Nod—when by sundry silent exhibitions of our skill at escalading, we have made our escape from the sacred precincts of authority, and are off to Sambo's Quarter, footing it with a fluttering heart beneath the uncertain starlight.

Now as we had been prohibited from joining in "night-hunts," first, on the ground that they injured our health, and secondly, on the ground that they were dangerous, and third and lastly, on the ground that it was highly undignified that young gentlemen "to the manor born," and just from college, too, should go out hunting with "the servants:" we of course, with the heavy portent of all these formidable indictments hanging over us, felt that discovery would be attended with just the requisite amount of danger to give piquancy to the commencement of an enterprise.

If our pulse was quickened, our heels were not less so by such considerations. We were sinning on the strength of our instincts, and we knew it! We pause at the several cross-paths on the way, to wait for the other young recusants who were to join us. One after another they come in, each usually attended by a favorite servant not far from his own age, who has been admitted to his confidence. Joyously enough we begin to gabble as the distance between us and the awful shadows of the "Big House" is increased. Soon the

> "——Long leveled rule of streaming light,"

for a sight of which the bewitched lady in Comus prayed, "visits" *us*, and as we approach, the *one* ruddy "level" divides itself into many a narrow fitful stream from the open doors and glowing hearths of the "Quarter!"

The crossing of shadows to and fro shows that all there is alert. We hear the subdued too-oot of a horn, and the low opening howl of the gathering dogs in answer. We begin to grow silent, and move faster. The horn is sounded more boldly, and the howls accompany it in a gathering cadence.

Now the scene has burst upon us through an opening of the trees!—There they are! Negroes of all degrees, size and age, and of dogs—

> "Mastiff, greyhound, mongrel grim,
> Hound or spaniel, brack or lym,
> Or bobtail tike, or trundle tail."

All are there, in one conglomerate of active, noisy confusion. When indications of the hurried approach of our company are perceived, a great accession to the hubbub is consequential.

Old Sambo sounds a shriller note upon his horn, the dogs rise from independent howls to a simultaneous yell, and along with all the young half-naked darkies rush to meet us. The women come to the doors with their blazing lamps lifted above their heads, that they may get a look at the "young masters," and we, shouting with excitement, and blinded by the light, plunge stumbling through the meeting current of dogs and young negroes, into the midst of the gathering party. Here we are suddenly arrested by a sort of awe as we find ourselves in the presence of old Sambo. The young dogs leap upon us with their dirty fore-paws, but we merely push aside their caresses, for old Sambo and his old dog Bose are the two centres of our admiration and interest.

Old Sambo is the "Mighty Hunter before"—*the moon!* of all that region. He is seamed and scarred with the pitiless siege of sixty winters! Upon all matters appertaining to such hunts, his word is "*law*," while the "tongue" of his favorite and ancient friend Bose is recognized as "*gospel.*" In our young imaginations, the two are respectfully identified.

Old Sambo, with his blanket "roundabout"—his cow's-horn trumpet slung about his shoulders by a tow string—his bare head, with its greyish fleece of wool—the broad grin of complacency, showing his yet sound white teeth—and rolling the whites of his eyes benignantly over the turmoil of the scene—was to us the higher prototype of Bose. He, with the proper slowness of dignity, accepts the greet of our patting caresses, with a formal wagging of the tail, which seems to say—"O, I am used to this!" while, when the young dogs leap upon him with obstreperous fawnings, he will correct them into propriety with stately snarling. They knew him for their leader!—they should be more respectful!

Now old Sambo becomes patronizing to *us*, as is necessary and proper in our new relations! From his official position of commander-in-chief, he soon reduces the chaos around us into something like subjection, and then in a little time comes forth the form of our night's march. A few stout young men who have obeyed his summons have gathered around him from the different huts of the Quarter—some with axes, and others with torches of pine and bark. The dogs become more restless, and we more excited, as these indices of immediate action appear.

Now, with a long blast from the cow's-horn of Sambo, and a deafening clamor of all sizes, high and low—from men, women, children and dogs, we take up the line of march for the woods. Sambo leads, of course. We are soon trailing after him in single file, led by the glimmer of the torches far ahead.

Now the open ground of the plantation has been passed, and as we approach the deep gloom of the bordering forest—

"Those perplexed woods,
The nodding horror of whose shady brows
Threats the forlorn and wandering passenger"—

even the yelpings of the excited dogs cease to be heard, and they dash on into the darkness as if they were going to work—while we with our joyous chattering subsided into silence, enter these "long-drawn aisles" with a sort of shiver; the torches showing, as we pass in a dim light, the trees—their huge trunks vaulting over head into the night, with here and there a star shining like a gem set into their tall branching capitals—while on either side we look into depths of blackness as unutterably drear to us as thoughts of death and nothingness. Oh, it was in half trembling wonder then, we crowded, trampling on the heels of those before, and, when after awhile the rude young negroes would begin to laugh aloud, we felt that in some sort it was profane.

But such impressions never lasted long in those days. Every other mood and thought gives way to the novelty and contagious excitement of adventure. We are soon using our lungs as merrily as the rest. The older dogs seem to know perfectly, from the direction taken, what was the game to be pursued for the night. Had we gone up by the old Field where the Persimmon trees grow, they would have understood that "possums" were to be had; but as old Sambo led off through the deep woods towards the swamps, it said "coons" to them as plain as if they had been Whigs of 1840.

The flush of blood begins to subside as we penetrate deeper into the wood, and as we hear old Sambo shout to his staff officers and immediate rear guard, "Hush dat 'ar jawing, you niggers, dar," we take it for granted that it is a hint, meant not to be disrespected by *us*, that silence is necessary, lest we should startle the game too soon and confuse the dogs.

All is silence now, except the rustle of our tramp over the dried autumn leaves, and occasional patter of the feet of a dog who ranges near to our path. Occasionally a white dog comes suddenly out of the darkness into view and disappears as soon, leaving our imagination startled as if some curious sprite had come "momently" from out its silent haunts to peep at us. Then we will hear the rustling of some rapid thing behind us, and looking round, see nothing; then spring aside with a nervous bound and fluttering pulse, as some black object brushes by our legs—"Nothin' but dat dog, Nigger Trimbush," chuckles a darkie, who observed us—but the couplet,—

> "And the kelpie must flit from the black bog pit,
> And the brownie must not tarry,"

flashes across our memory from the romance of superstition, with the half shudder that is the accompaniment of such dreamy images.

Hark, a dog opens—another, then another! We are still in a moment, listening—all eyes are turned upon old Sambo, the oracle. He only pauses for a minute.

"Dem's de pups—ole dogs aint dar!" A pause. "Pshaw, nothin but a ole har!"—and a long, loud blast of the horn sounds the recall.

We move on—and now the frosty night air has become chilly, and we begin to feel that we have something to do before us. Our legs are plied too lustily on the go-ahead principle for us to have time to talk. The young dogs have ceased to give tongue; for like unruly children they have dashed off in chase of what came first, and as the American hare ("*Lepus Americanus*") is found nearly everywhere, it was the earliest object.

Just when the darkness is most deep, and the sounds about our way most hushed, up wheels the silver moon, and with a mellowed glory overcomes the night. The weight of darkness has been lifted from us, and we trudge along more cheerily! The dogs are making wider ranges, and we hear nothing of them. The silence weighs upon us, and old Sambo gives an occasional whoop of encouragement. We would like, too, to relieve our lungs, but *he* says, "nobody mus holler now but dem dat de dog knows: make 'em bother!" We must perforce be quiet; for "*de dog*" means Bose, and we must be deferential to his humors!

Tramp, tramp, tramp, it has been for miles, and not a note from the dogs. We are beginning to be fatigued; our spirits sink, and we have visions of the warm room and bed we have deserted at home. The torches are burning down, and the cold, pale moon-light is stronger than that they give. One after another the young dogs come panting back to us, and fall lazily into our wake. "Hang coon hunts in general!—this is no joke; all cry and no wool!"

Hark! a deep-mouthed, distant bay! The sound is electrical; our impatience and fatigue are gone! All ears and eyes, we crowd around old Sambo. The oracle attitudinizes. He leans forward with one ear turned towards the earth in the direction of the sound. Breathlessly we gaze upon him. Hark! another bay; another; then several join in. The old man has been unconsciously soliloquizing from the first sound.

"Golly, dat's nigger Trim!" in an under tone; "he know de coon!" Next sound. "Dat's a pup; shaw!" Pause. "Dat's a pup, agin! Oh, niggers, no coon dar!"

Lifting his outspread hand, which he brings down with a loud slap upon his thigh; "Yah! yah! dat's ole Music; look out, niggers!" Then, as a hoarse, low bay comes booming to us through a pause, he bounds into the air with the caperish agility of a colt, and breaks out in ecstasy, "Whoop! whoop! dat's de ole dog; go my Bose!" Then striking hurriedly through the brush in the direction of the sounds, we only hear from him again,

"Yah! yah! yah! dat's a coon, niggers! Bose dar!" And away we rush as fast as we can scramble through the underbrush of the thick wood. The loud burst of the whole pack opening together, drowns even the noise of our progress.

The cry of a full pack is maddening music to the hunter. Fatigue is forgotten, and obstacles are nothing. On we go; yelling in chorus with the dogs. Our direction is towards the swamp, and they are fast hurrying to its fastnesses. But what do we care! Briars and logs; the brush of dead trees; plunges half leg deep into the watery mire of boggy places are alike disregarded. The game is up! Hurrah! hurrah! we must be in at the death! So we scurry, led by the maddening chorus—

"—while the babbling echo mocks the hounds."

Suddenly the reverberations die away. Old Sambo halts. When we get into ear-shot the only word we hear is, "Tree'd!" This from the oracle is sufficient. We have another long scramble, in which we are led by the monotonous baying of a single dog.

We have reached the place at last all breathless. Our torches have been nearly extinguished. One of the young dogs is seated at the foot of a tree, and looking up, it bays incessantly. Old Sambo pauses for awhile to survey the scene. The old dogs are circling round and round, jumping up against the side of every tree, smelling as high as they can reach. They are not satisfied, and Sambo waits for *his* tried oracles to solve the mystery. He regards them steadily and patiently for awhile; then steps forward quickly, and beats off the young dog who had "lied" at the "tree."

The veterans now have a quiet field to themselves, and after some further delay in jumping up the sides of the surrounding trees, to find the scent, they finally open in full burst upon the trail. Old Sambo exclaims curtly, as we set off in the new chase,

"Dat looks like coon! *but cats is about!*"

Now the whole pack opens again, and we are off after it. We all understand the allusion to the *cats*—for we know that, like the raccoon, this animal endeavors to baffle the dogs by running some distance up a tree, and then springing off upon another, and so on until it can safely descend. The young dogs take it for granted that he is in the first tree, while the older ones sweep circling round and round until they are convinced that the animal has not escaped. They thus baffle the common trick which they have learned through long experience, and recovering the trail of escape, renew the chase.

Under ordinary circumstances we would already have been sufficiently exhausted; but the magnetism of the scene lifts our feet as if they had been shod with wings. Another weary scramble over every provoking obstacle, and the solitary baying of a dog is heard again winding up the "cry."

When we reach the "tree" this time, and find it is another "feint," we are entirely disheartened, and all this excitement and fatigue of the night reacting upon us leaves us utterly exhausted, and disinclined to budge one foot further. Old Sambo comes up—he has watched with an astute phiz the movements of the dogs for some time.

"Thought dat ware a *ole* coon from de fust! Dat's a mighty ole coon!" with a dubious shake of his head. "*Ole* coon nebber run dat long!" Another shake of the head, and addressing himself to his "staff:" "Ole coon nebber run'ed dis fur, niggers!' Then turning to us—"Massas, dat a cat! —'taint no coon!"

The dogs break out again, at the same moment, and with peculiar fierceness, in full cry. "Come 'long, niggers!—maby dat's a coon—maby 'taint!" and off he starts again.

We are electrified by the scenes and sounds once more, and "follow, still follow," forgetting everything in the renewed hubbub and excitement. Wearily now we go again over marsh and quagmire, bog and pond, rushing through vines and thickets and dead limbs. Ah, what glimpses have we of our cozy home during this wild chase! Now our strength is gone—we are chilled, and our teeth chatter—the moon seems to be the centre of cold as the sun is of heat, and its beams strike us like arrows of ice. Yet the cry of the dogs is onward, and old Sambo and his staff yell *on!*

Suddenly there is a pause! the dogs are silent, and we hold up! "Is it all lost?" we exclaim, as we stagger, with our bruised and exhausted limbs, to a seat upon an old log. The stillness is as deep as midnight—the owl strikes the watch with his too-whoo! Hah! that same hoarse, deep bay which first electrified us comes booming again through the stillness.

"Yah! yah! dat ole coon am done for! Bose got he, niggers—Gemmen, come on!"

The inspiriting announcement, that *Bose* had tree'd at last, is balm to all our wounds, and we follow in the hurry-scurry rush to the tree. Arrived there, we find old Bose on end barking up a great old oak, while the other dogs lie panting around. "Dare he am," says old Sambo. "Make a fire, niggers!" There is but a single stump of a torch left; but in a little while they have collected dried wood enough to kindle a great blaze.

"Which nigger's gwine to climb dat tree?" says old Sambo, looking round inquiringly. Nobody answers. The insinuations he had thrown out, that it *might* be a cat, have had their effect upon the younger darkies. Sambo waits, in dignified silence, for an answer, and throwing off his horn, with an indignant gesture, he says,—

"You d—n pack of chicken-gizzards, niggers!—climb de tree myself!" and straightway the wiry old man, with the activity of a boy, springs against the huge trunk, and commences to ascend the tree.

Bose gives an occasional low yelp as he looks after his master. The other dogs sit with upturned noses, and on restless haunches, as they watch his ascent.

Nothing is heard for some time, but the fall of dead branches and bark which he throws down. The fire blazes high, and the darkness about us, beyond its light, is unpenetrated even by the moon. We stand in eager groups watching his ascent. He is soon lost to our view amongst the limbs; yet we watch on until our necks ache, while the eager dogs fidget on their haunches, and emit short yelps of impatience. We see him, against the moon, far up amongst the uppermost forks, creeping like a beetle, up, still up! We are all on fire—the whole fatigue and all the bruises of the chase forgotten! our fire crackles and blazes fiercely as our impatience, and sends quick tongues of light, piercing the black throng of forest sentinels about us.

Suddenly the topmost branches of the great oak begin to shake, and seem to be lashing the face of the moon.

"De cat! de cat! look out down dar!" The dogs burst into an eager howl! He is shaking him off! A dark object comes thumping down into our midst, and shakes the ground with its fall. The eager dogs rush upon it! but we saw the spotted thing with the electric flashing of its eyes. Yells and sputtering screams—the howls of pain—the gnashing growls of assault—the dark, tumbling struggle that is rolled, with its fierce clamors, out from our fire-light into the dark shadows of the wood, are all enough to madden us.

We all rush after the fray, and strike wildly into its midst with the clubs and dead limbs we have snatched, when one of *the* body-guards happens to think of his axe, and with a single blow settles it!

All is over! We get home as we may, and about the time

> '—— the dapple grey coursers of the morn
> Beat up the light with their bright silver hoofs,
> And chase it though the sky,"

we creep cautiously into our back window, and sleep not the less profoundly for our fatigue, that we have to charge our late hour of rising, next day, upon Bacon or the Iliad, instead of the "Night Hunt."

CHAPTER V.

AUDUBON—THE HUNTER-NATURALIST.

THE time had now come to my developed and overflowing passions when life must mate itself with destiny; when tastes and energies thus nourished in wild seclusion, should seek their legitimate direction—should break away on their own course to find their natural level!

And so they did, with a vengeance! For had the unconquerable instinct been wanting in my nature, there was one NAME that had so filled my life, that it alone would have been sufficient to inspire me with a giant's strength, had such been necessary, to burst all bonds and away upon the same free track!

Audubon! Audubon! Delightful name! Ah, do I not remember well the hold it took upon my young imagination when I heard the fragmented rumor from afar, that there was a strange man abroad then, who lived in the wilderness with only his dog and gun, and did nothing day by day, but follow up the birds; watching every thing they might do; keeping in sight of them all the time, wherever they went, while light lasted; then sleeping beneath the tree where they perched, to be up and follow them again with the dawn, until he knew every habit and way that belonged to them. That when he was satisfied, he would shoot them in some manner, so as not to tear their plumage, and then sitting down on the mossy roots of an oak, and with nobody to connoisseur for him but his wise looking dog, and the squirrel that stamped and scolded at him from the limbs above, would draw such marvelous pictures of birds as the world never saw before!

Oh, what a happy, happy being that strange man must be, I used to think; and what a strong and brave one, too, to sleep out among the panthers and wild cats, where the Indian whoop was heard—trusting only to his single arm and his faithful dog. I loved to speculate about that dog. He must be larger than my dog "Milo," I thought, and just about as gentle and true, but a *little* more knowing. How I envied him the happiness of such a master and such a life.

As for the master, what magical conjurations of a charmed fancy I loved to associate with him. He must be noble and good, and wear such lofty calmness upon his brow. I had an ideal of physical perfection, and below it could not bear to conceive that so heroic a philosopher could fall.

What a martyr-spirit his must be; and what a holy enthusiasm leads him on through tangled swamps, where the cougar yelled, alligators roared, and hideous serpents parted, with their wavy spotted lengths, the green scum of stagnant pools; up difficult mountains, where the rattle-snake sprung its deadly alarum amidst the mossy fissures of the crumbling stones, and the eagle whetted its hooked beak upon the crag-points; or, beneath the profound shadows of primeval forests, where the few sunbeams that straggled through at noonday, looked like gold dust scattered over the black earth—down the destructive flood of mighty rivers, or beside crystal lakes set in a columnar rim of giant cypresses; on the sky-bounded ocean-heaved prairies, or where the green and glinting ice-bergs thundered crashingly against the hoar cliffs "of fretted Labrador," or the "tropic gulf" hurled at the low "Keys" its foaming mountains—through, amidst, and over all, his dauntless spirit was passing, led always by the winnowing sound of wings.

What a poetical enchantment there was to me in such a life! What sights of awe and of beauty he must see. What images of touching truth—of odd, peculiar humors he must have stored. And that magical power he was said to possess, to tame in colors the very waves upon the leap, and the arrowy Albatross upon the plunge into its beaded crest!

All these were so surprising and miraculous to me, that I wondered, in my simplicity, whether such devotion was not sinful, and such surpassing works would not bring upon their author persecution and imprisonment for necromancy, as the story books told had been the case of old.

It seemed to me too much bliss and too many gifts for a single mortal to enjoy! I felt, not envious; but a deep emulation was stirred within me. I vowed, in my inmost heart, that I would first *see* all those things for myself, with my own eyes; where and *as* he had seen them—out upon the broad face of the extended world,—and then I could look upon his work and know, with an appreciative knowledge, whether he had wrought these miracles or not.

This resolve at once gave tone to my after life. Many a tie was rent, and much agony endured by my friends, when I became an unrecking wanderer through wild and distant regions. The uttermost arms of our tremendous seaward floods saw me amongst their springs. The salt and tumbling Gulf tossed me upon its southern shores, and broad savannahs swelled in my westward course into undulating plains; and they yet rose, across their wearisome breadth, into tall, rounded hills, that grew apace, with crags upon their heads, until heap upon heap far glinting through the clouds, the pinnacled sharp rocks climbed upwards, and the vast forest of crags spread its white bloomy tops among the stars.

My restless step was everywhere; my eager eyes saw all that our great continent could show. The grizzly bear and the tropic bird were equally known to me. The savage trooper and the Mexican slave had been familiars, as well as the fierce bandit, and the stern, simple-hearted hunter. Years of my earlier manhood passed in these erratic wanderings. I had grown familiar with all wild, grotesque and lonely creatures that populate those infinite solitudes of nature, "that own not man's dominion." The vision and the passions of my boyhood still haunted me, and the rustling of free wings by my ear yet awakened all pleasant images.

Now, I felt that I had a right to know and see, face to face, that remarkable man whose deeds and life had so much occupied my imagination—who had so made a living reality out of what had been to me the poetry of life—aye, a poetry which had proved with me, stronger

"Than stipulations, duties, reverences,

and driven me far and wide, an April shadow chased before the fitful wind!

Should I ever see him? The eager questioning lived about my heart whenever I heard his name. I returned home, "the prodigal son," my spirit much tamed and chastened; yet the old leaven fermenting deep beneath the calmer surface.

My restless steps had not long been still. I became again a traveler.

Our boat landed one morning about daybreak at Pittsburg

—that singular city, that looks as if it had been built over the very gates of Acheron. Soon as I made my appearance in the raw, foggy air, upon the wharf, early as it was, I was surrounded by scores of "strikers" and agents of the different hotels and transportation lines.

Amidst the yells and deafening clamors of contending claims on every side, I permitted myself to be bodily ravished into a coach, and hurried off, bag and baggage, for—the word of the Darky "Striker" being accepted—"the most splendiferous hotel in the city!" As it happened to be the one I knew, and had selected beforehand, I was content to take his definition of its superlative excellence.

Before I reached my destination, the coach was hailed from a street corner, and a fellow, muffled in a pilot cloth, sprang in and took a seat beside me. To my no little astonishment, he seemed to take the most sudden and peculiar interest in me, and, greatly to the exaltation of my inward consciousness of great deserts, plied me with a series of the sharpest questionings as to my whereabouts "when I was at home"—my destination, and above all, my route—with the roundest and most voluble protestations as to the affectionate interest he felt in seeing that all travelers, especially such looking ones as I was, were properly warned of the complicated impositions and knaveries practised habitually upon them, by the many transportation lines in this wicked city; and to wind up this touching exordium, he frankly assured me that the "Stage Route" across the mountains was the cheapest—the most safe—the "*most genteelest*"—and altogether the route he would recommend to such a gentleman as me!

The milk of human kindness was somewhat stirred in my veins, responsive to this gratuitous exhibition of a broad philanthropy—but as it happened that I had determined upon the "Canal Route," I waived, with the most thankful acknowledgments, any present committal, and gratefully accepted the card he thrust into my hand. But, as it most unfortunately occurred, I found the office of the "Canal Route" for Philadelphia, &c., was next door to our hotel, and I was tempted, weakly enough, no doubt! to go in and book my name "clear through." Insensate creature that I was. The canal boats would not start till after dark, so that I spent the hours allotted to daylight by the cathedral clocks, in exploring the streets of this dim Cyclopian city.

The incessant clang of sledge-hammers had become sufficiently monotonous when the evening closed in, and I was glad enough to take coach and be transported to the Canal Depot, when the usual vexations and delay consequent, had to be endured.

Finally, however, we got underweigh, with such a cargo of pigs, poultry and humanity, as even canal boats are seldom blessed with. I stood upon tiptoe for the fresh air in the cabin, until the time had actually come when people *must* go to bed; when that awful personage, the Captain, summoned us all together, and informed us that every man, woman and child aboard, must stow his, her or itself away along the face of the narrow walls, in the succession of their registration during the day. Now, it happened that as gentlemen are not usually up before daybreak, that I stood first upon the first list, and was of course entitled to the first choice of hammocks. We panted in the centre of the close-jammed crowd, waiting till the ladies, who always take precedence in America, had been called off. As it happened that this right of choice was finally definitive for the route, and determined whether one should sleep upon a hammock, or the floor, or the tables, for several successive nights—it was a matter of no little moment.

It occurred while the ladies were being disposed of, that I heard above the buzz around me the name of Audubon spoken. My attention was instantly attracted by that magical sound.

I listened in breathless eagerness. I heard a gentleman near me say—"Mr. Audubon is last on the list; I fear he will not get a bed, we are so crowded!"

I felt my heart leap.

"What," said I, leaning forward quickly, "is it possible Mr. Audubon can be aboard? I thought he was still on his Rocky Mountain tour!"

"We are just returning, sir," said the gentleman courteously, half smiling, as he observed the excited expression of my face.

"But, you are joking, are you not?" said I, hardly able to realize so much happiness. He cannot *really* be in this boat. Where? Which is he?"

"He *is* actually in this very cabin," said he, turning full upon me.

"The man of all others in the world I wanted to see most," I ejaculated, half inwardly.

"Well, there he is," said the gentleman, laughing, as he pointed to a huge pile of green blankets and fur which I had before observed stretched upon one of the benches, and took to be the fat bale of some Western trader.

"What, *that* Mr. Audubon?" I exclaimed, naively.

"Yes; he is taking a nap."

At that moment my name was called out by the Captain as entitled to the first choice of berths.

"I waive my right of choice in favor of Mr. Audubon," was my answer.

Now the green bale stirred a little—half turned upon its narrow resting-place, and, after awhile, sat erect, and showed me, to my no small surprise, that there was a man inside of it.

A patriarchal beard fell, white and wavy, down his breast; a pair of hawk-like eyes gleamed sharply out from the fuzzy shroud of cap and collar.

I drew near, with a thrill of irrepressible curiosity. The

moment my eyes took in the noble contour of that Roman face, I felt that it was *he*, and could be no one else. Yes, it was Audubon in his wilderness garb, hale and alert, with sixty winters upon his shoulders, as one of his own "old eagles, feathered to the heel,"—fresh from where the floods are cradled amid crag-piled glooms, or flowery extended plains!

He looked as I had dreamed the antique Plato must have looked, with that fine, classic head and lofty mien! He fully realized the hero of the ideal. With what eager and affectionate admiration I gazed upon him, the valorous and venerable Sage!

What a deathless and beautiful dedication his had been to the holy priesthood of nature! I felt that the very hem of his garments—of that rusty and faded green blanket, ought to be sacred to all devotees of science, and was so to me.

What an indomitable flame, that not

"The wreakful siege of battering years"

could quell, must fire that heroic heart. To think, that now, when "Time had delved its parallels upon his brow"—when he had already accomplished the most Herculean labor of the age in his "Birds of America"—still unsatisfied, he should undertake a new, and as grand a work, upon the animals; and now he was returning with the trophies of science gathered on his toilsome and dangerous journeyings!

Ah, how I venerated him! How I longed to know him, and to be permitted to sit at his feet and learn, and hear his own lips discourse of those loveable themes which had so absorbed my life.

I scarcely slept that night, for my brain was teeming with novel and happy images. I determined to stretch to the utmost the traveller's license, and approach him in the morning. My happy fortune in having been able to make the "surrender" in his favor, assisted me, or else his quick eye detected at once the sympathy of our tastes; be that as it may, we were soon on good terms.

Like all men who have lived much apart with nature, he was not very talkative. His conversation was impulsive and fragmentary:—that, taken together with a mellow Gallic idiom, rendered his style pleasingly titilating to a curious listener, as I was eager to get at his stores of knowledge, and compare my own diffuse but extended observation with his profound accuracy.

The hours of that protracted journey glided by as in a dream. I was forever at his side, catching with a delighted eagerness at those characteristic scraps that fell from his lips.

I was anxious to obtain an accurate insight into the man—the individual. I found rather more of the man of the world about him, than I was inclined to expect, though every inch of him was symmetrical with his character of naturalist, and many inches are there in that, growing through tall cubits into the Titanic girth.

He had several new and curious animals along with him, which he had taken in those distant wilds where I had myself seen them in their freedom, and now they looked like old acquaintances to me; and I soon got up an intimacy with the swift Fox, the snarling Badger and the Rocky Mountain Deer. He exhibited to me some of the original drawings of the splendid work on the Zoology of the continent, which his sons are now engaged in bringing out. I recognized in them the miraculous pencil of the "Birds of America." But I observed several personal traits that interested me very much.

The confinement we were subjected to on board the canal boat, was very tiresome to his habits of freedom. We used to get ashore and walk for hours along the tow-path ahead of the boat; and I observed, with astonishment, that, though over sixty, he could walk me down with ease.

Now, I was something of a walker, and was not very far

advanced in years, and though I do not exactly affect the nimbleness of Cleopatra, who was seen to

"Hop forty paces through the public street,"

yet I pretend to very respectable ambulatory powers. Though, I say, I would not enter in a match with Gildersleeve, Col. Stannard, Kit North, John Neal, or anybody else who has pedestrinated himself into an Olympic Crown; yet I do set up to be a walker, and I was not a little confounded at seeing this old man leave me, panting to the leeward.

His physical energies seemed entirely unimpaired. Another striking evidence of this he gave me. A number of us were standing grouped around him, on the top of the boat, one clear sunshiny morning; we were at the same time passing through a broken and very picturesque region; his keen eyes, with an abstracted, intense expression, an expression of looking over the heads of men around him, out into nature, peculiar to them, were glancing over the scenery as we glided through, when suddenly he pointed with his finger towards the fence of a field, several hundred yards off, with the exclamation,—

"See! yonder is a Fox Squirrel, running along the top rail! It is not often I have seen them in Pennsylvania!"

Now his power of vision must have been singularly acute, to have distinguished that it was a *Fox* Squirrel at such a distance; for only myself and one other person out of a dozen or two, who were looking in the same direction, detected the creature at all, and we could barely distinguish that there was some object moving on the rail. I asked him curiously, if he was sure of its being a *Fox* Squirrel. He smiled, and flashed his hawk-like glance upon me, as he answered;

"Ah, I have an Indian's eye!" And I had only to look into it to feel that he had.

These are slight but peculiar traits, in perfect keeping with his general characteristics, as the naturalist and the man. Of course, I never permitted that acquaintance to fall through, while he lived, and amidst the many and wearisome vicissitudes which have befallen since, I have retained fresh and unimpaired the memory of that journey through the mountains, as one of the green places of the past, where the sunlight always lives.

Thus it was I came first to meet him, laurelled and grey, my highest ideal of the Hunter-Naturalist,—the old Audubon! Ah, the grandeur of that man's life! though it had filled my own with poetic yearnings in my youth, yet they have lost nothing in fire and earnest upward through my maturer age! Now that he is dead, and I can look upon his career with sobered vision, undazzled by the prestige of presence, unbiassed by personal affection, and from the stand-point of wide experience and comparison with other men, still I can speak of as a reality what was once more like the thought of a boy's daydream,—that in all the world's history of wonderful men, there is not to my mind one story of life so filled with beautiful romance as this of J. J. Audubon, considered in the mere deatils of its facts. Take them in his own simple words as furnished by himself incidentally, in the text of his great work, and what a wondrous tale it is!

We will hear then from his own lips something of how the greatest of the Hunter-Naturalists was developed, catch glimpses of the boy-Audubon, artlessly conveyed through his own memories and impressions of early scenes, yearnings and impressions, up to the period of manly achievement; of doubts, of failure, and finally of gloriously consummated triumph! In his charming preface to the Biography of Birds, written the March of 1831, he says of himself:—

I received life and light in the New World. When I had hardly yet learned to walk, and to articulate those first words always so endearing to parents, the productions of Nature that lay spread all around, were constantly pointed out to me. They soon became my playmates; and before my ideas were sufficiently formed to enable me to estimate the difference between the azure tints of the sky, and the emerald hue of the bright foliage, I felt that an intimacy with them, not consisting of friendship merely, but bordering on phrenzy, must accompany my steps through life;—and now, more than ever, am I persuaded of the power of those early impressions. They laid such hold upon me, that, when removed from the woods, the prairies and the brooks, or shut up from the view of the wide Atlantic, I experienced none of those pleasures most congenial to my mind. None but aerial companions suited my fancy. No roof seemed so secure to me as that formed of the dense foliage under which the feathered tribes were seen to resort, or the caves and fissures of the massy rocks to which the dark-winged Cormorant and the Curlew retired to rest, or to protect themselves from the fury of the tempest. My father generally accompanied my steps, procured birds and flowers for me with great eagerness,—pointed out the elegant movements of the former, the beauty and softness of their plumage, the manifestations of their pleasure or sense of danger,—and the always perfect forms and splendid attire of the latter. My valued preceptor would then speak of the departure and return of birds with the seasons, would describe their haunts, and, more wonderful than all, their change of livery; thus exciting me to study them, and to raise my mind towards their great Creator.

A vivid pleasure shone upon those days of my early youth, attended with a calmness of feeling, that seldom failed to rivet my attention for hours, whilst I gazed in ecstacy upon the pearly and shining eggs, as they lay imbedded in the softest down, or among dried leaves and twigs, or were exposed upon the burning sand or weather-beaten rock of our Atlantic shores. I was taught to look upon them as flowers yet in the bud. I watched their opening, to see how Nature had provided each different species with eyes, either open at birth, or closed for some time after; to trace the slow progress of the young birds toward perfection, or admire the celerity with which some of them, while yet unfledged, removed themselves from danger to security.

I grew up, and my wishes grew with my form. Those wishes, kind reader, were for the entire possession of all that I saw. I was fervently desirous of becoming acquainted with Nature. For many years, however, I was sadly disappointed, and forever, doubtless, must I have desires that cannot be gratified. The moment a bird was dead, however beautiful it had been when in life, the pleasure arising from the possession of it became blunted; and although the greatest cares were bestowed in endeavors to preserve the appearance of nature, I looked upon its vesture as more than sullied, as requiring constant attention and repeated mendings, while, after all, it could no longer be said to be fresh from the hands of its Maker. I wished to possess all the productions of nature, but I wished life with them. This was impossible. Then what was to be done? I turned to my father, and made known to him my disappointment and anxiety. He produced a book of *Illustrations*. A new life ran in my veins. I turned over the leaves with avidity; and although what I saw was not what I longed for, it gave me a desire to copy Nature. To Nature I went, and tried to imitate her, as in the days of my childhood I had tried to raise myself from the ground and stand erect, before Nature had imparted the vigor necessary for the success of such an undertaking.

How sorely disappointed did I feel for many years, when I saw that my productions were worse than those which I ventured (perhaps in silence) to regard as bad, in the book given me by my father! My pencil gave birth to a family of cripples. So maimed were most of them, that they resembled the mangled corpses on a field of battle, compared with the integrity of living men. These difficulties and disappointments irritated me, but never for a moment destroyed the desire of obtaining perfect representations of nature.—The worse my drawings were, the more beautiful did I see the originals. To have been torn from the study would have been as death to me. My time was entirely occupied with it. I produced hundreds of these rude sketches annually; and for a long time, at my request, they made bonfires on the anniversaries of my birth-day.

Patiently, and with industry, did I apply myself to study, for, although I felt the impossibility of giving life to my productions, I did not abandon the idea of representing nature. Many plans were successively adopted, many masters guided my hand. At the age of seventeen, when I returned from France, whither I had gone to receive the rudiments of my education, my drawings had assumed a form. DAVID had guided my hand in tracing objects of large size. Eyes and noses belonging to giants, and heads of horses represented in ancient sculpture, were my models. These, although fit subjects for men intent on pursuing the higher branches of the art, were immediately laid aside by me. I returned to the woods of the New World with fresh ardor, and commenced a collection of drawings, which I henceforth continued, and which is now publishing under the title of "THE BIRDS OF AMERICA."

In Pennsylvania, a beautiful State, almost central on the line of our Atlantic shores, my father, in his desire of proving my friend through life, gave me what Americans call a beautiful 'plantation,' refreshed during the summer heats by the waters of the Schuylkill river, and traversed by a creek named Perkioming. Its fine woodlands, its extensive fields, its hills crowned with evergreens, offered many subjects to my pencil. It was there that I commenced my simple and agreeable studies, with as little concern about the future as if the world had been made for me. My rambles invariably commenced at break of day; and to return wet with dew, and bearing a feathered prize, was, and ever will be, the highest enjoyment for which I have been fitted.

Yet, think not, reader, that the enthusiasm which I felt for my favorite pursuits was a barrier opposed to the admission of gentler sentiments. Nature, which had turned my young mind toward the bird and the flower, soon proved her influence upon my heart. Be it enough to say, that the object of my passion has long since blessed me with the name of husband. And now let us return, for who cares to listen to the love-tale of a naturalist, whose feelings may be supposed to be as light as the feathers which he delineates!

For a period of nearly twenty years, my life was a succession of vicissitudes. I tried various branches of commerce, but they all proved unprofitable, doubtless because my whole mind was ever filled with my passion for rambling and admiring those objects of nature from which alone I received the purest gratification. I had to struggle against the will of all who at that period called themselves my friends. I must here, however, except my wife and children. The remarks of my other friends irritated me beyond endurance, and, breaking through all bonds, I gave myself entirely up to my pursuits. Any one acquainted with the extraordinary desire which I then felt of seeing and judging for myself, would doubtless have pronounced me callous to every sense of duty, and regardless of every interest. I undertook long and tedious journeys, ransacked the woods, the lakes, the prairies, and the shores of the Atlantic. Years were spent away from my family. Yet, reader, will you believe it, I had no other object in view, than simply to enjoy the sight of nature. Never for a moment did I conceive the hope of becoming in any degree useful to my kind, until I accidentally formed acquaintance with the PRINCE OF MUSIGNANO, at Philadelphia, to which place I went, with the view of proceeding eastward along the coast.

* * * *

In April, 1824, he sought for patronage in Philadelphia, and failing there, went to New York, with some better success; but weary and depressed, on the whole, he returned to nature for refreshing, and, ascending that noble stream, the Hudson, glided over our broad lakes, to seek the wildest solitudes of the pathless and gloomy forests.

It was in these forests that, for the first time, I communed with myself as to the possible event of my visiting Europe again; and I began to fancy my work under the multiplying efforts of the graver. Happy days, and nights of pleasing dreams! I read over the catalogue of my collection, and thought how it might be possible for an unconnected and unaided individual like myself to accomplish the grand scheme.

Eighteen months elapsed. I returned to my family, then in Louisiana, explored every portion of the vast woods around, and at last sailed towards the Old World. But before we visit the shores of hospitable England, I have the wish, good-natured reader, to give you some idea of my mode of executing the original drawings, from which the illustrations have been taken; and I sincerely hope that the perusal of these lines may excite in you a desire minutely to examine them.

Merely to say that each object of my illustrations is of the size of nature, were too vague—for to many it might only convey the idea that they are so, more or less, according as the eye of the delineator may have been more or less correct in measurement simply obtained through that medium; and of avoiding error in this respect I am particularly desirous. Not only is every object, as a whole, of the natural size, but also every portion of each object. The compass aided me in its delineation, regulated and corrected each part, even to the very fore-shortening which now and then may be seen in the figures. The bill, the feet, the legs, the claws, the very feathers as they project one beyond another, have been accurately measured. The birds, almost all of them, were killed by myself, after I had examined their motions and habits, as much as the case admitted, and were regularly drawn on or near the spot where I procured them. The positions may, perhaps, in some instances appear *outré;* but such supposed exaggerations can afford subject of criticism only to persons unacquainted with the feathered tribes; for, believe me, nothing can be more transient or varied than the attitudes or positions of birds. The Heron, when warming itself in the sun, will sometimes drop its wings several inches, as if they were dislocated; the Swan may often be seen floating with one foot extended from the body; and some pigeons, you well know, turn quite over, when playing in the air. The flowers, plants, or portions of trees which are attached to the principal objects, have been chosen from amongst those in the vicinity of which the birds were found, and are not, as some persons have thought, the trees or plants upon which they always feed or perch.

An accident which happened to two hundred of my original drawings, nearly put a stop to my researches in ornithology. I shall relate it, merely to show you how far enthusiasm—for by no other name can I call the persevering zeal with which I labored—may enable the observer of nature to surmount the most disheartening obstacles. I left the village of Henderson, in Kentucky, situated on the bank of the Ohio, where I resided for several years, to proceed to Philadelphia on business. I looked to all my drawings before my departure, placed them carefully in a wooden box, and gave them in charge to a relative, with injunctions to see that no injury should happen to them. My absence was of several months; and when I returned, after having enjoyed the pleasures of home for a few days, I inquired after my box, and what I was pleased to call my treasure. The box was produced, and opened;—but, reader, feel for me—a pair of Norway rats had taken possession of the whole, and had reared a young family amongst the gnawed bits of paper, which, but a few months before, represented nearly a thousand inhabitants of the air!

The burning heat which instantly rushed through my brain was too great to be endured, without affecting the whole of my nervous system. I slept not for several nights, and the days passed like days of oblivion,—until, the animal powers being recalled into action, through the strength of my constitution, I took up my gun, my note-book and my pencils, and went forth to the woods as gaily as if nothing had happened. I felt pleased that I might now make much better drawings than before, and, ere a period not exceeding three years had elapsed, I had my portfolio filled again.

America being my country, and the principal pleasures of my life having been obtained there, I prepared to leave it with deep sorrow, after in vain trying to publish my illustrations in the United States. In Philadelphia, Wilson's principal engraver, amongst others, gave it as his opinion to my friends, that my drawings could never be engraved. In New York, other difficulties presented themselves, which determined me to carry my collections to Europe.

As I approached the coast of England, and for the first time beheld her fertile shores, the despondency of my spirits became very great. I knew not an individual in the country; and, although I was the bearer of letters from American friends and statesmen of great eminence, my situation appeared precarious in the extreme. I imagined that every individual whom I was about to meet, might be possessed of talents superior to those of any on our side of the Atlantic! Indeed, as I for the first time walked on the streets of Liverpool, my heart nearly failed me, for not a glance of sympathy did I meet in my wanderings, for two days To the woods I could not betake myself, for there were none near.

Well received in England, he passes through to Scotland.

Gallant and beautiful spirit! there was no need of woods for thee to hide! The noble work of Wilson had not long been finished then, and men were not done wondering at this glorious achievement of the Paisely weaver, who had left their own shores years ago, a poor and obscure adventurer for the forests of the New World, when another pilgrim from those far wildernesses, made his appearance among the learned circles of the Scottish Capital. He carried a portfolio under his arm, and came, too, on an adventure to this seat of the mind's royalty and of voluptuous wealth. There was a look of nature's children about him. His curled and shining hair, thrown back from his open front, fell in dark clusters down his broad shoulders. Those bold features, moulded after

> "The high, old Roman fashion"—

those sharp, steady eyes, that straight figure and elastic tread, were a strange blending of the Red man and the pure-blooded noble. A curious trader he! But, when his wondrous wares were all unfolded and spread out before their eyes, what a delicious thrilling of amazement and delight was felt through those fastidious circles! A gorgeous show! The heart of a virgin world unfolded—teeming with rare and exquisite thoughts—that had been born in the deep solitudes of her young musings, and thus caught by this weird enchanter's pencil, as they gleamed past in all the bright hues and airy graces of their fresh fleeting lives—with flower and tree, and rock and wave, as beautiful and new as they, thrown in to make the fairy pageant real! It was a surprising revelation, and when they knew that it had all been the work—the obscure, unaided work, through years of enduring toil—of that young wanderer, they were filled with overwhelming admiration. They loaded him with adulation and with honors; they took him by the hand generously, and led him up to his success.

Such was the effect of Audubon's appearance in Edinburgh. In that glorious portfolio men felt that a great creation lay folded; in that modest backwoodsman they saw the first of the Hunter-Naturalists—in the simple grandeur of that presence they recognized the type of those masterful spirits of the race of the olden time, the stories of whose deeds are the histories of ages. They were awed, they loved him—they nourished and they cherished him—how could it be otherwise among a cultivated people?—for to such there is in genius a compelling sense that will bear through its purposes in their love.

But it is not on his triumphal progress through Europe, that we prefer to accompany him. Nor is it of so much interest to us to hear that such men as Cuvier and Humboldt—who alone were his peers—pronounced his work on Birds the most magnificent monument art had yet erected to ornithology. The world has long ago taken charge of his fame. It is of the man, the Hunter-Naturalist, out in the wilderness highways and byways of the unreclaimed earth that we would know more intimately. It is rather the methods of the workman that we would now see—for it is well enough known that never, in the annals of individual achievement, did unaided enthusiasm, through poverty and neglect, accomplish so much single-handed against such tremendous odds.

The world, by the way, has been told many times of the immense pecuniary difficulties to be overcome by him from the commencement—but not yet, perhaps, in his own touching language, have they heard some of the effects of these struggles upon his temper and feelings. He says in the introduction to the third volume—

Ten years have now elapsed since the first number of my Illustrations of the Birds of America made its appearance. At that period I calculated that the engravers would take sixteen years in accomplishing their task; and this I announed in my prospectus, and talked of to my friends. Of the latter not a single individual seemed to have the least hope of my success, and several strongly advised me to abandon my plans, dispose of my drawings, and return to my country. I listened with attention to all that was urged on the subject, and often felt deeply depressed, for I was well aware of many of the difficulties to be surmounted, and perceived that no small sum of money would be required to defray the necessary expenses. Yet never did I seriously think of abandoning the cherished object of my hopes. When I delivered the first drawings to the engraver, I had not a single subscriber. Those who knew me best called me rash; some wrote to me that they did not expect to see a second fasciculus; and others seemed to anticipate the total failure of my enterprise. But my heart was nerved, and my reliance on that Power, on whom all must depend, brought bright anticipations of success.

Having made arrangements for meeting the first difficulties, I turned my attention to the improvement of my drawings, and began to collect from the pages of my journals the scattered notes which referred to the habits of the birds represented by them. I worked early and late, and glad I was to perceive that the more I labored the more I improved. I was happy, too, to find, that in general each succeeding plate was better than its predecessor, and when those who had at first endeavored to dissuade me from undertaking so vast an enterprise, complimented me on my more favorable prospects, I could not but feel happy. Number after number appeared in regular succession, until at the end of four years of anxiety, my engraver, Mr. Havell, presented me with the First Volume of the Birds of America.

Convinced, from a careful comparison of the plates, that at least there had been no falling off in the execution, I looked forward with confidence to the termination of the next four years' labor. Time passed on, and I returned from the forests and wilds of the western world to congratulate my friend Havell, just when the last plate of the second volume was finished.

About that time, a nobleman called upon me with his family, and requested me to show them some of the original drawings, which I did with the more pleasure that my visitors possessed a knowledge of Ornithology. In the course of our conversation, I was asked how long it might be until the work should be finished. When I mentioned eight years more, the nobleman shrugged up his shoulders, and sighing, said, "I may not see it finished, but my children will, and you may please to add my name to your list of subscribers." The young people exhibited a mingled expression of joy and sorrow, and when I with them strove to dispel the cloud that seemed to hang over their father's mind, he smiled, bade me be sure to see that the whole work should be punctually delivered, and took his leave. The solemnity of his manner I could not forget for several days; I often thought that neither might I see the work completed, but at length I exclaimed, "My sons may." And now that another volume, both of my Illustrations and of my Biographies is finished, my trust in Providence is augmented, and I cannot but hope that myself and my family together may be permitted to see the completion of my labors.

How that prayer has been answered, the facts since, with which the world is familiar, have shown. He obtained one hundred and eighty subscribers to the work at one thousand dollars each; and lived not only to complete it, surrounded by his sons, but, as I have already mentioned, had by their aid commenced and even completed another great work on the Quadrupeds of America.

It is not the least extraordinary characteristic of this man's unexampled career, that he should, until even late in life, have been entirely unconscious of the powers he possessed. Indeed, he repeatedly asserts, that it was not until his meeting with Charles Lucien Bonaparte, on his visit to Philadelphia in 1824, that he had any thought, whatever, of publishing, or dreamed that he had been accomplishing anything very extraordinary. Bonaparte was astonished,—astounded, even, in looking over his portfolio of drawings, and exclaimed, in an irrepressible burst of admiration and wonder at the simplicity of his unconsciousness,—

"Mr. Audubon, do you know that you are a great man,—a very great man!—The greatest ornithologist in the world?"

It was this language that first filled him with the thought

of publishing, which, as we have seen, on his retirement to the solitudes of nature, near the sources of the Hudson, became gradually nourished into a purpose. But let us see the most touching instance of this unconsciousness in his own relation of the manner of his first interview with Wilson, the Ornithologist. He lived for two years in Louisville, Kentucky, which was then a comparatively small town. He was engaged in business as a merchant or trader, yet nevertheless says:—

During my residence at Louisville, much of my time was employed in my ever favorite pursuits. I drew and noted the habits of everything which I procured, and my collection was daily augmenting, as every individual who carried a gun, always sent me such birds or quadrupeds as he thought might prove useful to me. My portfolios already contained upwards of two hundred drawings.

One fair morning, I was surprised by the sudden entrance into our counting-room of Mr. Alexander Wilson, the celebrated author of the "American Ornithology," of whose existence I had never until that moment been apprised. This happened in March, 1810. How well do I remember him, as he then walked up to me! His long, rather hooked nose, the keenness of his eyes, and his prominent cheek-bones, stamped his countenance with a peculiar character. His dress, too, was of a kind not usually seen in that part of the country; a short coat, trowsers, and a waistcoat of grey cloth. His stature was not above the middle size. He had two volumes under his arm, and as he approached the table at which I was working, I thought I discovered something like astonishment in his countenance. He, however, immediately proceeded to disclose the object of his visit, which was to procure subscriptions for his work. He opened his books, explained the nature of his occupations, and requested my patronage.

I felt surprised and gratified at the sight of his volumes,

turned over a few of the plates, and had already taken a pen to write my name in his favor, when my partner rather abruptly said to me in French, "My dear Audubon, what induces you to subscribe to this work? Your drawings are certainly far better, and again you must know as much of the habits of American birds as this gentleman." Whether Mr. Wilson understood French or not, or if the suddenness with which I paused, disappointed him, I cannot tell; but I clearly perceived that he was not pleased. Vanity and the encomiums of my friend prevented me from subscribing. Mr. Wilson asked me if I had many drawings of birds. I rose, took down a large portfolio, laid it on the table, and showed him, as I would show you, kind reader, or any other person fond of such subjects, the whole of the contents, with the same patience with which he had shown me his own engravings.

His surprise appeared great, as he told me he never had the most distant idea that any other individual than himself had been engaged in forming such a collection. He asked me if it was my intention to publish, and when I answered in the negative, his surprise seemed to increase. And, truly, such was not my intention; for, until long after, when I met the Prince of Musignano in Philadelphia, I had not the least idea of presenting the fruits of my labors to the world. Mr. Wilson now examined my drawings with care, asked if I should have any objections to lending him a few during his stay, to which I replied that I had none: he then bade me good morning, not, however, until I had made an arrangement to explore the woods in the vicinity along with him, and had promised to procure for him some birds, of which I had drawings in my collection, but which he had never seen.

It happened that he lodged in the same house with us, but his retired habits, I thought, exhibited either a strong feeling of discontent, or a decided melancholy. The Scotch airs which he played sweetly on his flute made me melancholy too, and I felt for him. I presented him to my wife and friends, and seeing that he was all enthusiasm, exerted myself as much as was in my power, to procure for him the specimens which he wanted. We hunted together, and obtained birds which he had never before seen; but, reader, I did not subscribe to his work, for, even at that time, my collection was greater than his. Thinking that perhaps he might be pleased to publish the results of my researches, I offered them to him, merely on condition that what I had drawn, or might afterwards draw and send to him, should be mentioned in his work, as coming from my pencil. I at the same time offered to open a correspondence with him, which I thought might prove beneficial to us both. He made no reply to either proposal, and before many days had elapsed, left Louisville, on his way to New Orleans, little knowing how much his talents were appreciated in our little town, at least by myself and my friends.

Some time elapsed, during which I never heard of him, or of his work. At length, having occasion to go to Philadelphia, I, immediately after my arrival there, inquired for him, and paid him a visit. He was then drawing a White-headed Eagle. He received me with civility, and took me to the Exhibition Rooms of Rembrandt Peale, the artist, who had then portrayed Napoleon crossing the Alps. Mr. Wilson spoke not of birds or drawings. Feeling, as I was forced to do, that my company was not agreeable, I parted from him; and after that I never saw him again. But judge of my astonishment some time after, when on reading the thirty-ninth page of the ninth volume of American Ornithology, I found in it the following paragraph:—

"*March 23d*, 1810.—I bade adieu to Louisville, to which place I had four letters of recommendation, and was taught to expect much of everything there; but neither received one act of civility from those to whom I was recommended, one subscriber, nor one new bird; though I delivered my letters, ransacked the woods repeatedly, and visited all the characters likely to subscribe. Science or literature has not one friend in this place."

We will not add to the gloom which has followed the illustrious life of poor Wilson to his grave, by any officious comments upon the tenor of this short narrative. I will add, though, that it should be remembered, in forming any judgment of that strong, moody man, that he had bitter woes enough to contend with, not only in his friendless early days, but in the harsh isolation of his weary wanderings and unappreciated after-life, to have grown a gall beneath an angel's wing. Withal, the bursts of sunshine and exultation which shone through his eloquent writings often, show that his inner self had fed healthfully sometimes upon the pure and peaceful teachings of his gentle pursuits. He was a man whose profound genius, darkened by misfortune, was sombrely illuminated by a noble enthusiasm. He, too, may be accepted as a Hunter-Naturalist, but not as first among them all! To J. J. Audubon, undoubtedly, that high place belongs, though this has been disputed by many, and even Christopher North has been found to assert them as "equals."

This cannot be admitted here. Then how stands the case?

When the noble work of Wilson, the unknown Scotchman, began to make its appearance, Ornithology among us was in its infancy, and the freshness of his hardy original genius was promptly recognized and keenly relished abroad, in contrast with the stale, unprofitable treatment of the predominant school of the Technicalists.

It was at once perceived how much the attractiveness of his subject was heightened by the circumstances of his personal intimacy and association with the creatures described in many of the conditions of natural freedom.

His fine descriptions had a savor of the wilderness about them. His birds were living things, and led out the heart in yearning through the scenes of a primeval earth to recognize them in their own wild homes, singing to the solitude from some chosen spray, or plying, with careless grace, on busy wings, their curious sports and labors.

Here is the legitimate purpose of works of this character—to fill the mind with such pleasant images as will win the affections forth from the dull centre of mere human sympathies, through all the wonders of the outer world, up, with a wise and chastened adoration, to the Power that framed it. Wilson, to a greater degree than any man who had yet appeared, felt himself, and caused others to recognize, this apostleship of the true Naturalist.

It was an era, a happy era in philosophy, when art had linked its remoter teachings to the hearts of men; and to Wilson undoubtedly belongs the glory of having fairly pioneered its ushering. It is impossible to regard the labors of this man, even in a purely scientific light, without astonishment; but when we come to take into consideration all the pitiable afflictions and degrading misery entailed upon him by "caste," in his own country, we are lost in affectionate admiration of his indomitable genius, as we see the shrunk veins of the haggard emigrant swelling, when he has touched our shore, with a new life hardy enough to cope with the rude elements by which he found himself surrounded, and carry through triumphantly his remarkable undertaking.

Spirits with the vigor in them his possessed, ask only the vital air of freedom. Difficulties then are nothing. It is no wonder, when those trophies which he had wrestled for alone with Nature here in her bare and unhoused wilds, and had won through trials and poverty, unassisted, had been returned to Scotland, that country which drove him forth in rags, and it had been offered a share of his glory for its gold, that it should have poured out freely the dross upon him in very shame. Nor is it surprising, that in the eager reaction of its penitence, it should continue to exalt him too highly—claiming for him, to the detriment of others, more than his just dues.

We think it very natural, that glorious old "Christopher," puzzled between the heartfelt and generous recognition, he hardly conceals, of the out-of-sight supremacy of Audubon, and some compunctious qualms of a yet farther expiation due to the shade of the neglected Wilson, should have split the difference, by making them "brothers."

Well, and brothers they are, by all those sacred bonds which link the tall fraternity of genius—brothers they are in all the higher virtues of manhood—brothers they are in the yet more intimate sense, that the same objects and the same field have been labored upon by each; but, that they are equals in the sense of Christopher's "same stature," we altogether deny.

We should as well talk of elevating the knotted front of Gifford, of murderous Jeffery, or the sleek scalp of a modern Reviewer into that rare altitude—till "the crowns of their heads touch"—from which the broad brow of "Maga throned" smiles serenely down upon her empire.

They are not equal! By the same sign that Christopher, like another "bald" and "full-winged bird," yet holds the empyrean alone,—Audubon, though "last, shall be first."

First—in that, though Wilson displayed the noblest elements of greatness in the staunch, unconquerable vigor with which he met the difficulties in his path—Audubon exhibited quite as much "game," and in the proportionable grandeur of his scheme, had full as many trials to surmount.

First—in that, while the biographies of Wilson were full of natural spirit, of grace and power, greatly beyond all his predecessors, yet those of Audubon are far more minute and carefully detailed—introducing us, one after another, to a more intimate fellowship with each individual of the wide family of his love, through every piquant and distinctive trait of gesture, air, and movement, characterizing all the phases of their nature—without the faults of generalization, and too much credence in hear-say, or a gloomy and unphilosophic spirit—since the mild and loving geniality of childhood breathes through every line.

First, moreover, by the reason that, while the drawings of Wilson are advanced upon all that had yet been accomplished, are free and accurate in outline, and sometimes even elegant in finish, yet those of Audubon are superior to them beyond all measure of comparison.

And here is the clear ground of distinction on which the more powerful genius steps forth in the proper garb of its own striking and unmistakeable individuality, and appeals to the eye at once for a recognition of its creations, as alone original and apart from all others. Audubon's drawings are quite as singular and unapproached as any one of the phenomena of art by which we mark the ages.

Wilson's pencil has been content with a mere portraiture, correct, indeed, of proportion, and a color barely suggestive; but the pencil of the necromancer has not only caught the play of sunlight, shivered gorgeous in metallic hues from each particular fibre of their plumes, (in a word, created the true style of coloring,) but has stilled these arrowy cleavers of the elements amidst their own clouds, upon the very waves on which they loved "to sit and swing," by "the beached verge," on the precipitous perch, or twig and leaf and berry of the boughs that were their homes—stilled them, too, in all the character of passionate life—their loves, battles, chases, gambols, thefts—the grotesquery and grace, every mode and mood of their being amidst their native scenes.

Each plate is a full-length family portrait, with all the accessories historical. They are perfect in themselves, and tell the whole story more clearly than words could do. Taken apart, they are chapters in the "Illuminated Bible" of nature —and very pleasant is the creed they teach, full of merry thoughts that make the heart go lightly; and plumy shapes, of strange, undreamed-of beauty, come and go through the still air of musings, till we grow devout with thinking how

God has made the roughest places of our earth so populous with lovely things that can surprise us into joy.

But without rhapsodizing. Wilson's claim to originality, in having first conceived the magnificent design of illustrating the Birds of America, and led the van of Practical Science in its relations to Ornithology, is certainly a most imposing one, and one with which no after exertions of *mere talent*, however tireless, devoted, and successful it might be, could by any possibility compete. But genius can do what talent cannot. It is above all rules and "saws," and scorns the measure of an aphorism.

> "When the power falls into the mighty hands
> Of Nature—the spirit, giant-born,
> Who listens only to himself ——"

such things are effected, as an age of the leaden attainments of studied acquisition cannot accomplish.

Audubon, in the unique and striking originality of his drawings, and the whole treatment of his themes, has so far outstripped, in a bold freedom of design and execution, any thing of Wilson's which may be denominated suggestive even, as to leave scarcely any room for comparison in this last issue. If Wilson was original, our Ornithologist is infinitely more so.

Wilson has all the advantages in such a contrast. "He was first in the field," and with the world—that said, all is said. Whatever has been done since must be footed on to his account with fame, at least to the point of careful balance with that of any one who has chanced to come after him. This is not strictly just.

We admit cheerfully all that is righteously due to the Paisley adventurer. But we cannot perceive why—when the fact that he is not entitled to it, is clear as a sunburst to any observer—he should be thrust, rather than elevated into an equal rank with Audubon. It has been too much the way of the world to ease its conscience of present injustice and neglect of genius, by an internal reservation, that it will pile up posthumous honors mountain high.

Now it is surely to be apprehended that this genius, though "of so airy and light a quality," has yet something to seek "of the earth, earthy," in common with the rest of men—and that, therefore, the recognizing, with its own proper eyes, the just claims of an original mind, by the country to which it has added lustre, cannot be to it a matter of indifference. Audubon has nothing of glory to ask of us. But this his memory demands, that we, his countrymen, should guard his honors from even the shadow of infringement. We drove him to the embrace of a foreign land for patronage—but there, amidst all the pomp of courts and the intoxication of sudden success, he was still proudly the American Woodsman; nothing could damp that noble pride, and through every page he has written, we can still see it looking out with the same calm, abiding affection. We should not, then, be the last to vindicate such valorous faith. The man of his age, the illustrious Frenchman, has led the way in defining his supremacy, and yet the American mind, since Professor Wilson pronounced his autocratic fiat, that they "were equals," has been timid to say in plain words—No! our Audubon is regally the head and front of Illustrative Science; the dictum of Christopher to the contrary notwithstanding, he is in this *the* Ornithologist of the world, and the favorite Wilson must be content to stand below him.

But hear this same cannie Scot, Christopher North, dis course of Audubon *en dishabille*, with the straight-jacket of nationality thrown aside, and verily in his dressing gown and slippers, when it is man to man that speaks as the heart moveth, not Scot to Scot! Thus, in the *Noctes* he discourseth, sotto voce.

We were sitting one night, lately, all alone by ourselves, almost unconsciously eyeing the members, fire without flame, in the many-visioned grate, but at times aware of the symbols and emblems there beautifully built up, of the ongoings of human life, when a knocking, not loud but resolute, came to the front door, followed by the rustling thrill of the bell-wire, and then by a tinkling far below, too gentle to waken the house, that continued to enjoy the undisturbed dream of its repose. At first we supposed it might be but some late-home-going knight-errant from a feast of shells, in a mood "between malice and true-love," seeking to disquiet the slumbers of Old Christopher, in expectation of seeing his night-cap (which he never wears) popped out of the window, and hearing his voice (of which he is chary in the open air) simulating a scold upon the audacious sleep-breaker. So we benevolently laid back our head on our easy-chair, and pursued our speculations on the state of affairs in general—and more particularly on the floundering fall of that inexplicable people—the Whigs. We had been wondering, and of our wondering found no end, what could have been their chief reasons for committing suicide. It appeared a case of very singular *felo-de-se*—for they had so timed the "rash act," as to excite strong suspicions in the public mind that his Majesty had committed murder. Circumstances, however, had soon come to light, that proved to demonstration, that the wretched Ministry had laid violent hands on itself, and effected its purpose by strangulation. There—was the fatal black ring visible round the neck—though a mere thread; there—were the blood-shot eyes protruding from the sockets; there—the lip-biting teeth clenched in the last convulsions; and there—sorriest sight of all—was the ghastly suicidal smile, last relic of the laughter of despair. But the knocking would not leave the door—and listening to its character, we were assured that it came from the fist of a friend, who saw light through the chinks of the shutter, and knew, moreover, that we never put on the shroud of death's pleasant brother, sleep, till "ae wee short hour ayont the twal," and often not till earliest cock-crow, which chanticleer utters somewhat drowsily, and then replaces his head beneath his wing, supported on one side by a partlet, on the other by a hen. So we gathered up our slippered feet from the rug, lamp in hand stalked along the lobbies, unchained and unlocked the oak which our faithful night porter Somnus had sported—and lo! a figure muffled up in a cloak, and furred like a Russ, who advanced familiarly into the hall, extended both hands, and then embracing us, bade God bless us, and pronounced, with somewhat of a foreign accent, the name in which we and the world rejoice—"Christopher North!" We were not slow in returning the hug fraternal—for who was it but the "American Woodsman?"—even Audubon himself—fresh from the Floridas—and breathing of the pure air of far-off Labrador!

Three years and upwards had fled since we had taken farewell of the illustrious Ornithologist—on the same spot—at the same hour; and there was something ghostlike in such return of a dear friend from a distant region—almost as if from the land of spirits. It seemed as if the same moon again looked at us—but then she was wan and somewhat sad—now clear as a diamond, and all the starry heavens wore a smile. "Our words they were no mony feck"—but in less time than we have taken to write it—we two were sitting cheek by jowl, and hand in hand, by that essential fire—while we showed by our looks that we both felt, now they were over, that three years were but as one day! The cane coal-scuttle, instinct with spirit, beeted the fire of its own accord, without word or beck of ours, as if placed there by the hands of one of our wakeful Lares; in globe of purest crystal the Glenlivet shone; unasked the bright brass kettle began to whisper its sweet "under song;" and a centenary of the fairest oysters native to our isle turned towards us their languishing eyes, unseen the Nereid that had on the instant wafted them from the procreant cradle beds of Prestonpans. Grace said, we drew in to supper, and hobnobbing, from elegant long-shank, down each naturalist's gullets graciously descended, with a gurgle, the mildest, the meekest, the very Moses of Ales.

Audubon, ere half an hour had elapsed, found an opportunity of telling us that he had never seen us in a higher state of preservation—and in a low voice whispered something about the eagle renewing his youth. We acknowledged the kindness by a remark on bold bright birds of passage that find the seasons obedient to their will, and wing their way through worlds still rejoicing in the perfect year. But too true friends were we not to be sincere in all we seriously said; and while Audubon confessed that he saw rather more plainly than when we parted the crowfeet in the corners of our eyes, we did not deny that we saw in him an image of the Falco Leucocephalus, for that, looking on his "carum caput," it answered his own description of that handsome and powerful bird, viz: "the general color of the plumage above is dull hair-brown, the lower parts being deeply brown, broadly margined with greyish white." But here he corrected us; for "Surely my dear friend," quoth he, "you must admit I am a living specimen of the Adult Bird, and you remember my description of him in my First Volume." And thus blending our gravities and our gayeties, we sat facing one another, each with his last oyster on the prong of his trident, which disappeared, like all mortal joys, between a smile and a sigh.

How similar—in much—our dispositions—yet in almost all how dissimilar our lives! Since last we parted, "we scarcely heard of half a mile from home"—he tanned by the suns and beaten by the storms of many latitudes—we like a ship laid up in ordinary, or anchored close in shore within the same sheltering bay—with sails unfurled and flags flying but for sake of show on some holiday—he like a ship that every morning has been dashing through a new world of waves—often close-reefed or under bare poles—but oftener affronting the heavens with a whiter and swifter cloud than any hoisted by the combined fleets in the sky. And now, with canvas unrent, and masts unsprung, returned to the very buoy she left. Somewhat faded, indeed, in her apparelling—but her hull sound as ever—nor a speck of dry rot in her timbers—her keel unscathed by rock—her cut-water yet sharp as new-whetted scythe ere the mower renews his toil—her figure-head, that had so often looked out for squalls, now "patient as the brooding dove"—and her bowsprit—but let us man the main-brace; nor is there purer spirit—my trusty frêre—in the Old World or the New.

It was quite a Noctes. Audubon told us—by snatches—all his travels, history, with many an anecdote interspersed of the dwellers among the woods—bird, beast and man.

All this and more he told us, with a cheerful voice and animated eyes, while the dusky hours were noiselessly wheeling the chariot of Night along the star-losing sky; and we too had something to tell him of our own home-loving obscurity, not ungladdened by studies sweet in the Forest—till Dawn yoked her dappled coursers for one single slow stage—and then jocund Morn leaping up on the box, took the ribbons in her rosy fingers, and, after a dram of dew, blew her bugle, and drove like blazes right on towards the gates of Day.

His great work, says Professor Wilson, elsewhere, was indeed a perilous undertaking for a stranger in Britain, without the patronage of powerful friends, and with no very great means of his own—all of which he embarked in the enterprise dearest to his heart. Had it failed, Audubon would have been a ruined man—and that fear must have sometimes dismally disturbed him, for he is not alone in life, and is a man of strong family affections. But happily those nearest his breast are as enthusiastic in the love of natural science as himself—and were all willing to sink or swim with the beloved husband and venerated father. America may well be proud of him—and he gratefully records the kindness he has experienced from so many of her most distinguished sons. In his own fame he was just and generous to all who excel in the same studies; not a particle of jealousy is in his composition; a sin, that, alas! seems too easily to beset too many of the most gifted spirits in literature and scienee; nor is the happiest genius—imaginative or intellectual—such is the frailty of poor human nature at the best—safe from the access of that dishonoring passion.

Just and generously said, most loyal Christopher! may thy giant shadow never be less!

ALEXANDER WILSON.

CHAPTER VI.

AUDUBON AND BOONE.

I TURN from Audubon and his triumphs amid courtly scenes of the Old World, surrounded by the princely and the learned, to the Hunter-Naturalist at his labors in the wilderness of the New—the associate of the rugged Boone, and many another skin-dressed peer.

We may gather from his generous exhortation to younger naturalists to take the field, interesting features of what may be supposed to have been his own method of conducting his investigations when abroad with nature. Something of the sort of training by which his remarkable character was formed, and the modes and circumstances under which his works grew. After saying that the list of new species had been nearly doubled since the time of Alexander Wilson's work, and that he felt confident very many species remain to be added by future observers, who shall travel the vast wastes extending northward and westward from the Canadas, and along the western slopes of the Rocky Mountains, from Nootka to California; indeed, that he looks upon the whole range of those magnificent mountains as being yet unexplored—he addresses the young enthusiast:—

Therefore, I would strongly advise you to make up your mind, shoulder your gun, muster all your spirits, and start in search of the interesting unknown, of which I greatly regret I can no more go in pursuit—not for want of will, but of the vigor and elasticity necessary for so arduous an enterprise. Should you agree to undertake the task, and prove fortunate enough to return full of knowledge, laden with objects new and rare, be pleased when you publish your work, to place my name in the list of subscribers, and be assured that I will not leave you in the lurch.

Now supposing that you are full of ardor and ready to proceed; allow me to offer you a little advice. Leave nothing to memory, but note down all your observations with *ink*, not with a black-lead pencil, and keep in mind, that the more particulars you write at the time, the more you will recollect afterwards. Work not at night, but anticipate the morning dawn, and never think, for an instant, about the difficulties of ransacking the woods, the shores, or the barren grounds, nor be vexed when you have traversed a few hundred miles of country without finding a single new species. It may, indeed, it not unfrequently happens, that after days, or even weeks of fruitless search, one enters a grove, or comes upon a pond, or forces his way through the tall grass of a prairie, and suddenly meets with several objects, all new, all beautiful, and perhaps all suited to the palate. Then how delightful will be your feelings, and how marvelously all fatigue will vanish.

Think, for instance, that you are on one of the declivities of the Rocky Mountains, with shaggy and abrupt banks on each side of you, while the naked cliffs tower high over head, as if with the wish to reach the sky. Your trusty gun has brought to the ground a most splendid 'American Pheasant,' weighing fully two pounds! What a treat! You have been surprised at the length of its tail; you have taken the precise measurement of all its parts, and given a brief description of it. Have you read this twice and corrected errors and deficiencies? 'Yes,' you say. Very well; now you have begun your drawing of this precious bird. Ah! you have finished it. Now then, you skin the beautiful creature, and you are pleased to find it plump and fat. You have, I find, studied comparative anatomy under my friend, Macgillivray, and at least, have finished your examination of the œsophagus, gizzard, cocca, trachæ, and bronchi. On the ignited clay castings of a buffalo you have laid the body, and it is now almost ready to satisfy the longing of your stomach, as it hisses in its oderous sap. The brook at your feet affords the very best drink that nature can supply, and I need not wish you better fare than that before you.

Next morning you find yourself refreshed and reinvigorated, more ardent than ever, for success fails not to excite the desire of those who have entered upon the study of nature. You have packed your bird's skin flat in your box, rolled up your drawing round those previously made, and now, day after day, you push through thick and thin, sometimes with success, and sometimes without; but you at last return with such a load on your shoulders as I have often carried on mine. Having once more reached the settlements, you relieve your tired limbs by mounting a horse, and at length gaining a city, find means of publishing the results of your journey.

It requires very little exertion of fancy to see in this a felicitous sketch of his own mode of "ransacking the woods, the shores, and the barren grounds."

It is just such hardy methods wherein consist the immeasurable superiority of Mr. Audubon over the whole school of stuffed-specimen delineators, whose indigestible crudities and wretched figures have proven the very night-mare of Natural Science in the Old World.

The idea of mounting knapsack and gun, and trudging thousands of miles through brake and morass, over "sands, shores, and desert wildernesses," encountering and braving the "imminence" of many perils, exposed to all "the spite of wreakful elements," purely for love of nature, and scientific accuracy, would have set one of these philosophical amateurs to shuddering. To bespatter black coat and silken hose, get half starved, and catch a death cold in "collecting materials," were simply preposterous—when the Zoological gardens are close at hand, and the museums are filled with specimens.

To be sure they have been dead a few years, and owe their present forms very much to the taste of the ignorant tradesman who "wired" and stuffed them—but the colors are there; *they* do not fade—that is, *not much*—and by a slight exertion of fancy it will be easy enough to make them "sister nature's own shape" of birds again, so that shortly a magnificent five vol. illustrated work makes its appearance.

Contrast all such farrago with the language of a man who knew what he was doing. It was during those weary wanderings in which Audubon coursed back and forth "the seasons from equator to the pole," that in the far south he met with the "*Carracaras Eagle*," then a new bird to him. He says—

I was not aware of the existence of the Caracara or Brazilian Eagle in the United States, until my visit to the Floridas, in the winter of 1831. On the 24th of November of that year, in the course of an excursion near the town of St. Augustine, I observed a bird flying at a great elevation, and almost over my head. Convinced that it was unknown to me, and bent on obtaining it, I followed it nearly a mile, when I saw it sail towards the earth, making for a place where a group of Vultures ware engaged in devouring a dead horse. Walking up to the horse, I observed the new bird alighted on it, and helping itself freely to the savory meat beneath its feet; but it evinced a degree of shyness far greater than that of its associates, the Turkey Buzzards and Carrion Crows. I moved circuitously, until I came to a deep ditch, along which I crawled, and went as near to the bird as I possibly could; but finding the distance much too great for a sure shot, I got up suddenly, when the whole of the birds took to flight. The eagle, as if desirous of forming acquaintance with me, took a round and passed over me. I shot, but to my great mortification missed it. However, it alighted a few hundred yards off, in an open savanna, on which I laid myself flat on the ground, and crawled towards it, pushing my gun before me, amid burs and mud-holes, until I reached the distance of about seventy-five yards from it, when I stopped to observe its attitudes. The bird did not notice me; he stood on a lump of flesh, tearing it to pieces, in the manner of a Vulture, until he had nearly swallowed the whole. Being now less occupied, he spied me, erected the feathers of his neck, and, starting up, flew away, carrying the remainder of his prey *in his talons*. I shot a second time, and probably touched him; for he dropped his burden, and made off in a direct course across the St. Sebastian river, with alternate sailings and flappings, somewhat in the manner of a Vulture, but more gracefully. He never uttered a cry, and I followed him wistfully with my eyes until he was quite out of sight.

The following day the bird returned, and was again among the Vultures, but at some distance from the carcase, the birds having been kept off by the dogs. I approached by the ditch, saw it very well, and watched its movements, until it arose, when once more I shot, but without effect. It sailed off in large circles, gliding in a very elegant manner, and now and then diving downwards and rising again.

Two days elapsed before it returned. Being apprised by a friend of this desired event, instead of going after it myself, I dispatched my assistant, who returned with it in little more than half an hour. I immediately began my drawing of it. The weather was sultry, the thermometer being at 89°; and, to my surprise, the vivid tints of the plumage were fading much faster than I had ever seen them in like circumstances, insomuch that Dr. Bell of Dublin, who saw it when fresh, and also when I was finishing the drawing twenty-four hours after, said he could scarcely believe it to be the same bird. How often have I thought of the changes which I have seen effected in the colors of the bill, legs, eyes, and even the plumage of birds, when looking on imitations which I was aware were taken from stuffed specimens, and which I well knew could not be accurate! The *skin*, when the bird was quite recent, was of a bright yellow. The bird was extremely lousy. Its stomach contained the remains of a bullfrog, numerous hard-shelled worms, and a quantity of horse and deer-hair. The skin was saved with great difficulty, and its plumage had entirely lost its original lightness of coloring. The deep red of the fleshy parts of the head had assumed a purplish livid hue, and the spoil scarcely resembled the coat of the living Eagle.

I made a double drawing of this individual, for the purpose of showing all its feathers, which I hope will be found to be accurately represented.

This is the way in which one of the truest naturalists who ever delineated form of bird, beast, or creeping thing, considered it necessary to labor in his vocation, and this is *his* opinion about the evanescence of colors in the dead subjects, and, as is of course implied, of the undoubtedly wide play for the "fancy" in replacing them.

Hear, too, his account of the study of Water Birds. He says—

The difficulties which are to be encountered in studying the habits of our Water Birds are great. He who follows the feathered inhabitants of the forests and plains, however rough or tangled the paths may be, seldom fails to obtain the objects of his pursuit, provided he be possessed of due enthusiasm and perseverance. The Land Bird flits from bush to bush, runs before you, and seldom extends its flight beyond the range of your vision. It is very different with the Water Bird, which sweeps afar over the wide ocean, hovers above the surges, or betakes itself for refuge to the inaccessible rocks on the shore. There, on the smooth sea-beach, you see the lively and active Sandpiper; on that rugged promontory the Dusky Cormorant; under the dark shade of yon cypress the Ibis and Heron; above you in the still air floats the Pelican or the Swan; while far over the angry billows scour the

Fulmar and the Frigate bird. If you endeavor to approach these birds in their haunts, they betake themselves to flight, and speed to places where they are secure from your intrusion.

But the scarcer the fruit, the more prized it is; and seldom have I experienced greater pleasures than when on the Florida Keys, under a burning sun, after pushing my bark for miles over a soapy flat, I have striven all day long, tormented by myriads of insects, to procure a heron new to me, and have at length succeeded in my efforts. And then how amply are the labors of the naturalist compensated, when, after observing the wildest and most distrustful birds, in their remote and almost inaccessible breeding places, he returns from his journeys, and relates his adventures to an interested and friendly audience.

It is thus the miraculous fidelity which characterises his whole work, could only have been attained. His life is full of such incidents. It was indeed a habit from which he never deviated throughout the long years of his faithful dedication to his art, to make his drawings, if possible, on the very spot where the specimens had been obtained, without regard to heat, or cold, or storm. In making his drawings of the Golden Eagle, his incessant application through many hours of hurried labor, without rest, threw him into a violent fit of illness which quite nearly cost him his life. In many other instances he suffered greatly. He sometimes worked, while in Labrador, until the pencil absolutely dropped from his stiffened fingers, frozen in that bitter air; and so it was in the South, his exposure to the opposite extremes were quite as great.

But it is by contrasting his own accounts of his visit to Labrador and the Florida Keys, that we will best be enabled to apprehend the rugged zeal of his out-door methods in these widely separated regions. A visit to Labrador, which is the nesting-ground of a vast number of our migratory birds, having become necessary to the continuation of his work, the first volume only having been as yet issued, he chartered a small vessel, the "Ripley," at Eastport, Maine, for the purpose, and accompanied by four young gentlemen, fond of Natural History and adventure, set sail for the North. He describes his out-fit, mode of life on board and ashore.

We had purchased our stores at Boston, with the aid of my generous friend Dr. Parkman of that city; but unfortunately many things necessary on an expedition like ours were omitted. At Eastport in Maine we therefore laid in these requisites. No traveller, let me say, ought to neglect anything that is calculated to insure the success of his undertaking, or to contribute to his personal comfort, when about to set out on a long and perhaps hazardous voyage. Very few opportunities of replenishing stores of provision, clothing or ammunition, occur in such a country as Labrador; and yet, we all placed too much confidence in the zeal and foresight of our purveyors at Eastport. We had abundance of ammunition, excellent bread, meat and potatoes; but the butter was quite rancid, the oil only fit to grease our guns, the vinegar too liberally diluted with cider, the mustard and pepper deficient in due pungency. All this, however, was not discovered until it was too late to be remedied. Several of the young men were not clothed as hunters should be, and some of the guns were not so good as we could have wished. We were, however, fortunate with respect to our vessel, which was a notable sailer, did not leak, had a good crew, and was directed by a capital seaman.

The hold of the schooner was floored, and an entrance made to it from the cabin, so that in it we had a very good parlor, dining-room, drawing-room, library, &c., all those apartments, however, being united into one. An extravagantly elongated deal table ranged along the centre; one of the party had slung his hammock at one end, and in its vicinity slept the cook and a lad who acted as armorer. The cabin was small; but being fitted in the usual manner with side berths, was used for a dormitory. It contained a small table and a stove, the latter of diminutive size, but smoky enough to discomfit a host. We had adopted in a great measure the clothing worn by the American fishermen on that coast, namely, thick blue cloth trousers, a comfortable waistcoat, and a pea-jacket of blanket. Our boots were large, round-toe'd, strong, and well studded with large nails to prevent sliding on the rocks. Worsted comforters, thick mittens and round broad-brimmed hats, completed our dress, which was more picturesque than fashionable. As soon as we had an opportunity, the boots were exchanged for Esquimaux mounted mocassins of seal-skin, impermeable to water, light, easy and fastening at top about the midde of the thigh to straps, which when buckled over the hips secured them well. To complete our equipment, we had several good boats, one of which was extremely light and adapted for shallow water.

No sooner had we reached the coast and got into harbor, than we agreed to follow certain regulations intended for the general benefit. Every morning the cook was called before three o'clock. At half-past three, breakfast was on the table, and everybody equipped. The guns, ammunition, botanical boxes, and baskets for eggs or minerals, were all in readiness. Our breakfast consisted of coffee, bread and various other materials. At four, all except the cook and one seaman, went off in different directions, not forgetting to carry with them a store of cooked provisions. Some betook themselves to the islands, others to the deep bays; the latter on landing wandered over the country, until noon, when laying themselves down on the rich moss, or sitting on the granite rock, they would rest for an hour, eat their dinner, and talk of their successes or disappointments. I often regret that I did not take sketches of the curious groups formed by my young friends on such occasions, and when, after returning at night, all were engaged in measuring, weighing, comparing and dissecting the birds we had procured, operations which were carried on with the aid of a number of candles thrust into the necks of bottles. Here one examined the flowers and leaves of a plant, there another explored the recesses of a diver's gullet, while a third skinned a gull or a grouse. Nor was our journal forgotten. Arrangements were made for the morrow, and at twelve we left matters to the management of the cook, and retired to our roosts.

If the wind blew hard, all went on shore, and, excepting on a few remarkably rainy days, we continued our pursuits much in the same manner during our stay in the country. The physical powers of the young men were considered in making our arrangements. Shattuck and Ingalls went together; the Captain and Cooledge were fond of each other, the latter having also been an officer; Lincoln and my son being the strongest and most determined hunters, generally marched by themselves; and I went with one or other of the parties according to circumstances, although it was by no means my custom to do so regularly, as I had abundance of work on hand in the vessel.

The return of my young companions and the sailors was always looked for with anxiety. On getting on board, they opened their budgets, and laid their contents on the deck, amid much merriment, those who had procured most specimens being laughed at by those who had obtained the rarest, and the former joking the latter in return. A substantial meal always awaited them, and fortunate we were in having a capital cook, although he was a little too fond of the bottle.

Our "fourth of July" was kept sacred, and every Saturday night the toast of "wives and sweethearts" was the first given, "parents and friends" the last. Never was there a more merry set. Some with the violin and flute accompanied the voices of the rest, and few moments were spent in idleness. Before a month had elapsed, the spoils of many a fine bird hung around the hold; shrubs and flowers were in the press, and I had several drawings finished, some of which you have seen, and of which I hope you will ere long see the remainder. Large jars were filling apace with the bodies of rare birds, fishes, quadrupeds and reptiles, as well as molluscous animals. We had several pets too, Gulls, Cormorants, Guillemots, Puffins, Hawks and a Raven. In some of the harbors, curious fishes were hooked in our sight, so clear was the water.

We found that camping out at night was extremely uncomfortable, on account of the annoyance caused by flies and musquitoes, which attacked the hunters in swarms at all times, but more especially when they lay down, unless they enveloped themselves in thick smoke, which is not much more pleasant. Once when camping, the weather became very bad, and the party was twenty miles distant from Whapatiguan as night threw her mantle over the earth. The rain fell in torrents, the north-east wind blew furiously, and the air was extremely cold. The oars of the boat were fixed so as to support some blankets, and a small fire was with difficulty kindled, on the embers of which a scanty meal was cooked. How different from a camp on the shores of the Mississippi, where wood is abundant, and the air generally not lacking heat, where musquitoes, though plentiful enough, are not accompanied by carraboo flies, and where the barkings of a joyful squirrel, or the notes of the Barred Owl, that grave buffoon of our western woods, never fail to gladden the camper as he cuts to the right and left such branches and canes as most easily supply materials for forming a lodging for the night! On the coast of Labrador there are no such things; granite and green moss are spread around, silence like that of the grave envelopes all, and when night has closed the dreary scene from your sight, the wolves, attracted by the scent of the remains of your scanty repast, gather around you. Cowards as they are, they dare not venture on a charge; but their howlings effectually banish sleep. You must almost roast your feet to keep them warm, while your head and shoulders are chilled by the blast. When morning comes, she smiles not on you with rosy cheeks, but appears muffled in a grey mantle of cold mist, which shows you that there is no prospect of a fine day. The object of the expedition, which was to procure some Owls that had been observed there by day, was entirely frustrated. At early dawn, the party rose stiffened and dispirited, and glad were they to betake themselves to their boats, and return to their floating home.

Before we left Labrador, several of my young friends began to feel the want of suitable clothing. The sailor's ever-tailoring system was, believe me, fairly put to the test. Patches of various colors ornamented knees and elbows; our boots were worn out; our greasy garments and battered hats were in harmony with our tanned and weather-beaten faces; and, had you met with us, you might have taken us for a squad of wretched vagrants; but we were joyous in the expectation of a speedy return, and exulted at the thoughts of our success.

As the chill blast that precedes the winter's tempest thickened the fogs on the hills and ruffled the dark waters, each successive day saw us more anxious to leave the dreary wilderness of grim rocks and desolate moss-clad valleys. Unfavorable winds prevented us for awhile from spreading our white sails; but at last one fair morning smiled on the wintry world, the Ripley was towed from the harbor, her tackle trimmed, and as we bounded over the billows, we turned our eyes towards the wilds of Labrabor, and heartily bade them farewell forever!

He had previously visited the Florida Coast, alone, in 1831 and 1832, and during this expedition penetrated the interior by the St. John's River. All this region, but particularly the "Keys," is like its Boreal contrast, Labrador, of peculiar interest to the Ornithologist, as the resort of myriads of water-fowl and tropical birds of extraordinary splendor. He says:—

While in this part of the peninsula, I followed my usual avocations, although with little success, it being then winter.

I had letters from the Secretaries of the Navy and Treasury of the United States, to the commanding officers of vessels of war of the revenue service, directing them to afford me any assistance in their power; and the schooner Spark having come to St. Augustine, on her way to the St. John's River, I presented my credentials to her commander, Lieutenant Piercy, who readily and with politeness, received me and my assistants on board. We soon after set sail, with a fair breeze. The strict attention to duty on board even this small vessel of war, afforded matter of surprise to me. Everything went on with the regularity of a chronometer; orders were given, answered to and accomplished, before they ceased to vibrate on the ear. The neatness of the crew equalled the cleanliness of the white planks of the deck; the sails were in perfect condition; and, built as the Spark was, for swift sailing, on she went gambolling from wave to wave.

I thought that, while thus sailing, no feeling but that of pleasure could exist in our breasts; but, alas! how fleeting are our enjoyments. When we were almost at the entrance of the river, the wind changed, the sky became clouded, and, before many minutes had elapsed, the little bark was lying-to "like a duck," as her commander expressed himself. It blew a hurricane:—let it blow, reader. At the break of day we were again at anchor within the bar of St. Augustine.

Our next attempt was successful. Not many hours after we had crossed the bar, we perceived the star-like glimmer of the light in the great lantern at the entrance of the St. John's River. This was before day-light; and, as the crossing of the sand-banks or bars, which occur at the mouths of all the streams of this peninsula is difficult, and can be accomplished only when the tide is up, one of the guns was fired as a signal for the government pilot. The good man, it seemed, was unwilling to leave his couch, but a second gun brought him in his canoe alongside. The depth of the channel was barely sufficient. My eyes, however, were not directed towards the water, but on high, where flew some thousands of snowy Pelicans, which had fled affrighted from their resting grounds. How beautifully they performed their broad gyrations, and how matchless, after awhile, was the marshalling of their files, as they flew past us!

On the tide we proceeded apace. Myriads of Cormorants covered the face of the waters, and over it Fish-Crows innumerable were already arriving from their distant roosts. We landed at one place to search for the birds whose charming melodies had engaged our attention, and here and there some young Eagles we shot, to add to our store of fresh provisions! The river did not seem to me equal in beauty to the fair Ohio; the shores were in many places low and swampy, to the great delight of the numberless Herons that moved along in gracefulness, and the grim alligators that swam in sluggish sullenness. In going up a bayou, we caught a great number of the young of the latter for the purpose of making experiments upon them.

After sailing a considerable way, during which our commander and officers took the soundings, as well as the angles and bearings of every nook and crook of the sinuous stream, we anchored one evening at a distance of fully one hundred miles from the mouth of the river. The weather, although it was the 12th of February, was quite warm, the thermometer on board standing at 75°, and on shore at 90°. The fog was so thick that neither of the shores could be seen, and yet the river was not a mile in breadth. The "blind musquitoes" covered every object, even in the cabin, and so wonderfully abundant were these tormentors, that they more than once fairly extinguished the candles whilst I was writing my journal, which I closed in despair, crushing between the leaves more than a hundred of the little wretches. Bad as they are, however, these blind musquitoes do not bite. As if purposely to render our situation doubly uncomfortable, there was an establishment for jerking beef, on the nearer shores to the windward of our vessel, from which the breeze came laden with no sweet odors.

In the morning when I arose, the country was still covered with thick fogs, so that although I could plainly hear the notes of the birds on shore, not an object could I see beyond the bowsprit, and the air was as close and sultry as on the previous evening. Guided by the scent of the jerkers' works, we went on shore, where we found the vegetation already far advanced. The blossoms of the jessamine, ever pleasing, lay steeped in dew; the humming bee was collecting her winter's store from the snowy flowers of the native orange; and the little warblers frisked along the twigs of the smilax. Now, amid the tall pines of the forest, the sun's rays began to force their way, and as the dense mists dissolved in the atmosphere, the bright luminary at length shone forth. We explored the woods around, guided by some friendly live-oakers who had pitched their camp in the vicinity. After awhile the Spark again displayed her sails, and as she silently glided along, we espied a Seminole Indian approaching us in his canoe. The poor dejected son of the woods, endowed with talents of the highest order, although rarely acknowledged by the proud usurpers of his native soil, has spent the night in fishing, and the morning in procuring the superb-feathered game of the swampy thickets; and with both he comes to offer them for our acceptance. Alas! thou fallen one, descendant of an ancient line of freeborn hunters, would that I could restore to thee thy birthright, thy natural independence, the generous feelings that were once fostered in thy brave bosom. But the irrevocable deed is done, and I can merely admire the perfect symmetry of his frame, as he dexterously throws on our deck the trouts and turkeys which he has captured. He receives a recompense, and without smile or bow, or acknowledgment of any kind, off he starts with the speed of an arrow from his own bow.

Alligators were extremely abundant, and the heads of the

fishes which they had snapped off lay floating around on the dark waters. A rifle bullet was now and then sent through the eye of one of the largest, which, with a tremendous splash of its tail expired. One morning we saw a monstrous fellow lying on the shore. I was desirous of obtaining him to make an accurate drawing of his head, and, accompanied by my assistant and two of the sailors, proceeded cautiously towards him. When within a few yards, one of us fired and sent through his side an ounce ball, which tore open a hole large enough to receive a man's hand. He slowly raised his head, bent himself upwards, opened his huge jaws, swung his tail to and fro, rose on his legs, blew in a frightful manner, and fell to the earth. My assistant leaped on shore, and contrary to my injunctions, caught hold of the animal's tail, when the alligator, awakening from his trance, with a last effort crawled slowly towards the water, and plunged heavily into it. Had he thought of once flourishing his tremendous weapon there might have been an end of his assailant's life, but he forfunately went in peace to his grave, where we left him, as the water was too deep. The same morning, another of equal size was observed swimming directly for the bows of our vessel, attracted by the gentle rippling of the water there. One of the officers, who had watched him, fired and scattered his brain through the air, when he tumbled and rolled at a fearful rate, blowing all the while most furiously. The river was bloody for yards around, but although the monster passed close by the vessel, we could not secure him, and after awhile he sunk to the bottom.

Early one morning I hired a boat and two men, with the view of returning to St. Augustine by a short cut. Our baggage being placed on board, I bade adieu to the officers, and off we started. About four in the afternoon we arrived at the short cut, forty miles distant from our point of departure, and where we had expected to procure a wagon, but were disappointed. So we laid our things on the bank, and, leaving one of my assistants to look after them, I set out, accompanied by the other, and my Newfoundland dog. We had eighteen miles to go; and as the sun was only two hours high, we struck off at a good rate. Presently we entered a pine barren. The country was as level as a floor; our path, although narrow, was well beaten, having been used by the Seminole Indians for ages, and the weather was calm and beautiful. Now and then a rivulet occurred, from which we quenched our thirst, while the magnolias and other flowering plants on its banks, relieved the dull uniformity of the woods. When the path separated into two branches, both seemingly leading the same way, I would follow one, while my companion took the other, and unless we met again in a short time, one of us would go across the intervening forest.

The sun went down behind a cloud, and the south-east breeze that sprung up at this moment, sounded dolefully among the tall pines. Along the eastern horizon lay a bed of black vapor, which gradually rose, and soon covered the heavens. The air felt hot and oppressive, and we knew that a tempest was approaching. Plato was now our guide, the white spots on his skin being the only objects that we could discern amid the darkness, and as if aware of his utility in this respect, he kept a short way before us on the trail. Had we imagined ourselves more than a few miles from the town, we would have made a camp, and remained under its shelter for the night; but conceiving that the distance could not be great, we resolved to trudge along.

Large drops began to fall from the murky mass overhead; thick, impenetrable darkness surrounded us, and to my dismay, the dog refused to proceed. Groping with my hands on the ground, I discovered that several trails branched out at the spot where he lay down; and when I had selected one, he went on. Vivid flashes of lightning streamed across the heavens, the wind increased to a gale, and the rain poured down upon us like a torrent. The water soon rose on the level ground so as almost to cover our feet, and we slowly advanced, fronting the tempest. Here and there a tall pine on fire presented a magnificent spectacle, illumining the trees around it, and surrounded with a halo of dim light, abruptly bordered with the deep black of the night. At one time we passed through a tangled thicket of low trees, at another crossed a stream flushed by the heavy rain, and again proceeded over the open barrens.

How long we thus, half-lost, groped our way, is more than I can tell you; but at length the tempest passed over, and suddenly the clear sky became spangled with stars. Soon after we smelt the salt-marshes, and walking directly towards them, like pointers advancing on a covey of partridges, we at last to our great joy descried the light of the beacon near St. Augustine. My dog began to run briskly around, having met with ground on which he had hunted before, and taking a direct course, led us to the great causeway that crosses the marshes at the back of the town. We refreshed ourselves with the produce of the first orange tree that we met with, and in half an hour more arrived at our hotel. Drenched with rain, steaming with perspiration, and covered to the knees with mud, you may imagine what figures we cut in the eyes of the good people whom we found snugly enjoying themselves in the sitting room. Next morning, Major Gates, who had received me with much kindness, sent a wagon with mules and two trusty soldiers for my companion and luggage.

Availing himself of his letters again, he now went on board a revenue cutter, the "Marion."

As the "Marion" neared the inlet called "Indian Key," which is situated on the eastern coast of the peninsula of Florida, my heart swelled with uncontrollable delight. Our vessel once over the coral reef that every where stretches along the shore like a great wall, reared by an army of giants, we found ourselves in safe anchoring ground, within a few furlongs of the land. The next moment saw the oars of a boat propelling us towards the shore, and in brief time we stood on the desired beach. With what delightful feelings did we gaze on the objects around us!—the gorgeous flowers, the singular and beautiful plants, the luxuriant trees. The balmy air which we breathed filled us with animation, so pure and salubrious did it seem to be. The birds which we saw were almost all new to us; their lovely forms appeared to be arrayed in more brilliant apparel than I had ever before seen, and as they gambolled in happy playfulness among the bushes, or glided over the light green waters, we longed to form a more intimate acquaintance with them.

Students of nature spend little time in introductions, especially when they present themselves to persons who feel an interest in their pursuits. This was the case with Mr. Thruston, the Deputy Collector of the island, who shook us all heartily by the hand, and in a trice had a boat manned at our service. Accompanied by him, his pilot and fishermen, off we went, and after a short pull landed on a large Key. Few minutes had elapsed, when shot after shot might be heard, and down came whirling through the air the objects of our desire. One thrust himself into the tangled groves that covered all but the beautiful coral beach that in a continued line bordered the island, while others gazed on the glowing and diversified hues of the curious inhabitants of the deep. I saw one of my party rush into the limpid element, to seize on a crab, that with claws extended upwards, awaited his approach, as if determined not to give way. A loud voice called him back to the land, for sharks are as abundant along these shores as pebbles, and the hungry prowlers could not have got a more savory dinner.

The pilot, besides being a first-rate shot, possessed a most intimate acquaintance with the country. He had been a "conch-diver," and no matter what number of fathoms measured the distance between the surface of the water and its craggy bottom, to seek for curious shells in their retreat, seemed to him more pastime than toil. Not a Cormorant or Pelican, a Flamingo, an Ibis, or Heron, had ever in his days formed its nest without his having marked the spot; and as to the Keys to which the Doves are wont to resort, he was better acquainted with them than many fops are with the contents of their pockets. In a word, he positively knew every channel that led to these islands, and every cranny along their shores. For years his employment had been to hunt those singular animals called Sea Cows or Marratees, and he had conquered hundreds of them, "merely," as he said, because the flesh and hide bring "a fair price" at Havanna. He never went anywhere to land without "Long Tom," which proved indeed to be a wonderful gun, and which made smart havoc when charged with "groceries," a term by which he designated the large shot which he used. In like manner, he never paddled his light canoe without having by his side the trusty javelin, with which he unerringly transfixed such fishes as he thought fit either for market or for his own use. In attacking turtles, netting, or overturning them, I doubt if his equal ever lived on the Florida coast. No sooner was he made acquainted with my errand, than he freely offered his best services, and from that moment until I left Key West, he was seldom out of my hearing.

While the young gentlemen who accompanied us were engaged in procuring plants, shells, and small birds, he tapped me on the shoulder, and with a smile said to me, "Come along, I'll show you something better worth your while." To the boat we betook ourselves, with the Captain and only a pair of tars, for more he said would not answer. The yawl for awhile was urged at a great rate, but as we approached a point, the oars were taken in, and the pilot alone skulling, desired us to make ready, for in a few minutes we should have "rare sport." As we advanced, the more slowly did we move, and the most profound silence was maintained, until suddenly coming almost in contact with a thick shrubbery of mangroves, we beheld, right before us, a multitude of pelicans. A discharge of artillery seldom produced more effect;—the dead, the dying, and the wounded, fell from the trees upon the water, while those unscathed flew streaming through the air in terror and dismay. "There," said he, "did not I tell you so; is it not rare sport?" The birds, one after another, were lodged under the gunwales, when the pilot desired the Captain to order the lads to pull away. Within about half a mile we reached the extremity of the Key. "Pull away," cried the pilot, "never mind them on the wing, for those black rascals don't mind a little firing —now, boys, lay her close under the nests." And there we were, with four hundred cormorants' nests over our heads. The birds were sitting, and when we fired, the number that dropped as if dead and plunged into the water was such, that I thought by some unaccountable means or other we had killed the whole colony. You would have smiled at the loud laugh and curious gestures of the pilot. "Gentlemen," said he, "almost a blank shot!" And so it was, for, on following the birds as one after another peeped up from the water, we found only a few unable to take to wing. "Now," said the pilot, "had you waited until *I had spoken* to the black villains, you might have killed a score or more of them." On inspection, we found that our shots had lodged in the tough dry twigs of which these birds form their nests, and that we had lost the more favorable opportunity of hitting them, by not waiting until they rose. "Never mind," said the pilot, "if you wish it, you may load the *Lady of the Green Mantle** with them in less than a week. Stand still, my lads; and now, gentlemen, in ten minutes you and I will bring down a score of them." And so we did. As we rounded the island, a beautiful bird of the species called Peale's Egret, came up and was shot. We now landed, took in the rest of

* The name given by the wreckers and smugglers to the Marion.

our party, and returned to Indian Key, where we arrived three hours before sunset

The sailors and other individuals to whom my name and pursuits had become known, carried our birds to the pilot's house. His good wife had a room ready for me to draw in, and my assistant might have been seen busily engaged in skinning, while George Lehman was making a sketch of the lovely isle.

Time is ever precious to the student of nature. I placed several birds in their natural attitudes, and began to outline them. A dance had been prepared also, and no sooner was the sun lost to our eye, than males and females, including our captain and others from the vessel, were seen advancing gaily towards the house in full apparel. The birds were skinned, the sketch was on paper, and I told my young men to amuse themselves. As to myself, I could not join in the merriment, for, full of the remembrance of you, reader, and of the patrons of my work both in America and in Europe, I went on "grinding"—not on an organ, like the Lady of Bras d'Or, but on paper, to the finishing, not merely of my outlines, but of my notes respecting the objects seen this day.

The room adjoining that in which I worked, was soon filled. Two miserable fiddlers screwed their screeching silken strings —not an inch of catgut graced their instruments; and the bouncing of brave lads and fair lasses shook the premises to the foundation. One with a slip came down heavily on the floor, and the burst of laughter that followed echoed over the isle. Diluted claret was handed round to cool the ladies, while a beverage of more potent energies warmed their partners. After supper our captain returned to the Marion, and I, with my young men, slept in light swinging hammocks, under the eaves of the piazza.

It was the end of April, when the nights were short and the days therefore long. Anxious to turn every moment to account, we were on board Mr. Thruston's boat at three next morning. Pursuing our way through the deep and tortuous channels that everywhere traverse the immense muddy soap-like flats that stretch from the outward Keys to the Main, we proceeded on our voyage of discovery. Here and there we met with great beds of floating sea-weeds, which showed us that turtles were abundant there, these masses being the refuse of their feeding. On talking to Mr. Thruston of the nature of these muddy flats, he mentioned that he had once been lost amongst their narrow channels for several days and nights, when in pursuit of some smugglers' boat, the owners of which were better acquainted with the place than the men who were along with him. Although in full sight of several of the Keys, as well as of the main land, he was unable to reach either, until a heavy gale raised the water, when he sailed directly over the flats, and returned home almost exhausted with fatigue and hunger. His present pilot often alluded to the circumstance afterwards, ending with a great laugh, and asserting that had he "been there, the rascals would not have escaped."

Coming under a Key on which multitudes of Frigate Pelicans had begun to form their nests, we shot a good number of them, and observed their habits. The boastings of our pilot were here confirmed by the exploits which he performed with his long gun, and on several occasions he brought down a bird from a height of fully a hundred yards. The poor birds, unaware of the range of our artillery, sailed calmly along, so that it was not difficult for "Long Tom," or rather for its owner, to furnish us with as many as we required. The day was spent in this manner, and towards night we returned, laden with booty, to the hospitable home of the pilot.

The next morning was delightful. The gentle sea-breeze glided over the flowery isle, the horizon was clear, and all was silent save the long breakers that rushed over the distant reefs. As we were proceeding towards some Keys, seldom visited by men, the sun rose from the bosom of the waters with a burst of glory that flashed on my soul the idea of that power which called into existence so magnificent an object. The moon, thin and pale, as if ashamed to show her feeble light, concealed herself in the dim west. The surface of the waters shone in its tremulous smoothness, and the deep blue of the clear heavens was pure as the world that lies beyond them. The Heron heavily flew towards the land, like the glutton retiring at day-break, with well-lined paunch, from the house of some wealthy patron of good cheer. The Night Heron and the Owl, fearful of day, with hurried flight sought safety in the recesses of the deepest swamps; while the Gulls and Terns, ever cheerful, gambolled over the water, exulting in the prospect of abundance. I also exulted in hope; my whole frame seemed to expand; and our sturdy crew showed, by their merry faces, that nature had charms for them too. How much of beauty and joy is lost to those who never view the rising sun, and of whose waking existence the best half is nocturnal!

Twenty miles our men had to row before we reached "Sandy Island," and as on its level shores we all leaped, we plainly saw the southernmost cape of the Floridas. The flocks of birds that covered the shelly beaches, and those hovering over head so astonished us, that we could for awhile scarcely believe our eyes. The first volley procured a supply of food sufficient for two days' consumption. Such tales, you have already been told, are well enough at a distance from the place to which they refer; but you will doubtless be still more surprised, when I tell you that our first fire among a crowd of the Great Godwits laid prostrate sixty-five of these birds. Rose-colored Curlews stalked gracefully beneath the mangroves; Purple Herons rose at almost every step we took, and each cactus supported the nest of a White Ibis. The air was darkened by whistling wings, while, on the waters, floated Gallinules and other interesting birds. We formed a kind of shed with sticks and grass, the sailor cook commenced his labors, and ere long we supplied the deficiencies of our fatigued frames. The business of the day over, we secured ourselves from insects by means of musquito-nets, and were lulled to rest by the cacklings of the beautiful Purple Gallinules!

When we had lain ourselves down in the sand to sleep, the waters almost bathed our feet; when we opened our eyes in the morning, they were at an immense distance. Our boat lay on her side, looking not unlike a whale reposing on a mud-bank. The birds in myriads were probing their exposed pasture-ground. There great flocks of Ibises fed apart from equally large collections of Godwits, and thousands of Herons gracefully paced along, ever and anon thrusting their javelin bills into the body of some unfortunate fish confined in a small pool of water. Of Fish-Crows I could not estimate the number, but from the havoc they made among the crabs, I conjecture that these animals must have been scarce by the time of next ebb. Frigate Pelicans chased the Jager, which himself had just robbed a poor Gull of its prize, and all the Gallinules ran with spread wings from the mud-banks to the thickets of the island, so timorous had they become when they perceived us.

Surrounded as we were by so many objects that allured us, not one could we yet attain, so dangerous would it have been to venture on the mud; and our pilot having assured us that nothing could be lost by waiting, spoke of our eating, and on this hint told us that he would take us to a part of the island where "our breakfast would be abundant, although uncooked." Off we went, some of the sailors carrying baskets, others large tin pans and wooden vessels, such as they use for eating their meals in. Entering a thicket of about an acre in extent, we found on every bush several nests of the Ibis, each containing three large and beautiful eggs, and all hands fell to gathering. The birds gave way to us, and ere long we had a heap of eggs that promised delicious food. Nor did we stand long in expectation, for, kindling a fire, we soon prepared, in one way or other, enough to satisfy the cravings of our hungry maws. Breakfast ended, the pilot, looking at the gorgeous sunrise, said, "Gentlemen, prepare yourselves for fun, the tide is acoming."

Over these enormous mud-flats, a foot or two of water is quite sufficient to drive all the birds ashore, even the tallest Heron or Flamingo, and the tide seems to flow at once over the whole expanse. Each of us provided with a gun, posted himself behind a bush, and no sooner had the water forced the winged creatures to approach the shore, than the work of destruction commenced. When it at length ceased, the collected mass of birds of different kinds looked not unlike a small haycock. Who could not with a little industry have helped himself to a few of their skins? Why, reader, surely no one as fond of these things as I am. Every one assisted in this, and even the sailors themselves tried their hand at the work.

Our pilot, good man, told us he was no hand at such occupations, and would go after something else. So taking Long Tom and his fishing-tackle, he marched off quietly along the shores. About an hour afterwards we saw him returning, when he looked quite exhausted, and on our inquiring the cause, said, "There is a dew-fish yonder and a few balacoudas, but I am not able to bring them, or even to haul them here; please send the sailors after them." The fishes were accordingly brought, and as I had never seen a dew-fish, I examined it closely, and took an outline of its form, which some days hence you may perhaps see. It exceeded a hundred pounds in weight, and afforded excellent eating. The balacouda is also a good fish, but at times a dangerous one, for, according to the pilot, on more than one occasion "some of these gentry" had followed him when waist-deep in the water, in pursuit of a more valuable prize, until in self-defence he had to spear them, fearing that "the gentleman" might at one dart cut off his legs, or some other nice bit, with which he was unwilling to part.

Having filled our cask from a fine well long since dug in the sand of Cape Sable, either by Seminole Indians or pirates, no matter which, we left Sandy Isle about full tide, and proceeded homewards, giving a call here and there at different keys, with the view of procuring rare birds, and also their nests and eggs. We had twenty miles to go "as the birds fly," but the tortuosity of the channels rendered our course fully a third longer. The sun was descending fast, when a black cloud suddenly obscured the majestic orb. Our sails swelled by a breeze that was scarcely felt by us, and the pilot, requesting us to sit on the weather gunwale, told us that we were "going to get it." One sail was hauled in and secured, and the other was reefed, although the wind had not increased. A low murmuring noise was heard, and across the cloud that now rolled along in tumultuous masses, shot vivid flashes of lightning. Our experienced guide steered directly across a flat towards the nearest land. The sailors passed their quids from one cheek to the other, and our pilot having covered himself with his oil-jacket, we followed his example. "Blow, sweet breeze," cried he at the tiller, and "we'll reach land before the blast overtakes us, for, gentlemen, it is a furious cloud yon."

A furious cloud indeed was the one which now, like an eagle on outstretched wings, approached so swiftly, that one might have deemed it in haste to destroy us. We were not more than a cable's length from the shore, when, with imperative voice, the pilot calmly said to us, "Sit quite still, gentlemen, for I should not like to lose you overboard just now; the boat can't upset, my word for that, if you will but sit still--here we have it!"

Reader, persons who have never witnessed a hurricane, such as not unfrequently desolates the sultry climates of the south, can scarcely form an idea of their terrific grandeur. One would think that, not content with laying waste all on land, it must needs sweep the waters of the shallows quite dry, to quench its thirst. No respite for an instant does it afford to the objects within the reach of its furious current. Like the scythe of the destroying angel, it cuts every thing by the roots, as it were, with the careless ease of the experienced mower. Each of its revolving sweeps collects a heap that might be likened to the full sheaf which the husbandman flings by his side. On it goes with a wildness and fury that are indescribable; and when at last its frightful blasts have ceased, Nature, weeping and disconsolate, is left bereaved of her beauteous offspring. In some instances, even a full century is required, before, with all her powerful energies, she can repair her loss. The planter has not only lost his mansion, his crops, and his flocks, but he has to clear his lands anew, covered and entangled as they are with the trunks and branches of trees that are every where strewn. The bark overtaken by the storm, is cast on the lee-shore, and if any are left to witness the fatal results, they are the "wreckers" alone, who, with inward delight, gaze upon the melancholy spectacle.

Our light bark shivered like a leaf the instant the blast reached her sides. We thought she had gone over; but the next instant she was on the shore. And now in contemplation of the sublime and awful storm, I gazed around me. The waters drifted like snow; the tough mangroves hid their tops amid their roots, and the loud roaring of the waves driven among them, blended with the howl of the tempest. It was not rain that fell; the masses of water flew in a horizontal direction, and where a part of my body was exposed, I felt as if a smart blow had been given me on it. But enough!—in half an hour it was over. The pure blue sky once more embellished the heavens, and although it was now quite night, we considered our situation a good one.

The crew and some of the party spent the night in the boat. The pilot, myself, and one of my assistants, took to the heart of the mangroves, and, having found high land, we made a fire as well as we could, spread a tarpauling, and fixing our insect bars over us, soon forgot in sleep the horrors that had surrounded us.

Next day, the Marion proceeded on her cruise, and in a few more days, having anchored in another safe harbor, we visited other Keys, of which I will, with your leave, give you a short account.

The Deputy-Collector of Indian Isle gave me the use of his pilot for a few weeks, and I was the more gratified by this, that besides knowing him to be a good man and a perfect sailor, I was now convinced that he possessed a great knowledge of the habits of birds, and could without loss of time lead me to their haunts. We were a hundred miles or so farther to the south. Gay May, like a playful babe, gambolled on the bosom of his mother nature, and every thing was replete with life and joy. The pilot had spoken to me of some birds, which I was very desirous of obtaining. One morning, therefore, we went in two boats to some distant isle, where they were said to breed. Our difficulties in reaching that Key might to some seem more imaginary than real, were I faithfully to describe them. Suffice it for me to tell you, that after hauling our boats, and pushing them with our hands, for upwards of nine miles, over the flats, we at last reached the deep channel that usually surrounds each of the mangrove islands. We were much exhausted by the labor and excessive heat, but we were now floating on deep water, and by resting a short while under the shade of some mangroves, we were soon refreshed by the breeze that gently blew from the Gulf. We further repaired our strength by taking some food; and I may as well tell you here, that during all the time I spent in that portion of the Floridas, my party restricted themselves to fish and soaked biscuit, while our only and constant beverage was water and molasses. I found that in these warm latitudes, exposed as we constantly were to alternate heat and moisture, ardent spirits and more substantial food would prove dangerous to us. The officers, and those persons who from time to time kindly accompanied us, adopted the same regimen, and not an individual of us had ever to complain of so much as a headache.

But we were under the mangroves—at a great distance on one of the flats, the Heron, which I have named *Ardea occidentalis*, was seen moving majestically in great numbers. The tide rose and drove them away, and as they came towards us, to alight and rest for a time on the tallest trees, we shot as many as I wished. I also took under my charge several of their young, alive.

At another time we visited the "Mule Keys." There the prospect was in many respects dismal in the extreme. As I followed their shores, I saw bales of cotton floating in all the coves, while spars of every description lay on the beach, and far off on the reefs I could see the last remains of a lost ship, her dismantled hulk. Several schooners were around her; they were wreckers. I turned me from the sight with a heavy heart. Indeed, as I slowly proceeded, I dreaded to meet the floating or cast ashore bodies of some of the unfortunate crew. Our visit to the Mule Keys was in no way profitable, for, besides meeting with but a few birds in two or three instances, I was, whilst swimming in the deep channel of a mangrove isle, much nearer a large shark than I wish ever to be again.

"The service" requiring all the attention, prudence and activity of Captain Day and his gallant officers, another cruise took place, of which you will find some account in the sequel; and, while I rest a little on the deck of the Lady of the Green Mantle, let me offer my humble thanks to the Being who has allowed me the pleasure of thus relating to you, kind reader, a small part of my adventures.

Admitted by Nature to her most tender confidences, the Hunter-Naturalist seems also to have been chosen as the favored intimate of her convulsed and most terrible moods. We have seen him here ride unharmed amidst the hurricane of the Tropics, let us now turn to him standing secure "a looker-on," beside its fearful track in the West. He thus describes the scene:—

I had left the village of Shawney, situated on the banks of the Ohio, on my return from Henderson, which is also situated on the banks of the same beautiful stream. The weather was pleasant, and I thought not warmer than usual at that season. My horse was jogging quietly along, and my thoughts were, for once at least in the course of my life, entirely engaged in commercial speculations. I had forded Highland Creek, and was on the eve of entering a tract of bottom land or valley that lay between it and Canoe Creek, when on a sudden I remarked a great difference in the aspect of the heavens. A hazy thickness had overspread the country, and I for some time expected an earthquake, but my horse exhibited no propensity to stop and prepare for such an occurrence. I had nearly arrived at the verge of the valley, when I thought fit to stop near a brook, and dismounted to quench the thirst which had come upon me.

I was leaning on my knees, with my lips about to touch the water, when, from my proximity to the earth, I heard a distant murmuring sound of an extraordinary nature. I drank, however, and as I rose on my feet, looked towards the south-west, where I observed a yellowish oval spot, the appearance of which was quite new to me. Little time was left me for consideration, as the next moment a smart breeze began to agitate the taller trees. It increased to an unexpected height, and already the smaller branches and twigs were seen falling in a slanting direction towards the ground. Two minutes had scarcely elapsed, when the whole forest before me was in fearful motion. Here and there, where one tree pressed against another, a creaking noise was produced, similar to that occasioned by the violent gusts which sometimes sweep over the country. Turning instinctively towards the direction from which the wind blew, I saw to my great astonishment, that the noblest trees of the forest bent their lofty heads for a while, and unable to stand against the blast, were falling into pieces. First, the branches were broken off with a crackling noise; then went the upper part of the massy trunks; and in many places whole trees of gigantic size were falling entire to the ground. So rapid was the progress of the storm, that before I could think of taking measures to insure my safety, the hurricane was passing opposite the place where I stood. Never can I forget the scene which at that moment presented itself. The tops of the trees were seen moving in the strangest manner, in the central current of the tempest, which carried along with it a mingled mass of twigs and foliage, that completely obscured the view. Some of the largest trees were seen bending and writhing under the gale; others suddenly snapped across; and many, after a momentary resistance, fell uprooted to the earth. The mass of branches, twigs, foliage and dust that moved through the air, was whirled onwards like a cloud of feathers, and on passing, disclosed a wide space filled with fallen trees, naked stumps and heaps of shapeless ruins, which marked the path of the tempest. This space was about a fourth of a mile in breadth, and to my imagination resembled the dried-up bed of the Mississippi, with its thousands of planters and sawyers, strewed in the sand, and inclined in various degrees. The horrible noise resembled that of the great cataracts of Niagara, and as it howled along in the track of the desolating tempest, produced a feeling in my mind which it were impossible to describe.

The principal force of the hurricane was now over, although millions of twigs and small branches, that had been brought from a great distance, were seen following the blast, as if drawn onwards by some mysterious power. They even floated in the air for some hours after, as if supported by the thick mass of dust that rose high above the ground. The sky had now a greenish lurid hue, and an extremely disagreeable sulphureous odor was diffused in the atmosphere. I waited in amazement, having sustained no material injury, until nature at length resumed her wonted aspect. For some moments, I felt undetermined whether I should return to Morgantown, or attempt to force my way through the wrecks of the tempest. My business, however, being of an urgent nature, I ventured into the path of the storm, and after encountering innumerable difficulties, succeeded in crossing it. I was obliged to lead my horse by the bridle, to enable him to leap over the fallen trees, whilst I scrambled over or under them in the best way I could, at times so hemmed in by the broken tops and tangled branches, as almost to become desperate. On arriving at my house, I gave an account of what I had seen, when, to my surprise, I was told that there had been very little wind in the neighborhood, although in the streets and gardens many branches and twigs had fallen in a manner which excited great surprise.

Many wondrous accounts of the devastating effects of this hurricane were circulated in the country, after its occurrence. Some log houses, we were told, had been overturned, and their inmates destroyed. One person informed me that a wire-sifter had been conveyed by the gust to a distance of many miles. Another had found a cow lodged in the fork of a large half-broken tree. But, as I am disposed to relate only what I have myself seen, I shall not lead you into the region of romance, but shall content myself with saying that much damage was done by this awful visitation. The valley is yet a desolate place, overgrown with briars and bushes, thickly entangled amidst the tops and trunks of the fallen trees, and is the resort of ravenous animals, to which they betake themselves when pursued by man, or after they have committed their depredations on the farms of the surrounding district. I have crossed the path of the storm, at a distance of a hundred miles from the spot where I witnessed its fury, and, again, four hundred miles farther off, in the State of Ohio. Lastly, I observed traces of its ravages on the summits of the mountains connected with the Great Pine Forest of Pennsylvania, three hundred miles beyond the place last mentioned. In all these different parts, it appeared to me not to have exceeded a quarter of a mile in breadth.

But even this is not enough for Nature's child; he must be accepted playmate of the earthquake too, and calmly rock upon its waves. He tells us:—

Travelling through the Barrens of Kentucky (of which I shall give you an account elsewhere) in the month of November, I was jogging on one afternoon, when I remarked a sudden and strange darkness rising from the western horizon. Accustomed to our heavy storms of thunder and rain, I took no more notice of it, as I thought the speed of my horse might enable me to get under shelter of the roof of an acquaintance, who lived not far distant, before it should come up. I had proceeded about a mile, when I heard what I imagined to be the distant rumbling of a violent tornado, on which I spurred my steed, with a wish to gallop as fast as possible to the place of shelter; but it would not do, the animal knew better than I what was forthcoming, and, instead of going faster, so nearly stopped, that I remarked he placed one foot after another on the ground with as much precaution as if walking on a smooth sheet of ice. I thought he had suddenly foundered, and, speaking to him, was on the point of dismounting and leading him, when he all of a sudden fell a-groaning piteously, hung his head, spread out his four legs, as if to save himself from falling, and stood stock still, continuing to groan. I thought my horse was about to die, and would have sprung from his back had a minute more elapsed, but at that instant all the shrubs and trees began to move from their very roots, the ground rose and fell in successive furrows, like the ruffled waters of a lake, and I became bewildered in my ideas, as I too plainly discovered that all this awful commotion in nature was the result of an earthquake.

I had never witnessed anything of the kind before, although, like every other person, I knew of earthquakes by description. But what is description compared with the reality? Who can tell of the sensations which I experienced when I found myself rocking as it were on my horse, and with him moved to and fro like a child in a cradle, with the most imminent danger around, and expecting the ground every moment to open, and present to my eye such an abyss as might engulf myself and all around me? The fearful convulsion, however, lasted only a few minutes, and the heavens again brightened as quickly as they had become obscured; my horse brought his feet to their natural position, raised his head, and galloped off as if loose and frolicking without a rider.

I was not, however, without great apprehension respecting my family, from which I was yet many miles distant, fearful that where they were the shock might have caused greater havoc than I had witnessed. I gave the bridle to my steed, and was glad to see him appear as anxious to get home as myself. The pace at which he galloped accomplished this sooner than I had expected, and I found, with much pleasure, that hardly any greater harm had taken place than the apprehension excited for my own safety.

Shock succeeded shock almost every day and night for several weeks, diminishing, however, so gradually as to dwindle away into mere vibrations of the earth. Strange to say, I for one became so accustomed to the feeling as rather to enjoy the fears manifested by others. I never can forget the effects of one of the slighter shocks which took place when I was at a friend's house, where I had gone to enjoy the merriment that, in our western country, attends a wedding. The ceremony being performed, supper over and the fiddles tuned, dancing became the order of the moment. This was merrily followed up to a late hour, when the party retired to rest. We were in what is called, with great propriety, a *Log-house*, one of large dimensions, and solidly constructed. The owner was a physician, and in one corner were not only his lancets, tourniquets, amputating-knives and other sanguinary apparatus, but all the drugs which he employed for the relief of his patients, arranged in jars and phials of different sizes. These had some days before made a narrow escape from destruction, but had been fortunately preserved by closing the doors of the cases in which they were contained.

As I have said, we had all retired to rest, some to dream of sighs and smiles, and others to sink into oblivion. Morning was fast approaching, when the rumbling noise that precedes the earthquake began so loudly, as to waken and alarm the whole party, and drive them out of bed in the greatest consternation. The scene which ensued it is impossible for me to describe, and it would require the humorous pencil of Cruikshank to do justice to it. Fear knows no restraints. Every person, old and young, filled with alarm at the creaking of the log-house, and apprehending instant destruction, rushed wildly out to the grass enclosure fronting the building. The full moon was slowly descending from her throne, covered at times by clouds that rolled heavily along, as if to conceal from her view the scenes of terror which prevailed on the earth below. On the grass-plat we all met, in such condition as rendered it next to impossible to discriminate any of the party, all huddled together in a state of almost perfect nudity. The earth waved like a field of corn before the breeze: the birds left their perches, and flew about not knowing whither; and the doctor, recollecting the danger of his gallipots, ran to his shop-room, to prevent their dancing off the shelves to the floor. Never for a moment did he think of closing the doors, but, spreading his arms, jumped about the front of the cases, pushing back here and there the falling jars; with so little success, however, that before the shock was over, he had lost nearly all he possessed.

The shock at length ceased, and the frightened females, now sensible of their dishabille, fled to their several apartments. The earthquakes produced more serious consequences in other places. Near New Madrid, and for some distance on the Mississippi, the earth was rent asunder in several places, one or two islands sunk forever, and the inhabitants fled in dismay towards the eastern shores.

Nor was it alone amidst the "elemental rack" that he thus seemed to bear a charmed life. He was threatened with another, and as stern danger, at the hand of the red man once during his Western wanderings. This was, when returning from the upper Mississippi, he was forced to cross one of the wide prairies of that region. We must let him relate it in part. Toward the dusk of the evening, wearied with an interminable jaunt over the prairie, he approached a light that feebly shone from the window of a log hut. He reached the spot, and presenting himself at the door, asked a tall figure of a woman, whether he might take shelter under her roof. Her voice was gruff, and her dress carelessly thrown about her person. She answered his question in the affirmative, when he walked in, took a wooden stool, and quietly seated himself by the fire. A finely formed young Indian, his head resting between his hands, with his elbows on his knees, was seated in the centre of the cabin. A long bow stood against the wall, while a quantity of arrows and two or three black raccoon skins lay at his feet. He moved not: he apparently breathed not. Being addressed in French, he raised his head, pointed to one of his eyes with his finger, and gave a significant glance with the other. His face was covered with blood. It appeared, that an hour before, in the act of discharging an arrow at a raccoon, the arrow slipt upon the cord, and sprang back with such violence into his right eye, as to destroy it forever. "Feeling hungry," Mr. Audubon continues his narrative, "I inquired what sort of fare I might expect. Such a thing as a bed was not to be seen, but many large untanned bear and buffalo hides lay piled up in a corner. I drew a fine time-piece from my vest, and told the woman that it was late, and that I was fatigued. She had espied my watch, the richness of which seemed to operate upon her feelings with electric quickness. She told me that there was plenty of venison and jerked buffalo meat, and that on removing the ashes I should find a cake. But my watch had struck her fancy, and her curiosity had to be gratified with a sight of it. I took off the gold chain that secured it, from around my neck, and presented it to her. She was all ecstacy, spoke of its beauty, asked me its value, put the chain around her brawny neck, saying how happy the possession of such a chain would make her. Thoughtless, and, as I fancied myself in so retired a spot, secure, I paid little attention to her talk or her movements. I helped my dog to a good supper of venison, and was not long in satisfying the demands of my own appetite. The Indian rose from his seat as if in extreme suffering. He pinched me on the side so violently, that the pain nearly brought forth an exclamation of anger, I looked at him. His eye met mine; but his look was so forbidding that it struck a chill into the more nervous part of my system. He again seated himself, drew a butcher-knife from its greasy scabbard, examined its edge, as I would do that of a razor I suspected to be dull, replaced it, and again taking his tomahawk from his back, filled the pipe of it with tobacco, and sent me expressive glances whenever our hostess chanced to have her back toward us. Never till that moment had my senses been awakened to the danger which I now suspected to be about me. I returned glance for glance with my companion, and rested well assured that, whatever enemies I might have, he was not of the number."

In the meantime, he retired to rest upon the skins, when

two athletic youths, the sons of the woman, made their entrance. She whispered with them a little while, when they fell to eating and drinking, to a state bordering on intoxication. "Judge of my astonishment," he says, "when I saw this incarnate fiend take a large carving knife, and go to the grindstone to whet its edge! I saw her pour the water on the turning-machine, and watched her working away with the dangerous instrument, until the sweat covered every part of my body, in spite of my determination to defend myself to the last. Her task finished, she walked to her reeling sons, and said: 'There, that'll soon settle him! Boys, kill yon ———, and then for the watch!' I turned, cocked my gun locks silently, and lay ready to start up and shoot the first who might attempt my life. Fortunately, two strangers entering at the moment, the purpose of the woman was disclosed, and she and her drunken sons secured."

But before and during this most erratic period of Audubon's long life of vicissitude and exposure, these same solitudes amidst which he wandered, knew another shaggy presence even better than his own. The same earthquakes, the same hurricanes, and the same red foe had beset the path of Daniel Boone—and he, too, the rough, strong birth of nature, was a Hunter-Naturalist! Though his deeds and aims were not after the manner of those of Audubon, yet were they as grand, and their lives, how much alike! These remarkable men, one the Pioneer of Civilization and the other of Art and Science, in that great wilderness, through which the path of empire leads, did not meet until the career of each had been finally shaped, and then what grandeur was there in such meetings!

But we will trace rapidly the career of Boone up to these periods, and see how much resemblance in the outline of the gigantic proportions of these two men shall appear.

The great Pioneer was born in 1746, and, though a native of Maryland, had lived as a hunter in two other States—

Virginia and North Carolina—before he was twenty-three. Having reached eighteen, with rifle on shoulder and hunting-knife at belt, he first set off alone for the wilds of Western Virginia. He left his parents behind—since he had found that they were not to be reconciled to the wild, roving, solitary life to which he had been so incurably addicted from the time he was strong enough to handle his little rifle. Since then, the woods had been his home and the father's house his camp—though less and less frequently, as the years advanced, had it amounted even to so much of a tie.

It was not that the young Daniel was of either an ungentle or unloving nature that this apparent alienation and desertion occurred—the reverse is true, and his whole striking career has demonstrated him to have been the possessor of attributes as loyal and as generous as ever marked the man of great achievement. No, the instinct of freedom—freedom with God and nature—was as strong as life in him, and his tenacity of purpose as ungovernable as the law of gravitation.

His family was humble, and he had no educated purpose but what he had learned from the deep breathings of nature. What this purpose was, he never stopped to think—he only felt yearnings—ungovernably strong—the meaning of which he could not know—but which led him, deeper and deeper, with yet more resistless strength, into the cool profounds of the all-nourishing bosom of his primeval mother. Here was his learning—here he found a language with meanings enough to him—for each day had taught him to read with clearer and more unerring vision. He could not interpret this language any more than he could the purpose with which his life was filled; but, as with that purpose, he would feel it in his being. About all that he knew definitely concerning himself was, that he always had been a hunter, and always should be a hunter; and, as for what might happen farther, he gave no other thought than for the day or the hour.

His spirit—even at lusty eighteen—with the eye of a hawk

and agility of a young panther—was not a turbulent one. He rebelled against the life of usages—that we call society—not because he lacked the strength or the firmness to battle with it—but because he lacked the will or desire to do so. He was too young and too healthy for misanthropy; and, if he had been older and less healthy, the social conditions with which he was familiar were too simple for him to have realized that contamination of vice which sometimes goes far to breed distrust, disgust and hate in even strong natures.

No!—if ever a wild creature—gentle, and yet terrible in gentleness—went on two feet through the shadowed heart of forests, the young Boone was one! He knew nothing of any world but God's world—of any law but the right—of any conscience but his own—of any Power but that which dwelt above—in nature, and in his own good right arm and unerring rifle.

In a word, he was the Patriarch of that "Wild Turkey breed" of tameless wanderers peculiar to this Continent; and from the restless and wary instincts of which our progress towards almost boundless empire upon the hemisphere takes origin.

"He might have been civilized!" as a *gentleman*, of Chestnut or Broadway—inspecting through an eye-glass his powerful frame and ruddy cheeks—may be supposed to lisp! —but that would have spoiled a *man!*—a man of might! the father of a State.

You could not have tamed such a man as Daniel Boone into the mere conventional slave while there was "elbow room," as he memorably termed it, in the world. If he had been chained, that dogged perseverance—that invincible self-reliance—that deathless love for the natural and the free would have made him a most formidable galley slave;—under any institutions he would have been a terrible agent of revolution and overthrow.

Indeed, one great cause of the solidity of our government

at present is undoubtedly to be found in the fact, that our immense territories have as yet formed an outlet for such fierce unbending spirits, in the better work of pioneering, than the worse of *emeutes*, as in hampered France. Crowd such natures too much, and the friction assuredly causes an explosion! They are too combustible to be trusted near the fires which rage beneath such cauldrons as Paris! Give them air and "elbow room!" Cool them beneath the shadows of wide forests, and beside the rivulets that murmur, glistening here and there—or by the deep beds where mighty torrents roll and roar—then you make human beings of them—you temper down that savage restlessness of restraint which makes of them beasts and devils elsewhere. However stern the code their passions and necessities may cause them to adopt, yet it is sure to be based upon justice, and lead to wide utility. Society had always better let such men go—if they want to go—if it be even to "the fartherest Ind"—for it is as sure in that event to hear of them again for ultimate good, as it is certain, if they are restrained, to feel them for immediate evil.

Young Boone passed through Virginia until he reached the wooded slopes, dark glens, and lofty cliffs of the Alleghany Mountains. Here at last it was lonely and wild enough for him. Here he felt was home and peace. Parts of this region were singularly picturesque and lovely, as they indeed still are. The fine open woods, heavily sodded with a rich and nutritious grass, afforded at that time the most abundant pasturage for great herds of deer, while now these lovely slopes are covered with large grazing farms, sustaining some of the finest cattle in the world.

The young adventurer soon built him a little hut in a ravine on the side of a mountain, about twenty miles beyond what he then supposed to be the outermost boundary of settlement. He then quietly proceeded to explore the region round about—pursuing industriously, in the meanwhile, his chosen vocation of hunter. This was at that time a far more honorable and lucrative employment than can well be realized now, for although very many devoted themselves to it as a means of earning an honest livelihood, and the skins and meat of the animals slain by them found an important branch of traffic to the whole country—yet everybody was in addition more or less a hunter—so that, fortunately, for our struggles then and since, this might be called the chief occupation of the people, and we a nation of hunters.

He went in to the nearest trading post now and then, laden with skins and meat, to exchange them for powder, lead and other necessaries, returning as speedily as possible, for the very atmosphere of even such "crowded haunts," was oppressive to him, and the coarse voices of common traffic sounded harsh enough to ears accustomed only to those of nature.

His lonely explorations were first directed towards the sum mits of the great chain. He would make excursions of weeks together along the wildest and most inaccessible sides of the mountains—penetrating their deepest fastnesses, and camping wherever the game or other objects of interest attracted him for a time—then he would *on* again, to some newer and yet more difficult region within reasonable reach of his solitary cabin, and in a different direction.

Thus the whole year was unconsciously spent in scaling the Eastern side of those mountains—the descent upon the Western slope of which was to open to him a field of renown.

We next hear of him on the Frontier of North Carolina. Here he lived for over a year in the most entire seclusion—never being seen except when he came in to the nearest settlement for powder and lead; and here he seemed still more shy than before—but yet his unusual energy as a hunter, his skill in wood-craft, and his cool, reckless presence of mind, under all circumstances of danger, soon attracted the admiration of the Border men, and, in spite of his modesty and entire shrinking from all intercourse with his fellows that could be avoided, he found himself at twenty-one literally dragged forward into the position of a leader.

The frontier of North Carolina was at that time a good deal harrassed by Indians, but principally by white ruffians and marauders who assumed the guise of Indians to perpetrate their most infamous outrages. From his knowledge of wood-craft he was soon enabled to put a stop to this trick, and break down this dangerous combination. This gained him, in a still greater degree, the admiration of the borderers, and he was now regarded as a person of importance, and great confidence reposed in him, though so young a man.

Little was known, at this time, of the vast country beyond the Alleghanies to the West, but most especially of the wild and remote land of Kan-tuck-Kee, as it was termed from its principal river by the Indians.

It is true, that so early as 1543, the Spaniards who penetrated the northern country under the chivalrous and unfortunate De Soto, discovered Kentucky while descending the Mississippi; that on the Ohio and Mississippi sides it had frequently been merely touched by the French Canadians, and by Jesuit missionaries, but it seems that a Colonel Wood in 1654, was the first American who penetrated it so far as the Mississippi, through the interior.

In 1670, Captain Bolt, visited it from Virginia, then the famous Jesuit, Father Hennepin, visited it in 1680. He is followed by Captain Tonti, three years afterwards, who descended the Mississippi for the first time to its mouth, along with the famous Laselle. By the year 1739, the French Canadian traders had a regular trail through Kentucky by the Big Bone Lick. In 1750, Dr. Thomas Walker crossed the Alleghanies and explored to the Cumberland and Kentucky rivers; then James McBride, in 1754, descended to the mouth of the Kentucky river and left his name there carved upon a beech tree. But it was not until 1767 that the country could be said to have been really explored.

In this year a bold and enterprising man, who is only known as John Finley, with a small party of restless and reckless persons like himself, did penetrate the very heart of the land, and returning to North Carolina with the story of this new Eden, fired the spirit of adventure wherever he went.

By this time, young Boone had married the daughter of a brave and upright borderer. In 1769 he left his little family, and with this same John Finley for a guide, and accompanied by a small party in addition, he set off for the new Dorado. His restless spirit yearned for solitudes more vast and wild than any he had yet known. It was only in the excitement of action, constant and unresting, that he could live.

From this time the history of the young hunter is well known. A little over one month, from the first of May to the seventh of June, 1769, the party of Boone, consisting of five men beside himself, arrived on what was then called Red river, after having crossed the mountains and penetrated, on foot, full five hundred miles, the untracked wilderness. Here they formed a camp near where the guide, John Finley, had formerly camped when trapping and trading with the Indians on his last expedition.

They remained here for some time to recruit, and each day the young Boone wandered farther from the camp towards the west. He made an expedition of several days at last, and having found a much more convenient and lovely location, returned, broke up his camp and moved on to this place.

From this camp he made even wider excursions than before, and it was upon one of these when, alone, he came out upon a mountain steppe, and saw stretched beneath him, as far as eye could reach, the wondrous vision of Kentucky. Miles and miles away the fair and glorious land extended in flowery undulating plains, along which, here and there, stretched dark lines of heavy forest, above which, in thin squadrons, the pale morning mist was lifting slowly on the rising breath of odorous summer. It was a vision more rare than day dreams reveal to wild Utopian. The young hunter was overwhelmed. Here the mother that he worshiped had put on her beautiful garments at last, and revealed herself to him as God had caused her to be! Here he could realize the joy of worship, the soft terror of an overcoming awe, and transported, cry aloud in wonder!

The Father of Empire stood above his realm, and knew not, as his heart swelled and trembled while the majesty of this new land passed into and possessed his soul, what a heritage of renown it was to prove to him.

He lingered in rapturous musings until the night gathered, and then returned with a proud elastic step to the camp. He felt now, for the first time, a fullness of content. Here was a space before him apparently illimitable, and *all* nature, nothing but nature! For the dangers he cared nothing, he was already familiar with, and fully prepared for them; and in the fullness of his joy, only looked forward to that vast unbroken quiet of the ancient wilds, and that had so absorbed his life in its own stillness. He was no longer a youth now, but had become suddenly a man in this fruition, his life dream!

The camp was broken up next morning, and young Boone with his companions pushed on with great alertness to penetrate the new Eden, and explore its treasures. But poor Boone, who, in the eagerness of his new enthusiasm, urged on ahead of the rest of the party, in company with his favorite friend and companion, Stewart, was suddenly brought to a stand; for, surrounded by a large party of Indians, they were made prisoners as they carelessly ascended a steep hill. They were plundered, stripped and bound of course, for the Shawanees who held that portion of Kentucky then, were not a little remarkable for their want of ceremony in such cases.

The tact of the consummate borderers now showed itself, and Boone with his companion feigned content, with such a quiet resignation, that the savages were entirely deceived,

and gave them liberties which finally resulted in the desired opportunity of escape, and of which they skillfully availed themselves in time to get off. They found their camp broken and plundered, and, to their great dismay, that the rest of the party having become frightened by the appearance of the Indians, had returned to North Carolina. This was a great shock to Boone, but his nature was far too resolute to be deterred at all from the prosecution of his fixed purpose at the out-set, to explore and possess this whole region.

Soon after this, his brother, Squire Boone, joined them with a small supply of necessaries, of which powder and shot were the most important.

John Stewart seems to have been a doomed man from the beginning, and his blood was to be the first offered up in the savage and unnatural struggle which was about to begin between the Red man and his brother, the "long knife!" As yet only incidental traders, the Jesuit missionaries, the Canadian French, and a few explorers whom we have named, had penetrated here and there on the different sides of this lovely land, and had been met with that sort of surly endurance which characterizes, always, the first intercourse of the savage with the civilized trader or explorer. As yet no blood of the white man had been shed in Kentucky.

As Boone, his brother and Stewart were traversing the forest this autumn, they were suddenly fired upon by a large party of Indians from a cane-brake, and Stewart fell, mortally wounded! Resistance was useless, and the brothers fled from the overwhelming force, and the scalping-knife which was drawn around poor Stewart's skull, opened, with its gory trophy, one of the most obstinate and bloody wars that ever occurred between two races.

Heretofore the most powerful aboriginal tribes of the north and the south had made Kentucky the common battle-ground. Taking the bloody wars between the Talegans and the Lenaps, with the branch of the grand and famous tribe of Natches in West Kentucky, and with the Sciotos in East Kentucky; then the later wars after the breaking up of the great Lenap confederacy, between the Senekas, the Mohawks, the powerful tribes of Menguys, Wyandots, &c., down to the time of the great Shawanee confederacy, and this beautiful land of Kentucky had been the field and scene of all the darkest struggles; therefore it came to be called the "dark and bloody ground!"

Indeed, considering the tremendous struggle between the Otawas and the Shawanees for supremacy, in which the former conquered, and uniting that with those which had preceded, and with the still more deadly and ferocious contest which,—incipient with the appearance of De Soto on the banks of the Mississippi,—was precipitated here by the death of Stewart; I think Kentucky may truly be said to be entitled to the name.

The Council ground—the hunting ground—the battle ground of many nations—Kentucky may well feel that she has been "tried in the furnace!"—that she has a right to send forth some names of historic dignity—to have at least a place among her sisters! She does not boast of her heroes—*she only presents them!*

The two Boones were the only white men now left in this vast expanse of wilderness. They were cool and resolute persons; but it seemed a tremendous and almost infinite thing for them to be alone here, with the momentary prospect of collision with a foe who had just pronounced "war to the knife"—in the slaughter of Stewart; and, to make this more remarkable still, the brother of Boone returned for supplies—and with the purpose of bringing out all that was necessary, in the way of implements, for opening a settlement.

In the meantime, Daniel was left sole tenant of the wilderness. Think of it!—alone!—this single young man, with his rifle on shoulder, presuming to hold, "by right of possession," this great demesne against savage foes unnumbered. This dark rich earth had been colored by the blood of many nations poured upon it. Why should it not continue the scene of desperate and memorable struggle?

Alone!—in his own proper self he stood, the sole representative of the great world he had left. The Romulus of Saxon blood, he was founding a new empire, and, greater than he—was fed, not upon the "wolf's milk"—but upon the abundance of mild and serene nature—upon the delicious esculence of her forest game, and fruits of her wild luxuriant vines.

With all his ànxieties, he found repose here. He knew content to be where he was, at last, with none to rebuke him, none to say to him, nay.

His brother returned during the year, and they met at the camp where they had parted. The brave and noble brothers now explored the country more thoroughly, and to greater distances than before, as the younger had then brought in what was far more precious than silver and gold, powder and shot! The last of the year 1771, they returned for their families, having determined to remove to Kentucky. The renown of the young hunter and his discovery had now reached the settlements, and on the way back he was joined by forty stout hunters in Powell's valley.

They had reached the interior, when the party was attacked by a large force of Indians, and six of their number killed. Their cattle were scattered, and indeed the whole party disorganized by this incident, and in spite of Boone's exhortations, they persisted in returning upon their trail and retreated to a settlement on the Clinch river.

Boone was indignant, and buried himself in the depths of the forest, leaving his family in charge of the new settlement, and there remained alone, a hunter, for four years, revisiting his family occasionally.

He had now become generally known as *the man* of the frontiers, and his reputation had filled the ear of authority, and, by the energetic Governor Spottswood, of the State of Virginia at that time, he was employed in some surveys of importance, and from that period was considered the leading spirit of that part of the State territory.

In 1775, after numerous and important services to the Government and the emigrants, who had begun to flock into the country from all sections, in small parties, he arrived at a salt spring or lick, with a scattered fragment of his party, which had been much cut up by the Indians, and commenced building a fort on the site of what is now termed Boonsborough. They were much annoyed by the Indians during this time, and one man was killed by them, but they suffered most from want of provisions. The indomitable courage of Boone overcame everything; he finished his fort, and soon after removed his wife and daughter to the stronghold—and now these two women stood alone by his side, the first who had crossed the mountains yet—the first white women who had yet stood upon the soil of Kentucky! The mother of a state stood now beside the daughter!

I cannot follow up with minuteness the further details of the life of this remarkable man. His story is the history of the birth of states in our progress towards the Empire of the West. It is well known that so soon as Kentucky had grown, mainly under his fostering, to be able to take care of herself, and the smoke of his neighbor's cabin could be seen on the distant hills, the restless pioneer shouldered his rifle and pushed forward to find more room in the yet deeper and unviolated solitudes of Missouri.

But let us turn to Audubon's first meeting with him, as related by himself in his sketch of the progress of early settlement, and of the wild sports of Kentucky. He says:—

Kentucky was formerly attached to Virginia, but in those days the Indians looked upon that portion of the western wilds as their own, and abandoned the district only when forced to do so, moving with disconsolate hearts farther into the recesses of the unexplored forests. Doubtless the richness of its soil, and the beauty of its borders, situated as they are along one of the most beautiful rivers in the world, contributed as much to attract the old Virginians, as the desire so generally experienced in America, of spreading over the uncultivated tracts, and bringing into cultivation lands that have for unknown ages teemed with the wild luxuriance of untamed nature. The conquest of Kentucky was not performed without many difficulties. The warfare that long existed between the intruders and the Redskins was sanguinary and protracted; but the former at length made good their footing, and the latter drew off their shattered bands, dismayed by the mental superiority and indomitable courage of the white men.

This region was probably* discovered by a daring hunter, the renowned Daniel Boone. The richness of its soil, its magnificent forests, its numberless navigable streams, its salt springs and licks, its saltpetre caves, its coal strata, and the vast herds of buffaloes and deer that browsed on its hills and amidst its charming valleys, afforded ample inducements to the new settler, who pushed forward with a spirit far above that of the most undaunted tribes, which for ages had been the sole possessors of the soil.

The Virginians thronged towards the Ohio. An axe, a couple of horses and a heavy rifle, with store of ammunition, were all that were considered necessary for the equipment of the man, who, with his family, removed to the new State, assured that, in that land of exuberant fertility, he could not fail to provide amply for all his wants. To have witnessed the industry and perseverance of these emigrants, must at once have proved the vigor of their minds. Regardless of the fatigue attending every movement which they made, they pushed through an unexplored region of dark and tangled forests, guiding themselves by the sun alone, and reposing at night on the bare ground. Numberless streams they had to cross on rafts, with their wives and children, their cattle and their luggage, often drifting to considerable distances before they could effect a landing on the opposite shores. Their cattle would often stray amid the rich pasturage of these shores, and occasion a delay of several days. To these troubles add the constantly impending danger of being murdered, while asleep in their encampments, by the prowling and

---

* We have given the true account of the "Discovery" in the preceding sketch of Boone.

ruthless Indians; while they had before them a distance of hundreds of miles to be traversed, before they could reach certain places of rendezvous called *Stations*. To encounter difficulties like these must have required energies of no ordinary kind; and the reward which these veteran settlers enjoy was doubtless well merited.

Some removed from the Atlantic shores to those of the Ohio, in more comfort and security. They had their wagons, their negroes and their families. Their way was cut through the woods by their own axemen, the day before their advance, and when night overtook them, the hunters attached to the party came to the place pitched upon for encamping, loaded with the dainties of which the forest yielded an abundant supply, the blazing light of a huge fire guiding their steps as they approached, and the sounds of merriment that saluted their ears assuring them that all was well. The flesh of the buffalo, the bear and the deer, soon hung in large and delicious steaks, in front of the embers; the cakes already prepared were deposited in their proper places, and under the rich drippings of the juicy roasts, were quickly baked. The wagons contained the bedding, and whilst the horses which had drawn them were turned loose to feed on the luxuriant undergrowth of the woods, some perhaps hoppled, but the greater number, merely with a light bell hung to their neck, to guide their owners in the morning to the spot where they might have rambled, the party were enjoying themselves after the fatigues of the day.

In anticipation all is pleasure; and these migrating bands feasted in joyous sociality, unapprehensive of any greater difficulties than those to be encountered in forcing their way through the pathless woods to the land of abundance; and although it took months to accomplish the journey, and a skirmish now and then took place between them and the Indians, who sometimes crept unperceived into their very camp, still did the Virginians cheerfully proceed towards the western horizon, until the various groups all reached the Ohio, when, struck with the beauty of that magnificent stream, they at once commenced the task of clearing land, for the purpose of establishing a permanent residence.

Others, perhaps encumbered with too much luggage, preferred descending the stream. They prepared arks pierced wlth port-holes, and glided on the gentle current, more annoyed, however, than those who marched by land, by the attacks of the Indians, who watched their motions. Many travellers have described these boats, formerly called arks, but now named flat-boats. But have they told you, kind reader, that in those times a boat thirty or forty feet in length, by ten or twelve in breadth, was considered a stupendous fabric; that this boat contained men, women and children, huddled together, with horses, cattle, hogs and poultry for their companions, while the remaining portion was crammed with vegetables and packages of seeds? The roof or deck of the boat was not unlike a farm-yard, being covered with hay, ploughs, carts, wagons and various agricultural implements, together with numerous others, among which the spinning-wheels of the matrons were conspicuous. Even the sides of the floating mass were loaded with the wheels of the different vehicles, which themselves lay on the roof. Have they told you that these boats contained the little all of each family of venturous emigrants, who, fearful of being discovered by the Indians under night moved in darkness, groping their way from one part to another of these floating habitations, denying themselves the comfort of fire or light, lest the foe that watched them from the shore should rush upon them and destroy them? Have they told you that this boat was used, after the tedious voyage was ended, as the first dwelling of these new settlers? No, kind reader, such things have not been related to you before. The travellers who have visited our country, have had other objects in view.

I shall not describe the many massacres which took place

among the different parties of White and Red men, as the former moved down the Ohio; because I have never been very fond of battles, and indeed have always wished that the world were more peaceably inclined than it is; and shall merely add, that, in one way or other, Kentucky was wrested from the original owners of the soil. Let us, therefore, turn our attention to the sports still enjoyed in that now happy portion of the United States.

We have individuals in Kentucky, kind reader, that even there are considered wonderful adepts in the management of the rifle. To drive a nail is a common feat, not more thought of by the Kentuckians than to cut off a wild turkey's head, at a distance of a hundred yards. Others will bark off squirrels one after another, until satisfied with the number procured. Some, less intent on destroying game, may be seen under night snuffing a candle at the distance of fifty yards, off-hand, without extinguishing it. I have been told that some have proved so expert and cool, as to make choice of the eye of a foe at a wonderful distance, boasting beforehand of the sureness of their piece, which has afterwards been fully proved when the enemy's head has been examined!

Having resided some years in Kentucky, and having more than once been witness of rifle sport, I shall present you with the results of my observation, leaving you to judge how far rifle-shooting is understood in that State.

Several individuals who conceive themselves expert in the management of the gun, are often seen to meet for the purpose of displaying their skill, and betting a trifling sum, put up a target, in the centre of which a common-sized nail is hammered for about two-thirds of its length. The marksmen make choice of what they consider a proper distance, which may be forty paces. Each man cleans the interior of his tube, which is called wiping it, places a ball in the palm of his hand, pouring as much powder from his horn upon it as will cover it. This quantity is supposed to be sufficient for any distance within a hundred yards. A shot which comes very close to the nail is considered as that of an indifferent marksman; the bending of the nail is, of course, somewhat better; but nothing less than hitting it right on the head is satisfactory. Well, kind reader, one out of three shots generally hits the nail, and should the shooters amount to half a dozen, two nails are frequently needed before each can have a shot. Those who drive the nail have a further trial amongst themselves, and the two best shots out of these generally settle the affair, when all the sportsmen adjourn to some house, and spend an hour or two in friendly intercourse, appointing, before they part, a day for another trial. This is technically termed Driving the Nail.

Barking off squirrels is delightful sport, and in my opinion requires a greater degree of accuracy than any other. I first witnessed this manner of procuring squirrels, whilst near the town of Frankfort. The performer was the celebrated Daniel Boone. We walked out together, and followed the rocky margins of the Kentucky River, until we reached a piece of flat land thickly covered with black walnuts, oaks and hickories. As the general mast was a good one that year, squirrels were seen gambolling on every tree around us. My companion, a stout, hale and athletic man, dressed in a homespun hunting-shirt, bare-legged and moccasined, carried a long and heavy rifle, which, as he was loading it, he said had proved efficient in all his former undertakings, and which he hoped would not fail on this occasion, as he felt proud to show me his skill. The gun was wiped, the powder measured, the ball patched with six-hundred-thread linen, and the charge sent home with a hickory rod. We moved not a step from the place, for the squirrels were so numerous that it was unnecessary to go after them. Boon pointed to one of these animals which had observed us, and was crouched on a branch about fifty paces distant, and bade me mark well the spot where the ball should hit. He raised his piece gradually, until the bead (that being the name given by the Kentuckians to the sight) of the barrel was brought to a line with the spot which he intended to hit. The whip-like report resounded through the woods and along the hills, in repeated echoes. Judge of my surprise, when I perceived that the ball had hit the piece of the bark immediately beneath the squirrel, and shivered it into splinters, the concussion produced by which had killed the animal, and sent it whirling through the air, as if it had been blown up by the explosion of a powder magazine. Boon kept up his firing, and, before many hours had elapsed, we had procured as many squirrels as we wished; for you must know, kind reader, that to load a rifle requires only a moment, and that if it is wiped once after each shot, it will do duty for hours. Since that first interview with our veteran Boone, I have seen many other individuals perform the same feat.

On another occasion he says—

Colonel Boone happened to spend a night with me under the same roof, more than twenty years ago. We had returned from a shooting excursion, in the course of which his extraordinary skill in the management of the rifle had been fully displayed. On retiring to the room appropriated to that remarkable individual and myself for the night, I felt anxious to know more of his exploits and adventures than I did, and accordingly took the liberty of proposing numerous questions to him. The stature and general appearance of this wanderer of the western forests approached the gigantic. His chest was broad and prominent; his muscular powers displayed themselves in every limb; his countenance gave indication of his great courage, enterprise, and perseverance; and when he spoke, the very motion of his lips brought the impression that whatever he uttered could not be otherwise than strictly true. I undressed, whilst he merely took off his hunting shirt, and arranged a few folds of blankets on the floor, choosing rather to lie there, as he observed, than on the softest bed. When we had both disposed of ourselves, each after his own fashion, he related to me the following account of his powers of memory, which I lay before you, kind reader, in his own words, hoping that the simplicity of his style may prove interesting to you.

"I was once," said he, "on a hunting expedition on the banks of the Green River, when the lower parts of this State (Kentucky) were still in the hands of nature, and none but the sons of the soil were looked upon as its lawful proprietors. We Virginians had for some time been waging a war of intrusion upon them, and I, amongst the rest, rambled through the woods in pursuit of their race, as I now would follow the tracks of any ravenous animal. The Indians outwitted me one dark night, and I was as unexpectedly as suddenly made a prisoner by them. The trick had been managed with great skill; for no sooner had I extinguished the fire of my camp, and laid me down to rest, in full security, as I thought, than I felt myself seized by an indistinguishable number of hands, and was immediately pinioned, as if about to be led to the scaffold for execution. To have attempted to be refractory, would have proved useless and dangerous to my life; and I suffered myself to be removed from my camp to theirs, a few miles distant, without uttering even a word of complaint. You are aware, I dare say, that to act in this manner was the best policy, as you understand that by so doing, I proved to the Indians at once, that I was born and bred as fearless of death as any of themselves.

"When we reached the camp, great rejoicings were exhibited. Two squaws and a few papooses appeared particularly delighted at the sight of me, and I was assured, by very unequivocal gestures and words, that, on the morrow, the mortal enemy of the Red-skins would cease to live. I never opened my lips, but was busy contriving some scheme which might enable me to give the rascals the slip before dawn. The women immediately fell a searching about my hunting-shirt for whatever they might think valuable, and, fortunately for me, soon found my flask filled with *monongahela* (that is, reader, strong whisky). A terrific grin was exhibited on their murderous countenances, while my heart throbbed with joy at the anticipation of their intoxication. The crew immediately began to beat their bellies and sing, as they passed the bottle from mouth to mouth. How often did I wish the flask ten times its size, and filled with aqua-fortis! I observed that the squaws drank more freely than the warriors, and again my spirits were about to be depressed, when the report of a gun was heard at a distance. The Indians all jumped on their feet. The singing and drinking were both brought to a stand, and I saw, with inexpressible joy, the men walk off to some distance and talk to the squaws. I knew that they were consulting about me, and I foresaw that in a few moments the warriors would go to discover the cause of the gun having been fired so near their camp. I expected that the squaws would be left to guard me. Well, sir, it was just so. They returned; the men took up their guns, and walked away. The squaws sat down again, and in less than five minutes had my bottle up to their dirty mouths, gurgling down their throats the remains of the whisky.

"With what pleasure did I see them becoming more and more drunk, until the liquor took such hold of them that it was quite impossible for these women to be of any service. They tumbled down, rolled about, and began to snore: when I, having no other chance of freeing myself from the cords that fastened me, rolled over and over towards the fire, and, after a short time, burned them asunder. I rose on my feet, stretched my stiffened sinews, snatched up my rifle, and, for once in my life, spared that of Indians. I now recollect how desirous I once or twice felt to lay open the skulls of the wretches with my tomahawk; but when I again thought upon killing beings unprepared and unable to defend themselves, it looked like murder without need, and I gave up the idea.

"But, sir, I felt determined to mark the spot, and walking to a thrifty ash sapling, I cut out of it three large chips, and ran off. I soon reached the river, soon crossed it, and threw myself deep into the cane-brakes, imitating the tracks of an Indian with my feet, so that no chance might be left for those from whom I had escaped to overtake me.

"It is now nearly twenty years since this happened, and more than five since I left the whites' settlements, which I might probably never have visited again, had I not been called on as a witness in a law suit that was pending in Kentucky, and which I really believe would never have been settled, had I not come forward, and established the beginning of a certain boundary line. This is the story, sir.

"Mr. ——— moved from Old Virginia into Kentucky, and having a large tract granted to him in the new State, laid claim to a certain parcel of land adjoining Green River, and as chance would have it, took for one of his corners the very ash tree on which I had made my mark, and finished his survey of some thousands of acres, beginning, as it is expressed in the deed, 'at an ash marked by three distinct notches of the tomahawk of a white man.'

"The tree had grown much, and the bark had covered the marks; but, somehow or other, Mr. ——— heard from some one all that I have already said to you, and thinking that I might remember the spot alluded to in the deed, but which was no longer discoverable, wrote for me to come and try at least to find the place or the tree. His letter mentioned that all my expenses should be paid, and not caring much about once more going back to Kentucky, I started and met Mr. ———. After some conversation, the affair with the Indians came to my recollection. I considered for awhile, and began to think that after all I could find the very spot, as well as the tree, if it was yet standing.

"Mr. ——— and I mounted our horses, and off we went to the Green River Bottoms. After some difficulties, for you must be aware, sir, that great changes have taken place in those woods, I found at last the spot where I had crossed the river, and waiting for the moon to rise, made for the course in which I thought the ash tree grew. On approaching the place, I felt as if the Indians were there still, and as if I was still a prisoner among them. Mr. ——— and I camped near what I conceived the spot, and waited until the return of day.

"At the rising of the sun I was on foot, and after a good deal of musing, thought that an ash tree then in sight must be the very one on which I had made my mark. I felt as if there could be no doubt of it, and mentioned my thought to Mr. ———. 'Well, Colonel Boone,' said he, 'if you think so, I hope it may prove true, but we must have some witnesses; do you stay here about, and I will go and bring some of the settlers whom I know.' I agreed. Mr. ——— trotted off, and I, to pass the time, rambled about to see if a deer was still living in the land. But ah! sir, what a wonderful difference thirty years makes in the country! Why, at the time when I was caught by the Indians, you would not have walked out in any direction for more than a mile without shooting a buck or a bear. There were then thousands of buffaloes on the hills in Kentucky; the land looked as if it never would become poor; and to hunt in those days was a pleasure indeed. But when I was left to myself on the banks of Green River, I dare say for the last time in my life, a few *signs* only of deer were to be seen, and as to a deer itself, I saw none.

"Mr. ——— returned, accompanied by three gentlemen. They looked upon me as if I had been Washington himself, and walked to the ash tree, which I now called my own, as if in quest of a long lost treasure. I took an axe from one of them, and cut a few chips off the bark. Still no signs were to be seen. So I cut again until I thought it was time to be cautious, and I scraped and worked away with my butcher knife, until I *did* come to where my tomahawk had left an impression in the wood. We now went regularly to work, and scraped at the tree with care, until three hacks as plain as any three notches ever were, could be seen. Mr. ——— and the other gentlemen were astonished, and, I must allow, I was as much surprised as pleased myself. I made affidavit of this remarkable occurrence in presence of these gentlemen. Mr. ——— gained his cause. I left Green River forever, and came to where we now are; and, sir, I wish you a good night."

There are a thousand such characteristic anecdotes of Daniel Boone that might be given, but none of them would be so interesting in themselves or possess such attraction as this, coming from the lips of such a narrator—for Boone was never more remarkable for the development of the curious instincts of wood-craft, than was Audubon himself—who of all men was best qualified to appreciate such phenomena in another.

Not long after his removal to Missouri, Boone calmly laid down and died in 1818, and what is not the least extraordinary fact connected with his history, died poor! With all the opportunities his life had afforded him from the beginning, of amassing enormous wealth, by dealing in lands, the settlement of which he pioneered, he preferred a clear conscience and a stainless name, and only retained to the last what was his original inheritance, his rifle! Simple and generous hero—the turf of that wild distant grave must lie lightly on that broad and gentle bosom!

Audubon, too, as we know, is lately dead. But let us, before we pass to other themes, linger to look upon him once more at the moment, and in the scene of what he considered the greatest triumph of his long life—his discovery of the Bird of Washington. He says—

It was in the month of February, 1814, that I obtained the first sight of this noble bird, and never shall I forget the delight which it gave me. Not even Herschel, when he discovered the planet which bears his name, could have experienced more rapturous feelings. We were on a trading voyage, ascending the Upper Mississippi. The keen wintry blasts whistled around us, and the cold from which I suffered had, in a great degree, extinguished the deep interest which, at other seasons, this magnificent river has been wont to awake in me. I lay stretched beside our patroon. The safety of the cargo was forgotten, and the only thing that called my attention was the multitude of ducks, of different species, accompanied by vast flocks of swans, which from time to time passed us. My patroon, a Canadian, had been engaged many years in the fur trade. He was a man of much intelligence, and, perceiving that these birds had engaged my curiosity, seemed anxious to find some new object to divert me. An eagle flew over us. "How fortunate!" he exclaimed; "this is what I could have wished. Look, sir! the Great Eagle, and the only one I have seen since I left the lakes." I was instantly on my feet, and having observed it attentively, concluded, as I lost it in the distance, that it was a species quite new to me. My patroon assured me that such birds were indeed rare; that they sometimes followed the hunters, to feed on the entrails of animals which they had killed, when the lakes were frozen over, but that when the lakes were open, they would dive in the daytime after fish, and snatch them up in the manner of the Fishing Hawk; and that they roosted generally on the shelves of the rocks, where they built their nests, of which he had discovered several by the quantity of white dung scattered below.

Convinced that the bird was unknown to naturalists, I felt particularly anxious to learn its habits, and to discover in what particulars it differed from the rest of its genus. My next meeting with this bird was a few years afterwards, whilst engaged in collecting crayfish on one of those flats which border and divide Green River, in Kentucky, near its junction with the Ohio. The river is there bordered by a range of high cliffs, which for some distance follow its windings. I observed on the rocks which, at that place, are nearly perpendicular, a quantity of white ordure, which I attributed to owls that might have resorted thither. I mentioned the circumstance to my companions, when one of them, who lived within a mile and a half of the place, told me it was from the nest of the Brown Eagle, meaning the White-headed Eagle (*Falco leucocephalus*) in its immature state. I assured him this could not be, and remarked that neither the old nor the young birds of that species ever build in such places, but always in trees. Although he could not answer my objection, he stoutly maintained that a brown eagle of some kind, above the usual size, had built there; and added that he had espied the nest some days before, and had seen one of the old birds dive and catch a fish. This he thought strange, having, till then, always observed that both Brown Eagles and Bald Eagles procured this kind of food by robbing the fish-hawks. He said that if I felt particularly anxious to know what nest it was, I might soon satisfy myself, as the old birds would come and feed their young with fish, for he had seen them do so before.

In high expectation, I seated myself about a hundred yards from the foot of the rock. Never did time pass more slowly. I could not help betraying the most impatient curiosity, for my hopes whispered it was a Sea Eagle's nest. Two long hours had elapsed before the old bird made his appearance, which was announced to us by the loud hissings of the two young ones, which crawled to the extremity of the hole to receive a fine fish. I had a perfect view of this noble bird as he held himself to the edging rock, hanging like the Barn, Bank, or Social Swallow, his tail spread, and his wings partly so. I trembled lest a word should escape from my companions. The slightest murmur had been treason from them. They entered into my feelings, and, although little interested, gazed with me. In a few minutes the other parent joined her mate, and from the difference in size (the female of rapacious birds being much larger), we knew this to be the mother bird. She also had brought a fish; but, more cautious than her mate, she glanced her quick and piercing eye around, and instantly perceived that her abode had been discovered. She dropped her prey, with a loud shriek communicated the alarm to the male, and, hovering with him over our heads, kept up a growling cry, to intimidate us from our suspected design. This watchful solicitude I have ever found peculiar to the female:—must I be understood to speak only of birds?

The young having concealed themselves, we went and picked up the fish which the mother had let fall. It was a white perch, weighing about 5½ lbs. The upper part of the head was broken in, and the back torn by the talons of the eagle. We had plainly seen her bearing it in the manner of the Fish Hawk.

This day's sport being at an end, as we journeyed homewards, we agreed to return the next morning, with the view of obtaining both the old and young birds; but rainy and tempestuous weather setting in, it became necessary to defer the expedition till the third day following, when, with guns and men all in readiness, we reached the rock. Some posted themselves at the foot, others upon it, but in vain. We passed the entire day, without either seeing or hearing an eagle, the sagacious birds, no doubt, having anticipated an invasion, and removed their young to new quarters.

I come at last to the day which I had so often and so ardently desired. Two years had gone by since the discovery of the nest, in fruitless excursions; but my wishes were no longer to remain ungratified. In returning from the little village of Henderson, to the house of Doctor Rankin, about a mile distant, I saw an eagle rise from a small enclosure not a hundred yards before me, where the Doctor had a few days before slaughtered some hogs, and alight upon a low tree branching over the road. I prepared my double-barrelled piece, which I constantly carry, and went slowly and cautiously towards him. Quite fearlessly he awaited my approach, looking upon me with undaunted eye. I fired, and he fell. Before I reached him he was dead. With what delight did I survey the magnificent bird! Had the finest salmon ever pleased him as he did me?—Never. I ran and presented him to my friend, with a pride which they alone can feel, who, like me, have devoted themselves from their earliest childhood to such pursuits, and who have derived from them their first pleasures. To others I must seem to "prattle out of fashion." The Doctor, who was an experienced hunter, examined the bird with much satisfaction, and frankly acknowledged he had never before seen or heard of it.

The name which I have chosen for this new species of Eagle, "The Bird of Washington," may, by some, be considered as preposterous and unfit; but as it is indisputably the noblest bird of its genus that has yet been discovered in the United States, I trust I shall be allowed to honor it with the name of one yet nobler, who was the saviour of his country, and whose name will ever be dear to it. To those who may be curious to know my reasons, I can only say, that, as the New World gave me birth and liberty, the great man who insured its independence is next to my heart. He had a nobility of mind, and a generosity of soul, such as are seldom possessed. He was brave, so is the eagle; like it, too, he was the terror of his foes; and his fame, extending from pole to pole, resembles the majestic soarings of the mightiest of the feathered tribe. If America has reason to be proud of her Washington, so has she to be proud of her Great Eagle.

In the month of January following, I saw a pair of these eagles flying over the Falls of the Ohio, one in pursuit of the other. The next day I saw them again. The female had relaxed her severity, had laid aside her coyness, and to a favorite tree they continually resorted. I pursued them unsuccessfully for several days, when they forsook the place.

Stay yet, too, while we note this fine expression of the agonized travail of genius in the production of its mighty works. It is from the introduction to his fifth and concluding volume of the "Ornithological Biography."

How often have I longed to see the day on which my labors should be brought to an end! Many times, when I had laid myself down in the deepest recesses of the Western forest, have I been suddenly awakened by the apparition of dismal prospects that have presented themselves to my mind. Now sickness methought had seized me with burning hands, and hurried me away, in spite of all fond wishes, from those wild woods in which I had so long lingered to increase my knowledge of the objects they presented to my view.

Poverty, too, at times, walked hand in hand with me, and on more than one occasion, urged me to cast away my pencils, destroy my drawings, abandon my journals, change my ideas, and return to the world. At other times, the red Indian, erect and bold, tortured my ears with horrible yells, and threatened to put an end to my existence; or white-skinned murderers aimed their rifles at me. Snakes, loathsome and venomous, entwined my limbs, while vultures, lean and ravenous, looked on with impatience. Once, too, I dreamed, when asleep on a sand bar on one of the Florida Keys, that a huge shark had me in his jaws, and was dragging me into the deep.

But my thoughts were not always of this nature—for, at other times, my dreams presented pleasing images. The sky was serene, the air perfumed, and thousands of melodious notes from birds, all unknown to me, urged me to rise and go in pursuit of those beautiful and happy creatures. Then I would find myself furnished with large and powerful wings, and cleaving the air like an eagle, I would fly, and by a few joyous bounds, overtake the objects of my desire. At other times I was gladdened by the sight of my beloved family, seated by their cheerful fire, and anticipating the delight which they would experience on my return. The glorious sun would rise, and as its first rays illuminated the earth, I would cheer myself with the pleasing prospect of the happy termination of my labors, and hear in fancy the praises which kind friends would freely accord. Many times, indeed, have such thoughts enlivened my spirits; and now the task is accomplished. In health and in sickness, in adversity and prosperity, in summer and winter, amidst the cheers of friends and the scowls of foes, I have depicted the Birds of America, and studied their habits as they roamed at large in their peculiar haunts.

That concluding passage is far nobler than "*Veni, vidi, vici!*" as the simple expression of a proud triumphant consciousness; for, instead of the intense egotism which renders that repulsive as it is celebrated, this is modest and severely classic. What a day that was when he could say, "I find my journeys all finished, my anxieties vanished, my mission accomplished!" What a magnificent perspective could he look back through, down the past, more glorious than all royalties, than any heritage of earthly princes—and all his own! That day has now come in the fulness of time—and, glorious old man, thy mission is indeed accomplished!

CHAPTER VII.

THE HUNTERS OF KENTUCKY.

THE GRAVE OF THE SILENT HUNTER.

My native town, Hopkinsville, is in one of the southern counties of Kentucky, called Christian, which was for a long time one of the largest, if not the largest county in the State. This was no special matter of boast by the way; for although the southern portion, comprising about half the county which bordered upon the Tennessee line, was as rich, level and lovely a stretch of "barrens" as ever swayed its myriad wild flowers of countless hues beneath the labored beat of the south wind's odor-burdened wings, yet, immediately to the north of the county-seat—Hopkinsville—the whole character of the county changed at once. While five miles to the south was a paradise of flowers, or when cultivated, covered with crops of Indian corn ten and fifteen feet in height; tobacco, with leaves often three feet by two; and wheat, five to six feet; the same distance to the north brought you amidst rugged hills of sand or clay, that barely yielded the most meagre subsistence to the poor and simple inhabitants, who necessarily remained hunters. Their rifles supplied them with that provision which the ungrateful earth refused to yield to the plough and the hoe. As you penetrated further in this direction, the country became wilder and more broken at every turn of the narrow trail, until, even so late as twelve years ago, you came upon a country quite as wild and savagely unaltered as when the Indian war-whoop alone disturbed its echoes. Here your trails cease, and as you push into this formidable looking wilderness, which reaches to Green river—over forty miles—you shudder at the tremendous solitudes of its abrupt cliffs, that take away your breath when you come suddenly upon the verge of their deep gorges, winding far away, black with the "Bottom Forests," except where some stream that has leaped with a sullen roar from beneath you down the cliff, gleams sharply out from the shadow here and there; or when, in the distance, some huge "Pilot Knob" lifts its bare, conical crown so high into the hazy heavens, that it seems like one of old Nilus' Pyramids, set above the hills! The scene here, is indeed inexpressibly shaggy, wild and stern. These Pilot Knobs, of which there are two, are very famous in the early annals of Kentucky; and we may have more to say of them. They constitute the most peculiar features of this singular scenery, and there are many legends connected with them. Here the Indians lingered longest after being driven from their northern possessions, or hunting grounds rather; and here the raging hate of the two races spent itself in the last desperate collisions, before sullen conquered or conqueror could agree to part. Here the game lingered too, and still lingers, and must continue to linger for many a year to come; though what was once sole possession of the fierce, swarthy Shawanee, is now periodically intruded upon by the pale sons of the lordly planters of the tobacco lands to the south, who are accustomed to make up, yearly, "camping parties" to hunt in this region for a few weeks during the fall of the year.

Along the southern border of the rougher part of this wilderness, there are a few cabins of the old race of hunters, who belong to the times of Boone, and still boast that they continue to "hold their own," which means, being still "out of sight of the smoke of a neighbor's chimney!" It would indeed be rather a difficult feat to see this same smoke, it must be confessed, since the nearest neighbor is probably twelve miles off, and both their huts embosomed in steep crags!

I have never been a lover of, what they term so expressively in the West, "a crowd," particularly on hunting excursions; the chief charm of which has consisted in the entire separation from my race, permitted for the time, and the solitude that invites a refreshing communion with the primitive forms of the natural world. Many's the time have I forgotten to shoot, and let the stately deer go by unscathed, while I stood breathless to admire its graceful action, and the charming unity of its antlered presence here, with the swaying of old boughs and lapsing leap of streams. With such moods upon me, I could not bear to hurt the lovely creatures; it seemed as though a voice of our mother nature chid me: "Shame! shame! to slay the beautiful!"

But I was usually as keen a hunter as ever startled the ancient echoes with the rifle's shrilly ring. My boon companion at this time, some twelve years ago, was like myself, named Charles, or Charlie M., as he was everywhere called, from his merry, reckless, jovial character. Now Charlie *was* a character, sure enough, and just such an one you will meet with nowhere else in the world but in Kentucky; and even there it is nearly grown out by this time. A more loyal, gentle and generous spirit never lived, nor did a truer heart beat ever in the broad, roomy chest of a lion-man. He was as merrily reckless as a prodigious flow of physical energies, mirthful instincts, and indomitable courage could make him. He always took sides with the weak, it mattered not to him what the odds of the oppressor, or how strange both parties might be to him. He carried this feeling to amusing extremes in the defence of domestic animals; and many the scrape he has got into by taking the part of a poor horse or dog that was being cruelly beaten by a drunken beast of a master. He would never pass such a scene without stopping it, at all hazards to himself; he would never see a negro beaten, and never struck his own, but resented it as a personal injury to himself if another did. This man was the most passionately devoted to the chase of any one I had ever yet met with. His father had been very wealthy, and at the time he grew up, at Frankfort, the capital of Kentucky, the chase was the one fashionable and absorbing pursuit of the young men of his social rank. The greater part of his life was thus spent in the saddle; and a passion cultivated from boyhood is not easily shaken off in early manhood, particularly one so fascinating. Suffice it, he kept a splendid pack of hounds, the genealogy of every one of which he had at his tongue's end; and some fine hunters in his stable; and for years after I knew him—when he moved to the south—near my native town—he spent fully one-third of his time, night and day, in the woods on horseback following his hounds. He, too, was a genuine lover of Nature, and preferred to hunt alone. Charlie was indeed the very impersonation of a class of gay, dashing, reckless and accomplished sportsmen of the north of Kentucky, which is now nearly extinct. Whether, mounted on his tall and powerful hunter, that seemed almost a miracle of indomitable game and speed, he went sweeping through the thick, primitive woods at a pace that would have terrified any other sportsman on the open ground, clearing at flying leaps the most extravagant perils, without notice, and always close with the chase, cheering in ringing halloes his noble hounds; or, on our long rides to the distant hunting grounds by night, carrying chorus to some wild hunting song in the shrill blasts of his curled bugle, cr to some touching balled of the ancient chivalry, poured from his manly lips, rolling its soft accompaniment in mellowed clamors through the echoing hills, he was still the splendid and consistent ideal of the north-Kentucky fox-hunter of the generation following Clay and Crittenden!

We soon knew each other; and, as there were many points of earnest congeniality between myself and the wild hunter, we soon became frequent and inseparable companions, particularly on the long hunts to this rude region I have described.

It was now the last of November that we started with hound and horn for the hills, on the grand hunt of the year. A snow storm had commenced the over night, and none but a true hunter can realize the bounding delight with which the first snow storm is welcomed. Then only comes his enjoyments in highest perfection! Now the game of every kind is not only within his reach, but is in its highest condition. He can himself trace it for miles and miles away through the deep snow, until brought to bay at last, it falls before his unerring aim. He has an exulting consciousness of his independence, even of his dogs, for nothing can escape his practiced eye and tireless patience. The most exciting of all hunts are proverbially those in the snow; but in the northern States they become disgusting very soon, as they quickly degenerate into the merest butcheries, where the snow, from three to four feet, remains upon the ground for three or four months, with a crust over it just strong enough to bear a man on snow shoes, or his dog, and yet will let in the poor animal at every jump as deep as it can sink. Here it is like slaughtering sheep in a pen when hunters attack a "yard" of deer or moose, but in Kentucky the case is very different. The snow seldom or never falls deeper than two feet, and most frequently does not last a week. It never crusts sufficiently to impede, materially, the progress of large game, and all the sport is therefore confined to within the first few days; and the principal, if not only advantage the hunter gains, consisting in the increased facility with which the game is traced, either by himself or by the noses of his hounds. This makes the sport intensely exciting, for you sometimes pursue a single herd or sole animal for twenty miles before you get a shot; but as you are sure to get a glimpse of them, and hear their whistling snort of defiance as they bound on again every half hour or so, you are kept in a constant state of excitement, and beguiled, without heeding, over miles and miles that would otherwise have been weary enough to you. It is only when the coveted achievement has been really accomplished, and you have proudly thrown your noble quarry across the saddle, that you begin to realize fatigue in satiety, and self-reproach in the fatigue, as with aching limbs you turn your wearied horse through the strange, darkening woods towards the distant camp. Now the chill night wind whistles through the gnarled boughs, dashes the frozen snow in fine, sifted, searching particles into your face and bosom; now your hot blood chills and your fiery pulse sinks; the cutting nor'-wester searches the very "marrow of annoy;" and with sinking heart and shivering limbs, its very shadow as the owl sails by, causes your teeth to chatter, and its sudden hoot makes you almost leap from the saddle in nervous affright. Now, as the dreary way lengthens before you, the cheerful light of the solitary camp-fire seems far, far away, and an almost infinite distance of bog and bluff, of crag, ravine and tangled wood, seems stretched between you and that warm haven; then it is that conscience speaks through the downcast life, and we are forced to realize the brtual savagery of this miscalled "sport;" we have a foretaste of the aches and pains of the poor animals we have been chasing through the deep snow all day, already in our own chafed and suffering limbs, with the sure knowledge that the fruition is not yet, but must come when we rise sore, stiff and shivering, from, perhaps, a frozen couch in the morning. Ah, how the weary miles do stretch! It is in vain that a few spasmodic notes are sounded upon the curled bugle at our side; the echoes take on such stunning reverberations amongst the bare cliffs, that we are awed into silence! How many vows against cruelty to animals, against the indulgence of such tiger-passions, are muttered as our despair gathers with exhaustion. The moon wheels up her glittering disk, and at another time we should have been wild with delight to watch the glory of the shine her coming lays along the sparkling earth, and through the dark armed trees; but now, alas! it only taunts with its splendor; it cannot make the way more short! On, on we plunge; the miles grow longer, and the noble horse begins to stagger beneath his double load, and then the shuddering apprehension comes that he may give out, and leave us to trudge the live-long night through the snow to keep from freezing. If the fatal sleep overtake us, we must lie down and die, with our poor horse for a pillow, and the filmed eyes of the noble buck we slew fixed in a stonied gaze upon our own as they are glazed by the cold wind. Maddened by such horrid images, and nerved by despair, we raise the bugle to our stiffened lips once more; loud, long and high the peal rings out, shrill as a death-cry. My sagacious horse has stopped of his own accord, holding his breath, while with pricked ears he listens. Hark! that faint distant sound! Is it echo! He stamps his foot with an impatient neigh, and with blazing eyes and erect crest springs forward. No more staggering now,—fatigue is gone; it requires all my exhausted strength to hold him within anything like a moderate gait. A half an hour, and with an eager neigh he breaks into a run, under my not unwilling rein, for I, too, have caught a glimpse of a fire through the wood, and recognize the white face of yonder cliff, with the moon full upon it; and in another minute, with the warm blood rushing to my heart and brain, and a mad whoop of delight, I burst into the light of the camp-fire to be welcomed by the yells and combined howls of a dozen hounds, and a hearty cheer from the gallant Charlie!

Now the scene has changed, and by the warm fire and over the smoking roast of tenderest venison, the feats of the day are recounted with as much eager zest as if there had been no such thing as cold, fatigue, and nervous apprehensions. The terrors have all vanished within the charmed circle of that fire-light, and we threw ourselves upon our blankets to sleep, dreaming lustily of just such scenes to be gone through to-morrow; only the dreams some how gave only the bright side of the picture, and managed to leave out all about freezing to death, starvation, &c. So sunrise would find us with appetites only sharpened by the sufferings of the day before, and yet more ready to do full justice to the roast or living venison. Such are the strange inconsistencies of the hunter's moods, and such the charms of the vivid shifting excitements of his restless and tumultuous life! He is one moment worse than the most ferocious wild beast, and the next his head is turned aside to weep that he has slain "a thing of beauty," fresh from God's own hands. It was thus our lives had fared, in camp and out, for four or five days, when the weather changing suddenly, the snow commenced to disappear rapidly.

Our sport in the snow was now over; but we were not by any means satisfied, and Charlie proposed that we should strike our camp and make our way across the ridges to the hut of a famous hunter known along this border as Old Jake,

—what his other name was he had never heard, though he had been at his hut several times. He said the old fellow would be very glad to see us, and would furnish us with a "hill-boy," whom he kept in his employ, to act as a guide and driver for us. We intended now to change our mode of hunting. We were to be placed by the driver at different "stands," as they are called, meaning places at which, from his knowledge of the country, he knew the deer always passed out when roused by the dogs from their feeding-grounds. After placing us, he was to return along the ridge for a mile or so with the dogs, and then descending into the bottom, with sound of horns, yells of dogs and other noises, drive the frightened creatures before him to our stands. We found everything at Old Jake's as Charlie expected. We were received with true hunter hospitality by the family; consisting of the old man, his tanned and wrinkled dame, with two stout and comely daughters, who were the very impersonations of buxom good humor.

We had a merry time of it the first evening, and the next morning, early, were joined by our guide that was to be. He was a droll-looking specimen, surely! Lank, long, and lantern-jawed, he looked as if the fever and ague of the country bottoms had, in shaking him into a bag of bones, forgotten to joint him again when he was set up; yet, withal, it was marvellous to see the cadaverous-looking creature making his way over these rugged hills, far in advance of our active horses, while with every long stride his loose limbs actually seemed to be wrapping round each other. He was called Jabe, as I supposed short for Jabez, and carried a very long specimen of the old-fashioned rifle of our fathers. It was easy enough to see that he was a fine marksman, from the sharp, steady shine of his black eyes beneath the long, coarse, Indian-like hair that hung over them; indeed, I half suspected that the fellow was a half-breed, but had no opportunity of ascertaining! We had evidence enough of this afterwards. Placing ourselves with implicit faith under the patronage and guidance of this remarkable personage, we met with "sport" to satiety at last, within two days.

We had gone out as usual on the third, and in a different direction from any we had yet tried. The spot assigned me for a stand by Jabe was by far the most remarkable I had yet seen. Five miles back, we had, with considerable difficulty, climbed up the steep side of a lofty and wooded ridge, that seemed much higher than any one we had yet seen. We had found the top, or comb, apparently level; though as we rode on, I observed the surrounding country to be either sinking beneath the feet of the ridge, or else the ridge was rising rapidly above the country. Suddenly we came to what, I remember instantly reminded me of my boyish idea of the "jumping-off place!" The thing was so sudden that our horses reared backwards and snorted with affright. We were on the sheer verge of a precipice three hundred feet in depth, and the heavy forest below us looked almost like lichens clinging to stones, which were in reality considerable bluffs. It seemed as if the ancient basin of some ocean lay at our feet, stretching as far as the eye could reach on either hand and in front; while far away to the right, just under the rim of the horizon, we could distinguish the dark, heavy line of the wood bordering Green river; while to the left it shut down upon a blue serrated line of lofty Knobs. We were lost in wonderment, gazing over this extraordinary scene, when Charlie suddenly shouted, as he turned his head quickly:

"Hilloa, there!—you Jabe—where are you making off to, you tallow-skinned knave?—you havn't shown me my stand yet!"

But Jabe either did, or pretended not to hear, and only increased the celerity of his gait, as he went crashing through the brush down the steep ridge-side without turning his head, ever. Charlie was highly enraged, and bestowed upon him sundry expletives not of the choicest selection, but which it is hardly necessary to repeat. I laughed heartily at the incident, and Charlie at once forget his wrath in a loud burst of merriment, when I recalled to his recollection the droll way in which our guide had acted for the last mile. He had been up to that time striding just ahead of our horses, gossiping in the gayest possible of saturnine humors, asking us all sorts of unsophisticated questions about the ways of the "settlements," and telling us quaint anecdotes about Old Jake, who was the greatest man in the world, according to his estimation. Indeed, he had been keeping us in one continued roar of laughter at his simplicity, and a certain shrewdness combined, when suddenly a new thought seemed to have struck him. He had paused for an instant,—looked around him furtively, and then drawing over towards the left hand side of the ridge, had, from that time, commenced bearing down that side further and further, until when we had nearly reached this spot, he pointed here, without a word, and the next we saw of him he was "splitting it" down the ridge.

"You remember, Charlie, we could get nothing, not one word out of him, with all your merciless rallying, after he made that sudden stop! Depend upon it, there is some fun in this, and that fellow has got this bluff-point somehow mixed up in the ridiculous superstitions common to his class!"

After many merry comments upon this text, in the course of which, with our loud talking and laughter, we violated all the accepted rules of "driving," which require, peremptorily, the most profound silence on the part of the "stander" as he approaches his "stand," we came to the conclusion that as the mischief had no doubt already been done, and the deer turned back by the sound of our voices, we had just as well take it easy until the driver came in. So, seating, or rather stretching ourselves upon some mossy boulders, scattered around, we chatted away the next half hour very cozily, although an occasional eddy of the wind would bring up to our ears the distant babble of the hounds in the valley, and the long, mellow wail of the driver's horn, both showing the game was on foot; yet neither of us rose, even, so entirely had we become cloyed of this sport! Soon the full chorus of hounds burst upon us, seemingly close at hand, still neither of us rose. Suddenly we heard a heavy crashing through the underbrush, and before we had time to think, an enormous black bear rushed past us.

"Hah! new game!" I exclaimed, as we both sprang to our feet and fired our rifles after the unwieldy brute. It was evidently hit, but kept on with undiminished speed across the ridge. The dogs, with bristles erect, and savage yells, came pouring after, while we, thus unexpectedly aroused to the wildest excitement, shouted like madmen as we followed after on foot, loading our guns while we ran. We knew the bear was wounded, and would take to the first large tree it came to. The comb of the ridge was about a quarter of a mile wide here, and the ground a general level. We heard the dogs baying furiously now.

"He's tree'd already!" chuckled Charlie. "Let's approach cautiously."

We feared it might resort to its common trick when tree'd by the dogs;—seeing the hunters approach,—it rolls itself up into a ball, and dropping to the ground, makes off again. We, however, managed to get fair shots, and brought it down. It was a very large animal of the species, and we wound a merry blast, both loud and long, in honor of our unexpected triumph. We supposed that the sound of the guns and the recall of the horns would, of course, bring our faithful esquire, Jabe, to us. After listening for some time, and no answer, Charlie gave another louder and longer blast, with all the power of his lungs, and receiving no answer still, sent out his prodigious voice over the valley, with a force that filled it with reverberations. After listening a moment we could barely distinguish a feeble "too-oot! toot!" that seemed to come from no great distance, but what the direction might be, neither of us could tell; for Jabe, as it undoubtedly was, must surely have been stretched upon the ground in some hiding-place. I laughed heartily.

"Why Charlie, that fellow is frightened out of his wits by some ghost story,—we must get along without him!"

"More like the bear has scared him into a fit—the spindle-shanked hill-tyke!" growled Charlie, who was excessively wroth for a few minutes, but whose risibles could not withstand the slightest allusion on my part to that dolorously timid "too-oot! toot!" We accordingly went to work, in despair of any assistance from the redoubtable Jabe, and prepared our meat for transportation homeward. We had reached our horses, and while engaged in dividing the burden between them, who should come crawling cautiously towards us, out of the wood, but our gentleman of the asthmatic horn. As soon as Charlie saw him, he staggered in convulsions of laughter, and letting his burden fall, rolled over and over upon the leaves, scarcely able to articulate more than a word or two at a time.

"O Jabe! O Jabe!—the bear! the bear!—run Jabe—the bear!—what'll uncle Jake say!—Jabe!—run Jabe!—the bear!"

Jabe, in the meantime, was very cooly examining the bear, while his eyes fairly glistened at the sight of the fat, heavy hams.

"Gosh! he's a whopper! Killed jest sich a old 'un down in the truck-patch back er uncle Jake's, 'bout this time last winter. I was out choppin', and he com'd snuffin' at a hog-bone I'd brung out for a bite, and didn't seem to mind me,—so I stood still, and he kinder come too close at last, and I let him hev it across the nose! one lick turned him up, sir,—sure as a gun!"

I now remembered having heard uncle Jake refer to this feat of Jabe'—but it had been done incidentally, and in such a matter-of-course sort of a way, that I had not noticed it specially at the time. The simple way in which the young hunter now recalled it, and the enthusiasm which lit his eye the moment he saw our unwonted quarry, convinced me that Charlie had been entirely mistaken, and that there must be some other cause than the one he assigned for the evident alarm of a man who had already, and with such coolness, killed a full-grown bear with an axe only. I accordingly let Charlie have his laugh out; for he had no notion of listening to any but his own version of the affair, while I determined to take advantage of the garrulous excitement, caused in the mind of Jabe by the sight of this the most valued of all the game of the country, to draw out from him the real cause of his alarm. So we sat down on the ground to examine the bear more at our leisure, and winking at Charlie, I at last got him to comprehend something of my purpose. We drew him out as to his hunting feats in general,—but most especially with regard to those in this particular neighborhood. Gradually he seemed to forget himself, and watching the moment, I asked him, suddenly, if he had ever taken a "stand" here, where he had placed us, himself!

"I!" he exclaimed, with a look of amazement,—"I!—great jingo—no!—I wouldn't er tuck a 'stand' on this here Pint, fer all the bar on the Tennessee and Cumberland put together!"

"But, why not, Jabe?—we've seen nothing very wrong here!"

"O, you're strangers! but didn't *he* swar before he died that the fust hunter, as ought'er know, that com'd near enough that big black oak to see the little head-stone to his grave—that he meant to haunt him to death? Didn't he?—I tell you this aint the boy that would go in a hundred yards of that big oak on no consideration in natur?"

"But,"—said I, impatiently,—"Jabe, who was this person?"

"Why, Old Bill Smith—to be sure!—you never hearn of

Old Bill Smith? Why uncle Jake know'd him well—he's fit Injuns with him many a time; everybody down in these parts know'd him!"

"No doubt, Jabe—but you say he's buried under the big black oak;—was he buried there of his own wish?"

"In course!—they say he chose the place years before he died, and fixed the grave himself. Them as buried him say it's a mighty curius sort o' grave. He was one of Boone's men, and so was uncle Jake,—and uncle Jake helped three more on 'em to bury him. There 'aint bin a livin' soul belongin' round here since. He lived by himself more 'n two years, down by the big spring. That's since I ken recollect. He never spoke to nobody but our uncle Jake, and we never seed him more 'n three times a year, when he com'd in to git the powder an' lead uncle Jake had got for him."

"Now, Jabe," said I, in my most wheedling tone, "Jabe, my good fellow, won't you show us the grave?"

"I!—good!—why man, no!—not for all the money in your town!"

"But, Jabe, you need only go near enough to show us the tree,—you will not be violating the command in doing that, merely!"

He still continued to shake his head, dubiously, in spite of our united entreaties, and mutter:—

"Golly!—don't like this here ridge, anyhow,—don't think it's safe,—wish hadn't bin sich a dratted fool as to come this way;—forgot till I was most there!"

But Charlie and I, in whom the spirit of mischief on his part, and earnest curiosity on mine, had now been thoroughly roused,—determined to give poor Jabe no time for consideration, and plied him on both sides with such eagerness, that after a considerable degree of wavering and hesitation, we at last brought him up to the sticking point by the application of a few shiners to his palm. He started, though still with visible trepidation, to lead us to the grave. I could scarcely keep from giving way to my inclination to laugh again, as I watched the various expressions of dread, mingled with the most spasmodic efforts to express a courageous and devil-may-care sort of air, which were becoming more and more forlorn as we approached the scene of his apprehensions.

We had not walked more than a few hundred yards, almost immediately along the edge of the cliff, when he stopped, and pointing ahead to a very large black oak tree that stood somewhat apart from the more stunted growth of the ridge, and within a few feet of the precipitous verge we had been treading, he said in a tremulous tone,—

"Thar!—that's the tree!—wouldn't go any closer for a kingdom!"

"Well, Jabe, you'll wait here, won't you!" said I, as we walked on.

"'Spose I will,—don't like it, though!"

We laughed slightly as we looked back.

The moment the tree had been pointed out to us, I had remarked to Charlie, that I thought I recognized that tree; and when we reached it, judge our astonishment, to find it was the very one from which we had shot the bear a few hours before: and, on looking round, we perceived what had, during the excitement of the chase and conquest, entirely escaped our attention before, namely, that this was really the largest tree in sight, and that it stood exactly on the highest point of the ridge, and commanded a wider prospect than was possible from any other spot. These observations interested us not a little, and I looked around curiously for traces of the grave. Directly, Charlie uttered an exclamation.

"Here it is! I suppose this must be it—though it's a droll looking affair for a grave!"

I stepped towards him and found him kneeling on the bluff-side of the tree close to its roots, and peering between some flat rocks which he had partly uncovered of the mould and leaves.

"These flat rocks seem to be regular—this must be the sepulchre, coffin, or whatever you choose to call it!"—he continued, as he scratched away. "By Jove! look through that crack—I can see the skull!"

I knelt beside him, and sure enough a human skull was visible in the shallow sarcophagus. I immediately proposed to remove the stone, and take the skull out. I was at the time a vehemently ardent student of the new science of Gall and Spurzehim, and would cheerfully have risked my life for any such opportunity as this for examining the skull of a man whose character must evidently have been so very marked and extraordinary. It was no vulgar curiosity that caused me to disregard the slight remonstrance of Charlie, who muttered something about the pity to disturb the old fellow's rest. I reverently lifted the thin flat stone, about eighteen inches in length by six in breadth, which lay across the grave over the head, and could then see the structure of the whole as well as the great portion of the skeleton.

The grave was only about eighteen inches deep by about the same width, and was lined bottom and sides with flat unhewn stones of the same size of that I had taken from over the head, and the rest of the cover was the same, as well as what we call the head-stone, which stood an inch and a half above the surface. I immediately recognized the sort of stone sarcophagus or grave, which is to be found in thousands, covering sometimes miles of ground in the southern part of Kentucky and portions of Tennessee. The people adopting this curious mode of sepulture were extinct at a period earlier than the remotest reach of the tradition of the present *aboriginal* races, as we *vainly* enough call them! I have often examined these graves where you could not make a step for miles but upon one. It was evidently a pigmy race, for these graves average not more than three feet in length. It was from these ancient burial grounds that the old hunter had obtained his idea of sepulture. Who this singular people were, will probably never be satisfactorily discovered. In the meantime, men of sense will continue to laugh at the absurd theory, that they are the burying grounds of the Aztecs for their children. They must have been accommodating children to die by the thousand just about three feet high!

After examining the interior, without disturbing the limbs and body, I proceeded to lift the skull tenderly in my hand. I now stood erect, holding it off from me to study its proportions—when a sudden yell so startled me that I came near dropping it in the shock. I looked around quickly, Jabe uttering a second yell of horror, was in the act of throwing his long rifle from him—then bending his head forward and fighting desperately about his ears, as if attacked by a whole nest of hornets, he bounded with another wild screech into the thicket, and, as far as I could hear him, he seemed to give a screech for each bound. I turned an inquiring look upon Charlie, who was rolling upon the leaves half dead with smothered laughter.

"Has he got into a yellow jacket's nest, Charlie!" I inquired, very soberly, of the ridiculous fellow, for I did not feel much like laughing.

"No," he gasped at last—"but if you don't look out you will have got into one, by that phrenological whim of yours. Jabe saw you with the skull in your hand, and it frightened him to death almost. You may rest assured that he will not stop now until every man in the circumference of twenty miles knows of this. There are not many of them to be sure, but they will be troublesome fellows to deal with."

"Well, what would you advise, Charlie?"

"Why, that we both make a bee-line for home, right off? I think I can find the way out, and its no use meeting these fellows while they are exasperated. We'll return in a few weeks, when the thing has passed over; and as I have no hand in it, I'll make your peace with the superstitious fools, and we can have our hunt out, and hear Uncle Jake's story of this Bill Smith!"

"Well, I'm agreed—but stop a few moments, Charlie. As I have risked a lynching to get a sight of the old hunter's skull—I am going to have a good look at it now before we go!"

He uttered some exclamation of impatience, and sunk down upon the leaves again, when I was soon deep in the mystery of bumps.

I marvelled at that head! The skull was of rather small size, and ran up at firmness almost to a cone—secreetiveness was enormous, too, and destructiveness quite as excessive—but combativeness was not large—adhesiveness, benevolence and conscienciousness remarkably large. Of acquisitiveness he seemed to have nothing scarcely, and of what is called human nature, a great deal. He had prominent language, yet one of his sobriquets was, the "Silent Indian killer!" Of casuality there was little—but comparison was large—the organs between the eyes were large—form, locality, &c. Philoprogenitiveness was the largest organ, except firmness!

These were the hasty observations I had time to make before the impulsive hurry of my comrade compelled me to replace the skull. This was done with the most scrupulous care, in as exactly the position from which I had taken it as possible. The grave was also re-covered with the same care, and restored as nearly as I could get it to the condition in which I found it. We soon after mounted our horses, with the bear meat tied behind us, and set off rapidly on our return to town. During the whole ride I was thinking of this extraordinary head, and what had been no doubt its equally remarkable owner. What a man this must have been, and what a career!—for, obscure as it appeared to have been, it was evident from the awe and dread his very bones inspired in the mind of the simple hunter, that he must have possessed traits while living, quite as peculiar, as his taste in burial, or the shape of his head. What circumstances could have combined to drive one of his naturally strong and active social feelings into the terrible isolation of life and of death, in which I had thus far traced him.

Come what might, I vowed that at some future time I would make another effort to clear up this mystery of the "Hunter's Grave," and trace the story of this saturnine old warrior of the dark and bloody ground.

CHAPTER VIII.

OLD BILL SMITH, THE SILENT HUNTER.

I CARRIED out my resolution, to get at all that could be reached concerning the history of Bill Smith. On a new excursion, I saw and made my peace with Uncle Jake—the one of his old comrades who had most of his confidence, and who lived nearest to the concluding scenes of his life. My friend Charlie and myself spent a week with him this time, and we were even successful, after the first day, in reconciling to us our old acquaintance and guide, Jabe, in spite of the terrible fright we had given him through my phrenological enthusiasm. Jabe seemed to have come, finally, to the logical conclusion, that, as the ghost had not yet ridden us into our graves, that it meant to let us off, on the score of our being green-horns, "who didn't know no better!"

"But fur a *hunter*, who ought'er know'd sumthin, to do sich a thing—it would'er been more 'an his life or his sleep o'nights war worth!"

Without pretending to dispute the metaphysical views of Jabe, we proceeded as usual to avail ourselves of his really uncommon skill as a guide and driver, while I made it a point when we returned from the day's hunt, and when the evening meal had given way to pipes and segars, to bring old Uncle Jake round, by indirections, to the topic of which he was most shy, while I was most eager, namely, the story of this Bill Smith—for the more I heard of him the more curious the contradictions of his character appeared.

In furnishing this relation in my own language, I wish it expressly understood, that the whole is necessarily a sort of scraps and patch narrative, the general tone of which I take from Uncle Jake, but many of the important facts beside have been obtained in conversation with some others of the elderly survivors of that period, and who, too, had been associates of Smith. Other circumstances of interest I picked up in Washington City, and others more private, I gleaned in North Carolina. I have taken the liberty to throw all these things together, as to me "seemeth best," and as I have to trust entirely to my memory, am liable to some inaccuracies; but such as it is, I offer you this account of Old Bill Smith.

So far as I can make out the story, he seems to have been an orphan boy, thrown upon the charities of the kind world when quite young, by the sudden death of parents, whose only child he was, and who had lately come over with a ship load of other emigrants from Old England.

It was not to be expected that a child with such an unfortunate patronymic as Smith, was ever to be inquired after. He was lost in the undistinguishable and innumerable multitude of that great family. Of course the fate of the poor nameless child—for Smith can hardly be called a name!—was apprenticeship under the system of indenture which prevailed quite generally among the colonies. We hear of him as indentured to an old farmer in the northern part of North Carolina. He must have been eight years old or thereabouts at this time.

This old farmer, I suspect, was a veritable brute; for although the terms of indenture, besides a sufficiency of food and clothing, together with comfortable lodgings, expressly stipulated that the apprentice, thus bound for a term of years, for and in consideration of his services, was to be afforded the opportunity and allowed the necessary time for the acquisition of a good common school education.

This part of his bond and duty, it seems, the old curmudgeon never did or would fulfill, thinking, I suppose, that learning was only one of the worldly vanities, and would most likely turn the boy's head. William seems to have been, from the beginning, remarkable more for wilfulness than any other trait; and I suppose it was quite as much because old Saunders refused to send him to school as from any inherent love of learning, that he determined to learn to read anyhow.

Little blue-eyed Mattie Saunders, who seemed a stray angel by the fireside of the old beast who called her child, somehow or other divined the wishes and purpose of the young Smith; and as her excellent mother had taken care to learn her to read as soon as she could speak, from a sort of melancholy presentiment that she had not long to tarry with her, she proved a very capable and certainly remarkably successful instructress. Certain it is, that if he did not take to learning for learning's own sweet sake altogether, there proved to be a most salutary attraction in that little white and dumpy finger, gliding from letter to letter, to fix the attention of the wilful and headstrong boy.

He made such rapid progress that he soon became the teacher of his young mistress in turn; and as this relation between the young ones had to be kept scrupulously private, the pleasures of such stolen intercourse were greatly lightened.

This condition of things, charming enough, no doubt, to both parties, was most unpleasantly broken up by the accidental discovery of its existence by the old man, who, it seems, was furious thereat, and from that time commenced a series of petty and abominable persecutions, which almost drove the forlorn and wretched child mad.

The gentle consolations which he had heretofore received from sweet little Mattie, were now denied him. He was banished, in mid-winter, to the barn to sleep on the hay, with only a single thin and tattered blanket to cover his shivering body.

The heroic boy bore all this for eighteen months without a murmur, and all for the sake of his little mistress, with whom, in spite of the vigilance of the father, he managed to obtain occasional interviews, in which, with many tears on both sides, the testimonials of their pure and innocent affection were hurriedly exchanged.

Old Saunders had but the one child; and having amassed a considerable fortune by the most parsimonious and usurious practices, he was constantly haunted by the apprehension, even in her childhood, that every one who approached little Mattie did so with an eye to her money. The child was tender-hearted, meek, and confiding, as her poor mother had been before her; and the wretch remembered how even *he* had wrought upon the isolation of that poor woman, and induced her to confide to him her little all, as well as life, and he very properly concluded, that if such a creature as himself could thus win upon the confidence of the mother—even though it had only lasted for a few days after marriage—*who* might not aspire to win that of the child, that resembled her so closely.

He therefore watched her most jealously, and cut her off as much as possible from all intercourse with the outward world—even in the distant perspective of womanhood—the idea of her marriage and a dower was almost death to him. To part with any portion of his precious and ill-gotten gold was like wringing the drops of his heart-blood upon the thirsty sands. He at once became furious the moment he discovered the intimacy and childish sympathy between the boy Smith and his child. There was no knowing what such a thing might come to; and the starveling, whom he flattered himself he had apprenticed out of charity, might prove the viper upon his hearth.

Such were the barbarities practised upon the helpless orphan, that, although too manly himself ever to complain, they became the talk of the neighborhood; and, while some persons openly asserted that old Saunders was trying to kill the boy by inches, others had determined to have him presented to the next Grand Inquest that sat in the county, for barbarity and neglect of duty.

Before, however, this very necessary and proper step could be taken, these persecutions had grown beyond any further possibility of endurance, and in a fit of ungovernable despair, the miserable child made up his rags into a little bundle, in which he also secreted a few scraps of food, which little Mattie, to whom he had made known his purpose, had obtained for him. He then crept into her little room by the window at night, and after weeping long, as if their little hearts would burst—in each other's arms—for each felt that this parting was from the only friend they had in the world —the poor boy comforted the tender mourner by assuring her, in a tone of singular confidence, that when he got to be a great man he was going to come back for her and make her his little wife.

Even at the early age of thirteen the remarkable magnetic power which afterwards distinguished the man, was developed —for, in relating this occurrence himself in after-life, he said that when he spoke this in a bold, confident tone, the little trembler ceased to weep, and looking up into his face with a smile, said—

"Well, then, you may run along, Billy—I'll wait for you!"

He was off in an instant, and with her last pure kiss upon his lips, he plied his little legs as fast as they could carry him on the road which he had learned led to the capital of the State. His heart was light, his spirit bold, and the great world before him a shrouded mystery. He reached Raleigh in about a week, begging his way after his own little store gave out. He must have exhibited a great deal of audacity and address, for a child of his age, to have succeeded in getting through such a journey without being stopped by the authorities somewhere on the way. However, it is not more remarkable than many other of the events of his life.

After reaching Raleigh, his life was of course wretchedly precarious for some time. He prowled about the kitchens of the gentry at meal times, and lived upon such of the scraps of the tables as the negroes chose to throw to him in compassion—at night he crawled into some shed or stable to shiver in the straw till morning.

It happened that a kind-hearted old Judge of the Circuit Court—Campbell by name—who was a very early riser, and always went, the first thing, to see how the cattle and horses came on, found one morning a feeble looking child, with features ghastly and sharpened by hunger, lying in the trough of his cow-house, which was a close shed around three sides of the stable. He stopped, astonished, to gaze upon him. The little fellow had not rags enough upon him to cover his nakedness, and had drawn down some of the hay from the manger above to cover him, and the whole pile shook as he shuddered with the cold.

The old man gazed for a moment or two upon that troubled sleep, the irregular breathing, broken so often with faint moans, that they touched deeply, and as the tears sprang to his eyes, he murmured—

"This must not be so while I have a crust. Children must not starve in such a country as this!" So saying, he took the child gently in his arms, and bore it into his house, where his good old wife immediately took the dying orphan to her bosom, and soon warmed it into life again; but with the utmost exercise of her matronly skill, it was several days before the exhausted little one could recover strength enough to give any coherent account of himself.

Judge Campbell knew old Saunders well, and when he heard the boy's straight-forward story, he had every reason to believe that it was true, every word of it. In the meantime he had got up a great interest in this little *waif and estray*, which it had pleased Providence to cast in his path; and as the old couple had no children, but two daughters who were married and comfortably settled, they finally determined to submit to what seemed like a requisition upon them by the Father of all on behalf of the fatherless, and adopted little Smith into their family as a son.

The Circuits were some of them very large at that time, as was especially the case with that of Judge Campbell's. Soon after this event he started on his round, and what was his inexpressible delight to find the first case on the docket, in the county which had the honor of owning old Saunders for a citizen, marked "Commonwealth *vs.* Samuel Saunders, for abducting, murdering, or otherwise unlawfully making away with an indentured male child, known as William Smith," &c. &c.

The old man could scarcely contain his gravity upon the bench. He immediately ordered up the case—ruled down all quibbling attempts to obtain a postponement—and it was the general remark among the lawyers, that the usually lenient Judge was more severe and harsh this term than they had ever known him to be before in twenty years upon the bench.

The case came on. The Judge compelled the minutest scrutiny of all the facts, and a most damning case was made out from the evidence. His own lawyers were cowed, and the pale and frightened wretch listened with ghastly face, chattering teeth, and trembling hands to the Judge's charge to the jury, which sounded in its solemn tones and terrible denunciations much more like a sentence of death than a charge—when, as he was apparently about winding up with positive instructions to the jury to find the prisoner guilty—there was the sound of carriage wheels outside, and then a sudden commotion in the court.

In a moment the Sheriff stepped forward and placed a slip of paper in the hands of the Judge, who had paused at the first sound, and now read the paper calmly over twice; then deliberately throwing back his spectacles, he nodded assent to the Sheriff, who, with a sort of half smile upon his face, made his way out of the court room, and in a moment returned, pushing through the crowd, bearing in his arms the attenuated form of the missing boy, William Smith!

Such a thrill and murmur as ran through that court room,—the old miser, who had at first sprung to his feet, convulsively dropped, swooning, into his seat, for the child had been artfully draped in white, and looked as if it might have just come from the grave, and the hoary-headed villain really did not know whether it was dead or alive,—for Mattie! tender, timid, gentle Mattie!—had kept her little companion's counsel, as she had promised, in spite of all the threats of her father, and all the terrors of a public trial. Indeed, poor child, she did not know herself whether he was alive, and had been almost crying her life away because, in her innocence, she supposed the neighbors who had presented her father must of course have known the fact of his murder before they did it—he was in truth dead to her!

The scene that follows baffles description. Old Saunders was borne from the court room in convulsions, and shriek was heard following shriek from him until the doors of the jail closed upon him. The Judge then ran rapidly over the facts of the case as nearly as he could without detailing his own share in the plot,—which was entirely unnecessary, as his object had been to further the cause of justice and humanity by punishing this monster morally, if it could not be done legally,—and then exhibiting the boy to the jury, declared the bond of indenture to be forfeited, and that Saunders should be found in costs of suit, and compelled to give security for the support and education of the boy until he was eighteen.

Such was the eventful opening of the public career of "Billy," as poor Mattie called him. When we next hear of him he was a gay, voluble, dashing young lawyer, successful in his first case, and indeed in almost every other to which he put his hand. The old Judge, his adopted father, had retired from the bench upon a handsome competency, and though now very decrepid, could not resist the gratification of listening to the forensic triumphs of his "pet nursling of the cow-troughs," as he used to term William, humorously. Whenever William had an interesting case on hand, the old man's carriage was invariably seen to roll up to the court house door, and he to hobble in on crutches, when the dutiful young man was instantly at his side to assist him up the accustomed steps to the old accustomed chair, which still held its place for his occasional accommodation. After seeing him comfortably seated, and his gouty feet adjusted with scrupulous care, would return with redoubled energy to his case.

It was always noticed that when the venerable ex-judge was present, the face of the young lawyer flushed with anxious excitement, and then he made his very happiest efforts, and carrying everything before him by the impetuous vehemence of his oratory, never lost a case; and the father and patron, in one, would sit with half closed eyes, in a sort of rapt ecstacy of enjoyment, while his lips occasionally moved in unconscious approval as the young man let off his happier hits. Smith soon became exceedingly popular, and his clients learned to avail their causes of this noble trait of Smith, in something of the same spirit of the wretches who made fortunes off of the vice of poor George Moreland. When a new picture was to be wrung from their victim, they came to him with a pittance of ready gold in one hand and a brandy bottle in the other; and as the latter was always the more potent of the two, they made up the difference due in gold, in cheap and villainous brandy.

Smith, like Moreland, was too lazy to work under the ordinary stimulus of money, for which he never could be made to care, and when they found out this "beautiful weakness," as the mercenary knaves were in the habit of terming it, they never failed, when he was to speak on a doubtful case where there was much at stake, to have the old man informed of the day and hour, and thus drag him forth, well or ill—for go he would,—to act as a sort of spiritual brandy bottle upon his adopted son. They knew well that Smith would sooner lose his right arm than make a failure in a legal argument before his beloved and venerated patron. What is still more strange, neither Smith nor the old judge ever suspected this infamous game, although it was regularly practised upon them, until the death of the latter, and was well known to every one about the courts.

The Judge lived just long enough to bless the son of his adoption and his pride, who had been elected to the Assembly of the Province the very year he came of lawful age. The good man then lay down in peace to die, for now he had seen the fruition of his hope. He left his property divided equally between his two daughters and the adopted son. He was soon followed by his faithful dame, and now the young orphan stood once more alone in the world. Not entirely alone, spiritually, either, for Mattie was still steadfast to her childish affection, and would listen to no suitors that came. To be sure, had she been disposed to coquetry, the indulgence would have been something difficult, for old Saunders became more and more miserly as he grew older, and more watchful of his daughter.

William and she had, however, in spite of his vigilance, managed, through the good offices of a relation of Mattie's, who had learned to admire Smith, and had always loved Mattie, to keep up a sort of broken correspondence by letter, and even to obtain an occasional interview, which was sufficient, during the long period I have passed over, to keep always bright and unbroken the links of that subtle chain which seems from the first gradually binding their lives more inseparably in one.

Smith, though considered a rising young man with a good fortune already in hand, and every prospect of great honors and a greater fortune before him, and therefore, of course, greatly sought after by the highest ladies of the land, yet never for one moment did he falter or flinch in allegiance to his gentle mistress with the chubby fingers! When he came to realize that it was really love that he bore her, he felt at once the serenity of entire content; and that love was enough for him, it filled his being and he asked no other. The subject was never mentioned between them until after the death of his adopted parents, for William seems to have always felt as if his first duty was to them and gratitude,—love and himself afterwards.

He was now in such circumstances as permitted him to think of marriage; as it was utterly hopeless to expect the consent of the miserly old Saunders, he took the matter in his own hands, and in defiance married the sweet Mattie, who was now of age, almost under his eyes, and leaving him to rave, blaspheme and tear his hair at his own leisure, quietly installed his bride as mistress of the old town mansion left him by the Judge. Mattie proved a thrifty and a tender wife, and bore him sons and daughters, comely to look upon, and that gladdened their father's heart.

He, in the meantime, grew apace in manly honors, and at the time of the Declaration of Independence, was forty-five years of age, and one of the leading men, in a quiet way, of the patriot party.

Since his marriage, and up to this time, Smith's character seemed to have undergone a change, which was specially remarked by those who had watched his entrance upon public life. Up to the time of his marriage he had exhibited the most recklessly spendthrift disposition; although enjoying a lucrative practice, yet it was observed that he always wanted money. He had no such apparent habits of extravagance as could account for such expenditure, so that he had the full benefit of all sorts of dark hints and vague surmises, not one of which was in the neighborhood of true.

There were a few who knew him better, who could have told how the base vultures and harpies that always flock around where there is a great heart to be torn and fed upon, regularly fleeced him of more than half the dues for his services, by some servile and whining appeal to his well known magnanimity, and singular disregard of gold. He was systematically victimized by a whole flock of such foul birds, who chuckled over the thought that they were gulling the smart young lawyer; a great mistake!—for his intuition of character and motive was as quick as lightning.

His keen, gray eye was never at fault; and he gave them what they cringed for out of contemptuous disgust for the creatures and the filthy god they worshipped. He loathed the one as much as the other, and was equally anxious to get rid of both. His charities were just as reckless, though it began soon to be found that he was rather a dangerous person to task the patience of *too* far.

From the day he married Mattie he became a cautious, saving man; and the hungry wretches that had battened upon his lofty generosity, or rather, scorn, were soon scattered in dismay before the stern brow and powerful arm that hurled them right and left from his path. He had Mattie, beloved

Mattie, to provide for now, and her precious little ones; there was to be no more trifling. He became a rigid economist, or rather, Mattie economized for him, and all his expenditures were left entirely to her frugal and patient housewifery. He neither gave nor spent now without first taking counsel of his heart-elected monitress, and how skillfully she managed may be shown in the fact that in twenty years after their marriage Smith was accounted one of the wealthiest men in the province. With this change came another, which was accounted quite as droll by the wiseacres. As a young man, he had shown great ambition for political distinction, his prospects were extremely flattering, but he withdrew after serving one term, and steadily refused ever afterwards to be drawn into public life again.

But now that the great struggle for freedom was fairly entered upon, the William Smith of twenty-five was waked up again suddenly, after having slept the charmed sleep of domestic love and happiness for twenty years. Now again his contempt for gold, but as a medium of good, a mechanical means, exhibited itself as strikingly, but in a more rational and consistent manner than before; now his carefully hoarded wealth flowed like water, and the gentle Mattie saw it go and said never a word nor shed a tear. So long as her beloved was spared to her the gold might go. They had no right to it when the blessed Congress and brave army needed it. They had no right to keep William selfishly at home with them, to sleep in a warm bed when so many of our brave people were tracking the snows with the blood of their bare feet, and when General Washington himself was glad to sleep upon a snow bank with only his cloak for covering. "Let the gold go! let the gold go!" the brave woman was wont to say,—"it is all for liberty, and the children will be better for that than for all the wealth of the province!" and the gold did go!

Aye, there was no keeping back of the tribute there!

William Smith had always exhibited a remarkable disinclination for scenes of bloodshed, considering the character of the times. He did not, even now, join the patriot army; but, as the chief of the Vigilance Committee, did far better service with his prompt sagacity and profuse liberality than he could probably have done in the field. We cannot follow him through the details of the acts of this noblest period of his career; suffice to say, that when the war ended in our dear-bought independence,—he first took time to look upon the condition of his own affairs; the survey exhibited himself to to himself a *beggar!*

Everything had been swallowed up in the vortex, except some few fragments of landed estate; and they had only been spared him because nothing could be raised on them in such troublous times. He smiled upon Mattie as he looked around proudly upon five handsome, manly boys and three daughters, all pleasant variations upon her, and patting her still fresh cheek, said gaily,—

"Missus,—it's all gone!—I am proud of the way it went—we've gained our holy cause,—I am content!—what say you, woman?"

"Dear Billy, what should I say!—Am I not proud of it as you!"

"Well, missus, neighbor Daniel Boone has got back from Kan-tuck-ee, across the mountains, as he calls it. He says it's a great country, greater and more beautiful than any on this side the Alleghanies,—and Daniel's a reliable man, you know!—and that plenty of splendid land is to be had for the settling and defending it; our boys are good riflemen,—what say you, Mattie?"

Mattie turned a little pale, and laid her cheek against that of her husband, but answered in a firm, round voice,—

"I am ready, Billy, to follow you!"

And this is all that was said between them; it was settled!

This was a few years after the time that Daniel Boone and

his brother came in for their wives and families. The news of his wonderful discoveries had flown like wildfire throughout Virginia and North Carolina, in both of which States he was well known. It had caused a great and general ferment among all bold and reckless spirits in the old States, as well those of the border, as those whom a long war had unfitted for any other than a life of adventure. Various companies had been fitted out in different directions who had followed the return of the Boones. Settlements had been formed—forts built—and even municipal regulations commenced.

The place of general rendezvous was across the mountains, in what was called Powell's Valley, and the settlement on Clinch river was the Frontier fort. The emigrants assembled in Powell's Valley in the Spring of 1784, and when all collected, started on their long journey. Among them was the family of William Smith. He had converted all that was left him into live stock, implements, &c. Himself and his whole family—Mattie and the girls included—were in the highest spirits in view of the novelty and wild loveliness of the scene they were to traverse.

The emigrants numbered fifty souls, the great majority of them women and children. The journey, as they were prepared to expect, proved a rough and tedious one, but they saw nothing of Indians, as yet. They arrived on the banks of the Licking river in the ordinary time. Harrod, who had several years since built the fort where Harrodsburg stands, was now returning from a visit to Virginia; and he, with several other of the principal men, Smith among them, left their families, as they supposed, with a sufficient guard in camp, and pushed forward to find Boone, at either Harrodsburg or Boonesborough, and bring back some supplies.

Alas, for that parting! when they returned six days afterwards, as the day was breaking, having accomplished the object of their mission, they found the camp just broken up, and following on the scattered trail, caught up with the frightened remnant of the emigrants, in full retreat back for the settlements on Clinch river.

"Where is my wife? and where are my children?" demanded Smith, in a cold, stern tone, of the person under whose command the camp had been left.

"You will find them where you left them! Ask the Shawanees; they can tell you the rest."

"You have neglected your trust, and they are murdered," Smith replied, in a deliberate but trembling voice.

"And yet we find you retreating!—where is your manhood, wretch! coward!" he shrieked, as he sprang at the throat of the man, and hurled him to the ground with such furious violence that the blood gushed from his nose and mouth, and he was thought for a long time to be dying. Without pausing an instant to see what he had done, the unfortunate man turned, and with the speed of the wild deer, fled back to the deserted camp.

Several hours subsequent, Harrod and some others returned to look after the dead, and they found Smith stretched upon the bodies of Mattie and the children, with his arms spread in the endeavor to clasp them all in one embrace. He looked up with tearless eyes, and smiling with a terrible serenity, took the spade from the hand of the nearest person, and commenced digging a grave for them. The sturdy men around, moved and awed by the speechless silence with which he proceeded, offered in low whispers to assist him. He motioned them solemnly away, and would not be aided. He thus worked on for hours, until a grave wide enough and deep enough had been hollowed—then reaching the cold form of Mattie from the spot where it lay, he clasped it to his breast a moment—held it off for one long, fixed gaze—pressed those dear lips, and laid her gently down to rest. He then placed her first-born son upon her right side, and as he saw the frown of desperate battle still on his fair young brow, and the shattered rifle clutched in the grip of death, he smiled a strange and terrible smile. Her youngest born he lay next her heart, and to each, as he disposed the stiffening form in order, he gave the last embrace and farewell kiss. This done he stood on the side of the grave for some moments, gazing silently down upon the home, the earthly heaven he had lost, and then, without a word or groan, proceeded to fill up the grave. His comrades waited until he had finished, and had heaped a pile of stones to mark the place. They expected him to return with them now to the new camp which had been formed. He, however, took up his rifle, waved his hand in solemn adieu, and without speaking, disappeared on the trail of the Shawanees.

Little was generally known, and less said about Smith, from the time of this disappearance. It was generally believed that Boone, Harrod, and a few others, knew more of him than they chose to tell; the most that could be got out of any one concerning him, was, a significant touch of the forehead and shake of the head. Boone, in particular, was believed to have frequent interviews with him, as he would take with him at such suspected times a double supply of powder and lead.

For a year or two the mystery of his solitary life received no elucidation whatever, until a Shawanee, having been made captive by the people of Boones' Fort, they heard from him a terrible story of an Evil Demon that had been haunting the war-path of the Shawanees for nearly two years, and that from the hunting-trail and war-path together, more than thirty of their best braves, including several chiefs, had disappeared. The Shawanees believed that the Great Spirit was angry with them, and had sent a Medicine Spirit to punish them. They were nearly determined on this account to leave their hunting-grounds in Kan-tuck-ee forever. When questioned as to whether they had ever got sight of this Medicine, the answer was—that they had never seen it distinctly, but that of late their young men had pursued it often, and always came back with some of their number missing. They had never been able to overtake, or even to approach the mysterious and terrible Medicine Spirit.

After this report got abroad, men began to mention the name of Bill Smith again—but it was with a feeling of unaccountable dread, and in low voices that they spoke. The timidity and uncertain movements of desultory attack which began to characterize the warfare of the Shawanees, once the best organized and most formidable of the tribes, came now to attract attention, too. But all conjecture was set to rest, when, after awhile, Smith was seen to make his appearance at the Forts occasionally—but this was only when the Shawanees were known to be engaged in a foray. He usually came in ahead of the Indians, or after some unaccountable fashion, suddenly appeared in the midst of a battle with them.

He was at the Blue Lick, at the Raisin, threw himself into Brian's Fort when it was stormed; and, indeed, he was known to have been in nearly all the principal battles in which Boone was present.

He was never heard to speak to any one—he came without a greeting and went without farewell. He was regarded with a curious feeling of dread and respect by the Border people, none of whom ever ventured to address a word to him. The Shawanees were driven first across the Kan-tuck-ee River, then across the Green River.

Bill Smith disappeared, and never crossed Green River again; they thought towards the North that he must finally have fallen a sacrifice to his monomania of vengeance. It will be remembered by what accident I found his grave, and heard from old Uncle Jake Latham something with regard to his latter years.

After seeing the last canoe of the Shawanees launched upon the Ohio, and sending a death-messenger in farewell after it, the old man had built him a hut in the most inaccessible part of the Green River Hills, and there the remainder of his days were spent in solitary quiet. He hunted just enough to furnish him with food, and powder and shot—never went near any one but Uncle Jake, who made his purchases for him; and at the age of eighty-eight was found dead in his cabin. He seemed sleeping calmly, with a serene smile still upon his face, such as might have greeted his Mattie above, waiting for him. His face in death alone had lost that still and fearful expression of astonied ferocity, which was said never to have left it from the time of the death of Mattie and his children. Monomaniacs are proverbially known for the frequently marvellous cunning displayed by them in bringing about the accomplishment of the one object, which is the single thought of their lives.

"Vengeance is mine, saith the Lord!" Who, at this time, in weighing the acts of this remarkable man, while wasting under the long fever of his terrible vengeance, shall venture to forget, "Judge not, that ye be not judged!"

It was ever thus that our Fathers of the Dark and Bloody Ground were tried!

CHAPTER IX.

THE HUNTERS OF KENTUCKY.

JAMES HARROD OF HARRODSBURG.

After all the bombast of hero worshipers, it is astonishing how little it takes to make a real hero! Like many of those important discoveries in mechanics, which have revolutionized the world, the combinations are so simple, that whe nmen come to realize them, the general exclamation is, "Why, pshaw, I could have done that myself!" No doubt such wiseacres could have done it themselves, but somehow, they didn't do it! and what renders the parallel still more complete is, that when the humble mechanician has accomplished the work, has chained an element with a silken thread, he looks upon the mighty achievement as nothing, and is bowed down with shame that men should so wonder at a thing so plain.

Your true hero never understands why men should marvel that he has only done his duty, and the plaudits of the crowd are to him only a heart sickening commentary upon its own unworthiness. Why should they applaud him for only acting like a man? Had they expected him to act like a brute, and therefore been surprised into raptures? Or was it that they were conscious that they would have acted like brutes themselves under the same circumstances?

The world may say what it may of the natural equality of mankind, but there is often more in one large brain and large heart than in a whole nation. It is not by any means, learning, or station, or honors that constitutes this greatness; these are but the tinsel, the appliances, the outward show,—in a word,—

"The man's the man for a' that;"

and it was indeed among the early scenes of the settlement of Kentucky, that the fine gold was separated and that the man stood forth in the nude grandeur of the heroic virtues.

There was nothing of the pomp and circumstance here of adventitious place, to bolster up padded and pretentious nobility. State was trampled in the bloody mire of struggle, and all regalia, but such as nature had bestowed, turned into plough-lines and significant halters.

The contest here was hand to hand, and foot to foot, with foes too stern and real for a silken diplomate to soothe. In his unhoused wild condition, the strong man wrestled with the panther for its cave, and took its dappled hide for covering. Starched ruffs and white gloves would have served ill in such a battle. The death-hug, when the white man and the red man met, would have poorly become the voluptuous court, and the bleak, wintry winds would scarce have put a shirt on warm.

There was no dodging here, the axe was first swung by brawny arms, and then a shelter rose; and, before no dainty strength that fed on sylabubs, would those tall forests bow, that bread might grow! No shaky nerve, or eye dulled in the sickly glare of show, could hold the heavy rifle in a vice-like grasp, and guide it clear and sure as death's own arrow flies.

Here action was eloquence, with deeds for words, and the glib and oily art of demagogues learns no such language: the axe spoke louder than the honied phrase; and forests, thundering in their fall, rolled out the grandest sentences: the rifle cracked the sharpest jokes, and staggering buffaloes roared bathos best upon the bloody plain!

One of those men of nature, whose large brain and large heart, hard hands and giant thews, best fitted them to cope in mastery with such conditions, was James Harrod, the founder of Harrodsburg, Kentucky, and one of the noblest of the early companions of Boone.

Harrod was one of those persons who make their appearance in the world much as an oak tree comes into it: nobody hears it grow, sees it grow, or knows that it is, and has a being until suddenly a people look up and find themselves sheltered beneath its boughs, and nourished by the nuts it rains in benediction upon their heads.

So little was known of the youth James Harrod, that the histories of that time do not even name the colony from whence he came, nor even the precise year in which he emigrated; they only know that he came early with Boone, was most probably a Virginian, went back to that State and returned to Kentucky in 1774; joined Colonel Lewis and his followers on the way, and was with them in the battle at the mouth of the Kenhawa, and that in the next year he settled himself on the site of the present town of Harrodsburg. This is about the extent of the chronology bearing upon that early period of his history.

But for years before this period the name of the stalwart young hunter was familiar along the borders, and associated with that of Boone in many a feat of self-denying hardihood and generous chivalry. He was tall, strong, modest and simple. He had read no book but that of nature, knew no art but wood-craft, hated nothing on earth but an Indian and a pole-cat, and never said, "Boys, you do it!" but, "Boys, come on!" His rifle was the longest, the heaviest and the surest; his calm, frank eye was never at a fault to mark the distant game, to meet the gaze of deadly foe, or smile back truth to friend. His arm, resistless, as his tongue was slow. How can you make a hero out of a block so rough as this? We had nothing to do with the manufacture, God made him a hero, if he was one!

The unwritten history of that time tells many a touching narrative of the deeds of this young hunter; his skill on the war-trail, his vigilance and his wonderful powers of endurance, soon made him one of the chief supports of the feeble and shattered settlements, which then, in the name of God and civilization, dared presume to hold and occupy this wide land, which for its richness and its beauty had for many centuries been the golden apple of dispute between powerful tribes of savages, on the North and the South. The hardiness and simplicity of his habits, his fresh and unbroken constitution, his great frame, endowed with a natural strength remarkable, everywhere gave him supremacy even over those border sons of Anak, among whom he seemed to move as peer.

Such were his habits of incessant activity, and so cool his self-reliance, that he never waited for companions, on the longest and most dangerous of his expeditions. He would often be gone for weeks, and even months together, no one knew whither, or for what end, and the first thing heard of him would be his sudden appearance, to put the settlements on their guard against the approach of some Indian war-party. During these long absences his industry was untiring; all the game that he could kill was cured and stored, after the manner of the Indians, beyond the reach of wild beasts, or even of the sagacity of his teachers. To these stores he could resort at any time of scarcity, for supplies for the block-houses.

His knowledge of Indian life, and confidence, was such that he frequently continued to hunt alone, when he knew well, by the signs around him, that Indians were hunting on the same ground. The proud hunter would not give way, but took the chances with his red foe.

On one such occasion he had perceived several fine deer, grouped, feeding, in a small open glade in the forest, near the Kentucky river. He had approached them with much precaution, for a shot, and having gained the desired point, was kneeling behind a tree, and in the act of raising his rifle to take aim, when the buck of the herd lifted its head suddenly, and uttered the peculiar shrill whistle which indicates that they have either seen or smelt danger.

Harrod was too prompt a woodsman not to perceive instantly, from the direction in which the deer turned its head, that there was another foe present than himself. He remained motionless, holding his breath, when, at the sharp crack of a rifle from the opposite side of the glade, the startled buck sprang into the air and fell dead.

The report of Harrod's rifle followed so instantly that it seemed a mere prolongation of the first sound; a nobler quarry bit the dust, the ball of the back-woodsman met the proud heart of a Shawanee chief, who had leaned forward from his covert to fire. Harrod had known for several days that there was a hunting-party of Shawanees in the neighborhood.

At another time his own wary game was nearly played

successfully upon himself. He was on a great buffalo trail, leading to the Blue Licks. He had been hunting for several days with great success, and this time had seen no Indian sign, and was not aware that any had come down. He had wounded a large bull that had left the herd, and stood at bay several miles distant, in a thick wood; Harrod was obliged to approach it with great precaution, for the animal was now very dangerous, as is always the case when it is badly wounded.

He had gained his position, and when in the very act of firing, caught glimpse of a warrior taking aim at him from behind a tree. He fired, for it was too late to help that, but in the same instant dropped as if killed. The warrior fired, of course, and his ball made a hole through the wolf-skin cap of Harrod as he fell. He laid perfectly still, while the Indian, after stopping to load his rifle, as they always do before leaving cover, now approached him to get his scalp, but did so with characteristic wariness, leaping from tree to tree; he came near, and seeing that the body lay perfectly still, sprang forward, scalping-knife in hand, but as he stooped to grasp the scalp-lock, quick as lightning the long and powerful arms of Harrod were clasped about his neck, and with the sudden throe of a waking panther, the warrior was crushed in his herculean hug, and writhed helpless on the ground beneath him.

There is yet another anecdote of his individual prowess, with something of the same character as those given above, which, although a household story in Kentucky, is not so well known elsewhere.

The Shawanees had made several attacks upon Boone's station, against which settlement they had always expressed the bitterest animosity, on account, no doubt, of its having been the first white settlement held in the country. Boone was absent at the Licks, with a great part of the men of the station, making salt; the prowling parties of Indians had killed their cattle, driven in their hunting-parties, and so shortened their supplies of meat, that the little garrison was reduced to great straits.

At this juncture Harrod made his appearance unexpectedly, on his return from one of his long expeditions. Finding the condition of things, he first proposed to some of the remaining men, that they should accompany him to one of the nearest of his depots of meat. The risk was very great; and Harrod perceiving from the hesitation, that the men were not willing to go, left the station that night alone, telling the women to be of good cheer, that he would bring them back meat.

He found game very shy in the morning, and as there was plenty of Indian sign about, he determined to have the first meat he could get, and return with it as soon as possible to the relief of the station. He came in sight of a small herd of deer, which were moving as if they had been lately startled, and were still on the look out; this caused him to use great circumspection. It was not long before he came across signs, which induced him to think that there were several Indians close at hand. The daring hunter cared nothing for the odds, but coolly resolved to have one of those deer or lose a scalp, and of the latter there surely seemed to be a great likelihood.

This would have been foolhardiness with any other man, but with Harrod it was entirely a matter of course. He had never turned aside from his path for the red man, nor did he ever intend to do so. He claimed those hunting-grounds, too, and those deer were his, if he could win them, and his he intended they should be.

His circumspection was not a little increased on perceiving the marks of the mocassin on the trail of the deer. These were before him, and he might come upon them at any moment. This did not deter him, for he saw at a glance his advantage, as he was on the look-out for them, while they were on the look-out for the deer, and, evidently from the carelessness of the sign they left, entirely unconscious of his proximity. He had followed on in this manner for several miles, taking care to expose his body as little as possible, and indeed, advancing from tree to tree all the time, as if in a bush fight.

The sudden whistle of a deer, followed instantly by the ring of two rifles close on his left, gave him warning that the time for business had come. The Indians kept close, and as he was peeping cautiously round a tree, endeavoring to get a sight of them, a rifle ball from the right whizzed through the heavy mass of black hair that fell down over his shoulders, stinging his neck sharply as it grazed past. He crouched instantly, and all was as still as death for a long time, for the two on the left had taken the hint, and lay close, while the Indian on the right did the same, while he reloaded and watched for another chance.

Here was a fix certainly for any common man, beleaguered on two sides, and it might be on every side for all he could tell. But from what is known of Harrod's character, I have no doubt he enjoyed the fix; for it was just such a one as he delighted to get himself into, for the pleasure of getting himself out again.

The foot of the tree at which he crouched was surrounded by bushes or shrubs about three feet high, and he was obliged to lift his head above these before he could fire. He wore his famous wolf-skin cap, as usual; and after waiting till he was convinced that there was no chance of getting a sight of the cautious foe, he placed it upon the muzzle of his rifle, and, after some prefatory manœuvring among the shrubs, to show that he was getting restless, gradually and cautiously elevated the cap.

The ring of the three rifles was almost simultaneous, as it rose a little above the bushes, and before the echoes had died away, the death-shriek of the warrior on the right followed them into the shadows. Harrod lay still for a long time again before he concluded to try the manœuvre over; the cap was cautiously elevated again, and this time drew but one fire, for the Indians had taken warning. It effected all that Harrod required, however, for it disclosed the exact position of these two. He had only known the direction before, but not the position, as his eyes had been occupied in watching the one on the right—in less than half a minute, the Indian who had fired, exposed part of his body in sending home his rod. Harrod shot him through the heart.

The other Indian commenced a rapid retreat. He got off, but Harrod thought he carried a third ball with him. They had been entirely deceived by the manœuvre of the cap, and the survivor was clearly of the opinion, that, as they had killed two, there must be several white men there yet. Harrod proceeded at his leisure to dress the two deer they had brought down, and that night entered the station, to the great joy of all, with a full load of meat.

The benevolence of Harrod seems to have been equal to his energy. His hut, one of the first erected in the country, became at once the nucleus of a station—thither the surveyors, the speculators, the hunters and emigrants flocked for shelter and protection, and the names of Harrodsburg and Boonesborough became the first identified in the minds of weary adventurers of every grade, to this dangerous region, with the prospect of rest and the hope of security. Other huts had rapidly gone up around his, until more secure defences had become necessary, and a fort was built.

Thus, under the shelter of these two names, Boone and Harrod, the permanent occupation of Kentucky by the white race commenced.

These men, though both comparatively young, seem to have reproduced in themselves perfectly the primitive type of the ancient patriarchal character, which was so much needed in the elementary condition of the society they were organizing. All new comers were their children—they were received as such with open arms, they were watched over, guarded and guided, until they learned to stand alone and take care of themselves, and, what was still more remarkable, were allowed, without a murmur or a thought, to avail themselves of nearly all of the extraordinary labors and sufferings of their noble and unselfish guardians.

For example, Boone, who might, as I mentioned before, have been the richest man in the whole West, had he been as grasping as he was good and wise, entered no land, and died in wandering poverty, with no claim to one spot in that paradise into which he had led his countrymen. Harrod exhibited the same unselfish traits, as we shall see.

When a new settler came, he inquired for a locality; Harrod's knowledge of the surrounding country was at his service; he shouldered his axe, and helped the new comer run up a hut—the family out of meat, Harrod, by some necromancy peculiar to himself, had found it out. He was off to the woods, and soon a fine deer, or fat bear, or quarters of a buffalo, was placed at their disposal. Their horses had strayed in the range, with which the husband was not yet familiar, and no ploughing could be done—Harrod's incessant activity has made the discovery in passing, that something was wrong in the new clearing—his frank and manly voice is heard shouting from the fence, "Hilloa, Jones! What's the matter? No ploughing done yet, I see! Nothin' wrong, I hope?"

"Well, yes!—the old horse been gone these five days—can't find him down thar in that cane-brake range—been lost myself already two whole days in looking for him, and I've jest about gin it up."

"Never mind, Jones, you'll get used to that range sometime before long—that horse of your'n is a blood-bay, aint he?"

"Yes—snip down the nose, and left hind foot white—collar marked bad on the shoulders."

"Good morning, Jones!"

A few hours afterwards, Jones' horse, with his snip on his nose, is quietly driven up to the fence and turned in—James Harrod walks on.

News comes into the station that the Indians have attacked the house of a settler, five miles distant, and murdered all the family but the two daughters, whom they are hurrying off to a brutal and perilous captivity—the war-cry of Harrod is instantly heard.

"Come, boys! come, boys! we must catch those rascals—we can't spare our girls!"

While his dark complexion glows with enthusiasm, and his black eye flames again—the men know their leader, for he is off without them in a moment, and they are soon ready.

The swift and tireless pursuit, the wary approach to the camp, the night attack, with its short, fierce struggle, the rescue, the return, were all the not unusual incidents of their wild life.

In the capacity of spy, guide or ranger captain, his excursions into the Indian country were very daring and frequent. There was no enterprise too audacious for his enthusiasm, none requiring patience, dexterity, endurance of hunger, thirst and fatigue, too serious for his cool self-reliance to undertake, and that most frequently alone. He avoided, when possible, having other men with him, for, he said, they always complained of the hardships or the dangers before the fun was fairly commenced with him, and therefore it cost him more trouble to take care of them, than to do all there was to be done himself, twice over. This extraordinary love of solitary adventure was one of the marked characteristics of James Harrod. Indeed, the Indians christened him the "Lone Long-Knife," and dreaded his mysterious prowess very greatly.

He on several occasions entered their villages in the night to ascertain their plans; and once, when discovered by a young warrior, struck him to the earth with his huge fist, and then threw himself into the neighboring forest, not though without being seen and pursued; twenty or thirty warriors followed him, and so close were they upon his heels at the start, that their rifle balls showered like hail about him.

The swiftness of Indian runners has passed into a proverb, but they had a man before them more swift and tireless than they. He gained so much upon them that by the time they reached the Miami, which was ten miles distant, there were only three warriors who seemed to be continuing the chase.

Harrod swam the river without hesitation; as he reached the opposite bank they came up, and fired at him as he climbed the bank; the river was wide here, and the balls fell short. He now took a tree upon the edge of the forest, and removing the water-proof cover of deer's bladder from the lock of his rifle, prepared for them, should they attempt to cross the river. The Indians hesitated a moment, for it had now been some time full daylight, and they seemed to have some apprehension that he might make a stand, but hearing at this instant the coming yells of those who had fallen behind, they replied, and plunged into the stream.

Harrod waited until they were more than half across, when at the crack of his rifle, the foremost sank; the other two paused, then turned to go back, but before they could get out of range, he wounded a second desperately, who gave himself up to the current and was swept down. The third, by a series of rapid dives, like the manœuvres of a wounded wild duck, succeeded in baffling the aim of Harrod, even, and got out of range.

Harrod heard the furious howl of the main body of his outwitted pursuers, who had reached the river as he was making off again through the forest; the chase was not continued further.

What adds not a little to the dramatic interest of this adventure, is, that when, two hours afterward, Harrod struck the bank of the Miami again, he saw upon a pile of drift wood, which had collected at the mouth of one of the small tributaries of the stream, some living object, which he took for a large turtle glistening in the sun, as he struggled to drag his unwieldy body upon the logs to bask.

He stopped to gaze; and imagine his astonishment, when he saw a tall Indian drag his body slowly from the water, and finally seat himself upon the logs. He had lost his gun, and commenced endeavoring to stifle the bleeding from a bullet wound in his shoulder. Harrod knew that it was the second Indian he had shot, and who had most probably reached one of the pieces of drift wood of which the swollen river was at present full, and sustained himself by it all this distance, badly wounded as he was.

Here was a trial for such a man as Harrod; his foe was wounded and helpless; take him prisoner he feared would be impossible, and letting him escape he felt to be contrary to his duty to his own people. He thought within himself some little time before deciding upon his course, for shoot the poor wretch he could not.

His determination formed, he made a wide circuit, and crept cautiously upon the wounded warrior from behind; a large tree stood close to the drift, which being gained, Harrod laid down his gun, then suddenly stepping into full view from behind the tree, raised his hands to show that he was unarmed.

"Uguh!" grunted the astonished warrior, making a sudden movement as if to plunge into the water again. Harrod placed his hand upon his heart, spoke two words in the Shawanee tongue, when the Indian paused, and looking at him a moment earnestly, bowed his head in token of submission. Harrod helped him to the bank, tore his own shirt and bound up the wound with cooling herbs; and then, as he found the savage unable to walk, threw him across his broad shoulders, and bore him, not to the station, but to a cave which he used as one of his places of deposit. No one knew of the existence of this hiding-place but himself, and he had discovered it by the accident of having driven a wounded bear into it.

The entrance was very small and covered with briars; pushing these aside, you looked down into what seemed a deep well; when the eye became accustomed to the darkness, you could gradually discover a dry, white bottom. Harrod had descended into it by means of a pole ladder which he had let down; this ladder, which is essentially a frontier contrivance, consists merely of a stout sapling, which is thick set with limbs; the sapling being cut down, the limbs are chopped off within six inches from the trunk, thus leaving excellent foothold to climb by.

When you reached the bottom, which was about twelve feet below the surface, you found yourself in a small, but irregularly shaped room, the ceiling of which was hung with many beautiful and fantastic stalactites, from among which, and at the farther extremity of the room, a small, clear stream, poured steadily down into a white, round basin, which it had worn into the solid limestone.

The little stream, after passing across the length of the chamber, found vent through a dark hole in the wall, about large enough to admit a man, crawling in on his hands and knees. Here, over the whitest sand, it escaped into unknown caverns beyond. From the point of every stalactite on the ceiling a drop of water fell slowly upon stalactites rising to meet them, many of which had assumed the most extraordinary shapes. About twelve feet square of the ceiling and floor of this singular subterranean chamber was as dry as tinder.

I am thus particular in describing this cave, having once visited it, and been singularly impressed with the quaint peculiarities of the place. Among other things, the steady dropping of the water upon the white and ringing stalactites, formed a sort of low harmonicon, the sweetness of which I shall never forget.

In this strange hiding-place, as the story goes, Harrod concealed his wounded foe, for the generous hunter having once determined to aid him, possessed too much magnanimity to subject the proud warrior to the humiliation worse to him than death, of being paraded before his white foes as a prisoner. Harrod took care of him till his recovery, visiting him regularly on his hunting excursions. When the warrior grew strong again, Harrod gave him a supply of provisions, and pointing towards the North, bade him return to his people, and tell them how the "Long-Knife" treats his wounded foe.

Nothing was ever heard directly from this warrior again, though Boone, who was aware of the circumstance, and who was taken prisoner by the Shawanees a short time afterwards, always attributed the kind treatment he received from the Indians, and their good faith to eighteen of his men, to the good offices of this grateful savage. These men were engaged, under his command, in making salt at the saline springs, and surrendered at his own suggestion, he having been surprised and taken prisoner while hunting, and the promise of kind treatment and release having been pledged to him by the Indians. They, after taking their arms, ammunition, &c., permitted the men to return to the station unharmed. They took Boone with them, however, to Canada, where he was shortly ransomed.

The popularity of Harrod became very great; for these many extraordinary feats and kind acts were not his only claims on the now rapidly increasing population of Kentucky, for their respect and gratitude. His manly wisdom and counsel, was fully equal to his efficiency in the field; for though to the last he could barely write his name, and continued to be a man of few words,—one short sentence of his, direct, as it always was, and to the purpose, was of greater value in those times than all a mouthing demagogue could utter in a year.

He was elected Colonel, married happily, a genuine Kentucky girl, and was universally venerated and idolized, though yet scarcely past his prime. His modesty was unconquerable, and he shrunk from all honors which he could possibly avoid.

Strange to say, not even the endearments of his happy home, the love of his fellow citizens, or the charms of a society daily increasing in refinement, could win him from that singular passion for solitary hunting,—which seems to be general and peculiar to the Hunter-Naturalist, in whatever guise he may be found—for which Harrod was so remarkable. He would still, rifle in hand, bury himself for weeks, and even months, in some unpenetrated fastness of the wilderness, from whence he would return as unexpectedly as he went, laden with the trophies of the hunt.

Once he thus disappeared, never to return! By what casuality of the chase, or in what deadly contest with his Indian foes, no one could ever more than conjecture.

Thus died a true hero!—as he would no doubt have chosen best to die,—amidst those wild, stern scenes he had so dearly loved, and in fair battle with the chances that he gloried most in daring. Face to face, with God, the ancient nature and his foe, his noble heart was stilled, and his strong arm fell nerveless!

The wintry winds have moaned through stately mausoleums, indeed, but never yet wailed they a grander requiem, above a nobler grave, than that wild spot of rocks and forest where James Harrod lies! He left, I believe, one daughter; and a large and respectable family, descended from her, still live in Harrodsburg and the neighborhood.

CHAPTER X.

THE FOX—AND FOX HUNTING IN AMERICA.

Reynard is a famous fellow, to be sure!—it behooves me to be somewhat careful in making my approaches to a person of such world-wide celebrity.

He is eminently an historical character, and one not lightly to be dealt with, even from behind the ponderous shield of science. His fame has been recounted, not alone in the sober "chronicles of wasted time," but legend and romance have given their voices to commemorate his deeds, and poets have sung of them in high heroic strains. Witness that renowned and venerable epic of the nursery, "Reynard the Fox," for "what their antique pens would have expressed!"

But it must be confessed that your philosopher is a prodigious leveller. No antiquity is so remote that he will not brush off the green rime of ages, to count the wrinkles on its front; no fame so awful or overshadowing, that he will not, with familiar hands, stroke "the mane of darkness till it smiles," and renders up the secrets of its glory.

It is only from this point of view that we account for unconscious and remarkable coolness, with which astute Naturalists have seized Master Reynard by the nape of the neck, to drag him forth from beneath the misty obscurations of time, and hold him in the common light of day before the eyes of the astonished world. Seeing that they have done so, in spite of all savage growlings of his outraged historical dignity, even I can take courage, though with humility, to give him now an additional shake. I shall accordingly proceed to "beat out his fur," mathematically, so long as I can hold a sober face in dealing with a proverbially slippery and facetious customer.

There are about twelve well known species belonging to this genera, four of which are native to North America. There are many disputes among Naturalists with regard to the varieties of this animal. Instead of twelve, the number of species has been extended to sixteen. Mr. Audubon, in his new work, the Quadrupeds of America, has discovered that many of those animals which have been named and set down as distinct species, are only varieties. As for instance, the Cross Fox, the Black or Silver Fox, and the Red Fox, have each been classed as a separate species heretofore; but he has shown, I think, conclusively, that the two first are mere varieties of the last.

He found all three together in one litter. This fact in itself, is very strong proof that he is right, for the Gray Fox is never known to breed with either of these varieties; and the same is true of the Swift Fox and the Arctic Fox. This is somewhat singular, for the Red Fox is well ascertained to breed with the wolf and dog; while a mortal antipathy is thought to exist between it and the Gray Fox; so great, indeed, as to give rise to a common opinion, that the Gray Fox is exterminated by the Red wherever it makes its appearance.

Furthermore, the celebrated Dr. Richardson adheres to the same opinion, in common with the Indians, hunters and trappers, who have a saying, with regard to the Red Fox, "This is not a Cross Fox yet, but it is becoming so!" The European Fox is subject to similar varieties, and the *Canis crucigera* of Gessen, differs from it in the same way that our Cross Fox does from the Red one. On the whole then, I regard it as a safe conclusion, that the Red and Gray Foxes are the only distinct species we have within the present limits of the States.

The slight variations of pelage, which have given rise to the belief of the existence of so many species, are not at all extraordinary or peculiar; and, indeed, this is the common cause of a vast and unnecessary accession of species, which so complicates and involves the whole history of quadrupeds. Where such differences are not owning to age or sex, they are frequently to the accidents of disease, locality, climate, &c. I once saw three cubs taken from the bed of a Gray Fox, two of which were white as milk, and the other gray. It would have been very wise of me to have announced the discovery of a new species on the strength of these Albinoes!

There is a curious and interesting case in point, given from the personal experience of Dr. Bachman, the editorial associate of Mr. Audubon in the "Quadrupeds." After premising that the swiftness of the animal has most probably been greatly exaggerated, he says:—

In regard to the cunning of this variety, there may be some truth in the general opinion, but this can be accounted for on natural principles; the skin is considered very valuable, and the animal is always regarded as a curiosity; hence the hunters make every endeavor to obtain one when seen, and it would not be surprising if a constant succession of attempts to capture it, together with the instinctive desire for self-preservation possessed by all animals, should sharpen its wits and render it more cautious and wild than those species that are less frequently molested. We remember an instance of this kind, which we will here relate.

A Cross Fox, nearly black, was frequently seen in a particular cover. We offered what was in those days considered a high premium for the animal in the flesh. The Fox was accordingly chased, and shot at by the farmers' boys in the neighborhood. The autumn and winter passed away, nay, a whole year, and still the Fox was going at large. It was at last regarded by some of the more credulous, as possessing a charmed life, and it was thought that nothing but a silver ball could kill it. In the spring we induced one of our servants to dig for the young foxes that had been seen at the burrow, which was known to be frequented by the Cross Fox. With an immense deal of labor and fatigue the young were dug out from the side of a hill; there were seven. Unfortunately we were obliged to leave home, and did not return until after they had been given away, and were distributed about the neighborhood.

Three were said to have been black, the rest were red. The blackest of the young whelps was retained for us; and we frequently saw at the house of a neighbor another of the litter that was red, and differed in no respect from the common Red Fox. The older our little pet became, the less it grew like the Black, and the more like the Cross Fox. It was, very much to our regret, killed by a dog when about six months old, and as far as we can recollect, was nearly of the color.

The following autumn we determined to try our hand at procuring the enchanted fox, which was the parent of these young varieties, as it could always be started in the same vicinity. We obtained a pair of fine fox hounds, and gave chase. The dogs were young, and proved no match for the fox, which generally took a straight direction through cleared fields for five or six miles, after which it began winding and twisting among the hills, where the hounds on two occasions lost the scent, and returned home.

On a third hunt, we took our stand near the corner of an old field, at a spot we had twice observed it to pass. It came at last, swinging its brush from side to side, and running with great rapidity, three quarters of a mile ahead of the dogs, which were yet out of hearing. A good aim removed the mysterious charm. We killed it with squirrel shot without the aid of a silver bullet. It was nearly jet-black, with the tip of the tail white. This fox was the female which had produced the young of the previous spring, that we have just spoken of; and as some of them, as we have already said, were Cross Foxes, and others Red Foxes, this has settled the question in our minds that both the Cross Fox and the Black Fox are mere varieties of the Red.

Here I will dismiss this question, premising the conviction confirmed out of my own experience by the facts given above, that the three varieties, the Black, Cross and Red Foxes, will be found to be about as nearly identical as three specimens of the common American Skunk, taken from the same bed, one of which will be banded, another barred, and another mottled.

But the Editors of the Quadrupeds of America, have been, after some hesitation, bold enough to go with Cuvier in a most decided innovation upon the old formulas of classification.

They say, the characters of this genus differ so slightly from those of the genus canis, that they were induced to pause before removing it from the sub-genus in which it had so long remained.

I do not perceive that there was any special reason for doubt about the matter, for I have always been surprised that the foxes have not been recognized by Naturalists through all time as a separate genus. The common sense of mankind has always so placed them, but it seems that the common sense of Naturalists has been something different.

Nobody but a technicalist was ever satisfied with seeing the fox ranked as a sub-genus of canis. Apart from slight physical coincidents, it is so distinct in habits, character, &c., that we could quite as readily be content to see the humming-bird classed as a moth! There is about as much reason for the one as the other. The truth seems to me to be, that as the humming-bird, though distinct in its own character, forms the connecting link between insects and birds, so does the fox that between the genera canis and lynx; which last, it will be remembered, was once, in a like manner, classed as a Feline.

Here comes in a reflection which pertinently illustrates the ladder-like ascension of scientific inquiry towards truth. Before Linnæus, the methods of classification were so vague that nothing more definite could be said of them, than that food, size, shape and color were the principal rules. But the great classifier made an immense advance upon this loose mode, and his terse definitions are perfect, so far as external signs can go, or an accurate knowledge of habits substantiate them. Buffon, who repudiated systems, only made confusion worse confounded; and in the fierce collisions which ensued between his followers and their technicalists, (who swore by their master, the great Swede,) all systems of classification seemed to be in danger of being swept overboard.

Cuvier at once stepped to the helm and righted everything. He brought along with him, not alone the strong arm and the commanding eye, which wield success, but as well, a heavy ballast of fossil remains, and huge pre-Adamite bones, which soon steadied the storm-shaken vessel. Now, Naturalists were for the first time forced to realize, though unwillingly, that the only absolute and mathematical law of classification in Zoology, was to be looked for in the dental and osseous structure. The old methods are accepted as suggestive adjuncts, but by no means as absolute authority.

In the dental formula of the genus vulpes, there is only a slight, but decisive difference from that of the genus canis; the upper incisor being less curved. It was, however, sufficient to determine Cuvier. The other marked traits of difference are, that animals of this genus, generally, are smaller, and the number of species known, greater, than among the wolves; they diffuse a fœtid odor, dig burrows, and attack none but the weaker quadrupeds, or birds, &c. Yet, despite their courage upon this point, the venerable Editors of the "Quadrupeds," with characteristic caution, persist in what may be called "hedging their position," when they say:—

As a general rule, we are obliged to admit that a fox is a

wolf, and a small wolf may be termed a fox. Commend us to consistency,—say I!

The genus vulpes of Cuvier is now established,—has become a fixed fact of science among us, as it ought to have been considered long ago! The other two species, beside the Gray and Red, which go to make up the complement of four assigned to North America, are the Swift Fox and the Arctic Fox.

The Swift Fox inhabits the Missouri and Platte Rivers, west to the Rocky Mountains. It is a very extraordinary creature. Although the smallest of American foxes, it is by far the fleetest. In traversing the wild region where it is native, I heard from the hunters and trappers most marvelous tales of its swiftness, some of which placed it even alongside the horse and antelope in this respect, and far beyond any other animal on the plains. These stories are to be taken with considerable allowance. I saw it frequently, but had no fair opportunity of testing its speed thoroughly—though there is one observation which I made, that may be worth giving in this connection.

The vast bare extent and undulating surface of those plains seem to have had a somewhat remarkable effect in developing powers of flight and pursuit, in most of the creatures inhabiting them, and more particularly in the smaller ones; and there is quite as much of this exaggerated story-telling to be met with upon the lips of these same wandering hunters and trappers, with regard to the great-eared rabbit of the plains further South. This animal is represented by them as a miracle of speed; and I am, from my own observation, disposed to give a large proportion of credit to their representations.

I have witnessed in them such astonishing power of getting over the ground, that they almost seemed to defy pursuit. It was "more like flying than running," as the hunters say. The total absence upon these wild plains of any of those facilities for concealment, refuge or escape, which are afforded elsewhere, by trees, shrubs, rocks, holes, &c., renders the whole game of flight and pursuit a plain, straight-forward matter of hard running on both sides; so that it is no great wonder after all, if the heels of both the predatory and fugitive animals should be somewhat cultivated. As civilization is extended toward these remote regions, we shall know more of the habits of these fleet children of the solitudes, it is to be hoped.

The Arctic Fox is more familiar to us, though really far more distant, and living among more unpropitious and apparently inaccessible fastnesses, locked in by icebergs.

I shall merely say of it, that it is the only one of the genus which we think at all justifies the remark, that "a large fox is a wolf, and a small wolf may be termed a fox." It is much more like the jackal and wolf in its habits; like them, it is gregarious, when pressed with hunger, and is known, like them, to hunt in packs.

But the Red and Gray Foxes are the most interesting, for around them all the legendary and historical memorabilia of the genus cluster. This Red Fox must be the same mighty embodiment of quadrupedal treachery, upon whose sneaking head the indignant Chaucer loosened such an avalanche of bitter epithet and grand comparison—

> "O false morderour reecking in thy den!
> O newe Scariot, newe Genelon,
> O false dissimulour, O Greek Sinon,
> That broughtest Troye al utterly to roune."

And I fear he has not much improved in manners since; for so well is the slipperiness of his reputation understood, that his most earnestly solicitous friends, the sportsmen, not to speak of Naturalists, are to this day puzzled with regard to his identity. It is a question now of grave dispute, whether this "false morderour," denounced into immortality by Chaucer, be identical with the personage known by the same name among us—one party strenuously maintaining that the Red

Fox of America is entitled to the glory of such high descent, while the other sturdily contends that our Fox is an aboriginal Fox, and by no means deserving of such hard names as Chaucer used with regard to the English Fox.

This dispute is rather curious and amusing than serious. I shall look over some of the grounds of this interesting controversy. One party contends most earnestly that it is the European Fox, which was brought over by one of the Continental Governors, who was an ardent sportsman, and who turned a pair or more loose to breed on Long Island; that finally they escaped, they or their descendants, over to the main land, and have since migrated South and West.

The other party contends that it is a native species, and comes from the North, migrating—as many other species of quadrupeds and birds, as well as nations of men have done—towards the South.

The last argument appears to me to be the true one, because, in the first place, although there are many points of general resemblance, which might deceive any but careful Naturalists, yet it has been found, when the two animals have been brought together and critically compared by them, that they are quite clearly distinct. This, of itself, ought to be enough to settle the question; but when we come to remember, in the second place, that the Red Fox and all its varieties is a Northern animal, and that from its cunning and sagacity, it would always make a convenience of the neighborhood of man, for the purpose of preying upon his domesticated creatures, we can well understand how its progress South should have been quite as gradual as that of well stocked barn-yards and fat flocks of geese.

The case is to me a perfectly plain one; and the answer to the multiplied inquiries I hear from old sportsmen—"Whether it is that the Red Fox has degenerated, or that our hounds, through careful breeding, have been appreciated in speed?—since it is true that the Red Fox is now taken with ease in two hours at most, when we thought ourselves fortunate, when he first came amongst us, if we run him down in twelve,"—is equally plain. He is a Northern animal, and the fat living you give him, and your warm climate, have degenerated the gaunt starveling of the North.

Godman, in his American Natural History, disposes of the question in quite a summary manner, and, no doubt, greatly to his own satisfaction. He says:—

By the fineness of its fur, the liveliness of its color, length of limbs, and slenderness of body, *as well as the form of its skull,* the Red Fox of America is obviously distinguished from the common fox of Europe, to which, in other respects, it bears a resemblance sufficiently striking to mislead an incidental observer.

But to suppose this question of varieties settled, we may proceed in justice to say that with all his persecution Reynard has never been remarkable for ill-nature, except after the manner of a practical joker, who gives and takes; he has too great regard for his ancient and privileged character as a humorist, ever to show his teeth savagely, except when fully cornered, and then he dies game. No wonder the gall of bitterness should be stirred within him at the venal and unfair method of pursuit common in the Northern States, where the Cross Fox is hunted by countrymen on foot through the snow.

The dogs used are a mongrel cross upon the cur hound and grayhound. This animal is stronger and swifter than any thorough-bred, and better suited for this peculiar purpose—for the object is simply to get the skin and turn it into dollars and cents in the most direct possible manner. There is no poetry or chivalry in this kind of chase, of which Dr. Bachman gives the following account.

In the fresh-fallen and deep snows of mid-winter, the hunters are most successful. During these severe snow storms, the ruffled grouse, called in our Eastern States the partridge, is often snowed up and covered over; or sometimes plunges from on wing into the soft snow, where it remains concealed for a day or two. The fox occasionally surprises these birds, and as he is usually stimulated at this inclement season, by the gnawings of hunger, he is compelled to seek for food by day as well as by night; his fresh track may be seen in the fields, along the fences, and on the skirts of the farm-yard, as well as in the deep forest. Nothing is easier than to track the fox under these favorable circumstances, and the trail having been discovered, it is followed up until Reynard is started.

Now the chase begins; the half-hound yells out, in tones far removed from the mellow notes of the thorough-bred dog, but equally inspiriting, perhaps, through the clear frosty air, as the solitary hunter eagerly follows, as fast as his limited powers of locomotion will admit. At intervals of three or four minutes, the sharp cry of the dog resounds, the fox has no time to double and shuffle, the dog is at his heels almost, and speed, speed, is his only hope of life. Now the shrill baying of the hound becomes irregular; we may fancy he is at the throat of his victim; the hunter is far in the rear, toiling along the track which marks the course so well contested, but occasionally the voice of his dog, softened by the distance, is borne on the wind to his ear.

For a mile or two the fox keeps ahead of his pursuer; but the latter has the longest legs, and the snow impedes him less than it does poor Reynard. Every bound and plunge into the snow diminishes the distance between the fox and his relentless foe. Onward they rush, through field, fence, brushwood, and open forest, the snow flying from bush and briar as they dart through the copse, or speed across the newly cleared field.

But this desperate race cannot last longer; the fox must gain his burrow, or some cavernous rock, or he dies. Alas! he has been lured too far away from his customary haunts, and from his secure retreat, in search of prey; he is unable to reach his home; the dog is even now within a foot of his brush.

One more desperate leap, and with a sudden snappish growl he turns upon his pursuer, and endeavors to defend himself with his sharp teeth. For a moment he resists the dog, but is almost instantly overcome. He is not killed, however, in the first onset; both dog and fox are so fatigued that they now sit on their haunches, facing each other, resting, panting, their tongues hanging out, and the foam from their lips dropping on the snow.

After fiercely eyeing each other for awhile, both become impatient—the former to seize his prey, the other to escape. At the first leap of the fox the dog seizes him; with renewed vigor he seizes him by the throat, and does not loose his hold until the snow is stained with blood, and the fox lies rumpled, draggled, with blood-shot eye, and frothy, open mouth, a mangled carcase on the ground.

The hunter soon comes up: he has made several *short cuts*, guided by the baying of his hound; and striking the deep trail in the snow again, at a point much nearer the scene of the death-struggle, he hurries toward the place where the last cry was heard, and pushes forward in a half run until he meets his dog, which, on hearing his master approach, generally advances towards him, and leads the way to the place where he has achieved his victory.

There are yet more unfair modes of taking this gallant animal, known at the North, the very mention of which would make the warm blood of a genuine fox-hunter boil over with contemptuous indignation.

The fox is pursued over the snow by one of the scrubby mongrels above mentioned, until he is fairly earthed, when the *sportsman*, as he is facetiously called, comes up with spade and pick-axe on his shoulder, and after cooly surveying the ground, prepares to dig him out. His labor at this season is worth something less than a dollar a day, and if he succeeds in digging out the poor fox, he will receive from five to seven dollars for the valuable skin, which would be a considerable advance upon what he gets for fair and honorable labor.

Alas! poor Reynard, for all the dignity of ancient associations,

"To what base uses do we come at last."

The countryman throws off his coat, goes doggedly to work, and, after hours of digging, perhaps succeeds in dragging out and knocking the poor beast upon the head, and then swings the inglorious trophy upon his back to trudge away, triumphing in the prospective dollars. It may be he has to smoke poor Reynard to death in his hole, or else knock him on the nose as he rushes forth to the fresh air.

Truly this may be called "Crucigera," the cross-bearing variety of the genus, since it is subjected to such unorthodox and savage modes of persecution, which certainly entitle it to the crown of martyrdom, if not to the meeker glory of bearing the cross for the sins of all its wicked and witty family. Indeed, all the twelve tribes, in whatever part of the world they are found, may be said to "bear the cross" of slander and unmerited abuse from the whole quadrupidal kingdom.

But Reynard having somehow mysteriously, got a bad name for himself, is made amenable for all the cunning, sly, audacious things done among the animals, and is therefore considered, and really known to be, a grievously wicked person.

"It is no harm to abuse a poor devil whom the world unites in abusing," is the magnanimous motto of the mob, and poor Reynard has the full benefit of it, in an amount of obloquy and buffeting which would surely have been sufficient to chasten and reform the life of any but such an incorrigible.

I rather think he glories in bearing the cross, and courts martyrdom. I can perceive no symptoms of amendment.

He is still the glozing and subtle intriguant of the Greek fables. The old "romaunt" is still being enacted, and "all the beasts complain of the fox," daily and hourly, until king lion roars in wrath against his wily minister.

I fear there is no sober reform or hopeful redemption for the sad scamp, since his quaint malfeasances, instead of becoming more tempered and ameliorated by time, have grown only the more glaring and impudent as history brings him nearer to us.

Verily, it is a sad story that the records tell, for Chaucer found him still "a col fox, full of sleigh iniquitie," even in his day. The young poet, in the prattle of his "garrulous god, innocence," tells us a dreadful story of the morals and manners of Reynard in his time.

I think it should be blazoned now in the self-same words of him

> "Who first with harmony informed our tongue,"

that it may be kept before the eyes of all modern and juvenile Reynards, as a warning and example of the fearful consequences following upon the unrestrained indulgence of the predatory instinct they have inherited. It appears from Chaucer's evidence, that "Russel, the fox," *alias* Reynard, (for like all thieves and robbers he has an *alias*,) did

> "By high imagination forecast—"

(which hints, I suppose, at clairvoyance,) find his way

> "Into the yerde, there chaunticlere the faire
> Was wont and eke his wives to repaire."

This was of course only one of his accustomed jokes; and although he certainly seemed to be "on the sneak" when crouching

> "——— in a bed of wortes, still he lay,"

no intimate admirer of his ancestral glory would have suspected what dire and shameless purpose brought him there! The poet denounces him, as we have seen, with a just and dreadful denunciation, which, it would seem, must have been sufficient to arouse the conscience of anybody else, and send him with rebuked tail between his legs abashed away. But, nevertheless, observe how coldly it has fallen upon his deaf ear, and how, with oily words of glozing courtesy, he proceeds to assail the gallant and unsuspecting cock, upon his weak side of vanity and family pride. He tells him blandly—

"Save you ne herd I never man so sing
As did your fader in the morwening."

The silly bird believes him, and

"—— Stood high upon his toos,
Stretching his neck and held his eyen cloos,
And gan to crowen loud for the nones,
And Dan Russel, the fox, start up at ones,
And by the garget heute chaunticlere,
And on his back towards the wood him bere."

Then arises at sight of the daring depredator, the many-tongued hubbub of the barn-yard.

"The sely widow and her daughtren two,"

rush out in pursuit with broom-sticks and with staves, and cry "harow and wala wa, a ha, the fox!" and after him, too,

"Ran Colle, our dog, and Talbot and Gerlond,
And Malkin with her distaf in hire hond;
Ran cow and calf, and eke the veray hoggs."
* * * * * *
"They ronnen so hem thought their hertes breke,
They yelleden as fendes don in hell,
The dokes crieden as men would hem quelle,
The gees for fear flowen over the trees,
Out of the hive came the swarm of bees,
So hideous was the noise a *benedicte!*"

Shocking and abhorrent as is the view of the moral life of Russel, *alias* Reynard, here presented by the simple-hearted chronicler, there are yet more grievous and solemn charges laid to his door in the "Shepherd's Callender." I cannot but devoutly hope that the grand old Spencer is rather, in this case, after the confirmed manner of his "Faerie Queen," indulging in metaphor, than telling a veritable incident out of his own knowledge. His ominous words are concerning

"——A wily fox, that having spide,
Where on a sunny bank the lambes doo play,
Full closely creeping by the hinder side,
Lyes in ambushment of his hoped prey,
Ne stirreth limbe till seeing readie tide,
He rusheth forth and snatcheth quite away
One of the little younglings unawares."

This bloody, but cold and sneaking crime, wrought on innocence, so white-wooled, gaily, meek and unsuspecting, is too fearful to dwell upon. I can only drop the curtain here for the present, hoping that Reynard may not prove guilty, according to the poet's showing!

Certainly we are not much comforted when we take up the character of the "Gray Fox." Comparisons are proverbially odious, yet as an accurate historian, I have felt myself compelled to make them.

It must be admitted that the Gray Fox, as compared with the Red, is something of a sneak! They are both four-footed Jesuits, to be sure, but the latter is stouter, and besides has a family name, an ancestral glory to sustain! He is the Don Quixote of the foxes, and therefore we can well understand his hen-roost chivalry, not to speak of his barn-yard heroics!

Though we admit him to be great, we cannot help recognizing the Gray Fox as the special embodiment of all the blarney and lower cunning of the race. We are most familiar with him at the South, and feel a sort of local jealousy for his fame and character. We flatter ourselves that he can afford to be guilty of a few peccadillos, since they are contrasted by such extraordinary attributes.

Let anybody read the subjoined anecdote, by the Editors of the "Quadrupeds," and say afterwards, if he can, that the Gray Fox is not an extraordinary animal!

On a cold, drizzly, sleety, rainy day, while travelling in Carolina, we observed a Gray Fox in a field of broom-grass, coursing against the wind and hunting, in the manner of the pointer dog. We stopped to witness his manœuvres; suddenly he stood still, and squatted low on his haunches; a moment after he proceeded on once more, but with slow and cautious steps; at times his nose was raised higher in the air, moving about from side to side. At length he seemed to be sure of his game, and went straight forward, although very slowly, at times crawling on the earth; he was occasionally hidden by the grass, so that we could not see him very distinctly; however, at length we observed him make a dead halt. There was no twisting or horizontal movement of the tail, like that made by the common house-cat when ready to make a spring, but his tail seemed resting on the side, whilst his ears were drawn back and his head raised only a few inches from the earth.

He remained in this attitude nearly half a minute, and then made a sudden pounce upon his prey; at the same instant the whirring of the distracted covey was heard, as the affrighted birds took wing; two or three sharp screams succeeded, and the successful prowler immediately passed out of the field with an unfortunate partridge in his mouth, evidently with the intention of seeking a more retired spot to make a dainty meal.

We had a gun with us, and he passed within long gun shot of us. But we did not wound or destroy him? He has enabled us, for the first time, to bear witness that he is not only a dog, but a good pointer in the bargain; he has obeyed an impulse of nature, and obtained a meal in the manner in which it was intended by the wise Creator that he should be supplied. He seizes only a single bird, whilst man, who would wreak his vengeance on this poacher among the game, is not satisfied until he has killed half the covey with the murderous gun, or caught the whole brood in a trap, and wrung off their necks in triumph.

Condemn not the fox too hastily; he has a more strikingly carnivorous tooth than yourself, indicating the kind of food he is required to seek; he takes no wanton pleasure in destroying the bird; he exhibits to his companions no trophies of his skill, and is contented with a meal; whilst you are not satisfied when your capacious bird-bag is filled.

This anecdote is very curious and interesting for several reasons. In the first place, it exhibits the fox in a new character of higher intelligence, than he has credit for possessing, —and in the next, it goes far towards confirming the old Spanish legend, with regard to the pointer dog. This represents the pointer as a *made* variety, and not an original race.

The legend represents that a Spanish monk, first observed, in the wild dog of Andalusia, the trick of pausing before the spring upon its prey. As this pause was longer than in any other animal, the idea was at once suggested, that by training, this habit might be made useful. He accordingly tamed a number of these dogs, and finding them somewhat deficient in size, docility and scent, crossed them upon the nobler species of hound, and hence the pointer was derived.

I have always been inclined to regard this remarkable story as giving somewhere near the true origin of the pointer, and think it most likely that the wild dog mentioned, was a transition species between the wolf and fox. But apart from these conjectures, this incident illustrates from an entirely new point of view, the predatory habits of the species.

In the older States, as all other game has been nearly exterminated, these nine-lived creatures seem only to have become more abundant, more sagacious and more popular. Spencer, in his "Shepherd's Callender," very clearly intimates that this is not the first time in the history of men and foxes, that such a condition of things had existed. He says:

> "Well is it known that sith the Gascon King,
> Never was wolf seen, many nor some;
> Nor in all Kent nor in Christendome;
> But the fewer wolves (the sooth to sain,)
> The more bene the foxes that here remaine."

This animal seems to have been able to take care of itself, when all others have vanished before the exterminating tread of human progress. The game laws protect the Red Fox in England to an uncertain degree; but the Gray Fox protects itself here in a *certain* degree, without the aid of game laws, and seems in many districts, to defy all our efforts to exterminate it; while its sagacity, dexterity and cunning, seem only to have been increased by the difficulties and dangers of its environment.

Fox-hunting in the Middle and Southern States, is quite as much a subject of enthusiasm, as it has been in England; although it is neither so expensive nor so technical with us. We don't pay fifty guineas a couple for our hounds, or keep studs of "hunters" at prodigious cost; yet we are fox-hunters after a rude and untechnical manner; and although we do not ride in white tops and corduroys, yet we ride to the purpose; and through the rude and break-neck exigencies of thicket, forest, fallen trees, precipitous hills, rough rocks, precipices, quaggy swamps and fatal quicksands, we are still the eager and staunch hunters of a game as staunch. Our horses doubly trained in the deer and fox-hunt, are more wiry and active than the English hunters, although they may not be so heely in passing over open ground, or so well trained in leaping over hedges and ditches! And, finally, as for dogs, their genealogies have been quite scrupulously preserved in the old Scates. Even at this day, we frequently find the Shaksperian ideal of the dog, still carefully maintained:—

"My hounds are bred out of the Spartan kind,
So flew'd, so sanded; and their heads are hung
With ears that sweep away the morning dew,
Crook-knee'd and dew-lapped, like Thessalian bulls
Slow in pursuit, but matched in mouth-like bells."

From Maryland to Florida, and farther west, through Kentucky and Alabama to Mississippi and Louisiana, fox-hunting next to deer hunting is the favorite amusement of sportsmen, and the *chase* of that animal may in fact be regarded exclusively as a southern sport in the United States, as the fox is never followed on horseback in the North, where the rocky and precipitous character of the surface in many districts prevents the best riders from attempting it; whilst in others, our sturdy, independent farmers would not like to see a dozen or more horsemen leaping through fences, and with breakneck speed gallopping through the wheat-fields, or other "fall" crops. Besides, the Red Fox, which is more generally found in the northern States than the gray species, runs so far before the dogs that he is seldom seen, although the huntsmen keep up with the pack, and after a chase of ten miles, during which he may not have been once seen, he perhaps takes refuge in some deep fissure of a rock, or in an impenetrable burrow, which of course ends the sport, very much to the satisfaction of the fox.

In the southern States, on the contrary, the ground is, in many cases, favorable to this amusement, and the planter sustains but little injury from the passing hunt, as the Gray Fox usually courses through woods or worn out old fields, keeping on high dry ground, and seldom, during the chase, running across a cultivated plantation.

In fox-hunting, it is well known that the horse usually becomes as much excited as his rider; and at the cry of the hounds, I have known an old steed, which had been turned loose in the woods to pick up a subsistence, prick up his ears, and in an instant start off full gallop until he overtook the pack, keeping in the run until the chase was ended.

In the older southern States the modes of hunting the Gray Fox are much alike. To the sound of winding horns the neighboring gentry collect at an appointed place, each accompanied by his favorite dogs, and usually a negro driver to manage them and keep them from starting deer. Mounted on fine horses, accustomed to the sport, they send in the hounds and await the start, chatting in a group, collected in some by-road, or some high spot of open ground from which they can hear every sound borne upon the breeze. Thickets on the edges of plantations, briar patches, and deserted fields covered with bloom-grass, are places where the fox is most likely to have his bed. The trail he has left behind him during his nocturnal rambles being struck, the hounds are encouraged by the voices of their drivers to as great speed as the devious course it leads them will permit. Now they scent the trail the fox has left along the field, when in search of partridges, meadow-larks, rabbits or field-mice; presently they trace his footsteps to some large log, from whence he has jumped on to a worm-fence, and after walking a little way on it, leaped a ditch and skulked towards the borders of a marsh. Through all his crooked ways the sagacious hounds unravel his trail, until he is suddenly roused, perchance from a dreamy vision of fat hens, geese or turkeys, and with a general cry, the whole pack, led on by the staunchest and best dogs, open-mouthed and eager, join the chase. The startled fox makes two or three rapid doublings, and then suddenly flies to a cover, perhaps a quarter of a mile off, and sometimes thus puts the hounds off the scent for a few minutes, as when cool and at first starting his scent is not so strong as that of the Red Fox.

After the chase has continued for a quarter of an hour or so, and the animal is somewhat heated, his track is followed with greater ease and quickness, and the scene becomes animating and exciting. Now the masters dash into the chase, and with wild, eager yells of bursting excitment, they spur after the roaring pack and regardless plunge at headlong speed over and through the difficulties of the ground.

When the woods are free from underbrush, which is often the case in Virginia and the Carolinas, the grass and bushes being burnt almost annually, many of the sportsmen keep up with the dogs, and the fox is frequently in sight. He now resorts to some of the manœuvres for which he is famous; he plunges into a thicket, doubles, runs into the water, leaps on to a log, or perhaps gets upon a worm fence and runs along the top of it for a hundred yards, leaping from it with a desperate bound and continuing his flight in the vain hope of escape. At length he becomes fatigued; he once more drives into the closest thickets, where he doubles hurriedly; he hears and even sees the dogs upon him, and as a last resort climbs a small tree. The hounds and hunters are almost instantly at the foot of it, and while the former are barking fiercely at the terrified animal, the latter usually determine to give him another chance for his life. The dogs are taken off to a little distance, and the fox is forced to leap to the ground by reaching him with a long pole or throwing a billet of wood at him; he is allowed a quarter of an hour before the hounds are permitted to pursue him; but he is now less able to escape than before, he has become stiff and chill, is soon overtaken, and falls an easy prey, turning, however, upon his pursuers, with a fierce despair, and snapping at them indomitably, game to the last.

The extraordinary cunning and sagacity of the Gray Fox is so much the constant theme of Southern hunters, that we might collect quite a volume of well authenticated stories of its feats; but the best of the joke is, that wonderful as are the stories they tell of it, we in Kentucky, and wherever the Red Fox has yet made its appearance, manage to out-Herod

Herod in the wonders we have to tell concerning *it;* so, that on the whole, the question of rivalry may be set down as near about as long as it is short.

Admitting all the champions of the Red Fox desire, the Gray Fox must be acknowledged to be smart, decidedly smart! It frequently climbs trees with an awkward readiness, particularly in the summer time—but its favorite resort is to holes. Indeed, from what I remember of the Gray Fox, I should say emphatically that it was "of the earth, earthy," for in limestone regions, such as Kentucky, Tennessee, &c., where sinks or holes in the ground are abundant, the fellow only condescends to run for recreation, and takes to a hole precisely as soon as he becomes blown.

An incident occurred in my own experience, and in the southern part of Kentucky, illustrating the astonishing sagacity of this fox. I was enthusiastically addicted to fox hunting, and kept a fine pack of hounds. Several young men of the neighborhood kept packs of dogs also, and we used very frequently to meet, and join in the chase with all our forces.

There was a certain briary old field of great extent, near the middle of which we could on any morning of the year, start a Gray Fox. After a chase of an hour or so, just enough to blow the dogs and horses well, we would invariably lose the fox at a given spot, the fence corner of a large plantation, which was opened into a heavy forest on one side of this old field! The frequency and certainty of this event became the standing joke of the country. Fox hunters from other neighborhoods would bring their pack for miles, to have a run out of this mysterious fox, in the hope of clearing up the mystery. But no. They were all baffled alike. We often examined the ground critically, to find out, if possible, the mode of escape, but could discover nothing, that in any way accounted for it, or suggested any thing in regard to it. That it did not fly, was very sure; that it must escape along the fence in some way was equally so. My first idea was, that the animal, as is very common, had climbed upon the top rail of the fence, and walked along it to such a distance before leaping off, that the dogs were entirely thrown out. I accordingly followed the fence with the whole pack about me, clear round the plantation, but without striking the trail again or making any discovery.

The affair now became quite serious. The reputation of our hounds was suffering; and besides, I found they were really losing confidence in themselves, and would not run with half the staunch eagerness which had before characterized them. The joke of being regularly baffled, had been so often repeated, that they now came to consider it a settled thing that they were never to shake another fox again, and were disposed to give up in despair. Some of the neighbors had grown superstitious about it, and vowed that this must be a weir-fox, who could make himself invisible when he pleased.

At last I determined to watch at the fence-corner, and see what became of the fox. Within about the usual time, we heard him heading towards the mysterious corner, as the voices of the pack clearly indicated. I almost held my breath in my concealment, while I watched for the appearance of this extraordinary creature. In a little while, the fox made his appearance, coming on at quite a leisurely pace, a little in advance of the pack. When he reached the corner, he climbed in a most unhurried and deliberate way to the top rail of the fence, and then walked along it, balancing himself as carefully as a rope-dancer. He proceeded down the side of the fence next to the forest in which I was concealed.

I followed cautiously, so as just to keep him in view. Before he had thus proceeded more than two hundred yards, the hounds came up to the corner, and he very deliberately paused and looked back for a moment, then he hurried on along the fence some paces farther, and when he came opposite a dead, but leaning tree, which stood inside the fence, some twelve or sixteen feet distant, he stooped, made a high and long bound to a knot upon the side of its trunk, up which he ran, and entered a hollow in the top where it had been broken off, near thirty feet from the ground, in some storm. I respected the astuteness of the trick too much to betray its author, since I was now personally satisfied; and he continued for a long time yet, while I kept his secret, to be the wonder and the topic of neighboring fox-hunters, until at last one of them happened to take the same idea into his head, and found out the mystery. He avenged himself by cutting down the tree, and capturing the smart fox.

The tree stood at such a distance from the fence, that no one of us, who had examined the ground, ever dreamed of the possibility that the fox would leap to it; it seemed a physical impossibility; but practice and the convenient knot had enabled cunning Reynard to overcome it, with assured ease. I quote an incident from the Quadrupeds of America of nearly the same class.

Shortly after the rail road from Charleston to Hamburg, South Carolina, had been constructed, the rails, a portion of the distance, having been laid upon timbers at a considerable height from the ground, supported by strong posts, we observed a fox which was hard pressed by a pack of hounds, mounting the rails, upon which he ran several hundred yards; the dogs were unable to pursue him, and thus he crossed a deep cypress swamp, over which the rail road was in this singular manner carried, and made his escape on the opposite side.

The late Benjamin C. Yancy, Esq., an eminent lawyer, who in his youth was very fond of fox hunting, related the following:—A fox had been pursued, near his residence in Edgefield, several times, but the hounds always lost the track at a place where there was a foot-path leading down a steep hill. He, therefore, determined to conceal himself near this declivity the next time the fox was started, in order to discover his mode of baffling the dogs at this place. The animal was accordingly put up and chased, and at first led the hounds through many bayous and ponds in the woods, but at length came running over the brow of the hill along the path, stopped suddenly and spread himself out flat and motionless on the ground. The hounds came down the hill in pursuit at a dashing pace, and the whole pack passed, and did not stop until they were at the bottom of the hill. As soon as the immediate danger was over, the fox, casting a furtive glance around him, started up, and ran off at his greatest speed.

I knew an instance much resembling the last given; but this was a Red Fox. It was in the remarkable bluffs of the Kentucky river.

The fox had always been lost at the edge of one of these abrupt cliffs, which faced the river. The place had often been examined by the hunters, but as the descent was nearly a sheer perpendicular of several hundred feet, it had only to be looked over to convince the beholder that the fox must have wings to leap down it in safety. At last a hunter determined to watch the fox, and accordingly lay in wait. He saw the creature come to the edge of the bluff and look down. Ten feet below, there was a break in the perpendicular line, which formed a sort of steppe nearly a foot in width. The movement by which he let himself down to this, was something between a leap and a slide, but it nevertheless landed him safe on the shelf; and then it appeared that this was the mouth of a wide fissure in the rock. The most curious part of this story is, that the hunter discovered another and easy entrance to the cave from the level ground above. This the fox never used when the hounds were on his trail, as the more perilous entrance from the front cut short the scent, and prevented the discovery of his retreat. He could only get down that way and came out by the other opening from the level.

CHAPTER XI.

THE TEXAN HUNTRESS.

MY dissertation of the last chapter upon the Fox and Fox Hunting, though strictly germain to the general theme, has caused me in some measure to lose sight of the individuality of the Hunter-Naturalist in one of his favorite sports. Though I have turned aside, through many pages, to present nobler exemplars of the character, still I must be here permitted to resume that broken thread of personal narrative, in which I commenced to recount something of its humble and inner experiences on the rough highway of development; and now, evil, and wild, and stern as they may be, I shall continue to depict them with an unfaltering hand, for the lessons they should convey.

The rude and hardy sports in which my boyhood, youth and opening manhood had been spent with such devotion, had yet not been sufficiently engrossing to divert or turn aside that morbid revulsion of the passions, which inevitably supervenes upon their first fiery introduction—at this critical period—to reality outside the holiday world of Dreams and Books.

Indeed, I had scarcely stepped beyond the threshold of the closet, and found myself under the sun, out in the broad world, before the sickness of this spiritual revulsion came over me. I felt the thin wings of the delicate visions I had nurtured in scholastic shades, wilt and curl up, as I have seen the dew-flower petals beneath a flaming noon. Ah! a grievous sickness—almost unto death—that was, when I saw those exquisite frail things all dying.

They were the creatures of the soul's first spring-time, of softer glowing hues, and breathing fresher odors than ever come again; and what the sun had spared—when the tinkling trample of the curt, gray frost went over them—were snapped and strewn—stark in their own beauties—dead! The glory and the joy passed from the earth with them—a huge desolation spinning on its poles—I stood upon its wide blank, deaf and blind, with one word burning in ghastly light through darkened brain and soul!—*a curse!* It was a purpose—it was a savage ecstacy, to live and curse all,—God, woman, man! to walk through life until I *chose* to die, hating and defiant. I laughed hoarsely as I hugged the pleasant madness to my heart. O, rare and mirthfulest conceit! Revenge.

Hate! scorn! Ha! ha! I shouted in my bitterness; right royal brotherhood for the stout spirit. What a carnival the game of life will be to us—only we wont throw sugar-plums. *I* lie down upon the grass and sob and pule like a tripping Cupid over his crushed flowers? Manly employment that!

When here is a world swarming with fools to scorn; and a wide air, tremulous with the beat of hearts, to trample on; a Universe pregnant with some hideous Power to be defied! And then the proud exultation—to stalk on, beneath God's own lights, wronging his creatures, and taunting him to send his bolts.

A new energy was possessing me. Life became stronger than it ever had been before, though my body was wasting. When the first wild whirl of this delirious excitement had passed away, the horrible transformation was completed, for an ashy-pale cold twilight, which no sunshine could dispel or warm, had settled upon my whole being—an icy ring palpably clung around my heart, which beat sharply and fast in the centre—my forehead was cold, but the brain was seething and glowing behind it.

I felt a chill, unnatural, flaming in my eyes. I was afraid to look at them; I saw little children shrink in affright as they gazed at me. Then I knew there was hate and hell in them, and felt glad—for there was *some* of the old leaven left in spite of me—that innocence would be alarmed of its own instincts, and avoid me. I was stolidly sullen or hysterically merry, and felt the strangest inclination to laugh when I saw others weep. I would hide my face in my handkerchief, and laugh until my sides ached at what were to others the most touching exhibitions of grief.

I read incessantly, and out of all literature managed to extract the bitter waters. My sharpened and morbid fancy conceived that it could trace the creed of the logician, with its doubts, its sophisms, and its sneers, through "all records of all times." Yet I regarded the Berkeley, Volney, and Tom Paine school with profound contempt. These people attempted —vulgarly enough—to "reason" themselves into atheism and universal scepticism—nothing could have been more absurd; and Hume would have been placed in the same category, but that he took to sneering and generalization. Voltaire was the Bayard of these weapons, and his compeers learned to use them. Gibbon possessed a subtle insight, and wielded the borrowed thrust effectually.

I hated and scorned the Truths of Christianity not as "a Reasoner" but as an Idealist. I did not, in my morbid madness, regard, though familiar with them, the historic evidences of Christ's Godship and Mission. Had the same evidence proved that he came in a chariot, with blazing worlds for wheels, and myriad legions of the seraphim, with fiery swords about Him, that reaped a nation from the lap of earth, I should have been no more impressed by it than by the simple story of Calvary. Mere "Reason," I saw plainly enough, to be utterly incompetent to deal with the sublimity of that sacrifice, as I had seen it, and known it to be, with the simpler yet lofty devotion of common humanity.

No; regarding our world as a mere infinitesimal mite of the Infinite Universe, I impiously questioned, why and how the creative and governing source of these myriad worlds could recognize the atomies upon this speck of his dominions, as alone worth the sacrifice of His Son, and whether such a sacrifice had been made for the rebels of other worlds; and recognizing, too, in my philosophy, the separate entity of the soul, and the mere animal life—I insanely *demanded* those spiritual evidences and revelations His followers professed to receive, and which proved to them that the God of all was present here, regardful of every hair of our heads, and even of every sparrow that should fall upon this molecule of space! Unfortunately, these evidences could never come to such demands; with all the travail of an eager and presumptuous spirit, they had not yet appeared. My faith, or imagination, had been appealed to, yet, through nothing palpable it could lay hold of; and the earnest logician, who *starts* with doubt, will certainly never *reason* himself out of the labyrinth. The more he reasons the more he doubts.

The beginning and the end with him is doubt. He doubts

everything—the justice and the being of God—for he measures him, his entity, and his acts, by the human standard—the truth and virtue of his race—for he measures them by what he has felt and realized to be his own *capabilities* of evil; and so he goes on, until life—its purposes, its duties, its realities—becomes to him one vast lie—a monstrous illusion; and himself, with his passions and their ferocious cravings, the only actuality—his own volition, the focal power round which and for which, the universe revolves. This devouring egotism—though more, in my instance, an intellectual, than a moral vice—had swallowed up all social ties.

I could recognize society now, only as a masked battle-field, in which every man, as captain of his own passions, saw in each fellow man he met a sworn instinctive foe, leading his own cohort of selfish passions in the grand *melée* of life. The individual contests, then, were decided by the cool and wary subtlety of the Olympic wrestler. The genial virtues, family ties, friendship, love, benevolence, constituted the mere masquerade of the great central instinct, *selfishness!*

This infernal creed grew upon me, until I became, in plain words, a devil. Those who had known me and loved me as the gay, frank, confiding enthusiast, stared at my altered face and relentless savagery of manner—first in speechless astonishment, and then turned aside to weep! When I laughed at and mocked their tears, they tried to think me mad—but I was too coolly and rationally brutal for that. They could not put me in a strait jacket, but could only wonder and grieve.

The very fiends of hell would have been aghast at the awful phantasies which came and dwelt with me as matters of course. I could think of stabbing my own friend, as a common-place thing to be *calculated* upon. I became morose and vicious in my temper until my best friends avoided me, and those who had given me cause for enmity would turn aside from my path. I had become a downright nuisance, with my wicked, scornful gibing at everything men hold sacred. As to women—"to search the bottom of annoy," and gall, and pain them with the most studied and cruel raillery, was an especially pleasant recreation—the enjoyment of which was heightened in the precise ratio of their beauty and wit—or, as I pretended to myself, of their power to deceive and ruin the moral lives of others, as mine had been blasted by them. At last I sickened of such tame amusements.

I thirsted—my blood was on fire for sterner excitements—I longed to meet death face to face, and look on carnage. It was an anticipated ecstacy of proud and fierce delight—the thought of meeting my detested fellows openly at the weapon's point. I had champed with the social manacles on, over my stifled hate, until endurance was no longer possible. I looked around upon the world for the scenes and circumstances fitted to the gratification of such pleasant humors. Texas was a very paradise of monsters—the vicious, the desperate, the social and civil outlaws of all the world had gathered there.

Delightful fraternity of devils!—they were fighting among themselves, fighting with the Mexicans, fighting with the Indians, and for recreation—to keep their hands in—were battling with the wild beasts. Charming existence! How it attracted me! how I yearned to participate in its pleasures. I madly severed the few remaining ties, and started for this El Dorado of the ruffian.

My friends saw me go, I believe, with a mournful sense of relief. Though I had been guilty of no overt outrage against the laws of society, yet my moral presence had become pestilential, and they felt that the morbid disease which was withering up my soul, must find its own cure. I found myself in just the element I needed in this country. I met with men capable of all I dared to do—as hard and reckless, as God-defying and man-hating, as could be desired. I felt at home and at ease with such men—we understood each other!

We carried our lives in our hands—or, what is in other words the same thing—our weapons.

It added very much to my relish of the sense of being, the consciousness that I could get myself shot at any time by crooking my finger. It was a novel sensation—the having one's life so entirely at our command—at least the holding it in such complete dependence upon one's prompt right arm. And then the occasional divertisement of quelling some red-handed bully—as cowardly as he was ferocious. It was a refreshing exultation to unmask such villains, and see their white livers paling through their cheeks.

But the life in the cities and settlements was a mere foretaste. I must go to the frontier to meet the dusky chivalry of the mountains on the "Debatable Ground" of the plains. What, with the open struggle with these wild warriors,—gaunt, half naked, subtle—and guarding against the secret and murderous treachery of the Mexican,—I expected to find employment enough, and glut my passions with the tumult of strange perils!

Perhaps then my blood would grow cooler, the fever might go off, and leave me thinking and feeling more as I once did! for I longed at times to get back to the ground I had left, but could not now! The disease must have its course. I was plunging into all this madness to get away from my own consciousness, to hide from the frightful realization of my own doctrines!

I would say, parenthetically, that this recital is not intended for the sleepy, lymphatic denizens of the "namby pamby inane." Your "perfect people," who never had a sinful thought, a passion above beef-steak, or a higher adventure than overturning a poor woman's apple-stall,—their very blood would be congealed at the idea of reading a line from the pen of so wicked a wretch as I have described myself to have been. But *men* and *women* who have thought, felt, analyzed, seen, acted and remembered, will recognize the idiosyncracy of this case, as set forth, to be common to one of the necessary stages of the inner life's development. Suffice it! To the frontier I did go,—and now for the story of my adventurings there.

The incidents I am about to give are some of them familiar to leading men of Texas, though they have never been related in print. On my way out I had stopped to visit at the house of a friend, who was a planter, living high up on the Brazos River. Our time was principally occupied in hunting. As I had just arrived in the country, the abundant sport afforded by the numbers and variety of the game, with which it might be said literally to swarm, afforded a diversion to my morbid feeling, and kept me in a continued state of eager excitement. I was on my horse the greater part of the time.

Though not a raw woodsman, so far as making my way through the heavy forests of the West was concerned, yet finding myself for the first time upon the vast and unaccustomed expanse of the Southern Prairies, I was for a long time surprised that though excessively reckless, I should be here much perplexed, and even timid, in attempting to find my way.

The land-marks are so different, as well as the modes of using them, from those to which I had been accustomed, that I was frequently confused and overwhelmed with awe on finding myself left in the vicissitudes of the hunt, alone amidst the illimitable solitudes, with no experienced eye to see for me the course, where all was trackless.

When I would thus get "*turned round*," as it is called, and the consciousness that I had lost my course, would drive the blood to my heart: the startled sense of the revulsion is difficult to describe. Body and soul would seem for a moment as if sinking under the weight of a drear solemnity, and then the returning blood would leap back to the brow, thrilling every fibre with a shudder. A thousand stories of bloody deaths under the reeking scalping-knife of savage hordes, met in the wide wilderness of plains; of confused circlings day by day, always bringing the victim back to his own trail, until the dreary, lingering death of starvation relieved the bewilderment; of banded wolves with gaping jaws, hungry yells and tireless feet, pursuing the uncertain flight which has betrayed to their ferocious instinct a sure prey in the *lost* man; of grim, creeping panthers springing from the thicket upon the deep sleep of his fruitless exhaustion; of the wild, vague and unutterable horror of lonely, unavenged and unrecorded death in a thousand forms,—until self-possession reeled, and the mad impulse was to strike spurs into my horse and plunge blindly on amidst them all.

This singular sensation gradually loses its intensity, when, by a series of happy accidents, rather than instincts, we gain more confidence, and it requires a less forlorn struggle to recall ourselves to calmness and the cool consideration of the position in which we are thrown.

But let there be as many lessons as can well be crowded into a year or two of such wild experiences, yet he is a man of very strong nerve who can, even then, draw up his horse, after a heated chase of buffalo, deer, or wolf, or bear, and not feel much of this appalled startle when, the slaughter over, he looks around with aching eyes for the first time to see where he is.

A sinking sense of loneliness and awe is the reaction of the fierce and headlong excitement, under which he has been hurled, as it were, he knows not in what direction, or how far. He gazes around him in breathless silence and nameless dread for awhile; the contrast of the stilless, now that death has intervened, with the crashing, raging impetus which brought him here, is too oppressive, and he dares not make a sound; he almost shudders while the dim consciousness that he has just done murder in the sight of his peaceful mother, Earth, comes over him reproachfully amidst her voiceless calms; and the whole forest, with its straight stems, the broad plain with its flower eyes, the benignant sun, the wide air itself, all seem for one instant to have stood still to gaze upon the unholy deed. There lies the quiet victim! He feels their reproach as he looks upon its fixed, but undimmed eyes.

He cannot stand all this. I said it was but for one instant, and then his habitual hardness returns; the awe he throws off with a sneer; the carcass is slung upon his horse, and he turns its head towards the nearest high land to look how the country lies. If he recognizes no familiar land-marks, and he sees that he is out of his range, he then takes his course by the direction of the prevailing winds, the moss upon the trees, the position of the sun, the course of the streams or of the buffalo trails, by the flight of birds, or thousand other telegraphic characters which he has learned to read.

But then he has nevertheless experienced, however briefly, this vague feeling of terror and dread, to which we have alluded, and no one but an old skinny Trapper, whose whole life has been spent among the mountains, ever entirely loses this sensation on realizing that he is lost in these mighty solitudes; because, in the first place, he is never lost, and in the next, if he were, it would be all the same to him. He can live wherever a snail, a lizzard, or a raven can live, and he cares little if he never sees the face of man for a year or two; in that time he is sure to come out somewhere, even if it be on the Pacific coast! The deep gorges of the mountains afford him shelter and repose in winter; the open plain or forest glades a couch in summer; a rock is pillow soft enough for him, and piping winds do well for lullabies, though they do bring the thunder for their bass!

He starves until ravin makes him wild, and then his rifle is more inexorable than the bolts of death. The famishing wolf is merciful to him. Earth and her creatures are nothing, now, but fuel and food to glut his shriveled maw. Blood! blood! Blood is to him Ambrosia. The Nectar of the gods would not tempt him from the greasy esculence of "beaver tail!" He is ecstatic upon "buffalo hump," and sups his divinest inspiration from a gourd of "bar's grease." What knows he, then, of that "dim religious awe" within the natural temples of the Most High, at which I have hinted! Not he! He has become in these temples what the world calls a *practical* priest, and cuts up the "flesh offerings" like a saw, as harsh and as steely hard!

But to return to our story. The day's hunt had been an unusually exciting one. We hunted deer after the following fashion. These animals feed principally upon the open prairie, but about eleven o'clock, A. M. they may be seen in long lines sauntering towards the nearest wood, which usually, throughout Texas, grows upon the margin of the small lakes or banks of streams.

They are now going to water, and repose in the shade until three or four o'clock in the afternoon, when they come out to feed again. The deer of the prairies is a very swift variety, with smaller antlers than the common buck of our forests bears. We stationed ourselves some half a mile distant in the prairie on fleet horses, some who were most skilled with the common "lasso" of the country, and others with our holster pistols, as in my own case. A negro "driver," as he is called, was then sent in with dogs on the opposite side of the wood to drive the deer out upon the plain; for, contrary to the usage of the common deer, this creature of the plains makes always for open ground directly when pursued, and we awaiting their exit chased them by sight on our horses. We had but little time to wait, for within twenty minutes out burst a numerous herd. It was a splendid sight as they came plunging into the long grass and sunshine, out from the dark shadows suddenly, with their white throats, their "antlered pride" thrown back, and round ears laid sharp behind to hearken the pursuing cry of "bell-mouthed" hound. It is one of the most exciting scenes I know in the sports of our country.

We reined up our horses for the start; bending forward

with eager eye and bounding pulse to wait the instant when they should have passed us on their way into the illimitable plain upon which they trust to their flying feet for safety. But though those tiny hoofs be fleet enough to leave the Red Wolf far behind, or dart beyond the agile panther's leap, yet our good steeds, that champ and plunge impatiently, are far more fleet than they. Now they go bounding by with long, high leaps over the tall, embarrassing grass, and seem as if they half wore wings, and were afraid to use them. Now, too, with a wild shout of pent-up excitement, we are off on the chase, each man selecting his special prey. There is little use for the whip and spur in this hunt, for when a horse has once tasted its fierce and headlong pleasures, he needs no other stimulant after. They, like their riders, become furious with the excitement, and sometimes will bite the poor animal when they come up with it after a long chase.

The broad, white tails of the deer produce a droll effect as they rise and fall along the surface of the grass, and serve as a sort of fluttering beacon to the eye in the early part of the run; for, when they, at first sight of you, fairly straighten themselves in their frightened speed, they leave horse and rider far enough behind; but this does not last long; they are very fat at this season, the fall, and do not hold out at this rate. They soon begin to flag from the heat and dragging weight of the grass, which is now nearly as high as their backs. We gradually close upon them, and the herd begins to break up, scattering here and there and everywhere. Your eye has become fixed upon a particular one, a noble buck, whose powerful form has attracted you. Your horse has caught the same object, and divines you well as he turns his head to follow it, without regard to the course taken by the rest.

Now the excitement becomes a delirium of action; and as you find yourself farther separated from the other sounds of the chase, your own individual passions become more and more intensified upon the immediate object before you, and you rush on, you know not whither. My game on this day proved to be much more long-winded and powerful than usual, and I had, as the consequence, a tremendous race of it before I began to gain very rapidly upon its flight. At length the buck began to make leaps a little less long and high, and my horse, by this time thoroughly heated in the run, to snort with eagerness as he let out an additional link or two of speed. I closed rapidly with the quarry, and loosened my holsters for the shot which was to close the scene. Now my horse, with ears laid back, closes up alongside, and with trembling haste the pistol is snatched from the holster. With all its desperate speed we almost touch the hair with the muzzle before we fire—between the shoulders—and it is down! —tumbling, in the impulse of its flight, forward with broken neck bent beneath the body.

It is over! We are silent and still. The bloody work is finished, and I look around for the first time to see where I am, or what is in sight. I am amongst a wild Archipelago of islands, or "motts" of timber, with long, irregular vistas stretching between them in all directions. My victim lies at my feet quiet enough now. The strong breeze cools my heated forehead. The hush is profound at first, for every voice of nature has been frightened into silence by the violent scene which had just occurred to desecrate a peaceful home; but gradually, before my confused sense has time to realize the scene, the rap, rap, rapping of a wood-pecker's hammer stole timidly out from the nearest "mott," and then sound after sound, resumed in the same low key, hesitated forth from bird and insect, showing that Nature was yet alive, although just now so appalled.

I gazed around—with something of the dim confused perception of one awakening from the deep sleep of troubled dream —into the lengthening vistas stretching by uncertain glimpses into remotest distance—when gradually the overwhelming realization of the vastness came upon me, and then the shuddering consciousness that I was *lost!*—as utterly lost as if I had just dropped upon the planet from the moon, with a piece of green cheese in my fist. I had lost all idea of course, distance, or time during the chase, and now was completely "turned round." I immediately felt the full dangers of my situation. I knew the direction in which we had started, but knew, too, as well, that from the numerous turns the chase had taken, that I could no more tell which way to start back than if I had been physically blind, as I had, in fact, been mentally so.

I had imprudently come out without a pocket compass, and was a young *woodsman* lost upon strange *plains.* I did not know enough of the geography of the country to render what knowledge I had of natural signs of any avail to me here. I was, in a word, sufficiently panic-struck to act more like the inexperienced person that I was, than with the self-possession these circumstances so much required. My heart beat very loud and fast as I wheeled my horse, and with a sultry feeling of recklessness, spurred him into one of the narrow openings, without stopping one moment to consider which way or whither it should lead me. The poor deer I left upon the spot where it fell, for I was too much startled to think of dissecting it now—since, of all the terrible fates that could ever befall a human being, this of being lost in such a country, had always been most formidable to me.

I had known of so many instances of terrible suffering and dreary death from such a cause, at this early time,—when even individual settlements were sometimes eighty or a hundred miles apart in the direction of Galveston, and none in the oppcsite direction for thousands,—that now the chill revulsion seemed first like present annihilation, and then like such remote and undefined suffering as was far more formidable; so I urged on vaguely—hoping nothing, trusting nothing, but simply asking for action to distract—and a crisis to end the suspense.

My horse apparently sympathized with my terror and despair, for he rushed on with a frightened speed, which at any other time would have been frightful, but now was only congenial. I recognized no object that we passed—each melted into the other, forming on either hand a sort of back-running liquefaction of mountain and tree, of plain and sky, that seemed to be keeping time with my motion. I was riding through a dim land, where nothing looked real but all infinite—where the end was I did not know.

It was not long before I gained the open plain, upon which there was, indeed, nothing but grass and horizon, but which appeared to me the wide end of all things. It was like galloping on clouds toward the moon or "the jumping-off place"—the distance seemed so inappreciable! yet I urged on. The grass sparrow chirped and flitted, I suppose,—the deer turned round to stare, no doubt,—the partridge roared its sudden under-bass of wings and skimmed away, bending the grass-tops with its windy whirr, for all I know, but yet I saw them not but as we see swift shadows in a stormy dream. I shouted like a crazy man.

I fired my other pistol in the air, in the hope that some of the party of hunters might hear it—then I paused to listen. My frightened and impatient horse would chafe and plunge for a moment, and again, as if divining why I paused, would be still as death; and now with pricked ears, pointed stiffly here and there, seem listening round him for a sound—and then would snuff the breeze with his wide, eager nostrils, and with an impulse, headlong and impatient as my own, bound onward—as the steady, winging raven that followed, over head, our course, croaked an answer that sounded so like self-congratulation.

Away! away! away! and still no sight—and still no sound that came to us with any promise—a herd of mustangs would scurry off, snorting as we passed—a squad of buffaloes, wheeling sharp about, and like hogsheads inspired of hoofs, with tails stuck straight in air, go lumber away over the shaking plain—but nothing like human form appeared. The first madness had passed off—the instinct of the love of life had assumed its place, and the blurred vision had become intensified by the sharpening apprehension which the physical brought, of thirst, hunger and exhaustion.

I saw objects clearly now. Every line in the horizon was distinctly defined, and conveyed to me a sort of hope. All things, indeed, took their relations again, and I was unfrightened into calm. I knew my danger, in detail, and saw every blade of grass that marked my way towards—what? I heard the odd ejaculation of the long-necked blue cranes explode upon the silence like a distant pistol shot—I saw the flowers bend, and the meadow lark, with its dark feather-heart outside its musical breast, bound up from the grass with its low fluttering flight, to sing on wing most sweetly, of all joy, though filled with fear. The very sand rat that had darted with a faint squeak to its hole, I saw peep forth again as I went past, so minutely did my vision take in everything now.

I had ridden on for several hours, the country at each moment becoming still more strange. There were no objects in which I could detect the slightest degree of familiarity—my horse was beginning to fail, and dreading lest he would give out beneath me, I reined him up. This would, indeed, be a fate too terrible to contemplate—being left on foot in the midst of these great plains! I got down and stroked his panting sides and walked with him for an hour, until he seemed to be regaining his strength somewhat, for the morning's work had been tremendous, as I in my unrecking despair, had kept him urged to nearly the top of his speed during this foolish ride. Fortunately, he was one of those game and indomitable horses formed by crossing the mustang, which is an Arab, upon the larger-boned Northern horse, or he could never have survived such a run.

I had supposed that my only chance of escape lay in keeping one direction, for, that circling commenced, each turn made lessened the chances. But now that I came to reason somewhat coolly about my position, it became apparent to me, that in this time I had, in pursuing this straight line, passed over more than treble the possible distance to the plantation of my friend, and that, of course, I must therefore either have taken the wrong direction or have passed it without observing. Then commenced that fatal series of doubts, fears, surmises, trials, in this and that direction, which is usually the indication of syncope in this disease of getting lost. Each failure only bewilders you the more—each turn makes "confusion worse confounded." But, nevertheless, some change had become necessary. I might be every moment going away from the reach of help—getting deeper and deeper into the trackless waste! But which way shall I turn? I now remembered, for the first time, that I had failed to trust any thing to my horse in choosing my direction.

If I had done so in the first place, the chances were that the extraordinary instinct possessed by many of these animals, would have carried me right! I have, in frequent instances, found this instinct infallible, especially when the animal was closely crossed upon the Arab blood. That noble race, which bore the earliest children of Ham in the chase across the shifting deserts, inherits all the strange instincts, with regard to courses and distances, which the wild and perilous uses of their hunter-lords developed in them, through the centuries which have developed as well our civilization. They are, therefore, best suited, until the *camel* comes, to traverse with security the "unhoused wilderness" of the great south-west. That wonderful animal has not yet been introduced upon these plains, although much has been done by myself and others to awaken public attention to its importance. Such an advent will entirely revolutionize the commerce and travel of the plains. The camel must carry our civilization over these deserts, as it has brought that of the ancient east upon its uncouth back towards the triumphing West.

I stopped my horse entirely, and dropping the reins upon his back, urged him slightly with my spurs—very slightly. When he found himself free, he shook his head to realize it, and then, stopping, turned his gaze around and around him several times—but yet he seemed to be bewildered, and only moved hesitatingly, first in this direction and then in that. If he had taken his course at once, I should have felt some hope—but my heart sank in me as I saw from his manner that he felt what was expected of him, but had become confused. Had he taken any particular direction and pursued it steadily, with accelerated speed, I should have been entirely secure, because then I would have been impressed that he knew he was right, and could ultimately bear us through. His hesitation, however, convinced me that I was as utterly lost as ever rudderless ship, without a compass, was upon a shoreless sea—but yet I felt, too, that I had better trust to him than to myself. My imagination had confused me, while physical exhaustion had rendered his instinct too insecure.

He was evidently as afraid of being trusted as I to trust. However, after a pause of a few moments, he moved on, turning back nearly in the direction we had come. At first I was pleased with this selection, as it seemed to indicate the possible truth of my own surmise, that I had started nearly right, but had passed the plantation. This poor consolation, however, did not outlive the approach of night, which came in heavy shadows, portending a storm, such as thunders and rages along these southern plains occasionally. My miserable horse was now nearly exhausted, and staggered as he dragged his limbs heavily through the high grass. We were still in the prairie with nothing around us but the great ocean of grass, which was beginning to toss and sway with the advance winds of the coming tornado.

The black heaven of clouds came rolling up out of the south-east, and already I felt the cold breath that drove it on, dash with a fresh heavy chill against my face, like the spray of a cataract. The rush and roar that followed left me no time for thought. In a moment, horse and man were prostrate, helpless along the plain.

Such crashes!—such tremendous claps—such sheeting the horizon with swift piercing blazes—such beating, crushing floods, that but seemed a better medium to transmit the mighty clangor hurled around by the strong wind, with vast black clouds that dipped and spun like flakes of ebon down, or sudden fire above! Such an image of sublimest anarchy never before came to overwhelm an already desperate, wearied, and starving wanderer. I clutched at the strong rooted grass in the blindness of my astound, and knew not, in the horrid tumult, that my horse had fallen upon my leg.

I was so stunned that I did not feel the pain. I tried to look up to understand the awful clamor. Was the last day come? Had some God descended in the terror of his might? A keen shaft, in clattering zigzag, would pierce the chaos, blinding as it illuminated. The crashing of torn limbs, caught up miles away, and projected with the flooding rain—the stifling grass-tops, torn and hurled into my face—the bellowing moan of frightened buffaloes—the shaking trample of their struggling feet, all came commingled, as the only interludes to my confused senses.

My horse, at last, as terror-stricken as myself, burst forth, while he lay writhing upon my crushed leg, into a wild and strangely harrowing cry—peculiar to these animals when overcome by panic—and which now rose a weird shriek of agony into the tempest. I had never heard it before, and could not know its source; and the sudden coming of this shrill and unimaginable cry so close to my head, had an effect of the supernatural so absolutely appalling, that I fainted, and remember nothing more until the steady blazing of the early sunlight upon my eyes waked me to a sense of pain, weakness, and astonishment, amounting almost to fright—for stooping over me was one of the most unexpectedly strange figures that it had ever been my fortune yet to encounter.

"He's coming-to—the poor boy!"

This was spoken in a tone that startled me for some reason —I did not know what—entirely apart from the circumstances, and the unexpectedness of hearing a human voice at all, after and amidst such scenes. I looked up. What a face! Storm-seamed and bronzed, it was clearly a woman's bust—a woman's face!—that leaned over and looked kindly down upon me from beneath a sort of half cap and half hood of fawn's skin, with the spotted hair turned out.

"You are not wanting of a wet bed to make you grow—my green youngster! What in the Lord's name brought you here, child?"

The sort of half-grim pleasantry with which this was spoken, as I opened my eyes fully upon her, relieved to some degree my startled feeling of apprehension, and I faltered out feebly, with an attempt at cleverness:—

"I suppose I was blown here—or fell from the clouds!" She assisted me to a sitting posture with her strong hand.

"Nonsense! nonsense, boy!—your own foolish hastiness brought you here! get up!—Ah! I see you cannot rise yet! But you are hungry, perhaps!—I'll give you a slice of as fine a buck as ever was killed, and the taste of which one would think you ought to know!"

She drew forward a small wallet of dressed skin that was slung behind her singular costume of the same material, and took from it some pieces of roasted venison, with which she presented me. As I clutched them with a half-famishing eagerness, a low, quiet laugh from this personage caused me to look up at her again with a droll feeling of curiosity, which even excessive hunger could not repress.

"Taste it, boy! taste it! He! he! he!—you ought to

know that meat!" and she stooped to pick a rifle from the wet grass; and while, continuing to chuckle, she examined carefully the neat lock, I could see her whole figure fully as I ate. The form was unmistakeably that of a genuine woman. The figure, about five feet seven, had nothing of Amazonian stoutness at all apparent, although the manner in which the rifle was held and handled, would naturally lead one to suppose that those limbs must be very compact, indeed. The general outline, although obscured by the rude drapery, gave you the idea of that swift tenacity which round, small bone and taut-strung thews express in the young Indian runner of the North, without destroying a sort of "formidable grace" in its flexible natural movement.

You were surprised, and yet you were not, that she should be a woman of our own race. The features were plain, and here the lines were a little sharp, though not unmatronly. altogether. There was an expression of care, not faded, but eager, anxious, longing. The eye seemed so calm and frank, quick, open, large and blue, that that you could never have conceived the finely arched eye-brow as darkening of itself, but simply as drawn down by the possible contracting of a "dreary mouth austere" below. In a word, with her tanned, self-possessed face, her hair slightly tinged with gray, her half-hunter and half Indian-woman costume, her concise language, her sudden appearance, she was to me the most extraordinary mortal phenomenon I had yet met with. I was too hungry to philosophize or speculate, so there was nothing left me to do but live in the exhausted present, and wait for the future to enlighten me concerning her.

She leaned the gun, re-covering the lock with a buck's skin guard, carefully against my saddle, which I observed upon the grass, and seeming to be satisfied from her inspection that the tube was all right and the cap now entirely dry, she walked towards my horse, merely saying,—"Sleep again, boy, and you will be ready!" The curt injunction seemed almost unnecessary, for the unconquerable drowsiness which follows eating, after long hunger and excessive fatigue and excitement, was already upon me; and the last I saw of her she was standing by the side of my horse with caressing words and gestures as he nibbled feebly at the grass amidst which he stood, with an uncertain sort of air, as if he would just as soon lay down again, or rather fall down!—as not!

When I awoke again, the sun was getting low, and its shadows even fell over the damp bed upon which I had fallen. I raised myself to a sitting posture with a vigor apparently renewed, as I felt for the moment the deepest astonishment and mystified enough by what had been occurring. It all seemed like a dream. It could not be real! There was a vague image of a strange woman with a rifle in her hand, struggling through my brain, and I tried to remember her cool, patronizing words, and her plain, remarkable face, with the fawn-skin hood, and her hardy looking figure, with its anomalous dress of buck-skin; but it all seemed too unreal, and I found myself standing erect, with a sort of smiling consciousness that I had been having a very ridiculous dream; because, there was my noble gray standing the usual distance off in the deep grass, and browsing as if he expected a long day's work, and was laying in the necessary supply of provender therefor.

To be sure, the grass seemed strangely levelled and twirled about, and it was odd what a number of twigs and limbs of trees lay strewed around, considering there was nothing like a tree in sight; but yet I could make nothing out of it. How came my saddle off? How came Gray to look so comfortable? How came I so lame in my left leg that I could not step more than half an inch at a time after I got up, with a sort of numbed struggle, to my feet, and realized the extent and dreariness of the devastation in the midst of which I stood? The prairie presented the appearance of a thousand maelstromes congealed into green stillness, humbled by a Higher

Power as a fixed expression of abasement, with all the broken, jagged wrecks left obtrusive, sticking here and there and everywhere, just as they had been hurled in the rash rebellion that had provoked it.

What a scene of desolation for a dreaming man to awake to realize? I had risen from a blanket! It seemed as if I must have gone to sleep quite considerately!—there were evidences about me of my having partaken of food,—the proof was in the vigor that I felt in spite of my lameness! and then the whole terrible scene of the storm came back to me as I brushed my forehead impetuously with my hand. Ha! ha!—I have it all!—*That woman!* I turned my head, and there stood the strange figure, leaning on her rifle, within ten feet of me, chuckling inwardly at my bewilderment, with that same cool smile!

"Young man, are you ready now?" she asked, suddenly. I was still somewhat bewildered, and answered, "Ready for what?"

"To go with me!" was the abrupt reply.

"But go where? What would you have me to do? Who are you? Are you man or woman?"

"What is that to you, childish boy? Your questions are foolish. I have saved your life and wish to preserve it farther; you can never get out of this wilderness in your present condition. I will take you home with me until you are recovered sufficiently."

"But, have you a home?" I said, pertinaciously.

"Am I a wild beast?" she answered, taking off the strange head-dress, and showing a pure white brow, the feminine lines of which contrasted curiously with the dark, seamed bronze beneath. She smiled, I thought a little proudly, as she replaced it, and advanced towards my horse for the purpose of equipping him, which was done with perfect dexterity. She then led him to my side.

"Now, boy, will you mount?"

"How can I! I can scarcely move."

"O, never mind! your leg is not broken. I can help you!"

So without more ado, she lifted me into the saddle, with perfect ease to herself, but great agony to me. When once *in* the saddle, the pain subsided in a measure. She pointed me the course, and walking by my side, held my leg gently, so as to ease its position as much as possible. This considerate kindness had a most soothing effect upon me, and the simple act greatly alleviated my pain and restored me to confidence,—singular as had been the circumstances of this rencontre. I was even moved to speak to her as to a human being; for in my disturbed state she had really appeared a doubtful sort of being. I was not over clear in my mind as to where she came from, nor over sure what to expect from her; but this little act convinced me that I must be in good hands, at least, however unaccountable the use they were apparently put to might seem.

She appeared to comprehend the sort of dubiousness of feeling with which I had become possessed, and answered the question:—

"How far is this home of yours?"

"O! it isn't in a hole in the ground, in a hollow tree, or in a cave, as you will see!"

"Then, how far is it to C———'s plantation?" (My friend's.)

"You will find it far enough to need whole limbs to reach it."

"But how far may that be?"

"Boy! we have no surveyors here, with their steel chains laid along the earth, emblematic of the slavery to which it is doomed, to measure our miles for us. We measure them by our own free strides!"

"But that is no answer!"

"Ask no questions! I will show you when it is time enough for you to go!"

This was spoken with a sort of petulance, mingled with solemnity; and, as if declining further conversation, she urged on my horse and strode more rapidly, not forgetting her tender care of my leg, though she had dropped her head moodily upon her breast. I was compelled into silence, of course, but this abrupt sort of manner roused my pride somewhat.

I recalled the frequency with which she had spoken to me as a "boy," "child," &c., with some spleen, as I rode on in sulky silence, too. Why, I was a young man of twenty-one, and thought myself somebody! What was there entitling anybody to call me by diminutive names, in the stupid fact of my having got lost in a country of which I knew so little? "I dislike this sort of patronage, even if she has got some streaks of gray in her hair; she is not so oldish-looking after all, as to entitle her to speak like the mother of Methusaleh, even if she did drag me from under my horse when I was unconscious!" so I muttered to myself in a really childish spleen, the secret of which was mingled of mortified vanity and baffled curiosity. As she remained silent, I was foolish enough to give way to this feeling at last.

"Why do you persist in calling me 'child,' 'boy,' and the like names?"

"Because you are a child!" and she looked up into my face with a quick glance that had an expression of sternness in it, above that compressed mouth, that I shall never forget.

"Mere boy as you are, you think you are a man!—you might pass well enough in the tinselled dens and reeking sinks of civilization! Perhaps you *are* a boy-man!" This was said with a slight sneer that cut me to the very core.

"But, remember!—it requires something more than mere years—the vital breath of which has been poisoned—to make a man out here, in the presence of the ALMIGHTY, worthy to look up into his solemn Infinite, where Nature is the only delegated Presence! You must have wiser and riper experience, than those which caused a brave young man—no doubt!—to start like a madman across the plains, merely because he considered himself lost,—without taking time to cut the throat of the deer he had just shot, or to cooly examine his immediate neighborhood,—when, in that event, he might have seen me step forth, whose eye had been upon him, and relieve him from all trouble. You need to trust Nature more, and through her learn to trust yourself! She is full of amenities, and in the mild grandeur of her moods is merciful to all but human weakness. As she represents all that we know of God's physical to us, we must trust her in such relations as we trust him in the spiritual. You are old enough and know enough to have found your way back to your friends, if you had stopped to think a moment.

"You did not trust,—and though you might not have fled from mortal foe, you did fly from your own imaginations, for I was an unseen witness! I saw you scurry off, and before I understood the cause, you were beyond the reach of any sound I could produce. I laughed, and pitied you,—but found you this morning by accident."

"You are a strange person! What is the meaning of all these things you say to me?"

"Meaning, boy? That you children of civilization imagine yourselves *educated* when you have talked with books in dingy closets, and grown pale in the stagnant air in which your morbid dreams are generated, along with dull diseases! You have only commenced the true life. Neither the physical or spiritual are yet developed in you, although you may be what you call *learned!*"

"That I disclaim!" I could not help saying, with false and unnecessary modesty.

"Then, it is nothing to your credit! One kind of learning is as necessary as another!" she continued, with no change of intonation, but in a severe, rapid manner.

"You should know books as well as Nature. One is God's Book and the other man's!"

"That sounds polemical!" sneered I, having by this time become interested in her dogmatism, and feeling a sudden accession of the old profane propensity for cynicism.

"I am no vulgar heretic. I believe in all the sacrednesses of humanity, but I believe as well in those of Nature. The religion of the Bible is, perhaps, more of a religion to me than to you,—but the religion of Nature is an essential part of it, and, with me, the base, of course, as Eden had its base upon the earth."

"Well!" thought I, to myself, "Here's a droll preacher I have met with, any how!"

"But, you think it strange I should tell you that you do not know your own life, because you suffered your imagination to make a fool of you, in conditions from which your experiences showed you no mode of escape which you could understand?"

"Yes!"

"Well, that you *may* understand what I mean,—should you not have known how to read this great page of continent-stretching plain, as well as that other smaller page of your Human Learning, let it belong to what tome it may?"

"Yes; but you remember I have not had time yet to learn!"

"Then confess yourself a child! I have been taught to read your books, and have learned something of them, too. I can read the other book as well; and, instead of the faded decay of the mere scholar, you see the bronzed seams of a sterner and more hardy life. Woman as you say I am—I will outlive a dozen of them in the Life of Truth. Had I been cast upon the middle of the desert of Sahara by such a tornado as you met with last night, I should not have attempted to take a course until I had seen the sun rise. This would have been a base for faith, for observation, for calculation—nothing would have escaped me, however minute—from the character of a cloud to the position of the low sand-waves fixed around me, to tell how the prevailing wind had left them to wait its next coming—and that wind would tell a pregnant story, too, when it went by. I could almost judge with certainty 'whence it cometh or whither it goeth!' Not a starved and bitter shrub, but its fingers pointed a significance—or showed something on one side of the discolored bark—either the direction of the nearest water, or of the prevailing wind—not an antelope that darted past but would have led me the way to some Oasis!" She paused suddenly.

"That a man should utter such thought would not surprise me so much"—said I, hastily. "But that a woman should—"

"A woman should!" she interrupted. "Give a woman something to love and something to venerate—an idea to achieve—and what will she not accomplish! Now you show yourself a child again!"

"You make woman in yourself more infallible than man pretends to be, even in his proper and peculiar field!"

"Young man—I understand you! I could possibly get lost as easily as some men—but I could not get scared!"

"Thank you!" said I, with a poor effort at the magnanimous. But she went on without noticing.

"I should not have been flurried out of my common sense, and lost all the chance I had for getting out of the scrape—if I am a woman. There is too much yet to be accomplished to justify any one in throwing away a life. Mankind has yet to be redeemed. The world needs all its laborers!"

Here is the key-note to this strange anomaly—I thought!

"You will not do much to redeem it out here!" I ventured to hint.

She turned her head abruptly, merely muttering—

"You will know more some time!" and, as at the moment, a herd of deer, which had been lying down in the grass within range, sprang up from a low piece of the ground—her rifle was at her shoulder in an instant. A deer bounded into the air, and merely saying as she turned off—

"Wait for me!"—she proceeded to cut the throat of the animal—reloading her rifle as she went.

"Well!" said I, as I squirmed in my saddle, when she was out of ear-shot—"Here's a *free* specimen, with a vengeance! A sort of Amazonian-Siamese-Twins-of-a-personage—a double-shotted-she-fanatic run wild! She is surely sufficient unto herself?—Lord help the husband of such a woman—if she have one!" Then I felt mean.

"But, by Jove, how strangely she talks—and how kindly she has treated me—if she does patronize! I half suspect she's right about the *child!*"

The deer was dissected in short order, and she returned to my side bearing the hams still enveloped in the hide, which had been stripped from the fore-parts, which are not much valued in a country where venison is so abundant. She slung her burden across my horse behind my seat, merely remarking as we moved on—"This is a fat saddle!"

"But is it possible that you hunt on foot always?"

"Yes; I prefer it!"

"How do you get your meat home?—not upon your shoulders, I hope!"

"Yes—but why not, young man? My limbs are strong, my step is firm. I do not tire like the tottering creatures of rotten civilization. I who breathe God's pure air have the will—why not the deed?"

"But you are a woman," I persisted. "Your husband, if you have one, should do this?"

"Bah! What if I am a woman—I must work? My husband works! Works gloriously and nobly for mankind, and I, too, am laboring for mankind when I provide for him. He has no time for such menial labors; and if he had, he would be doing injustice to the necessities of the race if he gave it to anything but the high mission on which he has been sent!"

"This is a strange doctrine, it seems to me—you are reversing the savage code; for even with them, although the women perform the baser services, the men at least do the hunting."

"Young man, you speak like one who had been in the world just twenty-one years, and that, having eyes, had not seen. Do you not know that progress, like all other of God's great Laws, moves in the spiral—upwards? That it must bring us around again to the same conditions from whence we started—though above them. A close approximation to the savage life and virtues will be the highest civilization. It is the ferocious vices we shall have conquered, and the heroic virtues we shall have attained. These stern savage races go down before the wheels of progress because they will not bend; with the light that was given them, they are too faithful and too strong to yield. It is a bastard civilization that is really untrue—begotten of luxury or lust—its children are the true Neros of ferocity and brutality. The world needs brains now more than thews and sinews. The need is too great for true hearts to stop at conventional forms, which, after all, are the mere disguises of unbounded licentiousness. The millions groan, and we must work each in his own appointed way."

"But I do not understand from all this why the common relation of husband and wife should be reversed."

"Ah, yes! Then the constant tendency of this struggle of civilization toward the simpler forms and a purer light, is to intensify the action of the mental and spiritual natures, rather than the mere physical. The mental searches for the mechanical means of rescue, the soul for the spiritual. Both are maddened by the clamorous cries of suffering nations into a morbid activity—the results of which are most frequently 'confusion worse confounded'—and an unnatural development of the brain, or of the mental in relation to physical. Where this condition has supervened, it is the office of *love* to restore the equilibrium; and in the true marriage, upon whichever party the lot of extreme spiritual and mental development shall fall, the doctrine of Utility requires of him or her a life-dedication to the great *cause*, in whatever direction the strongest tendencies may be—and so upon whichever party, man or woman, the lot of greatest physical strength and activity should fall, the responsibility of all that species of exertion must devolve. Thus they both labor to the same end, through each other, and are unified in purpose and results!"

"This then is your reason for assuming the office of commissary! You are physically strongest, and have assumed the burden of the way?"

"He is strong in his own way, young man!" she answered drily—"But look! there is our little home!"

I had become so interested in this strange conversation—stranger even than the circumstances which had brought me into such relations—that I had not noticed what the direction was, or what the peculiarities of the ground we were passing over. I now looked around me, and even if my vision had not been sharpened by observing a sort of cynical smile upon her face as she pronounced the last words—I think my own memory would have been sufficient to compel me to recognize the scene, amidst the "Archipelago of motts," in which the deer had fallen, and from which I had fled so ignominiously—as it was turning out.

There was the very spot where I had left the deer, and the bones of the refuse parts lay strewed around upon the dank and bloody grass. Some wolves, which had been squatting in the neighborhood of their feast, made off as we approached. I looked in the direction in which the woman had pointed, but could perceive nothing like a house. She smiled at my puzzled gaze of inquiry into her face.

"You are back again, you see! I took off that deer's skin myself, and you ate some of its meat. The horse had more wit than the rider—you perceive he was coming direct!"

"Yes!" said I dolorously, as we were passing on—"but where is the house of which you spoke?" for my bruised limb—the pain of which I had almost forgotten during the excitement of our conversation—was becoming most oppressive, now that something had been said of home and rest.

"Do you see that small mott?" said she, pointing with her rifle to a clump of large live oaks upon a bit of rising ground, some half a mile ahead—and near to what, I now perceived, for the first time, to look like the heavy timbered bottom of a stream of some size.

"I see nothing but a mott!" said I impatiently. "Where is the house?" Her look brightened as she stepped on more briskly by the side of my horse, who seemed to have scented some familiar odor on the breeze, that quickened his step, for his ear was now pricked forward, and his gait confident and elate.

"You shall see!" and she smiled. We soon reached the mott, and passing beneath the long heavy drapery of moss that descended from the low wide limbs of the live-oak, we were at once in the dim cool twilight, which would have best become that religious atmosphere in which the Druidical rites were performed. In the midst of this, and almost hidden by the gray fantastic drapery of the great tree above,—I saw indistinctly the appearance of palisading, that seemed to be circular in form. Another moment she pushed aside the moss, and we were at the door. It was a round hut, the walls of which were composed of the small trunks of trees set perpendicularly in the ground—the interstices being filled with a sort of cement of moss and mud. The roof was thatched with bull-rushes, and the door was a frame of hickory saplings stoutly interwoven. There was no sort of picketing about it, as is usual in the country, to the small as well as large ranchos.

It seemed as if the shelter of the moss-draped oaks had been deemed sufficient—and so, indeed, it appeared to be, for its appearance of entire security, like some wild nest of lonely birds, was what first struck me as I saw it. The door was closed, and it looked silent as death. She held up her arms to assist me to alight, and then taking down her venison, she gave the lariate of my horse a turn around a limb of the sheltering oak, and assisted me toward the door. She called out in a low tone, "William?"

I heard a soft, unsteady tread respond to the call, and the door was opened. A pale man, with large head, bright gray eyes, broad shoulders, and small legs, made his appearance.

"What is the matter, Molly?" said he, with such a quiet look as his eye fell upon me, that one would have supposed I was his oldest son.

"Is the poor youth hurt that he leans upon you so?"

"Yes."

"Then, bring him in, in God's name, and we will shelter him until his strength returns!" and she assisted me to the door, when he clutched me with a strength of gripe that astonished me, and nearly lifting me towards a low couch of dried moss, laid me upon it without asking a question. He adjusted my position with a sort of awkward care, and when assured that I was comfortable, he went quietly to a rude ottoman composed of dressed bear-skins with forked stakes and small saplings for supports, and seated himself, with the most benign expression of serenity before a rude table covered with all sorts of odd implements; and taking, up, what appeared to be a microscope, commenced an attentive survey of some small object before him, which I could not distinguish. He had asked me no explanation, did not seem to be at all disturbed by my sudden appearance, and had fallen back into what seemed a routine, just as if nothing had happened. This, though not very complimentary to my vanity, only served to rouse my curiosity, in spite of my sufferings.

"Molly will take care of you directly!" he said, looking up; "She has gone to stake out your horse!" and he went on with his work. I thought of magii, necromancers, astrologers, alchemists, &c., all in a breath, as I stared at the strange, calm man, with the light from one small window, or port-hole rather, falling upon his table and his gray hairs!

The strange effect was not a little heightened by the surroundings of this person. I had now, in the unbroken silence, sufficient leisure to observe these appliances, which were entirely inexplicable to me at the time. First, I noticed a small rude furnace in one corner, near to which were scattered about some small hammers, files, tongs and other tools used in working iron and steel; while near the desk were some ten or a dozen small models carved from wood with great neatness, and having occasional springs, bolts, &c. of metal. Such a maze of wheels, cogs, cranks, balls, bolts and all that sort of thing was there, that one could form no idea of their meaning, not even whether they all belonged to the same machine, or were the parts of one whole, waiting to be put together!

On knots and pegs, in crannies, and strewed in all sorts of confusion about the floor and on rude shelves, were every conceivable variety of parts that appeared to have been formed for machinery of models or a model. These parts were principally of wood, as the metals seemed to have been used with every possible frugality, since they must, of course, have been very difficult to obtain and to transport in such a region. A few of the simplest of the common implements of carpentry were hung around the room or thrown about the floor. It seemed as if the tools and their creations had all been shaken in a bag together and then whirled around the room to roll together, to fall or stick, where and as they might. It was certainly a droll looking place, and there was one mysterious seeming recess which was hung with skins, but which was, as it appeared to me, too small for a bed, and added no little to my curiosity.

The woman now came in.

"He is bruised, William,—what shall we do?"

The man looked up, slightly.

"Did you bring in a deer, Molly?"

"Yes!"

"Is it cold?"

"All but the hams!"

"Then skin them, and wrap the warm parts of the skin around the bruised limb!"

"Yes, I know!" and she turned off, while he resumed his labor.

"Well!" thought I, "this is a case! Here I am about to be enveloped in a reeking deer-skin, warm from the carcass, by these wild cannibals. I wish the infernal tornado had finished me. I have heard of such usages, but they horrify me!" I felt most like getting up to run away, but there interposed the sad difficulty that I was unable to rise. After several ineffectual efforts, which, however, attracted no sort of attention from the rapt student at the desk, and many muttered anathemas against fate, fools and fanatics in general, I managed to subside, in a great degree, into a cooler mood, and became resigned, from sheer helplessness, to trust in anything but such Providence!—as I impiously sneered to myself.

The woman came now with the warm skin; and after some remonstrance on my part, the old man was roused from his absorbed labor to envelop my extremities in this novel poultice. I afterwards found that it was extensively used among the Indians, north and south, and have since learned that this first step towards the "pack" of wet sheet and blanket, claimed to be invented by Priessnitz, is one of the oldest uses of our race, and still practiced with wonderful effect in China, Russia, Germany, &c., by the lower classes, and sometimes by the higher, as was the case once with Murat, when he was crushed almost into a jelly by the fall of his horse down a precipice.

He was enveloped by his wise physician, in the hide of an ox, which was killed for the purpose, and after a long sleep, recovered, with nearly all trace of his bruises gone. I was not aware at the time, more than vaguely, in what good and ancient company I lay in my disgusting envelope; all I could know about it was that I went to sleep very soon, and slept, —Heaven knows how long! and awoke with the pain *gone!*

The old man released me, and leading me, entirely nude, out-side the door, astounded me by dashing a bucket full of the coldest water upon my person, which was reeking with perspiration, and before I had fairly recovered from the effects of this, it was followed by another and another.

This primitive sort of treatment had a wonderful effect; and when I again dressed, I almost thought myself born again, so free did I feel from the distressing consequences of my fall. I found in attempting to move about that there was still some stiffness in my leg, but it was so slight as not to be a matter of much importance. The bruises were gone, and the circulation of the limb temporarily restored in a great measure, and that was certainly miracle enough for the present.

Though the acute pain had been entirely banished by this novel process, yet, of course, the entire restoration was yet slow. The muscles and tendons had been seriously strained and injured by the weight and struggles of my horse, but, bathing the parts in cold water, as was directed by the old man, always soothed any painful return of inflammation.

There was a clear, beautiful spring in the rear of the house, underneath the huge live-oaks composing the mott. Here I limped several times a day to apply the simple restorative. The little brook made its shining way through the high grass down the slope, and at some periods of the day, glanced prettily in the sun from beneath the green tangles that drooped and met over it. The scene was very pleasant; for, seated on the mossy roots in the cool, dense shade, I could just trace its glimmering way by glimpses through the heavy draping of moss which depended nearly to the ground. The stillness, mildly stirred by the faint ripple, was so lulling, that if one did not sleep soon he was compelled to think, and in connected strains of thought, too.

Here I sat and mused much; for, in spite of myself and all my efforts at sneering, there was something in this woman's wild talk that impressed me,—and in the strange life, manners and surroundings of this remarkable recluse, that had aroused my deepest and most curious sympathy. These were new thoughts,—strange ideas—she had spoken. This was a new phase of life to me—this isolation—this devotion to a fixed purpose—this self-denial, which could sever two persons from all the common sympathies of their race, and send them off to remote and dangerous solitudes,—change the natural relations of the sexes, and exalt them into the incommunicative and apparently crazed condition of abstraction and devotion to a single idea!

"What *is* this *Idea?* What *do* these people hope to accomplish?" I asked myself a thousand times. "They talk of social wrongs,—but that is no new story,—it is simply as old as society, that those who can find no business of their own to attend to, should, and will employ themselves with the business of others, and go to work to *save* the world! They commonly make a good speculation of it, and are usually corrupt as they are loud-mouthed, vulgar and stupid,—but here seems an anomalous case. These people are clearly in earnest. Women do not run such risks for nothing, nor do men dedicate themselves with such singleness of purpose to what they merely expect selfish returns from! I must get at this idea—and get at it I will! These persons are evidently educated, for silent and abruptly incommunicative as they have been since I came, I have heard enough to convince me of this much, and unravel this secret *I will!*"

Such, I remember, were my musings, when, after having been tenderly cared for several days, I found myself equally puzzled as at first, to understand what this old man was doing, or expected to accomplish. He had made no explanations, and although uniformly kind, had taken no sort of notice of the various and ingenious hints by which I had endeavored to get at what was his object. I had slyly tried to understand for myself the meaning of the models which strewed the room, but could make nothing out of them all. Though my knowledge of mechanics was very slight, yet I had some idea of general principles, which ought to have been sufficient to give me at least a vague clue to the object attempted. I had given up in despair; and as I could not understand the meaning of the sort of hieroglyphico-transcendental language in which they spoke to each other upon the subject of the mysterious machine, I determined to win upon the sympathies of one or the other in some way, and get thus at the secret.

Accident favored me!

She had talked with me in the freest manner during the first exciting period after our meeting, but since I had become an inmate, her answers to my inquiry upon such subjects had all been abrupt and mystical in a degree which left me no wiser than before. The old man seldom left the house, even for exercise; but one morning, when I had almost entirely recovered, I was sitting in my accustomed place by the spring, when he came slowly walking towards me with the feeble gait of the partial paralytic; and, greatly to my surprise, bore my pistols along with his own gun, in his hands.

"What can this mean!"—thought I, rising hastily to meet him.

Giving the pistols into my hands, he merely said, with a quiet smile:—

"The Cherokee Indians are down, young man!—and we may have to defend our little home!"

"Is it possible!" said I, starting with surprise. "The Cherokees! Where are they? How did you hear?"

"O, Molly keeps a good look out!—she found their trail

about day-break, and has since seen them. She has just got in. They are on her trail now, I suppose, for we expect them here soon!"

The blood rushed to my heart, and it beat very loud and fast. I had never met the Indians of any sort, as yet. Here at once was a stern novely in the excitements that I had courted.

I had little time to understand the thing, for we now saw and felt the imminent necessity of hurrying towards the house before the approaching savages. I had to assist the old man, and the moment I got into motion, the blood rushed in a burning tide back to my head and face, and then every limb and fibre thrilled with a new sensation. Everything seemed confused around me for the moment. The trees spun, and the moss and grass were whirled together in a chaotic blending, most like that before the eyes of a drunken man; while the only objects that I saw with perfect and vivid distinctness, were the tall forms of eight or ten warriors that had suddenly appeared in the distance, and were gliding rapidly across a small opening between the oaks, evidently with the view of getting between us and the house, and thus cutting us off from shelter. When I realized this it caused a violent start that restored me, like an electric shock in a case of stupor, to the full possession of all my faculties, sharpened, indeed, into a greater than the natural coolness. The distance we had to pass was short, to be sure, but then the old man was paralytic, and I was still somewhat lame.

I saw in one quick glance our great danger—that the savages were urging their utmost speed to intercept us. A sudden strength—almost supernatural—possessed me at once. My eye took in every thing. The very undulations of the moss enabled me to track their course, when they quickly passed out of view behind it. I could now even hear the twigs crush beneath their feet—when feeling that our hope was a desperate one—I seized the old man in my arms, and forgetting my lameness, rushed with him towards the door of the house.

I reached it—and found it was closed for the moment. He still held on to his rifle, and as the door opened to admit us, he turned himself in my arms, and coolly presenting it, said in a low voice, "Stop!"

The word was not fully spoken, when the ring of several rifles from the wood was replied to by that of his own. He dropped heavily from my arms on his own door-sill. The Indians were upon us! I had stuck my pistols into my belt, and now I wheeled to face them, standing over the body. The clear ring of a rifle above my shoulder, and the staggering fall of one of the foremost warriors showed me that "Molly" was on hand. The Indians recoiled for a moment, for it was the chief of the party that fell beneath the shot—and then seeing only myself astride of the body—they rushed on me with a yell as vengeful as it was infernal.

I saw the fierce eyes of "Molly" blazing behind me as she screamed—

"Give it to the Cherokee dogs, my boy!" while she plied her ram-rod desperately—reloading for another shot.

I stood at bay with that strange flushed feeling which always attends the consummation of despair. It was a wild and furious struggle for a moment. The firing of my pistols was almost instantly followed by the report of her rifle again—this caused the Indians to hesitate slightly, which gave us time to drag in the body of the dead or wounded man—we did not yet know which. They saw us about to escape, and made a rush to prevent the closing of the door. Several of them were throwing themselves against it together, and had nearly succeeded in the effort—but the frantic woman seemed endued with nearly supernatural strength, and with a single stroke, felled the foremost with the butt of her rifle—while I held the door with all my excited strength. Though both of us were wounded, we succeeded in closing the bolt, while the Indians kept firing at the door, in the vain hope of hitting us through it. Hickory is a very tough wood, and the closely woven withs or poles of which it was composed were bullet-proof.

It was not, however, proof against hatchets, and instantly we heard the blows by which they were cutting their way through. We reloaded our weapons in silence. The door was frail hung, and could not stand such a general assault more than a few moments—but when we were ready, she looked up with a smile that seemed very strange at such a time.

"I prepared for them long ago!" she said, in a low, hissing voice—as she punched out a bit of mud from between two of the pickets of the house—and then thrust her rifle through what I now saw was a shrewdly disguised port-hole, bearing directly upon the door. She fired, and a yell of agony from the outside followed. As she withdrew her rifle, I also fired my pistol through the port-hole into the midst of the flurried and astonished group, which had gathered about a fallen warrior. Their discomfiture was now complete, and with gestures of furious menace, I could see they commenced a retreat more rapid than the charge had been, and as little expected.

The woman, who now appeared to have grown wild with rage, quickly sent after their retreat another shot from the door-way, which she had impetuously thrown open. She screamed her defiance, and shook her clenched hand at them like some crazed "Madge Wildfire," as they disappeared in yet greater confusion from her shot, and turning towards me with lips blue and compressed—until they were thin as wafers across her teeth—muttered faintly—

"They have slain my husband!" and staggering towards the still insensible body—her flashing eyes suddenly grew dim—her face deathly pale, and dropping her rifle to the floor, she fell upon the body, clutching it convulsively about the neck.

Now came the time for me to repay, in some measure at least, the kindness of this singular couple. They both lay stretched upon the floor insensible, and apparently dead. It was a horrid sight—for a moment I was stupefied as I gazed upon them—but the last few moments, in thoroughly rousing my whole life to new sensations, had learned me a stern lesson in presence of mind. I sprang first for some water, and dashed it into the faces of the motionless pair, and then kneeling beside them, rubbed their hands and feet with all my strength. It was but a little time before I convinced myself that neither one of them was yet dead. This relieved and encouraged me greatly, so that I urged my efforts to resuscitate them, and, after a few minutes more, commenced examining the old man's body, to find and staunch the wound.

I had seen no blood as yet, and therefore supposed it must, of course, bleed internally, and consequently be fatal. What was my hopeful surprise to find that it was apparently a graze-shot—as the ball had ploughed up the flesh along the hinder part of the neck near the base of the skull; and as it was, evidently, not deep when I probed it with my finger, I came to the conclusion that the bone had been merely indented —not shattered—and that the spinal chord had been more paralyzed by the shock than seriously injured. Warmed still more pleasantly by this discovery, I rapidly staunched the blood, which had been running down inside the collar of his buckskin coat, and was, therefore, not visible.

The wound of the woman was bleeding profusely. I soon found that it consisted of an ugly flesh wound in the right arm, which passed through into the breast, but whether into the chest or not I could only conjecture—but hoped for the best, as I saw it, too, bled externally and freely. I staunched the wounds as well as my poor skill in surgery would admit.

She gradually recovered from the swoon, and, half rising, stared vaguely about her for an instant—but her first words were—

"Is he alive?" This was spoken in a suffocating voice, while her lips trembled.

"He still lives, and I hope is not mortally hurt!"

"God be thanked, and let humanity rejoice!" she said solemnly, and with a start she sprang to her feet. "You are hurt, young man—I see blood upon you!"

I had been too much excited to think of my own wound, although I now felt that the pain had been considerable—however, it proved to be, upon examination, but slight, and gave me of itself but little trouble afterwards. It was merely a flesh wound in the thigh of the same leg that had been injured in the storm, and, as is frequently the case, rather accelerated the cure of that injury. The vital functions, thus extraordinarily aroused, it is well known, do often throw off the old as well as the new disease, by the one great effort thus concentrated upon the local seat of the disturbance. Be this as it may, I did not suffer from lameness much after this—although I had a great amount of exertion devolved upon me by this sudden catastrophe.

The woman, after assisting me in dressing my wound, said to me gravely—

"Now, young man, much depends upon you! You are not a great deal hurt—as God would have it—while I am grievously—and my poor William must probably remain long in this stupor!"

She was carefully examining him without disturbing my dressings, further than to saturate them with water.

"I can hope," she said, as she rose from the examination and drew a long breath—"I can hope that your opinion of the wound may prove correct—for his pulse, though slow, is strong enough yet—but it must be a long time before he recovers his faculties. His brain is so immense and so disproportioned to his physical strength, that his recovery must be very slow, if it come at all. Young man, I have dedicated my life without stint or reservation to him, and although it is impossible for me yet to tell the extent of the injuries I have received, yet I must not stop to regard them—I must win that glorious mind back to the world again, cost what it will to me. I count myself as nothing weighed in the scale with his usefulness. He *must* be saved at any rate, to finish his great work! I saved your life—a lost wanderer, beaten down by the tempest—helpless, bewildered, wounded and forlorn—and now all that I ask of you is, help to save *him!* Make no remonstrances!"—as I was proceeding to deprecate the disregard of self she spoke of,—"make no remonstrances, my son!" she said mournfully—"I must require it of you not to interfere with—but obey me—for the time. I cannot be moved—I will nurse him—you must provide us with food and water in the meanwhile. I want no farther assistance. I know him best—you can render no assistance to him personally. God only knows how far this ugly hurt of mine may prove injurious. I will be careful of it for his sake, at least!"

"I promise to obey you. I feel that I owe my life to you, and I will cheerfully resign it to serve you or your husband!"

"I knew as much, my child!—I knew as much—and was selfish of me to remind you of obligation when you had already more than trebly repaid whatever there might be, by saving that dear body which lies so placid there, from the defacing hands of those murderous brutes—who, as with those who stoned the Prophet of old—knew not what they did!—But it is no selfish anxiety for self that has thus made me forget what was due to hospitality—it was for *him!*—for his dear life!—I spoke so eagerly, forgetting all things else!—come, let us place him on the poor bed!"

We immediately removed him to his place upon a raised couch of dried moss and leaves, covered with skins, which had heretofore been resigned to me. As we laid him down, his pulsation evidently quickened, but his eyes were still unopened, and his limbs remained palsied. I brought water from the spring, which I freely used under the directions of the woman, who by this time had become too faint for farther exertion. The only immediate effect was a partial one, even with our slight expectation. He breathed still more freely, and slightly moved his head. I now had to apply the same remedy to herself, and soon had the satisfaction, after using the cold water freely, and enveloping her in skins, of which there was a large quantity piled on a sort of garret scaffolding near the roof, to see her fall into a deep but troubled sleep. I enveloped his body in much the same way, and then had leisure to look about me, and find what store of provision we had on hand.

I was greatly disappointed to find but little venison or meat of any kind stored in the house, and this filled me with uneasiness, for I did not yet feel myself strong enough to hunt, and could not help dwelling upon the frightful fate before us in the event of my wound proving worse than I anticipated. I did what I could for it until the most resistless drowsiness overtook me, and falling upon a pile of skins, I sunk into the deep sleep consequent upon extreme excitement and loss of blood.

I was waked by the shrill cries of the woman, and, as I sprang to my feet was horrified to perceive from the flushed appearance of her face, her wild ejaculations and even screams, that she was suffering from a raging brain fever. She tossed her body violently to and fro, moaning as she pressed her throbbing head convulsively between her hands, and occasionally shrieking at the top of her voice incoherently. It was a melancholy sight, indeed. I knew but one remedy in reach; and if there had been a thousand, perhaps none would have availed so well as the simple one to which I now resorted, almost upon compulsion! I hobbled to the spring for a fresh supply of its cooling waters. Returning with equal difficulty, I found the fever even gaining in violence. It was certainly an awful sight: this stern, heroic woman helplessly tossed in blinded struggles by the side of that calm and gray picture of death, which, unmoved by it all, breathed on like one in a sweet sleep. I could only reduce the fever gradually, for my strength was not sufficient to lift her, and for hours I sat beside her, soothing, as well as I was able, her convulsions, by constant applications of cold water. It was, or seemed at least, a weary time before I gained any ground, and my wound broke out afresh from the excessive fatigue; besides, I was fainting with hunger and horror combined. At last I thought I might venture to leave her awhile, as she grew more composed, and I sought some food. I took a portion of our small supply and rekindled the coals of the smouldering fire, but the bleeding seemed to increase, and I was compelled to attend to my wounds before I could cook the flesh. I stopped the flow of blood, and was eating sparingly of the spare meal, when I suddenly became aware of the fact that I was the keeper of a *maniac!*

Hearing a sudden noise behind me, I looked around. The woman,—with flushed face and glittering eyes, was rapidly endeavoring to disengage her butcher knife from the sheath where it hung on the belt of her bullet pouch, which I had taken off and suspended on its usual hook of buck's horn. She was muttering rapidly, "I will do it myself! yes! yes! I will do it myself! The wretches did not finish their work! They did not know how hard it was for a god to die! He is not dead—he suffers! It shall not be! They sent their bloodhounds to murder a true Christ! *He* who came to redeem them! They struck at him in wrath! They did not finish their work —but I will do it! and go with him!"

The knife was in her hand, and she was darting across the room towards the unconscious man, when I, who had risen in the meantime, seized her suddenly, and with a shriek as she gazed round at me, she struck desperately at my breast with the knife. I warded off the blow, and she dropped it! Then, with a still more harrowing cry, she fainted across the body.

Never was horror amplified to a more intolerable extreme of fear and dread than now, in all my experience before or since. She was crazed,—we were nearly out of food of any kind!—and could I dare, even if able, to go out and leave her here alone? It seemed just as shocking to me to confine her with thongs as to leave her alone. What might not the furious strength of a maniac accomplish?

Here was a climax! I acknowledge, I felt in no hurry to restore her from her fainting fit. Murder, madness, stupor and starvation, all rose in appalling succession before me.

"What could I do? What should I do? I bowed my head upon my hands and wept,—completely overcome by this tragic combination of fearful extremities.

A loud hurrah, accompanied by the clatter of horses' feet now broke the stifling stillness, and springing up, I rushed forward, or rather hobbled earnestly towards the door to see if it was yet secure.

As I reached it, it was burst open violently, and in rushed my friend C——, the planter! followed by several negros. He was a good-humored, vehement, boisterous man, and exclaimed, in a loud voice, as his eye fell upon me:—

"Caught at last!—Why what's all this, my good fellow?" looking round him, in astonishment and horror. "What sort of a d——l's den is this you've fallen into?—have you been playing the 'Kilkenny cats' out here in this droll-looking place? Are those two people dead? What's been happening?"

"We've been having a brush with the Cherokees,—these persons are wounded!"

"Hah! the very fellows I've just been drubbing. They carried the bodies of several killed and wounded. You must have had close work of it, my boy! We finished the business for them, though,—only three got off?"

"Glad of it,—but help that woman,—she has fainted."

"Great God!—a woman here,—and in that dress?"

He sprang forward to the bed and looked at her!

"It is so,—as I am alive. Boys,"—turning to the negroes who stood at the door, rolling up the whites of their eyes in wonder and awe,—"run, boys, and get some water,—you saw the spring out there as we came?" then turning to me, with a broad expression of amazement, he asked:—

"Who can these people be? Did they drop from the clouds? She's wounded! Did she fight too?"

"Indeed, she did,—she did the most of it!"

"But what are they doing here with all this droll trumpery? Did she faint from loss of blood? Is she badly hurt? This old man looks as if he were dead?" So he ran on, and without waiting for answer, and turning, stepped hastily to the door, and shouted at the top of his voice:—

"You Tom!—Scip!—Jim!—come along with that water! Here are these poor people dying, and you lazy vagabonds you—ah, here you are!" and the three negroes rushed forward to the door of the room, bearing each a brimming gourd in one hand and his rifle in the other. The foremost stammered out:—

"Heerd you, Massa,—was comin' fast as we could,—but Jim say he war afraid ob dem cu'rus folks and dem cunjuration wheels thar,—he was 'bout to slope, an I cotch he."

"Hang Jim and his conjurations!—give me the gourd, you rascal!"

"Da he am, Massa!" while Jim, thrusting his own gourd from behind, into the hand of Tom, *did* "slope" out, sure enough, rolling his big eyes behind him as if he expected to see some horrid witch in pursuit.

"Here's Jim's, too!—nigger, fool! He afeard! Here,

Massa, here's Scip's, too! He fool!" and the second darkie glided furtively from the door, looking over his shoulder.

The Planter in the meantime was stooping over the silent forms of the couple, and administering the cooling water to them, while Tom stood by and looked on with a sort of half grin of heroical indifference, not a little heightened in its effect by the conscious expression of superiority and trepidation which still lingered upon his face, since he looked after the hasty retreat of his sable comrades in arms.

"She recovers!" said the good-hearted Planter, eagerly, lifting his head. The woman opened her eyes and sprang half erect, uttering at the same time a sudden shriek, so shrill that I involuntarily placed my hands upon my ears. The Planter stepped backwards, and Tom, in spite of his heroism, vanished in a twinkle out of the door.

"What does this mean?" said C———, glancing quickly around at me. "Is she crazy?" and he sprang towards her, instinctively, forcing her down upon the bed, while he turned his head slightly to listen for my answer.

"Yes, she is,—hold her!—hold her firmly!—she is not sane now, and may do more mischief!"

"I understand scalping,—but this infernal den is too much for me!" exclaimed he, as he pressed her down to the bed again, while her shrieks redoubled, and her struggles became more furious. He was a very strong man, and yet all his strength was required to keep her down, and he turned to me with an expression of exhaustion and flurried distress, as he exclaimed,—"Why didn't you warn me of this?"

"I had no time!"

"One word would have sufficed!"

"And what good would that have done?"

"I might have understood something!"

"No!—you could not have known more after an explanation than you can see!"

"And what is that?"

"Why, you perceive that the woman is out of her head,—has a brain fever. She suffers from her wound, her anxiety for her husband, and the additional excitement of the late conflict, that is all!"

"What shall we do?" he asked, in dismay, as it became every moment more difficult to keep her down.

"I must call the negros back,—for I can be of little assistance to you!"

"The stupid fools!—you can't get them to come back!"

"Yes I can!" and seizing his rifle, I hobbled to the door and looked out. Tom was the only one in sight. I shouted to him, ordering his return. The fellow shook his head, and looked furtively askance towards me. I instantly raised the rifle, and, as I brought it to bear upon him, peremptorily ordered his return, under penalty of a ball through his woolly head. The habit of obedience conquered his fears in a measure, and he came back with a slow, unwilling step.

"Why, you cowardly rascal!" I said, in an angry and contemptuous tone, which I thought might sting and rouse his pride,—for I knew he was really a brave fellow, but superstitious, as were all his class,—"I thought you had some manhood in you,—a great big lubber like you to run away from a sick and wounded woman! I am ashamed of you, Tom. Come in here, your master needs you to help him hold her!"

"Dat!—dat!—dat!—no woman, Massa!" He stammered hesitatingly, as he looked up humbly for a moment. "Dat witch,—she make poor nigger die like rotten sheep if he touch um!"

"I tell you, you fool, the woman is no witch; she is a good woman, and has a bad fever, and does not know what she is doing!"

"But, Massa, what all dat conjure-wheels do dar if she am no witch?" he persisted, in a more cheerful voice, but still hanging back.

"Why, you stupid fellow!—did you never see a wheel, Tom?"

"Yes, Massa, but den dem aint' cart-weels!'

"Fellow!" said I, provoked at his tenacious stupidity, "those are parts of small machines, and can hurt neither you nor me. Come in, this moment, without another word, and assist your master to hold the woman!"

I seized him by the collar and pushed him in, saying, as I looked significantly at my rifle—

"Do as you are ordered, or remember this!"

The Planter, who was nearly exhausted by the continued violence of the convulsions, when he saw the cowering negro enter, saluted him with a wrathful oath, which we will be excused from repeating, and in a voice of thunder, ordered him to seize the woman's arms, enforcing his command with a furious kick, followed by gentle insinuation that he would dash his brains out, if he dared to let her up. Tom took hold evidently with fear and trembling, but still with all his might.

"What are we to do with this she-dragon?" gasped the poor Planter, wiping the sweat from his brow. "It will take half-a-dozen men to hold her at this rate—we shall have to tie her!"

At this moment an extraordinary change came over the face of the raving woman. The face of the negro—as he stooped above her, holding her arms and body down—was, of course, immediately over hers. The moment her eyes rested upon it she ceased to struggle, and lay—gazing fixedly up at it without moving lip or muscle. We both noticed it at the same moment, and almost held our breath to watch the result.

After some little while, she began to speak in nearly her ordinary tone, except that it was more measured. It had before been so shriekingly incoherent, that we could only distinguish here and there a phrase.

"Yes! yes! Poor child of persecution, you are here!

Your pale tyrant is gone—he was my tyrant, too! With his foot upon your neck, he clutched with bloody hands at mine. Then I was furious because I must be free! You come to console—because the oppressed have learned to know what gentle pity is. You have Cain's mark upon your clouded brow—but so has truth. There is the allegory! 'The meek shall inherit the earth!'—'He that was first shall be last!' That brow shall grow bright once more—the curse shall be annealed!—It shall grow pure and white with love and truth —not pale of fear—livid with murder, and flushed with the ghastly mark of bloody hands! I hate my guilty race!" she continued to murmur in a lower voice—"I hate our ferocious cowardice! We dare not be men like the hunting fathers of thy hunted race—the hairy children of the accursed Cain! We dare not meet brute force with brute force, and hand to claw grapple with the lion in his might! We sneak behind our cunning, and pervert the laws of mechanics—which govern the Universe, rule the destinies of men and the earth—into the horrible agents of wholesale destruction from behind our sheltered ramparts!"

"Why, what is the woman ranting about?" said the Planter nervously—turning to me with a bewildered look. "I 'most believe she is a witch myself! Who ever heard such wild gabble? And yet she talks very plain!"

She had stopped when he spoke, and deliberately turned her eyes upon him, and I saw nothing more in their expression now than I had noted from the first—a sort of calm, intense enthusiasm or stern elevation. So far as appearances went, the crazy fit had passed, and she, if not restored to sanity, had at least returned to her habitual mood and manner. She spoke very coldly—

"Yes!—'ranting about?'—a convenient word that! I rant when you either will not or *dare* not understand! I rant when I tell you truths you have not the soul or the heart to face! I rant when I tell you that you are either an insensate brute, a maudlin fool, or a selfish tyrant!—I do not mean that you are all or any one of these things in your own responsible deed—but I mean that you and I, and that young man there—*our whole race!*—deserve such epithets!—because we have and are conspiring together—without concert, even—but from the individual selfishness which has either been educated into us or has been deliberately assumed by ourselves in spite of experience—to oppress our fellow-men—not of one color—but of *all!*—of our own! Release me!" and with a sudden effort, she threw the terrified negro across the room and sprang to her feet. We both rose to seize her, but she walked with the utmost calmness of look and manner right up to the astounded Planter.

"Do not place your hands upon me again. I am perfectly myself now. I know I have been delirious—I am not so any longer. Forgive what I have said, that you did not understand, and done, that may have been rude and violent, for the paroxysm has passed, and I now know you as you are. You have no doubt been kind, and I shall thank you as a brother!"

My friend was entirely confounded by this sudden change, and stared at the woman with such an expression of almost ludicrous surprise, that I could not for the life of me restrain a slight disposition to smile—particularly when I caught a glimpse of the eager and abject form of Tom creeping stealthily behind her, and from a respectful distance, catching, with pricked ears, open mouth, and wide staring eyes, every word that fell from her lips.

"Does *he* live?" she said to me, as she turned slowly towards the old man, and bent over him—feeling his pulsation—before I could answer she looked up—

"Yes! it is all well as yet. Leave him to me—he will recover soon in my charge. Thank God!—he was insensible while I was so!—was he not?" she asked eagerly, turning her head.

"Yes; he has not moved yet!"

"We can't leave this poor woman here alone!"—exclaimed my friend, with returning self-possession—"We must remove them to my house and have them cared for!"

"No, friend—that cannot be!" said the woman—"We live here or we die here! If you wish to do any thing, send your slaves here with provisions and some simple comforts. Leave that young man with me, and we will nurse him ourselves!"

My friend was about to answer vehemently with his usual rough impatience of contradiction, but I appealed to him in a beseeching look for acquiescence—for the present at least. I found some difficulty, in the hurried and whispered conversation which ensued while she turned back to affectionate offices—in convincing him that it was best to let this strange and unmanageable woman have her own way—that we must humor her, or we could do nothing for her.

He finally consented, with evident reluctance, to remain with me, and send Tom back to the plantation for supplies. It was about twenty miles distant, and we might expect to hear something of our scout by mid-day to-morrow. When it was explained to Tom what was expected of him, he accepted the mission with astonishing alacrity, and expressed with eagerness, in his own quaint fashion, his readiness to do every thing that speed and energy could accomplish, for he said, with a shamed and sneaking glance at me—

"She aint no witch—Jim are jes the nigger fool I sed he war! She be a good woman, massa!—Tom will gib he's scalp fur hur any time!" and springing upon his horse he galloped away, rifle in hand, and alone across these dangerous wilds.

"Tom is all right now!" I said, with an attempt at a smile as we turned into the house.

"Yes; he's brave as a bull-dog, when he knows what he's doing," answered my friend, with a contemplative lo͝ok, as we turned towards the round house—"But, by heaven!—I'd like to know where he gets his sudden confidence from—for this woman seems now almost as much of a witch to me as she did at first to him! She must be either a witch or a mad-woman!"

"Nonsense!" said I, "she is neither!"

I reconciled our Planter, in some degree, to what, apparently, there was no mode of escape from, and on re-entering the house, he acted with considerable circumspection, not a little to my amusement!—I could not help perceiving that this caution was not a little tempered with awe.

The woman continued perfectly quiet—administered to her husband in many sagacious though unusual ways, and he evidently improved.

Tom returned punctually the next day, bringing with him a supply of creature comforts and leading my horse. I was greatly surprised to see the animal back again, and turning to my friend, stared him in the face, exclaiming—

"Why, where did Tom get my horse? This is the first time I've thought of him since the fight—I supposed he must have been carried off by the Cherokees!"

He laughed heartily, while Tom grinned his broadest grin.

"Yah! yah! yah, massa! Dat witch-er-woman witch he back agin!"

Tom had brought another companion, in whose pluck he had more confidence, I suppose, and they both laughed with great apparent enjoyment at this sally. My friend slapped me on the shoulder pleasantly—

"I'm afraid you would have gone off on a broom-stick sure enough, but that your horse was wiser than yourself, and knew his way home better! We took his back trail, expecting to find some of your bones, at least, and it brought us to this place!"

"Well, I shall learn to place my trust in horses more hereafter—that is all!" and we proceeded to arrange our stores. In finding places to deposite them around the single chamber,

I took an opportunity to examine the little recess of which I have made mention. I was not much surprised to find it filled with books—for that I was prepared to expect—but for the number of rare and valuable works upon ONE subject, I had never seen it surpassed, even in extensive and pretentious libraries. They were nearly all works upon Social Science, and especially in its relations to Mechanics. I had only time to glance hastily over the titles, but they impressed me quite as strangely as had the appearance of the room and its wheels and models in the first place. This discovery only served to increase my curiosity.

We soon had every thing arranged in some sort of rude comfort—and as it was too late for any body to return to the plantation, my friend consented to remain until morning. My wound proved less formidable, now that there were others to wait upon the wounded. The old man was gradually waking and the woman continued perfectly calm.

Tom was very active now, and quickly produced for us an admirable supper. He was very alert in serving the woman, and would jump eagerly at her slightest gesture, and ran to do any errand she might require. It was even amusing to observe how reverentially he watched her and obeyed the slightest word or movement of the hand, and even endeavored to anticipate her very thought.

She received it all as a matter of course, merely deigning the acknowledgment of a look. She seldom spoke to us, and then it was in an abrupt and almost imperative manner, which excessively disgusted my Planter friend—though he obeyed her with nearly the alacrity of Tom himself—and then would come back to me growling in an undertone, most furiously about—" A crazy harriden !—an insolent virago !—a ranting fanatic !—a wier-woman !—a witch !—a she-devil," &c. I did not pay much attention to all these expletives, for I felt how entirely impulsive they were, and how little they expressed of his real feeling about her.

We passed the night quietly, and had the satisfaction to find in the morning that the old man had opened his eyes, and after his bath, seemed entirely conscious—recognizing me with a smile, and my friend with a slight but placid movement of the head. He made no attempt to speak, and it soon became apparent that he had, temporarily, at least, lost the power of speech.

We were all greatly shocked at discovering this sad misfortune; but the woman, although I could clearly see that she shuddered at the discovery, remained apparently cool, and only remarked:—

"I said his recovery must be slow,—but whether it come or not, I shall be content, for his glorious brain has been spared; I can see that in his clear, firm eye, and if he only recovers the use of his hands and body, the great work may yet be accomplished!" and she turned off about her domestic duties, as he nodded a sublimely placid acquiescence,—at least so it seemed to me!

The Planter was early ready to return,—telling me that he would send over a servant every day, or come himself to see how we were getting on. He offered to leave Tom with us, but I had stoutly refused, and the woman peremptorily. Tom brought up the horses the Planter had mounted, and the other slave was also in the saddle, when Tom, who had been standing during the moments of leave-taking, came forward, and making a humble bow at his master's stirrup, said, in a faltering voice:—

"Massa!—you please to gib Tom leave to stay here and wait on dis gemmen and dat sick lady?"

"Why, Tom, she wont have you, my good fellow! I've offered to leave you already!"

Tom seemed greatly humiliated by this speech, and bowed his head with a look of deep mortification for a moment, and then lifting it suddenly, exclaimed, with a droll look of eager entreaty:—

"Dat no matter to Tom, Massa! He sleep under de tree outside, and bring de wood, and fetch de water from de spring, and no look at um if she no like it for Tom!"

I said to the planter, in a low voice:—

"Perhaps you had better let him stay! The poor fellow seems to be very much in earnest, and may be of assistance!"

"You know I wanted you to keep him,—but what will this virago inside say to it? I believe she has bewitched him already,—do you think she won't whisk him off on a broomstick, nor anything of that sort?"

"O, no! I'll make his peace with her,—I'll engage! but I want him to stay now,—because this sudden and unexpected sort of sympathy and veneration for this woman interests me, and I wish to trace its real cause,—at present it is entirely inexplicable!"

"O, very good! Tom, you may stay. It seems as curious to me as to you. I shall come over as often as I can to see you all,—but," he added, leaning down from his saddle and speaking in a whisper:—"I want you to beware how Tom hears any more of her fanatical talk about Cain and the darkies,—such things always lead to mischief, and I'm half afraid that is why Tom has so soon got over his scare about her!"

"Yes!—yes!" I answered, with a smile,—"I'll see to Tom's morals."

"Then, good-by, and look sharp for witches and Redskins!"

So saying, he struck spurs into his horse and gallopped off beneath the mossy hung boughs, followed by his servant, while Tom, with great glee, unharnessed his horse and led him off to stake him out near mine. His manner was comically exulting, as I watched him until nearly out of view. He would throw his head far back, seeming to be in a paroxism of low laughter,—the chuckling sound of which would just reach me; he would occasionally toss up his arms in exultation, or jump into the air, striking his heels together twice or thrice e'er he came down, and make sundry other antics, to the evident astonishment of his horse, who would suddenly jerk backwards, while Tom, in total unconsciousness, would tug away at the lariat, uttering some comical expletive, until he got him started again, and then go on rejoicing!

I did not mention the circumstance to the woman, having determined that she and Tom might settle the affair after their own fashion. For several days I could see nothing of him, though the wood and water necessary for us was regularly deposited at the door. The woman, or myself as it happened, would take it in; and, as she made no comment upon the obvious singularity of the circumstance, I did not, of course, allude to it. Indeed, the terms of our intercourse were so monosyllabic that I could only speak to her concerning matters of plain necessity. Her wound had to be cared for, but most of all that of the husband! She sometimes remembered to cook, but when she did not do so I attended to that necessary duty myself. My friend had not returned as I expected, nor had we heard a word from him as yet.

The husband grew better with unexpected rapidity, and when he finally was able, with slight assistance, to resume his accustomed chair, it was a grand occasion with us; for the woman had evidently clung with a pertinacity, which was still afraid to precipitate its despair, to the hope that when he had recovered the use of his constitutional strength sufficiently to be able to use his limbs for locomotion, the faculty of speech would return to him—therefore she had applied herself to the restoration of his physique exclusively, and had, with an obvious feeling of trepidation, avoided calling out from him the slighest attempt at using his voice. Now came the shock in full! We had seated him in the chair, and he glanced around with a beaming look upon the instruments of his labor. He even picked them up, such as were near him, with an affectionate familiarity, and seemed to think of resuming his labors where he left them off. Her eyes brimmed and glistened as she watched him, and when he took up his magnifying glass she leaned forward, suddenly, and asked, with an eager and hopeful expression:—

"William, is the light good?"

He nodded his head pleasantly, but spoke no word; she turned pale at this, and said, in an agonized voice, while with blue and parted lips she hung upon his answer:—

"William, why do you not speak?"

He made an inarticulate movement of the lips, raised his finger to them, and shook his head sadly. She clasped her hands and staggered backwards, but I caught her. For one minute she was motionless, except a slow shivering of the body; and with rigid features and lips compressed, leaned against me, with such an expression of hopeless abandon, that I could not help the tears springing to my eyes. She soon recovered her self-possession, and raising herself erect, she coldly remarked:—

"He can at least talk for humanity in deeds; his eyes have language enough for us to converse."

From this time she seemed to me as one stricken; she moved about in tearless silence,—never speaking to me, except when compelled, and then only in monosyllables.

She never attempted to speak to him again, except by looks or signs, of which they had in a few days established a simple but sufficiently significant system. I never heard this woman complain once of her wound, though it was clearly a severe one, and she must have suffered greatly. She went calmly on as usual, watching every want of her husband, and even anticipating many. He had recovered sufficiently now to be able to resume his labor, and she kept near him all the time, seeming to understand perfectly the effect of every new combination attempted, and the purpose which was to be attained.

So much was she absorbed, that she never appeared to notice the fact that we had heard nothing from my friend, the planter, and that still our stores of provisions, wood and water, did not appear to diminish in the least, and that I had only to hobble to the door to bring them in each morning. She asked no questions, and saw nothing but what was required for her husband.

My life now grew horribly monotonous. The eternal silence, broken only by an occasional word to me, which had sole reference to some one of the details of our material wants;—that dumb worker, so earnestly plying his curious and delicate labors;—that stern, and almost sleepless watcher, whose eyes were always upon him, and who scarcely seemed to be aware of my presence;—that noiseless guardianship over our necessities from without;—all taken together, had such an effect upon my imagination, that sometimes I really believed myself to be in a dream, and that the whole of these surroundings were unreal as drifting phantasmagoria through the skies of cloud-land.

I had noticed for some days past that the eyes of the woman shone with an unusual brightness, and that to all my questions with regard to her wound she gave either evasive or abrupt answers. The ball had not yet been extracted, to my knowledge, though I had good reason to believe that this stern being had attempted to cut it out herself in private. In so deep a wound there would be, of course, a severe and dangerous sloughing. She had given me no sort of opportunity to judge how far it had progressed, for, like a wounded panther, she went sullenly apart to live or die alone at the feet of her mate.

I was inexpressibly shocked to notice these dreary symptoms, and isolated and unsympathetic as our relations were, and had been, I wept like a child when I saw her at last fall upon the bed her husband had so lately occupied, and with the first expression of utter helplessness I had yet heard from her, exclaim :—"It is all over! The struggle is closed for me! *He* will finish the work alone!"

I reached her side as soon as possible. She was most painfully haggard, and her eyes were distended to a degree which made their expression seem peculiarly ghastly. She recognized me with a smile of such genial sweetness, as for the first time showed me directly the infinite depth and tenderness of that strong heart. She had never revealed herself to me before, so that I *felt* her recognition; she had kept all her sympathies with an austere exclusiveness for her husband, and those she had given to me were merely general, such as she would have given to any other member of the human family. She beckoned me to come to her. I came and threw myself on my knees by the side of her couch, she placed her hand upon my head, saying, in a low, solemn voice :—

"My son, while I am yet strong enough, I wish to explain much to you that you neither have nor could have comprehended. I seem to you, no doubt, a wild and incomprehensible fanatic—my husband a dreamer! Neither idea is the true one. We are both enthusiasts—and love our common purpose more than we love each other—for a great thought is, and should be, far more sacred than any passion. Love is only spiritualized in reality when two souls meet in the same *idea!* Animals have passions, even stronger than ours —but have they a purpose? They have the purpose of *living.* We have, or ought to have, a higher! We have something more to do than to 'live, and move, and have a being'—we have to *work!* Work for what? For its men and women—its animals, its birds, its insects, its fishes, its reptiles, its monsters, anthropophagi, and all!—Work to elevate, enlarge, expand—to beautify—to glorify! Work to make the flowers like those we know in dreams—the trees express our thoughts of overshadowing strength and love—the rocks, of grandeur

—the mountains, of sublime! We must unchain the winter —quell the torrid sun!—

> We must charm the water—make its sedges spread—
> Must win all bitter berries up and make them turn to bread!
> E'en the insensate sod
> Must wake to know its life,
> To feel it has a God,
> And join the upward strife!

So she spoke, in a rapid, distinct manner, for some moments, and then abruptly ceased. This wild and half-poetical rhapsody impressed me quite as solemnly as the mythical mutterings of a Pythoness would have done, and I could make no reply. Very soon she commenced speaking again, in a voice still more subdued.

"This sounds to you as altogether vague, because the thoughts are new. But do you know these thoughts are as old as humanity? Men have always thought so—when they had brains to think with; they have not, except in isolated instances, dared to speak what they knew! They have hidden their sense in allegories—they have spoken in double meanings—or they have demonstrated in words. This was not sufficient. Mankind requires something more than words! The hieroglyphics of our infancy, as a race, must not be rendered into demonstration alone—but into physical realities. We must speak in creations—like Gods!—if we wish to be worthy of our trust. We must prove that he—and we!—possessing the 'one talent'—(which simply means our earth)! are worthy; and that it may not be given to *him* possessing five! In a word, we shall not and cannot wrap that '*one* talent in a napkin!' We must work in our own despite and for our own self-respect—*must* be doing for the good of others, as well as ourselves!"

"But how?" said I, humbly—"It is easy enough to dig!"

"O yes!—to delve is the lot of our race! But we must

dig up hill—moles, and all low beasts and reptiles climb towards the apex. Aspiration has no wings!—It climbs!—it does not soar!—all that even Shakspeare says is, that

'Aspiration *breedeth* wings!'

We must cultivate the facility—the habit of going up will soon accustom us to new ideas and modes of thought that had never been suggested—but I wander! The relation which I intended to give you is a very simple one. You asked me how we should work? I will tell you how *I* have worked, and why?

"I was poor as strength always is! The knaves starve wisdom because it is child-like! I was a daughter of New England—I was proud and self-reliant—I determined very early in my life that I would support myself! My parents, from whom my plan met but little sympathy, of course opposed violently my purpose to go to some great cotton mill, and work there for my own support. They were poor, too, but proud of an ancestral position; they could and would not resign it, as they supposed, to ignoble associations! We had a long and bitter struggle—the amount of which was, that I learned to hate most heartily their cowardly apprehension of the 'say-so' of the world! I carried my point, and must acknowledge that, for *one day*, my romantic delusion with regard to the general idea of associated labor in public mills and manufactories, was nearly kept up—but the filth and want of ventilation first shocked me.

"In a few hours after the excitement of my new position had passed, I began to feel myself stifled—my mouth was dry and my lungs suffered from the cotton-lint, which filled the air in infinite particles. I nearly fainted when we were turned loose late in the evening, and the sensation was little decreased when I returned to my room in one of the regular boarding houses. It was an affair of seven by six, without a pretence of ventilation, and contained two beds.

22

"The food was horrible! The mercenary wretches employed to grind, and starve, and rot the life out of several thousand helpless girls, proved worthy of their employers! They were just as ruthless barterers in human flesh as hell could ask, or millionaires applaud!

"Since, I have walked in the track of plague, leprosy, cholera, and fever—but I have never seen any thing so humiliating to personal dignity—so oppressive to individual health—so brutal in regard to the ordinary sympathies as the whole system of these mills. The poor children of strength and poverty die off, as regularly as the moths of the silk-worm, in three or four years at the most—or else they congeal into a sort of old-maid-withered state, which, in its wrinkled and horrid distortions, is more monstrous than any thing this side the English colliers!—*according to Parlia mentary Reports!*

"I could not be a slave! I would not be a minion. I left the mills—I left my family with the determination to work somehow—to redeem the earth from this great evil.

"This was a vast undertaking for a poor forlorn female. But, nevertheless, I had strong feelings that something could be done, even by one so humble as myself. But first I had to earn my own bread, and as my education had been good, and I had read eagerly since my early childhood, I thought myself qualified to act as governess, and advertised. I soon found a place. It happened to be in a rich and visionary family, every member of which had mounted some particular hobby of its own. I thought myself in heaven for awhile, but soon began to perceive that hobbies are hobbies.

"I found this family of *world-saviours*—for no one of them was any thing short!—the most intense *self-ists* I had ever met. The only merit they possessed was obstinacy. Each one held to his or her opinion with a ludicrous pertinacity, and the house was one continuous Babel of controversy. All the reform topics of the day were thus continually dinned into my ears, and the running commentary upon this anxious care for humanity was furnished in the dissolute habits of the family. A more vicious, mean, and cowardly set of knaves and beasts I never saw congregated in one household. It was a perfect epitome of the vices of civilization. With an immense inherited fortune and entire leisure, they united untameable passions and great intellectual activity—without one particle of faith or of honor. Each mounted a hobby because it was the fashion, and rode it until 'the galled jade winced!' The passion for notoriety, which predominated among them, was inexorable. All the lustful vices a corrupt humanity ever dreamed of, were practised among them. These were absolutely carried to hideous excesses, and I became a victim.

"The family were very handsome, and the oldest son was magnificently so. He early cast his eyes upon me. His advances were very subtle. He discovered my tendency towards what are called liberal views, and upon that key-note his skill was Satanic as his will was invincible. He imbued me fully with the knowledge of all modern *isms*—libertinism among the rest—in the end! Nothing that clairvoyance has guessed, Swedenborg dreamed, or Fourier idealised, but that I heard it all in his soft musical tones, breathed insidiously against my cheek. I believed it all, and believed him. My ruin was the consequence, as I have hinted. I bore him a child! The wretch had removed me from my place, and deserted me before the child was born! Why should I describe the sufferings of a strong nature under such a wrong? Like natures understand them better without description! A friend who knew and loved me, a just and righteous man, adopted the child of shame, and has done well by him.

One dark night, beneath a murky lamp, I met and stabbed the villain, in the place where I had awaited him for hours. He knew me as he fell, and I laughed in his dying ear. I fled the country, of course, and came to Texas. In Galveston

I met this man—my husband. I had lived there for several years, teaching the only regular school they had in the country. I had, after a fearful struggle, gained a sort of resignation.

"But once I heard some ribald fellows of that rude society ridiculing a "crazy old cove," as they called him. They said he did nothing but 'work! work! work! all day; and that nobody could understand what the poor old fool was doing with his wheels and his stupid machines.'

"I at once determined to know this man! To be abused by such fellows was enough to persuade me in his favor. I went to see him. I found him as you have seen him—a mighty intellect with a feeble physique! We became friends at once. My enthusiasm had only been 'driven in'—so to say, and now came rushing back to the surface of expression. I found him alone, and almost helpless. He had no one to care for him, and could not care for himself—for, although he possessed some means, he was too much abstracted to notice minor details of comfort—so he lived in the most painfully squallid manner. He did his own cooking, and made his bed once a week—for he would not have a servant about him, because he feared he might disturb his work—the apparent chaos of which was his *order!*

"I talked with this man,—for he talked then! long and eagerly. He told me much that satisfied me. He showed me that the reform, for which so many true and devoted spirits were really laboring, was a different thing from the cant of the *professional reformers.* They prayed in public places to be "seen of men;" they, who are in earnest, pray in deeds, and not in words; and neither do they let the right hand know what the left hand doeth!

"He showed me that the popular schemes of reform were all purely theoretical. That they could, and would accomplish nothing *direct!* That all true reforms must begin in the physical! That men were moved only through material means, and that it was through such means that the material was to be reached and elevated. That the laws of Mechanics were the laws of the universe *in dimuendo!* and that the hatreds, the oppressions, the crimes, the monstrosities of our social system, were only to be reached through Mechanics! The law of order was supreme, and this law required a material medium. Mankind was only to be emancipated into leisure to cultivate the spiritual by the aid of *machinery!*—of rail-roads, canals, &c.! Then the working classes would have leisure, leisure to think and feel; leisure to cultivate the arts; to make the flowers grow!

"But, yet, as he taught, they need a higher Mechanics! They have steam, and air and electricity,—they have appropriated the water and the gasses,—brutes, minerals, vegetation,—all!—but one *Power!* superior to them all!

"*The law of gravitation is the law of labor, of life, and of progress!* This great law remains to be conquered! We have conquered the elements and made them our slaves!—how slow they carry us! We want to rein the law that governs spheres!

"He was making the audacious attempt! He overwhelmed me with the calm profundity of his knowledge—he dazzled me in a very different sense from that first dazzle, which was delirious, and simply, simple!"

She placed her hands upon her eyes, and they looked very thin and feeble! A shudder passed through her frame. She muttered:—

"He dared attempt the '*perpetual motion,*' and I dedicated my life to him—but more to the *great* thought! We came apart from civilization, and made us a home here by the unaided labor of our own hands. Here he has worked and I have slaved, to the mighty thought that *God* may reveal himself in *Mechanics!* as well as by other revelations,—and the children of Eve be thus released from *all slavery!*"

She fell back upon her pillow, and, as I started to my feet, a strange, dull cry came from the husband!

She was dead! I turned my head in horror from the realization of the scene, and there was Tom, crouching close beside me, with his eyes rolled up in such an expression of horror and sympathy, that I was even more profoundly moved. He had evidently crept in, and been listening to everything she said!

Poor Tom! He buried this strange woman with many tears, and then we took the old man back to the Planter's house, with all his wheels and models; but he soon fell into idiocy, and died not long after, leaving his life's labor in the hands of strangers, to *come to nothing!*—as all attempts must do at asserting the prerogative of Divinity Himself—whose life is the *only perpetual motion that can exist in the Universe!* Here was a sad and stern first lesson of the presumption which goeth aside in the confidence of its own strength to search after the "strange gods,"—yet, alas, it was in vain for me, as I only came forth from this experience a more cold and impious doubter.

CHAPTER XII.

METAPHYSICS OF BEAR-HUNTING.

THERE are those who can learn nothing through the experiences of others, however impressively presented; who must hear, see, taste, smell and feel for themselves, before they can understand the most self-evident truths. The knock-down argument is the only one that has availed with me for evil or for good; and that, it seems, I was to have the full benefit of, before the frantic scepticism, which had fastened upon this period of my life, could be reached. The passion of the hunter-naturalist for solitary communion with the soul of nature, which had strengthened the life of my childhood and youth into the holier calms of full contentment, had now become so morbidly distorted that this solitude was terrible, unless filled with the action and excitement of danger. My late adventure, from the still farther confusion in which it involved my spiritual and mental sense, proved only the incentive to yet more blind and headlong plunges, into—I knew and cared not what—desperate extremes of adventure. I hurriedly parted with my friend C———, determined to push on to the uttermost verge of settlement, or even beyond if might be!

Now, by way of parenthesis, as to this novel metaphysics, upon an exposition of which I am about to enter, I would say, if there be sermons in stones, and the minnow-rippled, silvery-gabbling brooks be all oracular, and the mute trees yet pantomime of homilies,—not to speak of the obstreperous tongue, nimble-stroked, of "cross, quick lightning," which, "in the dead vast, and middle of the night" doth fright us with its ethics,—if, I say, these have, every one, high teachings of their own, why may there not be more in the metaphysics of bear-hunting than has been dreamed of in any fire-side philosophy?

I am human enough to love this linking of the invisible with forms; this association with the material gives it to the palpable. Every thought of mirth, or vision of delight, is ours forever, when, clothed in fit habiliments, we have given it "a local habitation and a name."

"These are the adept's doctrines; every element
Is peopled with its separate race of spirits;
The airy sylph on the blue ether floats,
Deep in the earthy caverns skulks the gnome,
The sea-green Naiad skims the ocean billow,
And the fierce fire is yet a friendly home
To its peculiar sprite, the Salamander!"

Now, though I have no special dealing at present with the Sylph, Naiad, Gnome, or Salamander, I would submit whether the century-lived glory of that antique Faith be not referable to this "bodying forth" of rare ideals, with all the circumstance of an "earthly house," a name—of the chisel and the pencil! So in these latter times, when a truth comes to us out from the Infinite, that is to abide with us, it is sent, not with the destroying splendors of its source, but through the gross types of sense, wearing the shapes of most familiar creatures, or acting through the common elements of things.

Miracles
Are so impounded now by the stern laws
Of sentient things, that poor short-sighted reason,
Yielding the divination up to Faith,
Submits these revelations under rule,
As only given to her far ken!

Miracles are above us, around us, and beneath us; it is only when the higher sense bends its inner vision upon them, that we recognize them so. The very triteness of the incidents and imagery through which they appeal to our eyes, "ever staring, wide-propped, at marvels, or lazily glouting on the moon," prevents the recognition of their import. But are they the less miraculous, that our own stultification will not permit us to see them thus?

There are times, though, when they come to us right solemnly, in sternness, in strangeness, through chastenings,—when the veil is torn aside, and we are made to look in awe on holy, hidden things, to tremble and believe. In such times our stolidity is no refuge; "we know that we do see!"—and when that time has passed, what are the symbols and the images through which that truth dwells forever after with the soul? The incidents through which the Godhead came, the material forms through which He was made visible! be they pigmy or huge in man's esteem, they ever, henceforth, in one certain collocation, must stand linked, the eternal, moveless, silent witnessess of that Revelation, and of God, against the soul.

When we would reproduce for other wayfarers the lessons vouchsafed to us, how, in what better way can it be done, than by dragging from under the broken seals of the past, that deep-lined imagery, in the array God stamped it on our life, that brother souls may regard it.

Perhaps they, too, may *see the miracle*, and be moved by it as we have been. Though a thousand eyes might look on the same facts, and sneer that you talk of *God!* yet there *are* those with the "gift and faculty divine" who know when to sneer wisely, if they sneer at all! Such will understand us, when we aver that faith can find "the evidence of things unseen" only as it is mated with the actual. How can it be thought or expressed otherwise? This necessity for the actual, is the true old Pantheistic element, though modern ethics will be gravely horrified by the profane juxtaposition! The elder Penates were things, ours are words; but not the less things for all that, if they be sacred.

But though this be a "bear story," why may it not convey a lesson of higher import and severer teaching than the name would promise? Why may it not be made to trace and arrange the progress of incidents which led to a new birth of the spiritual life within me? Which taught me, raving doubter that I was, through the simplest and most natural means—curiously enough presented, indeed—that first and most sublime of truths—God is! Which has linked the "pathless desolation" and "the lowly instrument" forever with my memories of adoring gratitude, of love and awe, and left them to me, the sentient demonstrations, strong as proof of Holy Writ, of a benevolent and active *Providence*—wielding appreciable laws inscrutably on my behalf! But to return to my narrative.

A solitary and perilous journey brought me to San Antonio de Bexar, then the extreme frontier post of Texas. On my arrival, I found the company of reckless scamps who called themselves Rangers, and made this old town their headquarters, in a very bad humor—what would you conjecture was the cause? Simply that there had been no fighting to do for a whole month!

I had never heard a spoiled belle complain half so pathetically of a decaying season, and the scarcity of victims, as did these petulant amateurs, of the late difficulties, in the way of raising a fight! They seemed to imagine the whole world was conspiring against them—that a coalition, including not Mexicans and Indians only, but even "His celestial highness, the brother of the sun," had been formed for the express purpose of killing them off, through a stagnation of blood, supervening upon the horrible monotony of an endless peace! Rather than die so base a death, they were just vowing to rush into any alternative extreme—sack some village or Catholic Mission on the other side of the Rio Grande—or go up into the mountains and burn an Indian town, and see if that would not stir the hornets and give them something to do.

After the deliberation due in so dire a strait, Hays, their good-natured little captain, too much moved, perhaps, by the tenderness of his sympathy, and a desire to give them full amends for all they had endured, decided upon the latter of these alternatives.

Lither of them was promising enough; but he, as in duty bound, of course selected that around which clustered the fullest fruition in perspective! To form some idea of his accommodating temper and their insatiable gourmandie, imagine a party of eight white men and two Mexicans, traversing an almost desert prairie, three hundred miles in width, with the purpose to reach the mountainous region near the sources of the San Saba river, in which lay the fastnesses of those formidable tribes that scour the plains of Mexico and Texas—intending, when gained, to penetrate them, and destroy some one of the towns hid away in their gorges—with, furthermore, the pleasant prospect of having thousands of infuriated warriors howling on their trail back to the very square from which they started—that is, if, contrary to all probabilities, they ever should reach it again. If possessed of a vivid imagination, after grasping all that this view presents, you may form some faint conception of what these remarkably moderate young gentlemen were contented to consider sport!"

For myself, being, as has been perceived by this time, just in the mood for so reasonable and matter-of-fact an undertaking, I was delighted at having arrived in time to join the party, and nothing the less delighted at the extravagant gusto with which the fellows seemed to relish the idea of this highly seasoned joke.

Captain Hays had thrown out a hint, as the climactric attraction to any one who might need further incentive or dream of hesitating, that if we had not seen *too* many Indians by the time we reached the foot of the San Saba ridge, we would recreate there a day or so in killing bears, which animals were reported to be wonderfully abundant, and collecting wild honey, to be drunk with the oil!

This last mellifluous argument proved too much for a rotund and doughty little Doctor—like myself, lately from the States—who had been slightly affected by some natural qualms of prudence; but now, "in fine phrensie rolling," his inner visuals were all preoccupied and inspired by the scenes round the camp-fire—himself, with sleeves rolled up—the sharp knife in his dumpy red hand—the fat streaks falling off beneath his strokes upon the napkin of leaves—the steam, "like rich distilled perfumes," that rose as they hissed upon the spit before the cheery fire. Then the brown honey in stately liquid flow from the tin cups, strewed over the tenderly crisped flesh! Oh! it was too delicious! What cared he for Comanches after that rapt vision! Yes, go he would, though they swarmed by thousands to turn him from his bliss!

The best of the joke, though, was, that after this we could not get the Doctor anyhow to realize that there would be

Indians to fight. He would not and could not conceive the possibility of the tawny rascals interposing "betwixt the wind" and that odorous revelation. "Faugh! give me an ounce of civet!" good apothecary, he would ejaculate, with the parenthetic addition, "or bear-steak and honey would do as well," whenever the thing was mentioned by us. Remonstrate as we might, he would see and know of nothing else ahead but these rare delicacies; nor could he be induced to make provision in his equipments for any thing other than securing them. He had gotten hold of something he called a bear spear, which a wag had quizzed him into believing to be an infallible weapon in hunting that animal; then, in addition, slinging a small axe to his saddle-bow, to be used in cutting out the honey, along with a huge pair of holster-pistols, he declared himself, with great vivacity, "Ready, boys!"

We tried to induce him to throw away his spear and take a gun. "Never! What, would you have me unsteady my nerves by lugging a great gun? How shall I then be able to dissect with that nicety of skill so indispensable to attaining the true flavor of a bear-steak? You are surely demented gentlemen!" and spurring his bob-tailed and vicious-looking pony into a canter, he led the way out of the square. We were all soon clattering after him.

It requires precious little time, after an expedition has been determined upon, for a troop like this to get ready for it; with his rifle, his pistols, his bowie knife, his tin cup, "water gourd," buffalo robe, lariat, Mexican bridle, saddle and spurs, the jolly Ranger feels himself prepared to go wherever his horse can carry him, and to meet "all imminence the gods address their dangers in!" He never troubles himself to-day about what he shall eat or what he shall wear to-morrow; for, so long as his eye is true, and his aim steady, his good rifle will supply him with meat for food, and skins for clothes; and what more could any reasonable mortal ask?

In truth, we were an odd-looking set—each one dressed in buckskin, fashioned and trimmed very much to suit individual taste, with no sort of respect to uniformity—our whole equipment making up a singular amalgamation of Mexican, Indian and American costumes, while our arms were of almost every conceivable stamp. The most experienced hunters carried the old-fashioned long-barreled rifle, single-barreled pistols, and a heavy knife; while those of us just from the States, were loaded down with the newest inventions—six-shooting revolvers, double-barrels, and all sorts of new-fangled notions, which we supposed were to make us, individually, a host—for which unwarranted supposition we got ourselves laughed at most heartily, and were afterwards glad to have time for repentance.

Our horses, some of them mustangs, others American, had been carefully selected with reference to their speed and endurance; and all, with the exception of the Doctor's nondescript pony, were fine looking animals.

After clearing the narrow streets of the dilapidated town, and gaining the open prairie, which lay stretched like an ocean before us, with its long waves stilled upon the leap—it was a glorious intoxication to feel the noble brutes exulting in their strength beneath us, as they bounded over the undulations; and, in one full ringing shout, our pent-up spirits greeted the mountain winds that came dashing their cool welcome against our faces!

Ho! for the mountains! ho! away!
For merry men are we!

A short but rapid ride through a lovely region—whose diversified features shifted in panoramic changes every moment as we dashed by—brought us to a small stream, which was to be our camping place for the night; and here, we must confess, that as is invariably the case on the first night out, there was a sort of intoxication rife round our camp-fires very different from that healthy exhilaration we have spoken of. Our "water-gourds" we had discovered would hold "nouya" and "absynthe" just as well, and the time was decidedly at a discount for the evening, which was spent in as gay and reckless a carouse as ever chased the "lagging night-shades," with songs and laughter through the "sma' hours."

Of course, in such a state of things, there was no watch set—and we all felt very foolish, on waking the next morning, to find some of our best horses gone—among them my own gallant American. Some of the thieving Mexicans of Bexar, having in view the well-known custom of the Rangers, to commence all long and perilous expeditions with a spree, had slunk and crawled upon our trail, since we left town, and having ascertained our camping ground, kept themselves invisible until we were far gone in the profound sleep which followed our excesses; then cre t near the camp, and cutting the lariats of those horses on the outside, rode them off!

Great as our vexation was, a general burst of laughter rung out on all sides when it was discovered that an attempt had been made to carry off the Doctor's pony, too; but from the indications, it was plain that the vicious little rascal had been too much for the thief—for it had compelled that luckless personage to leave his "sombrero" under its heels, and the print of his prostrate form was plain enough on the damp grass.

Pony rose a hundred per cent. in the estimation of all parties, forthwith, and his quaint owner with him. There was nothing for it but to wait patiently until those who had horses should return, and replace the stolen ones by purchases from the nearest "Cavayard." As they had nearly a thousand to select from, we were consoled by the hope that we should get at least passable horses.

The return of our messengers late in the evening was awaited by myself, as well as the other unfortunates, with great anxiety, for all that could be hoped of either pleasure or security, on an expedition such as this, depended very much upon the character and mettle of our horses. It was in vain to regret the noble fellow I had lost, for he would be across the Rio Grande in the shortest possible time. I could only mutter vengeance against Mexican horse thieves in general, and hope he might be at least tolerably replaced. It will be seen in the event, that we did not attach too much importance to this circumstance.

When the detachment arrived, I was agreeably surprised to find a powerful, wild-eyed, fine-looking animal assigned to me; but my pleasure was not a little dashed at discovering, as soon as I undertook to handle him, that he had never had a saddle on his back! Here was a poser with a vengeance! What was I to do with an untamed Mustang, as strong as a buffalo, and vicious as a wild cat? After enjoying a laugh at my chap-fallen, chagrined look, on realizing this astounding fact, my tormentors suggested to me the only alleviation, which was to pay one of our Mexican guides a dollar, mount his horse, and let him take mine in hand for a day or two, in which time he would make him "*cabello de buena rienda*" for me.

In a little while the copper-skinned knave was careering like the wind over the plains on my frantic steed, while the mischievous Rangers comforted me with the assurance, that we would probably catch up with him "in a day or two!" However, he came into camp late at night, with the horse sweltering in foam, and nearly exhausted by a run of some ten miles and back, and assured me that he was "muey buena" —very good!—that is, he had been able to stand this tremendous race, without falling dead in his tracks, which constituted the Mexican standard of excellence in these cases. I was eager to mount him myself next morning, for I did not fancy the idea of having his wind broken, by this Mexican and summary process of taming.

I was approaching him incautiously, without paying any

attention to the guide's reiterated "*No! no! por Dios!*" when he suddenly threw out his heels in such devilish earnest that they clattered together just above my forehead, and reminded me that "prudence was the better part," &c., so far as he was concerned, yet awhile. I turned off with a feeling of high indignation at this ungrateful reception of my kindly intentions, and consigned him over to the tender mercies of the Mexican, with the petulant and unnecessary injunction, to "kill him, or ride that devil out of him!" I have some times since thought that the horse must have understood this cruel speech, and to have bided his time to avenge himself right royally—and he did it, too, as you will presently see!

Our westward march was now resumed. We soon recovered that careless buoyancy which had somewhat been checked by the unpromising "first night." The scenery was glorious, the air deliciously fresh and bracing, the Doctor and his pony irresistibly comic; and the grouse was soon startled, whirring up from its grassy couch by the joyous bursts of tameless merriment. That same Doctor, and his better part, on four legs, were enough to have kept an army in a roar. I say better part, for the pony was as self-opinionated as he was cross-grained, and scarcely an hour passed that he and his rider had not some misunderstanding to settle, in the final adjustment of which "bobtail" generally managed to get the best of it. On the slightest matter of offence being given, the irrascible little wretch would stop and bite at the Doctor's short legs; when he, of course, jerking them back suddenly to avoid snaps, his armed heels would prick the pony's flank, who would spring forward with several quick successive leaps, which would sadly discommode his rider's equilibrium, and, not unfrequently, would keep them up with such rapidity, that the tight, round personalities of the Doctor, after a flying ascension over his head, would plump into the grass; but as that happened to be very thick, and the ground very soft, nothing worse would come of it than a smart jolt, which the Doctor would aver, with the most indomitable good humor, "assisted his digestion."

Pony never seemed to feel at liberty to desert his friend, after he had demonstrated his affection in this curious fashion, but would stand perfectly still, and with a very demure, repentant look, take the kick which the Doctor always favored him with before remounting.

I have laughed till my sides ached at this quaint couple. The Doctor was the strangest compound of simplicity and good humor that can be conceived.

The Rangers were most of them gentlemen, in breeding at least, so that the days of our travel glided by delightfully, enlivened with pleasantries and tales of curious adventure, to which I was a most untiring listener. I had, in the meantime, received my horse at the hands of the Mexican, and was very well pleased at his behavior. The character of the scenery was now entirely changed. It had been agreeably diversified before, but now we had stretched around us to the horizon, the fatiguing monotony of a dead-level, sterile plain, covered with coarse thin grass, with only once in fifteen or twenty miles a clump of stunted bushes to relieve the eye. This continued for several days.

At last, however, just as we were beginning to be excessively bored by it, a dim broken line looked in the lilac distance before us like a great bank of clouds. This, to our great relief, was announced to be the San Saba Hills.

"Now," said the little Doctor, who had been looking somewhat disconsolate, but brightened up when he heard this, "Now for the bear-steaks! And I warn you, gentlemen, that I shall win the first that are eaten, with this same spear of mine, which has been the subject of so much wit among you all! You need not laugh, I shall confound you before to-morrow night."

And saying this, he plunged his spurs into the sides of

bobtail with such unwonted energy, that he, feeling himself furiously insulted, commenced a series of caperings even more vivacious and complicated than usual, and persevered in them with such determination, that, after a hard struggle, the Doctor was fairly somerseted, bear-spear and all, amidst a roar of merriment. He got nimbly to his legs again, dealt two kicks this time, with a little more vigor than usual, and remounted.

By night, we could clearly distinguish the different knobs, and the shaded valleys between them. We camped in high spirits, for no traces had yet been discovered of Indians, and we were near enough the hills to reach them in time for sport in the morning.

Bright and early we were under way—our arms all overhauled and in fine order—with a keen relish for the rough work before us. As we neared the hills, they presented singular features. They rose directly and abruptly from the level of the plain we had been traversing. It seemed to be a succession of ridges, marched out like an army of Titans upon the meadows—the lowest in front—rising higher and higher as the eye traced each line back until it grew up into the clouds; and, from the level, we could look into the deep, cool, green valleys that went winding among their feet.

Those in front were by no means precipitous, but rose from the valleys with a gentle curve, clothed all the way to the top with mighty live oaks, bearded like patriarchs, whose trunks stood far apart to give room for their long knotty arms, festooned with silvery moss, to spread, over the girth, not unfrequently of half an acre. As these trees forked very soon, and as there was no underbrush beneath, the heavy drapery of the moss hung drooping as from a low-roofed temple of the Druids; and the thick green sward spread under it, mellowed the gray shades deliciously. The trees became gradually smaller and more sparse, as the eye descended to the valleys, and then in the centre of each was a strip of prairie of the deepest verdure, open to the sun, which produced the illusion of a gold and emerald flood, stilly creeping beneath the grim towering shadows. A few small trees were scattered along the feet of the ridges a short distance out into our prairie. We were all entranced into gazing upon this marvelous scene, which opened in new traits of surpassing loveliness and grandeur as we approached.

The awed silence which had fallen round the party was broken by a quick, vehement exclamation of the Doctor,—"Egad! there they are! I'm into 'em, boys!" and away he dashed, with "bobtail" at his best speed, and flourishing the spear above his head!

Looking around in astonishment for the cause of this sudden outbreak, I saw the whole party bending forward in the act of letting out their horses, while their eyes were strained with a half eager, half comic look after the Doctor. Following the same direction, I could distinguish, three or four hundred yards ahead, several black, unwieldy-looking objects, that seemed to be rooting in the long grass, just at the foot of one of the low Knobs, and a little distance out in the prairie. One of them raised its head at the moment, and I saw that is was a bear! Hays exclaimed, as he spurred his horse—"Boys, we're lucky! They come down to feed on the snails!" at the same moment the company broke off like madmen. I followed, but having been pre-occupied, and less on the alert, was soon among the hindmost.

The valiant Doctor had between fifty and eighty rods the start of us. His fiery little pony carried him straight up to the nearest bear, which stood upon its hind feet stupidly snuffing the air, evidently greatly puzzled what to make of these new visitors! The gallant Æsculapian dashed up to it, and was raising his spear to strike, before the astonished animal had concluded to turn tail, which, when it did, it waddled off with great speed. But, as the Doctor drove away manfully at its shaggy back with his weapon, in his eagerness he had ridden so close that pony, too, entering into the spirit of the affair, was biting with great vigor at its haunches.

Such a combination of assailants was too much for Bruin's patience, and it wheeled so suddenly, that, before pony could dodge, it had given him a wipe with his tremendous paws which brought him to his knees. This unexpectod stoppage, of course, sent the Doctor vaulting over the head of his beast. His dumpy figure looked so natural, so much like the old trick, as it went sprawling through the air, that one universal yell of laughter broke impulsively from every throat in spite of the imminent peril of his predicament!

Happily for the Doctor, the pony, as the largest object, distracted the attention of the bear from him for an instant, and gave him time to regain his feet, and make for a low live oak which stood near. Into this he mounted with inconceivable nimbleness, but the bear was close at his heels. He ran out upon a limb, but the inexorable monster still pursued. He finally got out so far as the limb would sustain his weight, and there he stood, swayed to and fro in the air, holding on with one hand to the branches above him, while with the other he was pushing away most vehemently at the bear's nose with his spear, endeavoring to keep it at a respectful distance. This arrangement Bruin did not seem to feel disposed to agree to, but was cautiously and slowly pushing his way out on the limb, for the purpose of making a closer acquaintance. To complete the picture, pony was prancing, stamping his feet, looking up into the tree and whining most furiously, as if he fully appreciated his master's danger, and was eager to get up to the rescue.

The whole scene occupied but a few seconds. The foremost of the party seeing the Doctor mount the tree, had gallopped on, laughing, in pursuit of the other bears; while we were so much convulsed with merriment, that I verily believe the creature might have eaten the poor fellow whole, before any of us would have recovered sufficiently to shoot, but for the interposition of Hays. He, by a great exertion of his remarkable self-command, so far recovered as to be able to send a ball through its head, which brought it to the ground.

There were now four bears in sight, who were making for the Knobs, and seeing that the Doctor was safe, without pausing, we all swept by in headlong career, to arrest these fellows before they left the plain. The last I saw of the Doctor for many a day, he was dangling from the end of that live oak limb, in the act of driving his spear into the body of the wounded bear, while pony, with his ears laid back, was kicking most vehemently at its writhing body!

The intensity of individual excitement was all now given to the chase. Our party had broken up into four groups, each of which had selected for pursuit one of the unwieldy brutes, who were getting over the ground with astonishing speed in a direct line for the Knobs. We pushed them so hard, though, that instead of attempting to ascend the ridges, they all diverged into some one of the narrow valleys I have spoken of. It happened that a young Virginian and myself had selected the same animal, and, before we entered the gorge, up which he ran, all the others of the party had disappeared into gorges of the same character, which led them to the opposite sides of the ridges. I now began to notice, for the first time, that there was trouble brewing with my horse. He had caught scent of the bear, and seemed to be terribly alarmed, snorting and bouncing up from the ground with a short, stiff spring, that almost jerked me out of my seat. Though his natural action was fully as great as that of the Virginian's horse, yet he, somehow or other, contrived not to get over much ground, and would not keep up. His manœuvres made me feel a little curious, though I am, and was then, a practical horseman.

I saw my companion closing upon the bear, which suddenly diverged from the valley, up the hill, and lost sight of both behind an immense live oak hung to the very ground with moss. In another instant he had fired two shots in quick succession. The idea of losing my shot entirely, made me desperate, and reining the horse's head with all my strength, I plunged the spurs furiously into his flanks.

Three or four frantic bounds, and he had brushed through the dense moss curtain under the live oak, and came through on the other side, within five paces of the object of his terror, the bear, the loins of which had been broken by the two shots, and it was swaying its huge carcass to and fro, and gaping its great red mouth with roars.

Had my horse been suddenly turned to stone he would not have been more rigid than he became the instant his feet touched the earth. There was something positively awful in the paralysis of fright which seized him. His skin had been perfectly dry, and in a second, big drops had started, running off to the ground. His legs were set and stiff; his nostrils prodigiously distended, but motionless; his eyes shot out, and fixed, in the fascination of terror, upon the hideous object. I was shocked. I drove my spurs into him with redoubled strength, wrenching at the bit at the same time. His head felt like a rock, and only a slight quiver of the muscles answered the spur. I fairly yelled with rage as I struck him over the head with my gun barrel. The blow sounded dull and heavy, but there was no motion, not even of an ear. I never felt so strangely in my life. I was frightened myself.

At this instant, for all had passed in an instant, just as the Virginian was leveling his pistol for a third shot, our attention was arrested by the quick succession of firing, like a platoon, from the other side of the ridge, followed up by the stunning clamor, which has only to be heard once to be remembered forever, of the Comanche war-whoop! and then, above us, the heavy tramp and rush of a troop descending the hill directly towards us! There was no time for deliberation! "The Indians! take care of yourself, Kentuck!" hastily exclaimed my companion, as he wheeled his horse and dashed down the hill for the valley. Cold comfort that—"take care of yourself," indeed!

I made one more desperate and unavailing effort to break the trance of the vile brute I strode, then sprang from his back, ran under the drooping moss, stepped up into the live oak, the forks of which were not over three feet from the ground, ran along up one of its massive limbs, and had barely time to conceal myself behind a dense cluster of the moss, when, with deafening whooping, a bronzed and feather-bedizened crew of some twenty Comanches swept into the valley just beneath me. They paused for an instant on seeing my horse, who was standing as I left him, and one of them took the lariat from the saddle-bow, but just then they caught sight of the flying Virginian, and, with a yell that made the very leaves shiver, dashed on in pursuit of him.

This broke the spell upon my Mustang, and, with a sudden start and shrill neigh, he plunged wildly through the crowd, dragging the warrior who held the lariat from his seat, and nearly unhorsing two or three others; then, as if the very fiends were lashing him with red hot steel, he flew, rather than ran, out of the valley into the plains, neighing louder than the savages howled, till he was out of sight! In a little while they, too, had disappeared; a gun or two followed at momentary intervals, and then the echoes faded into pulseless and oppressive silence, broken only by the sobbing moans of the wounded bear beneath me.

I was stupefied. These events were so strange, and had followed each other so rapidly, that I was dizzy and utterly confounded. Was it enchanted land? Here was I, three hundred miles beyond the remotest outskirts of civilization, perched in a tree; my horse gone; friends scattered or scalped; this infernal silence weighing upon my lungs. No! There is the dismal moan again! I must go down and stop that, or it'll run me crazy, sure enough! Ha! ha! this is a funny joke! what a laugh I'll have with the fellows when we all get together again! Oh! they have all hid as I have done, and we will all meet out there at the mouth of the gorge after awhile!

Pooh! the Fates merely mean to try my nerves! Curse that moaning! I must go down and kill that bear. Pity to kill him, too; it's a sort of companionship! Doleful friends we'll be! Confound it, if it wouldn't whine so piteously I could stand it! Pshaw! the fellows will be here directly, and what will they say to find I have been so unmanned by a little silence, that I could not finish a wounded bear, when I came all this way to hunt it? So down I went! The great monster, I found, was too far gone to be savage. He merely stared at me through half-closed eyes, then tossed his head about, gaped his jaws, and moaned. I went close up to him. I wanted him to show fight and excite me. It looked like cold-blooded murder to kill him so, and we the only live things near: but he wouldn't notice me.

His back was broken, and he had enough to occupy him. Wouldn't it be merciful to put him out of pain? Yes! but who's going to be merciful to me when I'm starving, after my ammunition gives out! I felt jealous of the bear's good luck, in having me there with a large knife to kill him at once!

All my logic wouldn't do. Sophise as I might, the awful conviction was settling about my brain that the party had been hopelessly scattered, and that I was left alone, with no experience to guide me back, and no hope of getting back on foot if I had possessed experience. But it wouldn't do to let this feeling gain the ascendant. I must have something to employ me. They *might* come yet.

So, I deliberately split the bear's skull open with my bowie-knife, and went to work very formally to dissect him. I managed to protract this operation to such a length, that, when I looked up, I was surprised to find that the sun was setting. But I had no longer to complain of the stillness. This was the signal for the voices of the wilderness to break forth.

A long, screeching cry, that seemed right at my ear, made my blood curdle. I looked around. The limbs of a live oak, near, were rustling and swaying, as under some great weight. The head of a panther peered out from between two bunches of moss. We looked at each other very coolly. He stretched his white throat from the covert, turned up his nose and snuffed towards me. He smelt the blood. His eyes were very large and gleaming, but he looked innocent enough; his face seemed so good-natured and familiar, that I felt for the moment we must be old acquaintances, that I ought to offer to take his paw. There's no harm in him!

He stretched his jaws to scream again, and I saw his long, white fangs: the cat tribe are well furnished about the jaws. But, horror! his cry has a dozen echoes all around, far away and near. What a caterwauling! God of heaven! it is said they like man's meat the best! Oh! but these are simple boors, uncontaminated by luxurious tastes. They won't know any better, unless they have heard the tradition. But, then, it is something of a risk if they haven't. What shall I do? Shoot that meek-looking panther in the eyes? Dead panthers tell no tales!

No, the Indians will hear the gun, and I shall have them swarming through the ridges, to-morrow, sky-larking. That won't do. What then? Why, I'll climb to the top of this live oak, so that these nimble gentry can't get above me, unless they jump out of the moon; and I'll tie myself up there, and swing about 'till morning. So long as I'm above 'em, I'm safe, for I can see their eyes as they come up, and rake down the limb.

This conclusion was forthwith acted upon. I didn't like that panther to stand there watching me, though, for he would be sure to tell, and I should be besieged all night; so I picked up some round pebbles that were strewed along the hill side, and took deliberate aim at his broad, innocent face. The first one cut the moss, just above his head. He looked up, with a quick movement, and low growl, evidently wondering prodigiously where it came from. He had no suspicion of me at all, and looked down again very friendly, and very inquisitive.

I tried it again. This time I struck the limb near him, and the stroke rang sharply. He clapped his paw over the place, clawed it and smelt. The simple fellow didn't look at me, at all. I felt almost ashamed to be imposing upon him so. But while he was thus engaged, I sent another, this whistled past him on the other side. He wheeled and clawed at the sound. At last I struck him, plumb! He saw the pebble fall, and go rolling down the hill, and with a savage growl leaped out of the tree after it, and went chasing it down into the valley. It was clear he thought the place bewitched; for he didn't come back again until it had grown quite dark, if he came even them!

I took some of the choicer pieces of the bear and hung them to a swinging limb, where they would be out of reach, and then ascended the live oak. I climbed and climbed until I got so high, that, by standing straight, I could look out above the top, and see the stars twinkling in a very sleepy sort of fashion, as if they had been called up too early, and had not decided whether they should wake at all, yet a while.

The moon was just wheeling up her chaste disc from behind the mountains. They all looked too much like old times to be pleasant just then; so I dodged my head beneath the shade of the moss again, and made my arrangements with the most accommodating forks for the night. That settled, I went to sleep counting the answers to the nearest panther's cry, guessing how many there were to the acre;

or conjecturing whether wolves learned to howl by gamut, and how many quavers made their endless bars, or wondering whether "rattle! rattle! snap! snap!" was considered a legitimate chorus to "tu whit! tu whoo!" by the San Saba owls.

I got tired conjecturing about the owls, for they seemed to have taken that matter in hand with regard to me, and came flapping and hooting about the tree tops, and shining their great eyes curiously at me, as they went by, till I almost foamed with spite, because I couldn't punch them out. The moon got up over head at last, and that narrow little valley, which looked so pretty in the morning sunshine, now lay along the deep bosom of the shadow, in the light, braiding them like a silver ribbon. Those graceful little creatures stepping across it, one, two, three, they are ocelots, spotted like a pard. What a carouse is going on down there over that bear's carcass. The brutes are about to hold a carnival here to-night, in celebration of my release from the thraldom and restraints of civilization. Confound 'em, if they hadn't such rakish ways about them, I would come down and do the "honors" for them genteelly, as a civil host should! Can't trust 'em, though! How their eyes do sparkle and flash green flames, as they spit and claw at each other over the bones. The panther rules the roost down there. I wonder if the puma is going to come.

I wish he would. There'll be rare scintillating fire-works from their eyes should they get to battling. I suppose I should see all the cat family by the light, sitting on their haunches around, connoisseuring. That would be funny, for they are a sober, demure-looking generation. Look at that pack of wolves sitting off there in the moonlight. How they fidget, and whine, and lick their chops. They dare not come nearer! Good for them, the sneaking grave-robbers! Those panthers are gleaming their eyes up this way. Have they scented? Can it be they suspect? There go the gleams shooting up. What can it mean? Ha! the greedy rogue! He is jumping up at the tit-bits, that I hung on a limb. He's welcome to them if he can get them—if that'll satisfy him so far that he wont attempt to make tit-bits out of me.

Ha! ha! strange that that quaint song about the fairies should be buzzing through my brain now:—

"From the silver tops of the moon-touched trees,
Where they swing in their cobweb hammocks high,
And rocked about in the evening breeze ——"

I'd make a good-sized courtier for Queen Mab's

"Hall of state in the lilly's cup."

I wonder how the "wee people" would fancy buckskins. I'm "rocked about in the evening breeze" with a vengeance. I wish I had "cobwebs," or something stouter in proportion, to lash my "hammock" a little more securely—

"Ye Gods!—
From fairies and tempters of the night
Guard me!"

Rather heathenish rendering that of—

"And now I lay me down to sleep," &c.

I fear I am no better than a heathen, anyhow! But bless us, they say a fairy is

"Something betwixt heaven and hell,
Something that neither stood nor fell—
Something that through thy wit or will,
May work thee good, may work thee ill."

i. e. it is a "betweenity!" But hush! they are "pesky folk," and won't stand being spoken of disrespectfully. They "may work thee ill," I am ill enough off already!

Curious notions to get into a body's head! I wonder if

there should be any angels, whether my predicament does not remind them something of the young Hebrew they saw in the lion's den, three thousand cycles ago—except that I am a trifle higher up than he was. But lions didn't climb then. I believe they haven't learned yet so well as panthers —cases mightily alike, anyhow! The angels pitied him, for they are said to be very compassionate; and maybe they'd pity me, too, if I were not such an unmitigated sinner, and didn't feel ashamed to ask their pity. I have no hope in that direction, for I never believed in them; though it *would* be a comfort now. I have sneered like a devil about their "harping on their harps," when they had never done me any harm—and I didn't want their help—even if I was to be overtaken with a belief in them now—I don't fancy such times as this for repentance and begging—don't think they would either.

Roar away down there—that's right! Saturnalia of the grizzly fiends! That's the music for the brave Sceptic! His religion is to hate and to defy! Pooh! I'm getting a little cracked, I believe, and sleepy, too. Ticklish place this, to dream, unless it is of hugging! Wonder what effect Mrs. Mab's chariot wheels, driven athwart one's nose, would have upon dreams up here? Warrant her "time out of mind coach makers," "joiner squirrel and old grub," are plenty enough out this way. Ha! ha! to think of her "team of atomies" galloping across the panther's snout.

Plague this unruly member! I can't keep it from prating about God! I'd like to know how high the Doctor roosts to-night? I'm afraid that it is in Abraham's bosom! I wonder if he has pony with him? Pity he couldn't have had a bear-steak, with honey, before he went; I think he'd have gone without a murmur then. But they say that milk and honey flow through the streets up there—no account of bears though. Sleep! "balmy sleep! tired nature's sweet—" Sleep, indeed! I fear I shall never go to sleep again. I find I shall have to take care of myself, and see fair play. Things are almost getting serious.

Just to think how long that panther's teeth were! He keeps them very white, considering!

I wonder if its daylight up in old Kentuck now, and what they are all doing. That good old man is trimming grape vines. He has prayed for me this morning. He can pray! And the girls,—weeding flowers, I warrant. And Willie, that glorious boy, with the seraph struggling through his great eyes,—pranking! pranking! like an elf. That's a catamount mewing; how soft his voice is—butter wouldn't melt in his mouth. Confound this drowsy fit—I had like to have fallen. This nodding "'twixt earth and sky" is rather more serious than, in my college days, I considered Homeric nods to be.

At it again down there! "Celestial Syren's harmonies!" you are discord to it! Howling, growling, snarling, yelling, spitting, snapping—whew! how the bones crack—sweet-tempered family these Felines! They are giving each other farewell salutes and embraces—affectionate creatures!

But, thank Fate! it is the order of nature that day *must* come, though it does seem to be a hundred years. And it has come at last. The wassailers of the night, striped, dotted, frecked, spotted, one and all, shrink away with mean, guilty looks, while

> "The morn, in russet mantle clad,
> Walks o'er the dew of yon high eastern hill."

Those surly panthers, though, unwilling to go, stop in full view under an oak, to lick their paws, and are looking back wistfully as if they would have thanked daylight to tarry yet awhile. But it will not do, you are not Joshuas, and the sun can't stand still for your convenience. Good-by! When you revisit the glimpses of the moon, "making night hideous," I am sorry to say I shan't be here! "Such sweet compulsion doth in music lie," I shall be compelled to travel away from yours! Well, as the coast is clear, I'll go down!

A pretty muss they've made of it down here. Fur, and blood, and bones! That salient thief did get my tit-bits, sure enough. Well, it is said there is such a thing as starving possible! I suppose I am beginning to feel something like the premonitories. I have tasted nothing since daylight yesterday morning; but they say an empty stomach for long wind, and I am likely to need all the wind I can raise before I get across this prairie. Some of the boys will be in sight though, by the time I reach the mouth of the gorge. It can't be that they are all scalped, and they must know that I am here. Oh, yes, I shall see them, and what a laugh we'll have comparing roosts.

I set off down the valley, reached the prairie, strained my eye over the desolate expanse, and not a living thing was to be seen. I went to the tree where I left the Doctor dangling; the wolves had stripped the bones of the bear, and were still lingering around them. That immortal spear was sticking between the ribs, where he had driven it, no doubt, with splenetic vigor. I looked around for some trace of his bones, but none were to be seen.

Great God, it *can't* be they are not coming! Foolish expletive! when one neither believes in the greatness or the Godship. Instinct of education! Bah! one needs something more get-at-able and substantial than instincts and old wives' tales at such times as this!

I climbed the tree to the top-most bough, and strained my eyes till they ached again. Wide and terrible solitude; not an insect chirped, not a leaf stirred. The pulses of my heart sounded like the throes of a mountain; I began to imagine it the centre of all vitality—the only thing that throbbed and felt beneath the sun; and that His great fire burnt alone for me. Pity that one couldn't live on beams, as they say the poets do.

I wish I was a poet! If things have been here, just as they look now, since the Flood, I wonder if the grass, and trees, and sun, have not become tired of each other's faces, everlastingly by the same. It must be quite a relief to them to have me here.

Who—what hears me when I talk? The earth, these stolid hills, or the solemn oaks, or the bowed grass? They all have "airy tongues," and mysterious whisperings have been heard between them. It is evident if they talk they must hear, and if they hear, they surely must pity me. Pity! I must be whining of pity! What have I to do with it? Have I been pitiful to friend or foe? Have I not swelled, till I was nigh to burst with ravings of defiance to the heavens above and the earth beneath, of the proud mastery of my own will? Where is it now? Cowed by silence! Egad! I did not know, that as he lay in his "old couch of space and airy cradle," this "silence" was so awful! I wish I had Atlas' shoulders—that old couch and airy cradle are terribly heavy as they lean upon me!

What is this silence and this awe? Oh, is it God's presence? Is this the way he looks and comes—with a fearful calm upon him! Is there a God out here in these tremendous wilds? I cannot see Him—unless this vast stagnation, this breathless, bare infinitude of waste, this huge, levelled corse be He! I cannot feel Him, unless it is He, striving to crush my life out with this hideous weight of stillness! Hah! He is not, or He is a God who loves to torture. They will not come. I have been set apart for an awful death, that His dread hate may gloat upon my agonies, because I have defied Him.

It shall not be. I will not starve, I fairly screamed; life is strong in me, and where the wolf lives, I can live. I'll be subtler than the serpent. My scent shall be keener than the sleuth-hound's, my sight than the vulture's. I'll run swifter than the deer. I will wrestle hand to claw with the prairie wolf, that I may tear out his heart to eat—but I will baulk that imperious Malignity. Die by inches? Not I. I'll set the prairie on fire to beacon the Comanches, and dare them to battle for my scalp, or give me food.

And so the infidel fiend within me mouthed its impotent ravings, in the face of Heaven's Majesty, until I almost fainted with exhaustion.

I slid out of the tree, and threw myself upon the grass. Long I lay there, half stupefied; my blood raging and brain whirling with fearful images. A solitary raven "tolled in his hollow beak," and aroused me. I knew it was one of the "ill birds," though I had never seen or heard one before. I looked up. It sat upon the oak just over me, and the limbs were swaying with its weight. It "tolled" that "sick man's requiem" again, then turned its head aside and stared, with "grave inquisition" in its black, glittering eyes, down upon me. You've come too soon, you ebony wizard! Not dead yet, I thank you! and I stared at its carnal glance. Its gray, scaly legs had stains upon them—hairs were clotted on its claws, and the fellow had not even wiped his sharp, wedge-like beak clean.

Think how slovenly, when he came to offer the services of the instrument to pick my eyes out! What wonder I felt indignant, and the life began to wake up in me again. I did not want him go! It was a ghastly companionship, but then I had always felt strangely curious about them, for they are wonderful creatures. They live where nothing else can be seen to live—out in the trackless desert—vast wildernesses of desolation—where even the clouds have fled away, and there is nothing but the sky and sun above, and sands and rocks beneath; the winnow of their black wings stirs the dead air, and their harsh, sepulchral croak, startles the torpid echoes from a sleep of ages. "He that feedeth the young ravens!" I felt now the striking sublimity of that figure.

Dark-plumed spirit of the desolation, in what grim wild hast thou thy home? Thou hast snuffed the slaughter from afar, and been coursing with death around the world. Yet there are wide throats gaping with ravin in that foul nest of thine. How dost thou live, and how art they fed, while thou art crossing continents, the mate of famine? Waugh! waugh! woo-a-ugh! he "tolled" again, and spread his black wings and flapped indignantly away! The omen of his coming is not ill to me; where he goes there must be *something* to live upon.

It is no miracle that gives refreshing to these tireless wings. Ha! I have it. The snails! Hays said the bears came down to feed upon them. I rose, with new hope, examined the ground about me, and, to my great joy found, scattered here and there over the surface, quite a number of snails, some of them as large as my thumb. Ah! ha! I said, I should not starve! and a gleam of exultant triumph shot through my inmost soul.

Defeated! defeated! I shouted, as I impiously shook my clenched, paltry hand toward the fathomless wide heavens; I shall neither die of starvation, nor, unless I will it, at the hands of the Indians. There is game in the hills to be had for the shooting, but I do not choose to turn "root-digger," as I should have to do when my ammunition gives out. I burrow with my claws for the gratification of no one. The first shot would bring the Comanches upon me, and I am not ready for them yet! I shall go back among men, and show the cowards how much a haughty purpose can accomplish. With nothing to creep behind, deer could not be approached on the dead level of the plain before me.

These snails, that ghostly-eyed, jolly old croaker has helped me to, will last so long as the sterility and the sand continue. What a fool I was to have lain there mumbling like a toothless crone, who pleads with death for one hour more of palsied life, when my veins are full of life. I am strong, and there is enough to eat scattered over the earth A child could hardly ask for more! I soon collected enough to make a meal. Oh, ye epicures, tell me not of your crustaceous delicacies, out of the deep sea. Snails—snails that grow upon the sands for me; though they *are* rather light food for a walk of three hundred miles, it must be confessed.

Being refreshed in my inner man, I looked at matters very coolly. The plain must be crossed; it lay between me and life; and the sooner the attempt was made the better. So I girded up my loins and started towards the sunrise. All that I knew about the course was, that we came west, and therefore east must be the direction back.

There were no objects to assist me in keeping the right line. I must walk with my shadow behind me in the morning, and before me in the evening, looking steadily at the horizon, my gaze fixed upon some slight feature, a wave or curve of its contour just under the sun. All day long I walked with my eyes fixed on something, which turned out to be nothing that could be distinguished from the vast level plain around when I reached it. Yet, I felt that I had kept the line, and that was a great deal. I had always to stop before it grew dark, to look for snails and water. For a day or two the snails were abundant, and I came to water at least once a day, but then they both began to grow scarce. The gnawings and parchings of hunger and thirst commenced at the same time. I could no longer keep my course steadily, for my eyes must be employed all the while in looking for food and water. A herd of Mustangs would go by now and then, stop a moment to shake their silky manes, snort and stare in startled wonder, and then sweep on before I could approach within gun shot. The deer would rise lazily from their couches of "knot-grass, dew be-sprent," prick their ears, toss their slight heads, whistle and bound away. The awkward cranes would stalk to and fro, gesticulate with their long necks, and croak; then stop, spread their broad wings, and go with their long shanks dangling behind them. But I could never kill them; for, though hunger made me reckless at last, and I could fire, I would hear the shot rattle smong their thick feathers: but it availed nothing. They still sailed croaking off.

These were the only living things, except "horned frogs," that I saw; and while my strength held out, I would chase the last, nimble, ugly little creatures, with an eagerness inconceivable. Yes, there were wolves, too; but they are minions of the devil, not honest, living things. Some of them were on my trail all the time, determined to be in at the death. Oh, how fiercely I hated them. I tried all manner of devices to lure them within gun-shot, but it was of no avail. They were too subtle. The hairy ghouls! they have the "second sight." They can see death before he strikes, and they will slink and creep with horrid patience in his wake, for one lap of blood. It would make me shiver to turn and see them, like my shadow, forever trailing me. And then at night they would sit around and howl and moan for hours and hours, as if they were determined I should learn my own requiem by heart!

Snails and water were becoming yet more difficult to obtain, and I weaker and weaker every hour. Still I travelled on, though my gait was staggering. I had drawn my hunger-belt, until I looked like a wasp. My senses became painfully acute. The clang of a crane's wing, or his croak as he rose, would thump and crash against my tympanum like thunder, and roar through my brain in reverberations for minutes after. The earth's smell became rank and oppressive; and when the breeze swept by, it sounded like the whirring of ten thousand wings. I began to see strange sights on the prairie. Armies with banners would hurtle by, and their tread would shake the earth. It would turn out to be a flying troop of mustangs. Great lakes of water would glimmer in the sun before me, and when I would reel along a little faster to reach them, they would still travel on, and I could not lessen the distance between them and me.

I was too weak to curse, but I thought of heaven-doomed Tantalus! The star-beams hurt me with their icy keenness, and the moon's light made my teeth chatter; mist forms of those I loved would sail along the air, solemnly and slow, their still eyes fixed on me. The wail of the accursed wolves would sound like the clamoring volume of agonies rolled up from a teeming bell-pick, or the moaning of a northern ocean through cavernous icebergs. The blood tingled sharply and stung along my veins; while my stomach was cold as if it were dead. I felt as if I were cut in two, and my head and feet acting from different volitions. At night, I would lie with my mouth open and tongue out, gasping for the dew. I would eat the grass like a beast, before the sun had dried it.

Yet I travelled on, for while I was in motion, I felt the horrors less; and sometimes my body seemed to drink in unnatural vigor from the atmosphere, giving me ecstatic visions. The most delicious moments of my life would crowd upon me, bringing all familiar faces, wearing the expression I loved best to remember them by. But they were spiritualized, and seemed to be the angels of old joys; and they looked with such pitying tenderness into my eyes, that tears would gush from them in hot torrents. And then all mirthful phantasies would dance and gleam about me, in such quaint shapes of sparkling beauty, that I would laugh aloud and stretch my arms to clasp, that I might kiss them. But when, from sheer exhaustion, I was compelled to lie down, then the awful hell of torture would commence to rage within me; and famine would tear and wrench at my vitals. Thirst, fiery thirst, would seethe, and boil, and shoot like electric flame along my veins.

In this condition I had been moving along like one in a dreadful dream, for two days, and yet no alleviation. I still clung to my gun; but, merciful heavens! how heavy it had become. It felt like Goliath's beam; sunk into my flesh, and seemed to be crushing the very bones. Yet I would not give it up. I could not bear the thought of being killed without the opportunity of revenge. It would have been a glorious happiness to have met the Comanches, and died defiant. Those fiend-whelps, the wolves, to have them snarling their white fangs over me, while I was yet alive, was too horrible.

I had almost lost the capability of further wrestling with inevitable fate, when I suddenly noticed on the prairie before me, that which appeared like a cluster of trees. I was strong again in an instant. My feet seemed to be shod with some buoyant principle. "Water! water! water." my parched lips articulated at every step. As I approached, I could perceive there were other "motts" scattered at wide intervals of miles in a line across the plain. This I knew indicated the presence of a stream; and oh, what a thrill of hope, for I was humbled now, it sent through my weakened frame.

In an hour I reached the nearest "mott,"—a cluster of scrubby timber, covering about thirty square feet—and I almost screamed with eager delight, as I saw from the gully on which it stood, the gleam of water. I dropped my gun, tumbled down the bank, threw myself prostrate on the brink, and plunged my head up to the shoulders in the clear fluid. I gulped several huge rapid swallows on the instant; but when I paused for breath—horror of horrors!—Great God! it was as salt as brine! It all came up in an instant, and it was like tearing out my vitals. The blackness of darkness came around my brain. I was insensible.

I cannot tell how long I lay there, but I fell with a portion of my body in the water, and this revived me. I waked to consciousness, with my brain clearer than it had been for several days. I felt that the game was all up now, and a strange calmness took possession of me. I smiled even, to think what a wild feverish struggle I had gone through to preserve a boon so utterly worthless as life now seemed—and how foolishly obstreperous and bitter I had been about things that now appeared as mere conventional whimsicalities! To die! why it is a sweet, a glorious prospect! What was life without the joy and happiness of dying? To die of starvation! It will be deliciously pleasant, as being lulled to sleep by the roundelays of home.

Strange! I never thought of God now but as a name; it was an inevitable law of being I obeyed, gladly and meekly! The fancy took possession of me that I wanted to lie down on the green moss under the trees. I must make one more effort to get there. I attempted to crawl, but was too weak, and fell! I lay for some time, and still that fancy haunted me so singularly, that my powerless limbs regained a partial vigor; I crawled on my hands and knees up the bank. It took me a long time to do this. I felt as if it was my last duty, and desperately I struggled to accomplish it. I passed my gun and dragged it along with me. I thought of the wolves, and wanted to go to sleep in peace.

I reached the mott. There was one bright green spot, under the largest tree, in the centre. That's the place. It will be a lovely couch. I managed to reach it, and stretched myself upon my back, with my gun by my side, and my head resting on a cushion of moss near the root. My eyes were closed. An indescribable sense of weakness pervaded my being. I felt that I should never rise from that place again. But I was happy. The agony was over; the "fitful fever" had grown calm, and was slowly sinking me to rest. The loved faces of that far away home came around me for the farewell. Others stooped from the clouds and beckoned and smiled for me to come on. They wore wings—oh, how I longed to be with them. It was a pleasant trance. I felt that I should never lose sight of them again: that before many hours I should feel myself, buoyant as they, rise up from the damp earth, and float away towards the stars. A sunbeam, struggling through the leaves, fell on my closed lids, and shocked me back to earth again. I opened my eyes for one more look at the glad sun and beautiful earth. I looked up.

What! can it be? Strange! strange! There *is* a God! That very being *I*—poor I—had thought to scorn, is here in the sublimity of mercy. He has work for thee to do, and has willed thou shalt not die yet!

Directly above me, within six feet of my face, crouching close to the body of the tree, was a large Fox squirrel. The instant my eye fell upon it, I felt that I had been reprieved, and life and all its objects rushed back upon my heart again. Not a shadow of an idea crossed my mind that there was even a possibility of the creature escaping me. I felt as well assured that I should get back to Bexar, and home, as if I had already been sitting in the old rocking chair. I felt awed, too, for here was the rebuke, broad and bright as the sun's path, of my feeble and impious presumption!

Who shall sound Thy compassion with a plummet, thou marvelous Majesty of Heaven? His hand—the hand of the God of Jacob! This is His act! I have looked upon that hand, and in that act have heard his pitying voice. "Go, thou poor worm,—live, and sin no more!" I lay perfectly still several minutes, watching it breathe, and thinking how its poor life had been given for mine. I had been too weak to raise my hand before, now I slowly, and with care, lifted my gun with one hand, without changing my position at all, raised it without aim, for I felt I couldn't miss it, and fired. It fell upon my breast. I sat up, drew my knife, cut it up deliberately, and ate as much as I cared at once, raw! and then, with the first prayer of Faith, of thanksgiving, and of praise that ever breathed upon my lips, sunk back, and was sound asleep in a moment.

I slept for twenty-four hours, as near as I can judge. On waking, I finished the remainder of the squirrel, and felt quite able to walk again; though, on attempting to rise, I staggered sorely for awhile. But the conviction that I should meet with no further difficulty, had become a matter of such positive certainty, that I never dreamed of a doubt.

"The evidence of things unseen" had reached me through the material at last. Faith looked farther and higher than the senses. I knew that I knew! The Penates of the soul, the image of the desolation and the humble instrument, had assumed their holy niches! I was happy, full of love, and humble. Spring-time visions came again. The brazen, glowing sky, and the red, cloudy earth, had passed from before my eyes, and the blue heavens and a natural sun were over me. The ice-ring melted from around my heart, sense and thought and brain were clear again! The madness had passed away. I clapped my hands and laughed aloud for joy!

In about two hours I saw two men on horseback, herding a drove of cattle. I was not surprised. I expected something of the sort. The men rode towards me. I saw they were Mexicans. I knew there was nothing to expect from these traitorous wretches, by fair means, so I concealed my gun by running it up my hunting-shirt, and waited for them to come within range. They approached very cautiously, and when they were within thirty paces of me, I drew my gun suddenly forth and brought it to bear upon them. They were desperately frightened, and would have wheeled and galloped off, but something in my look showed that I was not joking. I ordered them up to me, dismounted the one on the best horse, took his seat, waved my hand in adieu to the chapfallen-looking scoundrels, who had expected to plunder me, and galloped off.

The motion of the horse was dreadful. I remember dropping the bridle, and seizing the high pommel with both hands, while the horse dashed off towards the eastward, at the top of his speed. The next thing I remember was being lifted off by the Rangers at the door of Johnson's, in the square of Bexar. I heard some of them say, "Poor fellow! I thought it was his ghost."

The days were a blank then for several weeks. My next waking was in a pleasant room, in bed, with the little Doctor bending anxiously over me. I was safe—the crisis was past! The Doctor had been wounded, and was now a spare, thin little body. I supposed *he*, too, had seen his troubles.

It appeared that the body of Comanches had been very large. They had attacked the different detachments of our scattered party, very nearly at the same time, and so entirely dispersed it, that not more than two ever got together again. Two men had been killed, and several others wounded. Hays had saved the Doctor's life, with the faithful aid of pony; and it is said the Doctor means to have pony embalmed when he dies. All had a hard time coming in; but my case was rather the most desperate.

The sagacious critic will no doubt smile at the importance I have attached to these simple incidents. He is free to sneer—they are *facts*, and the most remarkable under the circumstances that ever came under my observation. This "mott" was not more than thirty feet square; the trees dwarfish, and none of them nut-bearing. It was fully six miles, above and below, to the other motts, and they were not so large as this one, and were thirty miles from any other timber.

The sterile prairie produced nothing which I could perceive to be natural food for such an animal. It may have been migrating, but they generally do so in large numbers, keeping near the water; there was none in this region. How the creature got there, and how it lived, will always be a positive mystery to me. The impression made by this combination of singular circumstances—the fact of its being there *at all*—then of my seeing it, just at the crisis when I thought I was dying—its crouching so close to me as to make it a matter of impossibility almost for me to fail of killing it, even in my feeble condition,—all together, it can never fade from my memory.

CHAPTER XIII.

HUNTING PECCARIES IN TEXAS—A BEAR-HUNT WITHOUT THE METAPHYSICS.

NATURALISTS are very fond of calling our American animals cowardly. This sweeping statement is only a partial truth; and I, for one, have got tired of hearing it reiterated. The animals of this continent were originally just as ferocious towards man,—if that's what they call bravery, and the fear of him cowardice!—as were any of the most formidable of the Eastern hemisphere, in proportion to the size and strength of the races.

Our forefathers, with their terrible rifles in hand, found our wild beasts quite sufficiently disposed, for their comfort, to dispute ascendency with them in the land. They had been accustomed to grapple with the Red man, armed only as he was with lance and bow, and in these conflicts, the animals were by no means unfrequently the conquerors. Now they are compelled to battle with a new and invisible power—an agent as mysterious in its operations, as it is terrible in its effects—which, as it overawed and intimidated their ancient foes, the Red men, might well be expected to fill them with the panic of an indefinable dread.

The growth of this wholesome fear has been very gradual and slow. The rifle had driven them from frontier to frontier of all the older States, before any marked change in their respect for the *genus homo* began to be apparent.

The Panther, which at first made fight with the hunter wherever he met him, had learned to be more circumspect, and instead of becoming the assailant, and leaping from the limb whereon he crouched above, down on his foe below, was content to let him pass, and stand entirely upon the defensive; even the Black Bear, who formerly had been notorious for his unceremonious habit of pushing his cold nose into whatever he might perceive going on before him, be the actors who they might, became almost a proverb of prudence. The wild cat, who sometimes lost his temper in love-making time, and challenged any buck-skinned intruder he might meet on the war-path for a fight hand to claw, now contented himself with "giving the road" as his sagacious nostrils recognized the smell of gunpowder ahead.

Now these changes should not by any means be stigmatized as the result of cowardice, but be honorably set down to the credit of a cautious reasoning: they had found an enemy armed with an agency, the nature or effects of which they could neither comprehend nor counteract; they therefore wisely concluded to avoid it—just as any other logical thinkers, reasoning from experience, would have done.

However, let any of those believers in the cowardice of

our wild animals, even at this late day, venture into the fastnesses of the Dismal Swamp, or any of those enormous cane-brakes locked up within the sluggish embrace of the bayous of the Mississippi, and propose to shake hands with the first Panther he meets, or offer the fraternal hug to Bruin, and he will see what a reception he will find?—let him be armed with as many guns and pistols as he can carry, I'll engage he will need to make the most of them, the first time he comes within spring of a panther, or treads on the tail (?) of a bear.

The fact is, the introduction of fire-arms, in modifying the face of the whole globe, physically as well as morally and mentally, has not failed, of course, in its effects upon savage animals as well as savage men. If it has thundered civilization or extermination into the ears of one, it has as well detonated circumspection into the ears of the other.

Before the East India conquests of the British introduced fire-arms, the bold and open ravages of lions, tigers, and other wild beasts, were frequently carried to such a formidable extent, that whole villages of the imbecile natives were depopulated by a single animal, to destroy which armies had to be assembled; and even they have been beaten back from the jungles, without effecting their object more than partially. When British officers first commenced lion and tiger hunting, it was considered the most dangerous sport in the world; and the records and correspondence of that period teem with fearful tales of bloody deaths at the horrid jaws of those animals. At that time, the tiger, without hesitation, attacked large parties of men, leaping into their midst from the jungle, and carrying off a victim without regard to epaulettes or color: while the lion charged boldly into camps, carrying off men, oxen, or any other dainties that happened to suit his taste.

In hunting on elephants, it was so exceedingly rare to find one who would charge a jungle after the scent of the tiger had reached him, that such an animal commanded the highest prices. Now the tables are so entirely turned, that we never hear of any one being carried off by these animals, whether native or not, except in the remote interior of the forests of Bengal and Africa, into which the heavy and formidable rifle of the British sportsman has not yet carried its ounce-ball terrors. While hunting on elephants has become a sport, attended with so little danger, that even the placid nerves of a clerk from Threadneedle street may now venture to partake of the indulgence, fortified with a little cotton stuffed in his ears to drown the roars of the brute, and a little sal volatile to stay his spirits when the blood begins to flow.

The dreaded tiger now skulks in caves and deepest jungles, until frightened forth by the maddening and incessant play of rockets, grenades, and every other species of torturing fire-works. While the lordly lion waits behind the bush for the assault of his foes, and is not known to charge, even until several times wounded. In yielding to the mastery man has thus established, these animals have lost nothing of their original characteristics, except so far as their relations to him are concerned—and in this the difference is rather, as we have before remarked, to man the mechanical intelligence, than to man the animal.

Nor are these gradual ameliorations of temper and habits, so far as mankind are concerned, confined to quadrupeds alone—birds, and all other creatures, partake of them, in degrees proportioned to their intelligence. It is notorious how soon game birds, and the whole family of rapacious birds, learn to distinguish a man with a gun from a man without a gun, and with such sagacity will they do this, too, that we are seldom able to surprise them, by any stratagem of concealed weapons.

And yet the white-headed eagle remains the white-headed eagle, so far as its relations to the rest of the world are concerned. It continues to thrash the vultures, to make them disgorge their food—robs the fish-hawk of his shining prey with just as splendid audacity as ever, and continues with quite as ferocious astuteness to tear out the eyes of any wounded deer or buffalo cow that it may perceive go aside from the herd.

But, all rules have their exceptions—and it was to treat concerning one of these exceptions, that this chapter has been written. Certainly, however much other wild animals may have yielded to the awful supremacy of that dread machine, behind which man has entrenched his physical inferiority, the Peccary cannot be accused of the same weakness; for of a verity, it does seem to me that if those same formidable tubes were to pour forth the thunders and fires of Hecla itself, instead of the respectable little volcano, of which they at present can boast, the belching of this huge and noisy chaos would only increase the irate valor of this curious little animal. It seems to be entirely insensible to all those sudden influences, the unexpected supervention of which are sure to cause panic in other animals. Ungovernable rage seems to take the place of this panic—a rage quite as headlong and as blind. Though scarcely more than eighteen inches high by two and a half feet in length, it is yet, really, one of the most formidable animals belonging to our hemisphere. It is gregarious, and goes in droves of from ten to fifty. Its jaws are armed after the manner of the wild boar, with tushes, but they are of very different shape, and if possible, more to be dreaded. They stand straight in the jaws, instead of curving upwards, and have the form as well as keenness of the lancet blade. Their motions are as quick as lightning, and with shoulders, head and neck possessing extraordinary muscular power, they manage to slash and gash in the most horrible manner with these villainous little weapons, which are only about an inch and a half in length. As they do not hesitate to attack any thing or any body, big or little, provocation or no provocation, that may chance to cross their paths, men and animals very soon learn that their only safety is in flight. As they rush upon the object in a body, and fight until the last of their number is slain, it is fruitless to stop and battle with them, as they would cut either a man or the largest animal, so badly, before they could all be despatched, that the victory would prove a dear one indeed.

There is no wild animal that will stop to fight them, and men, dogs and horses run from them in the most ridiculous consternation—indeed, they are the very terror of hunters.

This droll creature seems to be exactly the intermediate between the family of hedge-hogs and that of the wild boar, or common hog. Its general form, so far as the body is concerned, resembles rather more that of the hedge-hog, while its hair, which is about the average length of the bristles of the common hog, is thinly set in a rough skin, and flattened and sharp, as are the spines of the hedge-hog, and of the same bony consistenee in appearance, though so thin as not to be prickly to the touch, except very slightly, when erected—as they always are if the animal is enraged, after the manner of the whole family of porcupines. These thin spines, or hairs, are also parti-colored—being barred with the muddy white and bluish chocolate, producing the general effect of a roan—they are destitute of a tail, (excepting merely a fleshy protuberance,) in common with the hedge-hog, and have that curious gland which is vulgarly called the "navel on the back." They have no appearance of the navel underneath; and this depression of the spine, which is directly over the loin, looks more like a navel than anything else, though it contains a deposite of a certain musk, which the animal gives forth when excited, and which assimilates it again with the civet-cat of the East. Its shoulders, neck and head resemble the wild boar quite closely in conformation, though the outline, of course, is much more delicate, and sharpened at the snout. Its legs and feet, also, are much like those of the boar. Its food partakes of the character of that of both the boar and the hedge-hog, consisting of mast, wild fruits, grains, grasses, shoots of cane, roots, herbs, reptiles, &c.

But, with all its other peculiarities to answer for, the drollest is yet to come. I refer to their mode of sleeping. They usually frequent those heavy cane-brakes, through which are scattered, at wide intervals, trees of enormous size and age. These, from their isolated condition, are most exposed to the fury of storms, and, therefore, most liable to be thrown down. We find their giant stems stretched here and there, through the cane-brakes of Texas, overgrown with the densest thickets of the cane, matted together by strong and thorny vines. In these old trees the Peccaries find their favorite lodgings. Into one of these logs a drove of twenty or thirty of them will enter at night, each one backing in, so that the last one entering stands with his nose at the entrance. The planters, who dread them and hate them—as well on account of the ravages on their grain crops which they commit, the frequent destruction or mutilation by them of their stock, their favorite dogs, and sometimes horses even, as on account of the ridiculous predicaments, such as taking to a tree, or running for dear life, ect., to which they have been subjected themselves by them,—seek their destruction with the greatest eagerness. When a hollow log has been found, which bears the marks of being used by them, they wait with great impatience till the first dark, cloudy day of rain. A dark drizzle is the best, as it is well known that on such days they do not leave their lodgings at all.

The planter, concealing himself just before day carefully out of view, but directly in front of the opening of the log, awaits in patient silence the coming of sufficient light. Soon as the day opens, peering cautiously through the cane he can perceive the protruded snout and sharp watchful eyes of the sentinel Peccary on duty, while his fellows behind him sleep. Noiselessly the unerring rifle is raised, the ring of its explosion is heard, and with a convulsive spring the sentinel leaps forward out of the hole, and rolls in its death struggle on the ground. Scarcely an instant is passed, a low grunt is heard, and another pair of eyes is seen shining steadily in the place the others had just held. Not a sound is heard, the planter loads again with such dexterity that not even a branch of the embowering cane is stirred. Again, with steady nerve, the piece is fired, out springs the second victim, as the first had done; then another takes its place, and so on to the third, fourth, fifth, or twentieth, even to the last of the herd; unless he should happen, by some carelessness, to make a stir in the cane around him, when out it springs, with a short grunt, without waiting to be shot this time, and followed by the whole herd, when they make a dash straight at the unlucky sportsman, who is now glad enough to take to his heels, and blesses his stars if he should be able to climb a tree or a fence, in time to save his legs. If, during the firing, the sentinel should happen to sink in the hole without making the usual spring, the one behind him roots out the body to take its place. They do not understand what the danger is, or whence it comes. Neither do they fear it, but face its mysterious power dauntless to the last. They never charge towards unseen enemies, until guided either by the sight of some disturbance caused by a motion in the thicket, or by those sounds, with which they are familiar, indicating their position. Incredible as this account may appear, it is actually the method in which the settlements along Caney Creek and on the Brazos Bottoms have been, of late years, in a great measure relieved of this dangerous annoyance. When one is taken in a snare or trap, it is torn to pieces by the others in their eagerness to get it free. The planters amuse themselves very much by relating these adventures, as there are many mirth-provoking scrapes connected with them.

My first adventure with the peccaries I shall never forget. I was stopping with a planter on Caney Creek for a few days of rest and recreation. He was an old friend from my native State, had been one of the early emigrants to Texas, and was now settled with his brothers on a magnificent plantation, of which their joint enterprise had made them possessors. I was yet comparatively a new-comer, young, eager, and withal the tragic incidents of my late initiation to such life, an enthusiastic sportsman. Of course, I listened curiously to their many relations of adventures in the chase, which always form the chief topic of the social intercourse of the border. It happened that the Peccaries had lately been doing much mischief to their crops of grain, and as they had been hunting them with great zeal and wrath, they formed the principal theme of denunciation and narrative. Their invective became quite amusing as they took me out to show me several of their finest dogs, which had been disabled by the shocking mutilation received in accidental meetings with this fierce little animal. I say accidental, because no dog could be found hardy enough to hunt it, after having had one taste of its quality. The eldest brother told me of a meeting with them the day before. He had walked out with his rifle into a field of grain, on the border of the plantation, to look for fresh traces of the bear, which, together with the Peccary, had almost utterly destroyed his corn. Here, by way of parenthesis, he exclaimed, "And I did find the tracks of a whopping old *he!*"

"Let us go hunting him then, this morning!" we all exclaimed in a breath.

"Well, well, we'll see."

When near the outside fence, he suddenly came upon a drove of Peccaries in the very act of demolishment. It was too late to retreat decorously, for he had already been seen, and as is usual, they came charging headlong upon him, grunting and snapping their white tusks at every jump. It was useless to stop to shoot, taking to his heels was his only chance. He made for the fence, which he succeeded in climbing before they reached him. The foremost of them reared themselves on their hind legs, endeavoring to reach him, cutting at his feet with their sharp tusks most viciously. It was a loose worm fence, and not very high, and they kept him there for a few moments, dancing, to use his own expression, "like a hen upon a hot griddle," while he fired as rapidly as he could load. He had killed several, without any diminution of their ferocity. It rather indeed seemed to be increased, if possible, when suddenly, to his unutterable consternation, the frail fence broke down, and he measured his length backward, in the cane outside. He sprang to his feet, as you may imagine, with some celerity, and, before they could reach him, over the ruins of the fence, had fairly vacated. After a hearty laugh at this ridiculous misadventure, the preparations for the bear hunt immediately commenced.

We were soon mounted and under weigh, four of us, and attended by a negro "driver" on horseback, who, with his long cow's-horn swung about his neck, was to "put out" the pack. The dogs were a fine and powerful breed, used exclusively for bear hunting, and came of a cross of the bull-dog on the fox-hound—they were all scarred with the tusks of the Peccary and the claws of the bear. On our way across the plantation my friend was particular in counselling me how to behave in the event of any unpleasant rencontre with the Peccaries—for he assured me flight was my only alternative, unless I desired to have my horse ham-strung, or every leg hopelessly gashed. I promised to be very prudent, of course, but with the opening yell of our dogs, all recollection of the existence of such creatures as Peccaries vanished.

There was a nobler quarry on foot, and we plunged our horses eagerly into the narrow tracks opening into the cane-brake in the direction of the chase. We soon found ourselves riding beneath the matted arches formed by the meeting of the cane-tops, bound together by vines, ten or twelve feet above our heads. The cane on either side formed a wall so close, and seemingly so impregnable, that it seemed to me that a starved lizard would have found difficulty in making its way between the stems. So long as we could remain in the paths, of which there were but few, it was all very nice and exciting to listen to the fitful music of the chase; but when it came bursting on us with a roar of fitful yells, that made our horses shiver with eagerness, and we scattered each man for himself, trusting to his own ear, to enable him to intercept the chase, and win the honor of the first shot, then the rough and fierce realities of a bear hunt began to be realized. My fiery horse plunged into the thickest of the brake, requiring my whole strength to keep him within anything like bounds. Now the bear had commenced circling in short turns through the tallest and most dense of the cane; and very soon, when the thundering chase went crashing past me, utterly invisible, though within fifteen paces, my horse became entirely unmanageable, and in three or four furious bounds, I was torn from the saddle by the interlacing vines, through which he was endeavoring to burst his way. I held on to the reins, and recovered my seat, without stopping to count bruises; but the shock of the fall had brought me to my memory. I now did what I should have done at first, had I retained my self-possession, drew my heavy bowie knife, and commenced cutting my way through the brake. Ho! the chase has made another tack; and followed by the yells of my half-crazy comrades, the wild route turns crashing and roaring towards me again. This time my horse was even worse than before. At the first plunge he again became entangled in the vines, and whirling round and round in his furious efforts to release himself, I soon had the satisfaction of finding myself and horse twisted up in a net that would have defied the strength of Samson to have burst. The pleasure of this predicament was not a little increased, by the sight of the bear rushing past at a few feet distance, with the whole pack biting at his heels.

Alas for my prowess! in what a helpless case was I. The moment my horse saw the bear, he uttered a wild neigh—it was the first one he had ever faced—and backed with such ungovernable terror and strength, that I was almost torn to pieces by the vines, and choked in the bargain. However, at the expense of my coat sleeve, which was torn out at the arm-hole, my bleeding right arm was freed from the infernal mesh, when a few desperate strokes of my bowie-knife freed us from our desperate thraldom. Now came, from near at hand, the deafening clamor of baying, of shrieks, and hoarse growling, which told that the bear had stopped to fight the dogs. Now is the chance for the coveted shot, and it required no spur to urge my horse in that direction. I commenced hewing my way towards the scene, which seemed to be at the foot of a large tree. I heard the shouts of my friends, who seemed to be urging their way towards the same point. At about the same moment two of us burst our way through the wall of cane into the open space, about twenty feet in circumference, that had been beaten down by the weight of the enormous bear, during the battle. And such a scene as it was! The bear, hearing our approach, had made an attempt to climb the tree, and the dogs, encouraged by the same sounds, had made a simultaneous rush, and were literally all over his huge carcass, having hold of him on every side; our guns were instantly presented, but we feared to fire lest we should kill the dogs.

While we stood thus hesitating, and the bear was tossing

the poor dogs like shuttlecocks to the right and left, quicker than thought, a troop of grunting Peccaries came rushing in, and charged headlong upon bear, dogs, and all. Such yells, and screams, and roars of pain, and such a medley helter-skelter rout as now occurred, would be difficult to describe. The wounded dogs, with tails between their legs, came skulking towards us. The bear, frantic with pain, rolled his great carcass to and fro, and gaped his red mouth, as he struck blindly about him here and there. The grunting and rushing patter of an addition to the herd coming in behind us, waked us from the sort of stupor this unexpected scene had thrown us into for the instant. "Run, run!" shouted my friend, with a voice half choked with mingled rage and laughter, and such a scurrying on all sides, for the other hunters had just come in, and the cry of "Peccaries! Peccaries! run! run!" and the popping of our guns all round at them, as we urged our horses to escape through the cane, closed this eventful scene, of my first introduction to the Peccaries!

CHAPTER XIV.

THE BUFFALO.

BUT the wildest scenes to be witnessed on this hemisphere are those connected with buffalo-hunting on the great plains. This huge and shaggy brute affords a strong contrast in size with the fierce and bristling little peccary, though in many respects the formidable character of the two may be traced to a single and similar cause. The "downward eye," common to them, is this cause. Neither of them, from the stiff and peculiar structure of the neck and placing of the eye-balls, can, without an effort, see beyond the direct plane of vision presented to the habitual carriage of the head.

Whatever is thus exhibited to the peccary that has motion, if it be merely the legs of an animal, it charges upon, as we have seen; while the buffalo, which is less spontaneously pugnacious, may regard the same as an object of stupid suspicion, or of headlong, blundering terror. The buffalo must be wounded to turn upon the pursuer, and then the charge of the goaded and frantic monster, being always in a straight line, is disarmed of half its dangerous character, as the hunter is thus readily enabled to elude the effects by a quick side motion.

The eye of the horse being more prominently placed, it is enabled soon to acquire this facility of advantage; and it is most surprising with what wary confidence the trained steeds of a Black-feet, Sioux, or a Comanche will dash in and through an interminable herd of these prodigious beasts, winding in and winding out, amidst the surging tumult of horns and heels, without receiving a scratch.

On no other conditions could this powerful animal be assailed with sufficient effect to answer the requisitions of the numerous tribes upon it for their yearly subsistence. Were they able only to assail the outskirts of the herds, the foraging they might do would be meagerly enough eked out upon the weakly bodies of the sick and wounded and superannuated lingerers.

Indeed, were the buffalo possessed of the same alert, high-headed and agile motions of the mustang, in addition to the "bovine rage" with which it seems so easily inspired, the weight of the fore-parts of its body, and of the closely-packed, incalculable columns in which it moves, of choice, would make it the most formidable brute on earth, and enable it to trample the mightiest armies of men like grass in its path. There is no object in nature so terrible as the headlong advance of a great herd of these animals thoroughly aroused by terror. Niagara itself is not more tremendously resistless than that black, bellowing torrent which is thus sometimes poured through narrow defiles of Rocky Mountain steppes, or which is suddenly turned loose like a new roaring flood, to overwhelm the slant and trembling plains.

No sights equalling this are witnessed elsewhere on the face of the earth, though South Africa exhibits an approximating parallel in the migratory movements of the Springbock and other antelopes, to which we shall refer. A herd of elephant bulls, may be, and is properly esteemed "pro-di-gi-ous," by English adventurers in that direction, but the oceanic mases in which the native bison of our plains are accustomed to move, have no real parallel except those in which our people urge and act towards a given point of empire!

When we come to think that at a rough estimate, more than seventy thousand souls of our native tribes upon the plains depend, the year round, solely upon the slaughter of buffalo for food, covering, and in a great measure, implements, and then put this together, with the consideration that probably not more than one out of twenty of the animals slain is consumed, beyond the mere hide or hump, by these thriftless and wasteful people, some estimate may be formed of the aggregate increase necessary to keep up a supply for the demand in this one quarter.

The inroads of our own race upon them, though great, are as yet comparatively insignificant. We are merely guided by the utilities, and have slaughtered them rather as objects of necessary food, than of commercial interchange and profit. The wealth and dignity of the Indian warrior, on the other hand, is nearly proportioned to the number of buffalo robes he can afford to dispose of to the traders, and therefore this article is to him the representative of value. Hence he follows upon the track of the migratory herd, and when undisturbed, continues to slay them with the sole and improvident reference to the value of the skins at the nearest trading post; while the object of food, amidst its reeking abundance, is merely an incidental one. As it may chance he merely cuts out some tit bit from the individual slain, or leaves it, after stripping the skin, to the wolves who follow faithfully in the wake of their sure purveyor.

The extent to which this reckless massacre is, and has been habitually carried by the prairie Indians, can hardly be computed; yet we have the strange and significant fact that they have among them no tradition even of an appreciable diminution in the numbers of the buffalo thus wantonly slaughtered by them from remotest periods, which antedate the first appearance of the white man upon their plains with his sulphurous and panic-spreading engines of destruction. From this ominous event the tribes date those fatal refluxes in the stated periods and courses of migration of the herds, which have been attended by most disastrous famines among their people. Before this hated coming they and their fathers had been accustomed to calculate, with the same certainty with which the sailor does the ebb and flow of ocean tides, these annual migrations, and could move with or follow them at leisure and with confidence; but suddenly the mighty herds have snuffed some hidden danger on the tainted breeze, and breaking away in mad and scattered career over the plains, have defied pursuit, to gather again in some remote and unaccustomed pastures beyond the reach of this vague, indefinite dread which has met them on the coming air.

Thus all calculations for the usual supply of the season having been thrown entirely out, the tribes are left to struggle with the precarious chances of again finding the buffalo. They, too, have been accustomed heretofore to watching the signs of the seasons, and could even scent a drought as far as the grayest muzzle of the leaders of these herds, and could, with unfailing sagacity, foresee what variation from the usual trail this would cause with them. But now a new sign was in the heavens, a prognostic of evil, which, as it could only be felt in dread by their savage souls, was now first more nearly interpreted by the sure instincts of their brute co-occupants of these great solitudes and in these wild panics, distant, so unaccountable to them at first, they soon learned to recognize a mysterious apprehension of the remote advance of that destroying Power, the realization of which has now, though later, come to them more clearly. The brute sense proved surer than the man's in this, as in all other instances in which circumstances have enabled us to measure its actions and their results in regard to the approaches of our race into the wildernesses of earth with the fearful appliances of civilization. The shudder of approaching dissolution has already passed through all those vast herds, as well as felt in the awed souls of these savage hunters.

Of all the modes of hunting the buffalo practised by the prairie tribes, there is no one, the accompaniments of which are of such characteristic and terrible wildness, as that of which the lithograph given is a strikingly accurate delineation. The Indians are driving a maddened herd of buffalo over the edges of one of those tremendous prairie rifts or *cañones*, as they are sometimes incorrectly called by the border men. These are vast yawning fissures, which suddenly open on the great *Plano Estacado*, which stretches in one prodigious plain from the foot of the Rocky Mountains to the head waters of the Red River, Arkansas, &c. Mr. Kendall's description of this scene in his Santa Fe Expedition, is so nearly accurate, that I give it here in his own words.

We had scarcely proceeded six miles, after drying our blankets, when we suddenly came upon another immense rent or chasm in the earth, exceeding in depth the one we had so much difficulty in crossing the day before. No one was aware of its existence until we were immediately upon its brink, when a spectacle, exceeding in grandeur any thing we had previously beheld, came suddenly in view. Not a tree or bush, no outline whatever, marked its position or course, and we were all lost in amazement, as one by one we left the double-file ranks and rode up to the verge of the yawning abyss.

In depth it could not be less than eight hundred feet, was from three to five hundred yards in width, and at the point where we first struck it, the sides were nearly perpendicular. A sickly sensation of dizziness was felt by all as we looked down, as it were, into the depths of the earth. In the dark and narrow valley below, an occasional spot of green relieved the eye, and a small stream of water, now rising to the view, then sinking beneath some huge rock, was foaming and bubbling along. Immense walls, columns, and in some places what appeared to be arches, were seen standing, modelled by the wear of the water, undoubtedly, yet so perfect in form that we could with difficulty be brought to believe that the hand of man had not fashioned them. The rains of centuries, falling upon an immense prairie, had here formed a reservoir, and their workings upon the different veins of earth and stone had formed these strange and fanciful shapes.

Before reaching the chasm we had crossed numerous large trails, leading a little more to the west than we were travelling; and the experience of the previous day had led us to suppose that they all terminated at a common crossing near by. In this conjecture we were not disappointed, for a trot of half an hour brought us into a large road, the thoroughfare along which millions of Indians, buffalos and mustangs had evidently travelled for years. Perilous as the descent appeared, we well knew that there was no other near. The leading mule was again urged forward, the steadier and older horses were next driven over the sides, and the more skittish and intractable brought up the rear. Once in the narrow path, which led circuitously down the descent, there was no turning back, and our half-maddened animals finally reached the bottom in safety. Several large stones were loosened from their fastenings by our men, during this frightful descent; these would leap, dash and thunder down the precipitous sides, and strike against the bottom far below us with a terrific and reverberating crash.

We found a running stream on reaching the lower level of the chasm, on the opposite side of which was a romantic dell, covered with short grass and a few scattered cotton-woods. A large party of Indians had encamped on this very spot but a few days previous, the wilted limbs of the trees and other "signs," showing that they had made it a resting-place. We, too, halted a couple of hours to give our horses an opportunity to graze and rest themselves. The trail, which led up on the opposite side, was discovered a short distance above us, to the south, winding up the steep and rugged sides of the acclivity.

As we journeyed along this dell all were again struck with admiration at the strange and fanciful figures made by the washing of the waters during the rainy season. In some places perfect walls, formed of reddish clay, were seen standing, and were they any where else, it would be impossible to believe that other than the hand of man formed them. The veins of which these walls were composed were of even thickness, very hard, and ran perpendicularly; and when the softer sand which had surrounded them was washed away, the veins still remained standing upright, in some places a hundred feet high, and three or four hundred in length. Columns, too, were there, and such was their appearance or architectural order, and so much of chaste grandeur was there about them, that we were lost in wonder and admiration. Sometimes the breastworks, as of forts, would be plainly visible; then again the frowning turrets of some castle of the olden time. Cumbrous pillars of some mighty pile, such as is dedicated to religion or royalty, were scattered about; regularity was strangely mingled with disorder and ruin, and Nature had done it all. Niagara has been considered one of her wildest freaks, but Niagara sinks into insignificance when compared with the wild grandeur of this awful chasm—this deep, abyssmal solitude, as Carlyle would call it. Imagination carried us back to Thebes, to Palmyra, and to ancient Athens, and we could not help thinking that we were now among their ruins.

Our passage out of this place was effected with the greatest difficulty. We were obliged to carry our rifles, holsters, and saddlebags in our hands, and in clambering up a steep pitch, one of the horses, striking his shoulders against a projecting rock, was precipitated some fifteen or twenty feet directly upon his back. All thought he must be killed by the fall; but, strangely enough, he rose immediately, shook himself, and a second effort in climbing proved more successful—the animal had not received the slightest injury!

By the middle of the afternoon we were all safely across, after passing some five or six hours completely shut out from the world. Again we found ourselves upon the level prairie, and in looking back, after proceeding some hundred yards, not a sign of the immense chasm was visible. The plain we were then upon was at least one hundred and fifty miles in width, and the two chasms I have mentioned were the reservoirs of the heavy body of rain which falls during the wet season, and at the same time its conductors to the running streams. The prairie is undoubtedly the largest in the world, and the cañons are in perfect keeping with the size of the prairie. Whether the waters which run into them sink into them, or find their way to the Canadian, is a matter of uncertainty—but I am inclined to believe the latter is the case.

This description is accurate as the language is striking—no language, indeed, can fully convey the sudden appal with which this gaping waste of piled and torn immensity fills one coming upon it for the first time. It forms a stern and most characteristic feature of these dreary steppes, that climb through thousands of miles by imperceptible slopes towards the white soaring crests of the Rocky Mountain chain.

The buffalo trails leading from every conceivable direction to centre at the far separated crossing places, are, most probably, as old as the face of the continent, and are frequently themselves worn into deep and impracticable gullies, as you approach the point of convergence, by the tramp of myriad hoofs through unrecorded centuries.

Nothing more strongly indicates the fatuitous recklessness of the Indian tribes, whose sole dependence is upon this animal, than the constant recurrence of such wanton and wholesale massacres as this of which we give an illustration. Although the buffalo, for causes at which I have hinted, are yearly becoming less accessible to them—whether their numbers be so appreciably diminished in reality or not, yet they persist, as of old, whenever they can come upon a herd, however immense, feeding in such relative position to one of these rifts as to offer the inducement of possible success, in urging the panic-stricken masses over the sudden abyss, where, bounding from rough point to point—down! down!—their great bodies are piled in a huge hecatomb of blackened, writhing, sweltering slaughter, such as could rejoice only these Red Demons of destruction.

Next to this, in wholesale wantonness, among the methods of hunting buffalo peculiar to their Indian foes, is the "Prairie Surround." The widely scattered line of the Surround, enclosing some valley containing a herd, is rapidly closed up by the yelling warriors composing it, who drive the frightened animals from its circumference, urging towards a centre, where, precipitated in the headlong crush upon each other, the helpless mass sways, bellowing—while amidst the dust-clouds of their collision, the forms of the warriors, who have leaped from their horses upon the backs of the buffalo, may be dimly seen treading the horned tumult with fierce gestures, and wielding the long lance as a rope dancer does his balance pole, with the slight difference, that with nearly every step they thrust its sharp point down through joint and marrow, between the spine and skull of some new victim, whose shaggy back they have but pressed in passing with their moccasined feet. Thousands are thus slaughtered in a few moments.

This scene, as weird and wild as it is real, tames, by contrast, all midnight phantasmagoria beneath the blaze of the noon-tide.

CHAPTER XV.

PANTHERS, AND OUR OTHER FELINES.

In preceding articles I protested against any wholesale denunciation of the native wild beasts of our continent as naturally cowards. It sounds like a sort of imputation upon our soil, that it is not strong enough to have grown even wild cats, panthers, bears, etc., with the full instincts of destructiveness peculiar to their species elsewhere.

Mr. Audubon and Dr. Bachman, the editors of the new work on the Viviparous Quadrupeds of North America, entirely discredit what they call "the stories" of its boldness in attacking larger animals, men or even children. I agree that caution is a highly commendable trait in the character of the Naturalist, but it may carry him into absurdities, too. What is here asserted may be true enough of such poor persecuted feeble specimens of these animals as may be met with occasionally, lurking still about the borders of swamps in the old States, and even at no great distance from some of our southern cities—but that the wild cat did, and does still, in remote localities, and during the rutting season, attack grown up men with a prompt and formidable fierceness, there is abundant evidence.

I have spoken fully of that salutary effect which the terror of our formidable rifle has gradually impressed upon such creatures in the progress of our civilization—but the frontier settlements furnish many indubitable instances of their natural ferocity. Indeed, I have myself heard from the venerable lips of some of the honored compeers of Boone, in the settlement of Kentucky, relations of personal encounters held by themselves on unexpected meetings with creatures of this feline family, for which they were unprepared, and from which they necessarily came off terribly mutilated.

I remember particularly one instance in which the wild cat was met by the narrator in the narrow path which led from his cabin to the spring. The hardy hunter, though he had no weapon upon him but a common belt or sheath-knife which he always carried, met his assailant with that, and although he was fearfully wounded in the struggle, and would, undoubtedly, have had his bowels torn out, but for the partial protection which his stout buck-skin dress afforded him, yet he succeeded in despatching it with this small weapon.

The venerable soldier, who, by the way, is the ancestor of a very large and respectable family in Kentucky, showed me the plain scar of wounds from its claws and teeth upon his person. All corroborative circumstances which family reminiscences and the character of the man furnished, left one no hook to hang a doubt upon in this case, and left me more inclined to believe the many anecdotes of the same kind, which are as familiar to us of the southwest as household words.

Nor are such relations to be thus summarily disposed of, as old wives' tales; the hearsay and hap-hazard gossip of the borders, for they are sound, substantial realities—just as much historical truths of those times as the battle of the Horse Shoe, of the River Raisin, or of the Blue Licks, or any other collision that might be named between the white race and a foe quite as savage as even I can suppose the most ferocious of these animals to have been, and like them rapidly disappearing before our coming.

There can be no question that the port of the civilized man, even without the adventitious aid of the fearful engines he wields, is in itself sufficient, when he chooses to assert his God-like supremacy upon a physical world, to overawe and subdue the most untameable brutes; utterly changing their relations to himself, by the majesty of his presence and his will!

The Editors of the Quadrupeds of America give, in a short anecdote, an illustration to the point:

During a botanical excursion to the Edista river, our attention was attracted by the barking of a small terrier at the foot of a tree. On looking up, we observed a wild cat, about twenty feet from the ground, and at least three times the size of the dog, of whom he did not appear to be much afraid. He seemed to have a greater dread of man, however, than of this diminutive specimen of the canine race, and leaped from the tree when we drew near!

Yet with all the timidity this anecdote is intended to illustrate, the wild cat, from its desperate fighting and cunning, affords a very exciting sport to the hunter. When overtaken by the dogs, several of them are frequently killed by it, and Mr. Audubon gives some instances of its subtlety in eluding pursuit, which would do credit to Reynard himself. One of them is, that he makes for some half dried swamp or pond, and runs into the most sticky clay, seeming to be aware that the stockings with which his legs would be defended when he came out, would prevent the scent being deposited from his feet, and dull the trail! A shrewd conjecture that! but not, as I think, particularly plausible, for in a few bounds the mire would be rubbed off the soles of his feet, from which alone the scent is emitted, and leave him badly off as ever. I have described the cunning strategy of this creature, in the Night Hunt of an earlier chapter.

But I know hundreds of well authenticated instances in which the cougar or panther attacked the early hunters—springing upon them as readily from ambush, as they would have done upon a deer.

I should not feel authorized to mention at second-hand any incident of the many I could command, as entitled to stand among the facts of natural history, but that in my own personal experience I have so frequently witnessed such, that I am compelled to allow some of these a weight proportioned to their authority.

In an excursion towards the Rocky Mountains, I have met all our most formidable animals under the most varied circumstances of sudden collision. On this expedition we saw several skins and two specimens in the flesh of the puma, which is yet unrecognized by any American Naturalist. It is evidently a transitional genus, partaking of the characters of both the lion and the cougar. It has clearly the rudimental mane and tufted tail, which characterizes the former, while its habits approximate those of the latter.

I once, while hunting around a camp on one of the head streams of the Red River, encountered a puma, in a manner much resembling the instance of the wild cat given above. I had gone out in the early morning to hunt, with a comrade, and we were carelessly walking through the thick woods in

Indian file, when I, who was behind, suddenly observed a creature, which I supposed to be a panther, in the act of springing from the low limb of a bending tree on my companion—who was a few feet in advance of me. I shouted in warning to him, when he sprang forward, and I fired. The ball struck the creature "on the leap" just between the eyes, and it fell at my feet. The eyes were burst from the sockets, and its yells and dying struggles were terrific. On firing another load into it, these struggles ceased.

After our surprise had subsided, I examined it coolly, and found it to be entirely distinct from the cougar, both in size, which I am convinced was considerably greater, (I took no measurement,) and color, which instead of tawny, was a light roan, or mingled red and dull white. Then the head was of greater size in proportion to the body, and the rudiments of a mane and tufted tail were sufficiently distinctive. I regret that I was not more careful at the time, for my measurement might have substantiated a new species.

A hunter attached to Sir William Drummond Stewart's Expeditions, was assailed by a Puma leaping down upon him from off the face of a bluff, as he rode beneath. He was walking his horse slowly, when his attention was aroused by the rolling down of a pebble or some fragment of rock. Looking up quickly, the terrible brute was crouching above him, with ears laid back close upon its head, and he saw the wavy stir of the tail in the grass, and brambles above. To whip out his holster was the act of an instant, and he fired into its face, as the yellow glare of those eyes was almost against his own in the descent of its leap. He was considerably torn by its claws in the death-struggle, but the heavy ball of his holster had crushed its skull to pieces.

Mr. Miller afterwards made a sketch of the scene of this occurrence on the spot, and it is given at the head of this chapter.

But what is more in point, we saw several skins of these

creatures, which had been killed near San Antonio de Bexar, in Texas, which is a very old Spanish town; yet, on the most careful inquiry, we learned from the hunters, that they were quite as cowardly, and averse to attacking man as the cougars, which yet linger in the swamps of the Mississippi, the pine woods of the Carolinas, or along the course of our Western rivers, are known to be.

The secret of this is, that the creatures we met on the remote waters of the Red River, where the hunter's rifle had probably been never heard, were in fact living in entire unconsciousness of its formidable prognostics and accompaniments.

I had also an adventure once with the oceolet, which fully illustrates the progress this sort of intimidation has made in altering our relations to such creatures.

The oceolet—which is, next to the common house cat, the base of the felines, and has always been set down in old books of natural history as, in proportion to its size, one of the most incorrigibly fierce of its tribe, and which may still with truth be called the most untameable, as it is the most beautiful of all—yet showed itself to be even more timid than I, in a sudden rencontre!

I was hunting with a friend near his ranche, on the San Antonio river, one morning. The two untrained dogs which accompanied us soon ran off far enough ahead down the course of the heavily timbered river bottom. We were walking through a field which had been opened into the timber, and which being now uncultivated, was fringed by a thick briar-path. As we approached this, some creature sprang up from its outer edge, where it had probably been sunning itself, and we heard it rattling away into the adjacent forest, which at this place was below where we stood.

On looking down over the top of the thicket, we saw the beautifully mottled form of an oceolet, clinging to the trunk of a large cotton-wood tree, some ten feet from its base, with its striped face turned back over its shoulders, curiously regarding us. It was in short point blank range, and I immediately fired. It dropped out of view, and when I forced my way through the thicket and reached the foot of the tree, it had disappeared. There was a large hollow in the foot of the tree, into which we supposed the creature had fallen, for I felt sure of my aim.

On looking down, I saw it extended along the bottom, apparently dead. I was anxious to obtain its skin, and accordingly, after reloading my rifle, I, by a side-way movement, pushed my arm, shoulders and head with difficulty into the narrow gap, in hope that I should be able to reach and draw it out. My head had scarcely been introduced before a pair of flaming eyes looked up into mine from the darkness, apparently within a few inches. I, of course, struggled out as quickly as possible, under the impression that the creature I supposed to have been killed was only stunned. I put the muzzle of my rifle down the hollow—and fired, as I thought, directly between the glowing eyes. When the smoke was dissipated, I ventured to look in again, and there lay the same creature, as I supposed, stretched, and still in the old position.

I now determined on a second trial to draw it out. I had forced in—arms, shoulders and head—so far as they would go, when suddenly the fiery eyes made their appearance again, so close to mine that they seemed almost to burn them! I scuffled desperately to extricate my person, for the idea of a pair of long white claws stuck into my phiz, was not the most pleasant that could be conceived. I was just in time; for, as I drew my face out, plump against it came the heavy crush of soft fur, with a strong body behind it, and I was prostrated on my back.

I was roused from the stun and fright together, by the loud guffaws of my companion, who was too much convulsed with laughter to be able to shoot the cat, which we saw going off through the woods at full speed. On examination, I found the roots of the great tree had been hollowed far under and beyond the line of vision, and concluded that the shot into the hollow had missed aim, as I found the first animal dead, which I had seen lying from the first. We now called the dogs, which soon traced the fugitive to another hollow tree, from which we smoked it down—as is the practice in taking hares when they are "treed!"—and shot it dead as it sprang out. We found this to be the dam, while the first was a cub just grown.

It is a somewhat curious commentary upon the nature of these animals, that the cub was found to have been so badly torn by the teeth of the dam as to render its skin useless. I suppose its falling into the den so suddenly and unusually, was the cause of this unnatural act on the part of the mother, who mistook it for some assailant. I have no doubt I should have been badly mutilated by this creature had the incident occurred any where but in this neighborhood, where it had been thoroughly initiated into the terrors of gunpowder and the rifle.

The genus Lynx is very celebrated in those classic and European legends, which, under the name of facts, have come down to us as Natural History. The metaphor in which a "Lynx's eye" is represented as being able to pierce through stone walls, is familiar to our childhood. From very ancient times, it has been known through curious and various associations. It is a sort of anomaly—neither canine or feline, strictly, but holding an intermediate position both in grade and notoriety. Though it has been much identified with the old world progress and story, yet it is even more intimately connected with the associations of the new world pioneer life. With us, north or south, every body has heard of the *Lynx rufus*, (or common wild cat,) even though some may have identified it with the Canada Lynx, and others, puzzled by its varied marking and size, may have called it by sundry names, such as catamount, etc. In truth, even Naturalists have been sadly perplexed with regard to the true place of this genus, and we should not wonder that the common people of all countries should be as well. It is unquestionably the transition species from the more defined genera, felis and canis, and consequently, as a sub-genus, its definitions have become more involved. In the dental arrangement, there is only the slight variation from that of the felines of one molar less on each side above; for the rest, they have shorter bodies in proportion to the length of the legs, and shorter tails. Their resemblance to the genus canis (to which those of lupus and vulpes are sub-genera,) seems to be less defined. They approach the dogs, not by very distinct stages of transition, through both these sub-genera. They live more like the fox, on the ground, and approach its associations more in choice of localities and manner of taking its prey. It resembles the dog in its fleetness, and more particularly in its acute sense of smell, which no doubt gave rise to the legend about its being able to see through a stone wall—the acuteness of one sense being vulgarly substituted for that of another. But the true physical characteristic, which distinguishes this from all the other genera, is the tuft or pencil of hair which appears, when they are in full pelage, on the points of their ears. This is the most prominent character of the genus, which I have left to be considered last, because it varies so much with the shedding time and seasons, that it has been the most fruitful source of confusion in classifying the animal. At one time it is long, and at another scarcely visible—hence careless observers have insisted upon a most complicated subdivision of the genus.

Certainly this difficulty has quite naturally been increased, by the extraordinary variations in markings or color, which are peculiar to the *Lynx rufus;* although the Canada lynx is more strictly defined. Rafenesque even confounded it into fifteen varieties; and when a Naturalist is led into such errors, it is not astonishing that the popular judgment should make mistakes. Indeed, I myself for a long time held the opinion, based not only on the varied size, markings, length of tail and ear-tufts, of the specimens which I had either killed, or seen others kill, but as well upon a patient survey of thousands of skins at the fur warehouses in St. Louis—that the catamount, or common wild cat, was a cross upon the oceolet and Canada lynx. The oceolet is a true feline. Indeed, all these singular variations have had their effect on me, for I had seen the tail from one inch to four, and the pelage not alone faintly banded, but mottled, through such regular transitions, from plain olive brown to distinct markings, and then to the very peculiar black and unmistakable rosette, which belongs to the pelage of the oceolet, that I could not help thinking that the Canada lynx and the oceolet may have perpetuated a middle species, partaking, as well in habits as in markings, the characteristics of the two. The authors of the Quadrupeds of America, however, take a different view of the subject. They certainly bring up many formidable instances to show that they are right; and until I have spent as many years as they have in personal dedication to such investigations, I shall fully accept their nomenclature. They remark, in general terms, concerning the "pelage:"

There are, however, at all seasons of the year, even in the same neighborhood, strongly marked varieties, and it is difficult to find two individuals precisely alike.

Some specimens are broadly marked with fulvus under the throat, whilst in others the throat as well as the chin is gray. In some, the stripes on the back and spots along the sides are very distinctly seen, whilst in others they are scarcely visible, and the animal is grayish-brown above, with a dark dorsal stripe.

There are six species of lynx known to the old world, and,

as they say, *only two* to North America! I am surely right with regard to the old world, but whether they are, upon this knotty point, right as to *this*, we will leave for future investigation to determine. Be scientific truth on which side of the controversy it may, the animal itself is a very interesting one, and intimately associated with the legend and character, not only of the pioneers, but of the older population of our wide country, for it is found every where, from the middle to the extreme southern and southwestern limits of settlement. The Canada lynx, which is so frequently identified with it, extends from the mountains of Pennsylvania to the northern districts of Canada. With regard to the habits of the *Lynx rufus*, the authors of the Quadrupeds of America say:

The general appearance of this species conveys the idea of a degree of ferocity, which cannot with propriety be considered as belonging to its character, although it will, when at bay, show its sharp teeth, and with outstretched claws and infuriated despair, repel the attacks of either man or dog, sputtering the while and rolling its eyes like the common cat. It is, however, generally cowardly when attacked, and always flies from its pursuers if it can; and although some anecdotes have been related to us of the strength, daring and fierceness of the animal, such as its having been known to kill, at different times, a sheep, a full grown doe, attack a child in the woods, etc., yet in all the instances that have come under our own notice, we have found it very timid, and always rather inclined to beat a retreat, than to make an attack on an animal larger than a hare or young pig.

Dr. Bachman, Associate Editor of the Quadrupeds of America, describes with some minuteness and reality the most common mode of hunting the wild cat by daylight, when undertaken in set fashion by the southern gentry, with all the appliances of "hound and horn," etc.; but his chase is wound up by the shooting of the exhausted animal by some one of the huntsmen.

In a southern foxchase there can be nothing more unorthodox than such an expenditure of ammunition, for the hunters would have been somewhat dangerously furious, and the hounds themselves ready to tear in pieces the unlucky marksman who should have dared to interpose between their heated ferocity and a legitimate consummation of the chase, in "the death!" The wild cat injures the dogs, though, so much, that after losing a few of the most valued leaders of the pack in the bloody death-struggle with this savagely formidable creature, the huntsmen soon learn to differ from our friend Dr. Bachman's opinion concerning its courage, and become very cautious how they run the risk of having their dogs overtake it. They easily tell, from the cry of the hounds, when it is becoming exhausted, and has reached its short doublings; and, as by this time they have enjoyed the excitement of a long chase, they can very well afford to listen to the dictates of prudence in shooting it, as described above.

The dogs used in a night hunt are not the full-blooded hounds of the chase above. A cross of the fox or stag-hound upon the fiercer, snapping, wire-haired cur, which seems to be peculiarly the dog of the negro, makes a far more swift, though not so long-winded or so sure a hunter; and, from its strength and activity, is considered a much better fighter than the aristocratic hound, which is owned solely by the master. Indeed, the half-breeds of this and various other crosses are almost exclusively used for the chase and destruction of the carnivorous animals throughout this country—the game "full-bloods," which, when heated by their long chases, habitually rush in, closing instantly with their quarry, when it has been brought to bay, suffer terribly when it turns out to be wild cat, panther or bear; and, if permitted to chase these animals, the pack is soon exterminated by them.

It is curious to observe the instant change in the appearance of all dogs used in the chase, on striking the trail of any one of these animals, but more especially that of the wild cat or panther. The hair "roughs," as the hunters term it, that is, stands on end over the back and tail; and their cry becomes a sort of eager growl. The drivers understand these signs well, and when beating for deer or fox they immediately call the dogs off the dangerous scent.

As a hunter, the bay lynx exhibits a good deal of cunning and sagacity—quite as much, it would appear, as Reynard himself. Dr. Bachman gives some curious relations upon this head. One incident, which occurred at the plantation of Dr. Desel, in South Carolina, is worth giving. It seems that "the drove of geese were nightly lodged near the house in an enclosure which was rendered apparently safe by a very high fence. As an additional security, several watch dogs were let loose about the premises; besides, an excellent pack of hounds, which, by an occasional bark or howl during the night, sounded the alarm in case any marauder, whether biped or quadruped, approached. Notwithstanding these precautions, a goose disappeared almost every night, and no trace of the ingress or egress of the robber could be discovered. Slow in attaching suspicion to to his servants, the Doctor waited for time and watchfulness to solve the mystery. At length, the feathers and other remains of his geese were discovered in a marsh, about a quarter of a mile from the house, and strong suspicion was fastened on the wild cat! *Still, as he came at odd hours* of the night, all attempts to kill or shoot him proved, for a time, unavailing. One morning, however, he came about daylight, and having captured a good fat goose, was traced by the keen noses of the hounds."

The hounds tracked him up, and he was finally shot; but his subtle in-goings and out-comings sound to us very like the German stories of the witch or weir-wolf. It was surely ticklish walking, though his toes be padded, for the wary plunderer amid so many foes. But his astuteness and dexterity are quite as remarkable in those wild wood forays, which the editors of the "Quadrupeds" have had an opportunity of witnessing. Such examples are confirmed by my own experience.

When this animal discovers a flock of wild turkeys, he will generally follow them at a little distance for some time, and after having ascertained the direction in which they are proceeding, make a rapid detour, and concealing himself behind a fallen tree, or in the lower branches of some leafy maple, patiently wait in ambush until the birds approach, when he suddenly springs on one of them, if near enough, and with one bound secures it. We once, while resting on a log in the woods, on the banks of the Wabash river, perceived two wild turkey-cocks at some distance below us, under the bank near the water, pluming and picking their feathers; on a sudden one of them fled across the river, and the other we saw struggling in the grasp of a wild cat, which almost instantly dragged it up the bank into the woods and made off. On another occasion, we observed an individual of this species almost nine miles from Charleston, in pursuit of a covey of partridges—(*Ortyx Virginiana*,)—so intent was the cat upon its prey, that it passed within ten steps of us, as it was making a circle to get in advance, and in the path of the birds; its eyes were constantly fixed on the covey, and it stealthily concealed itself behind a log it expected the birds to pass. In a second attempt, the marauder succeeded in capturing one of the partridges, when the rest, in great affright, flew and scattered in all directions.

The Canada lynx is something larger than the bay lynx, and though more formidable-looking, is not so fierce, bold, or restless. Indeed, it seems to be quite remarkable for a shy timidity, even when far removed from the neighborhood of man. It is not mottled as the bay lynx, but is gray above, a little clouded with irregular dark spots, and lighter beneath. It is well protected against the cold of its northern home by its long fur. It is very dexterous in capturing the grouse, hares, squirrels, and other small creatures, which constitute its habitual prey. It has even been represented as having killed a deer—though I conjecture it must have been a wounded one. It is true there is less known of its habits than of those of the southern species; but on the whole, I am disposed to regard it as a less enterprising, and therefore less interesting species.

Indeed, it is by no means through the character of this gray northern animal, that the wide-spread notoriety of the wild cat, in connection with border life, has obtained in this country. It is to the more fierce, predatory, and pugnacious temperament of its tawny and mottled brother of the south, that the family reputation is mainly owing. The panther, (or cougar,) with even its greater size and more formidable attributes, is not more entirely identified with our wildest legends, scenes, and adventures, than is this bay lynx.

I give, in conclusion, a characteristic paper, in which a Cougar hunt is described by Mr. Audubon. This, as affording an additional glimpse of the adventurous out-door life of the great Naturalist, possesses a greater interest than any relation of personal adventure I could give, although such are abundant enough. He says:—

There is an extensive Swamp in the section of the State of Mississippi which lies partly in the Choctaw territory. It commences at the borders of the Mississippi, at no great distance from a Chickasaw village, situated near the mouth of a creek known by the name of Vanconnah, and partly inundated by the swellings of several large bayous, the principal of which, crossing the swamp in its whole extent, discharges its waters not far from the mouth of the Yazoo River. This famous bayou is called False River. The swamp of which I am speaking follows the windings of the Yazoo, until the latter branches off to the north-east, and at this point forms the stream named Cold Water River, below which the Yazoo receives the draining of another bayou inclining towards the north-west, and intersecting that known by the name of False River, at a short distance from the place where the latter receives the waters of the Mississippi. This tedious account of the situation of the Swamp, is given with the view of pointing it out to all students of nature who may chance to go that way, and whom I would earnestly urge to visit its interior, as it abounds in rare and interesting productions: birds, quadrupeds and reptiles, as well as molluscous animals, many of which, I am persuaded, have never been described.

In the course of one of my rambles, I chanced to meet with a squatter's cabin on the banks of the Cold Water River. In the owner of this hut, like most of those adventurous settlers in the uncultivated tracts of our frontier districts, I found a person well versed in the chase, and acquainted with the habits of some of the larger species of quadrupeds and birds. As he who is desirous of instruction ought not to disdain listening to any one, who has knowledge to communicate, however humble may be his lot, or however limited his talents, I entered the squatter's cabin, and immediately opened a conversation with him respecting the situation of the swamp, and its natural productions. He told me he thought it the very place I ought to visit, spoke of the game which it contained, and pointed to some bear and deer skins, adding, that the individuals to which they had belonged, formed but a small portion of the number of those animals which he had shot within it. My heart swelled with delight; and on asking if he would accompany me through the great morass, and allow me to become an inmate of his humble but hospitable mansion, I was gratified to find that he cordially assented to all my proposals. So I immediately unstrapped my drawing materials, laid up my gun, and sat down to partake of the homely but wholesome fare intended for the supper of the squatter, his wife, and his two sons.

The quietness of the evening seemed in perfect accordance

with the gentle demeanor of the family. The wife and children, I more than once thought, seemed to look upon me as a strange sort of person, going about, as I told them I was, in search of birds and plants; and were I here to relate the many questions which they put to me in return for those which I addressed to them, the catalogue would occupy several pages. The husband, a native of Connecticut, had heard of the existence of such men as myself, both in our own country and abroad, and seemed greatly pleased to have me under his roof. Supper over, I asked my kind host what had induced him to remove to this wild and solitary spot. "The people are too numerous now to thrive in New England," was his answer. I thought of the state of some parts of Europe, and calculating the denseness of their population compared with that of New England, exclaimed to myself, "How much more difficult must it be for men to thrive in those populous countries!" The conversation then changed, and the squatter, his sons and myself, spoke of hunting and fishing, until at length tired, we laid ourselves down on pallets of bear skins, and reposed in peace on the floor of the only apartment of which the hut consisted.

Day dawned, and the squatter's call to his hogs, which, being almost in a wild state, were suffered to seek the greater portion of their food in the woods, awakened me. Being ready dressed, I was not long in joining him. The hogs and their young came grunting at the well known call of their owner, who threw them a few ears of corn, and counted them, but told me that for some weeks their number had been greatly diminished by the ravages committed upon them by a large *Panther*, by which name the cougar is designated in America, and that the ravenous animal did not content himself with the flesh of his pigs, but now and then carried off one of his calves, notwithstanding the many attempts he had made to shoot it. The *Painter*, as he sometimes called it, had on several occasions robbed him of a dead deer; and to these exploits the squatter added several remarkable feats of audacity which it had performed, to give me an idea of the formidable character of the beast. Delighted by his description, I offered to assist him in destroying the enemy, at which he was highly pleased, but assured me that unless some of his neighbors should join us with their dogs and his own, the attempt would prove fruitless. Soon after, mounting a horse, he went off to his neighbors, several of whom lived at a distance of some miles, and appointed a day of meeting.

The hunters, accordingly, made their appearance, one fine morning, at the door of the cabin, just as the sun was emerging from beneath the horizon. They were five in number, and fully equipped for the chase, being mounted on horses, which in some parts of Europe might appear sorry nags, but which in strength, speed and bottom, are better fitted for pursuing a cougar or a bear through woods and morasses than any in that country. A pack of large ugly curs were already engaged in making acquaintance with those of the squatter. He and myself mounted his two best horses, whilst his sons were bestriding others of inferior quality.

Few words were uttered by the party until we had reached the edge of the Swamp, where it was agreed that all should disperse and seek for the fresh track of the Painter, it being previously settled that the discoverer should blow his horn, and remain on the spot, until the rest should join him. In less than an hour, the sound of the horn was clearly heard, and, sticking close to the squatter, off we went through the thick woods, guided only by the now and then repeated call of the distant huntsmen. We soon reached the spot, and in a short time the rest of the party came up. The best dog was sent forward to track the Cougar, and in a few moments, the whole pack were observed diligently trailing, and bearing in their course for the interior of the Swamp. The rifles were immediately put in trim, and the party followed the dogs, at separate distances, but in sight of each other, determined to shoot at no other game than the Panther.

The dogs soon began to mouth, and suddenly quickened their pace. My companion concluded that the beast was on the ground, and putting our horses to a gentle gallop, we followed the curs, guided by their voices. The noise of the dogs increased, when, all of a sudden, their mode of barking became altered, and the squatter, urging me to push on, told me that the beast was *treed*, by which he meant that it had got upon some low branch of a large tree to rest for a few moments, and that should we not succeed in shooting him when thus situated, we might expect a long chase of it. As we approached the spot, we all by degrees united into a body, but on seeing the dogs at the foot of a large tree, separated again and galloped off to surround it.

Each hunter now moved with caution, holding his gun ready, and allowing the bridle to dangle on the neck of his horse, as it advanced slowly towards the dogs. A shot from one of the party was heard, on which the Cougar was seen to leap to the ground, and bound off with such velocity as to show that he was very unwilling to stand our fire longer. The dogs set off in pursuit with great eagerness and a deafening cry. The hunter who had fired came up and said that his ball had hit the monster, and had probably broken one of his fore-legs near the shoulder, the only place at which he could aim. A slight trail of blood was discovered on the ground, but the curs proceeded at such a rate that we merely noticed this, and put spurs to our horses, which galloped on towards the centre of the Swamp. One bayou was crossed, then another still larger and more muddy; but the dogs were brushing forward, and as the horses began to pant at a furious rate, we judged it expedient to leave them and advance on foot. These determined hunters knew that the Cougar being wounded, would shortly ascend another tree, where in all probability he would remain for a considerable time, and that it would be easy to follow the track of the dogs. We dismounted, took off the saddles and bridles, set the bells attached to the horses' necks at liberty to jingle, hoppled the animals, and left them to shift for themselves.

Now, kind reader, follow the group marching through the swamp, crossing muddy pools, and making the best of their way over fallen trees and amongst the tangled rushes that now and then covered acres of ground. If you are a hunter yourself, all this will appear nothing to you; but if crowded assemblies of "beauty and fashion," or the quiet enjoyment of your "pleasure-grounds," alone delight you, I must mend my pen before I attempt to give you an idea of the pleasure felt on such an expedition.

After marching for a couple of hours, we again heard the dogs. Each of us pressed forward, elated at the thought of terminating the career of the cougar. Some of the dogs were heard whining, although the greater number barked vehemently. We felt assured that the Cougar was treed, and that he would rest for some time to recover from his fatigue. As we came up to the dogs, we discovered the ferocious animal lying across a large branch, close to the trunk of a cotton-wood tree. His broad breast lay towards us; his eyes were at one time bent on us and again on the dogs beneath and around him; one of his fore legs hung loosely by his side, and he lay crouched, with his ears lowered close to his head, as if he thought he might remain undiscovered. Three balls were fired at him, at a given signal, on which he sprang a few feet from the branch, and tumbled headlong to the ground. Attacked on all sides by the enraged curs, the infuriated Cougar fought with desperate valor; but the squatter advancing in front of the party, and almost in the midst of the dogs, shot him immediately behind and beneath the left shoulder. The Cougar writhed for a moment in agony, and in another lay dead.

The sun was now sinking in the west. Two of the hunters separated from the rest, to procure venison, whilst the squatter's sons were ordered to make the best of their way home, to be ready to feed the hogs in the morning. The rest of the party agreed to camp on the spot. The cougar was despoiled of its skin, and its carcass left to the hungry dogs. Whilst engaged in preparing our camp, we heard the report of a gun, and soon after one of our hunters returned with a small deer. A fire was lighted, and each hunter displayed his *pone* of bread, along with a flask of whisky The deer was skinned in a trice, and slices placed on sticks before the fire. These materials afforded us an excellent meal, and as the night grew darker, stories and songs went round, until my companions, fatigued, laid themselves down, close under the smoke of the fire, and soon fell asleep.

I walked for some minutes round the camp, to contemplate the beauties of that nature from which I have certainly derived my greatest pleasures. I thought of the occurrences of the day, and glancing my eye around, remarked the singular effects produced by the phosphorescent qualities of the large decayed trunks which lay in all directions around me. How easy, I thought, would it be for the confused and agitated mind of a person bewildered in a swamp like this, to imagine in each of these luminous masses some wondrous and fearful being, the very sight of which might make the hair stand erect on his head. The thought of being myself placed in such a predicament burst over my mind, and I hastened to join my companions, beside whom I laid me down and slept, assured that no enemy could approach us without first rousing the dogs, which were growling in fierce dispute over the remains of the cougar.

At daybreak we left our camp, the squatter bearing on his shoulder the skin of the late destroyer of his stock, and retraced our steps until we found our horses, which had not strayed far from the place where we had left them. These we soon saddled, and jogging along, in a direct course, guided by the sun, congratulating each other on the destruction of so formidable a neighbor as the panther had been, we soon arrived at my host's cabin. The five neighbors partook of such refreshment as the house could afford, and dispersing, returned to their homes, leaving me to follow my favorite pursuits.

CHAPTER XVI.

CAPAIN DAN HENRIE; HIS ADVENTURE WITH THE WOLVES.

EERY body remembers the famous escape of Capt. Dan Henie at Encarnacion. This reckless and daring Ranger probbly passed through a greater number of perilous and singur adventures than any other man of the same age in the srvice. Though one of the most light-hearted mortals that te warm sun ever smiled upon, yet he had a careless knackf getting into the most desperate scrapes on every possibl occasion, and then, of course, fought his way out again ith the most dashing gallantry.

Marlyou, Dan never got into scrapes with his own people;

he was far too kindly and generous for that; but he had a hatred for the "cussed yaller bellies," and "copper heads," as he called the Mexicans and Indians, which was refreshingly orthodox. His hatred of the Mexicans was amusingly bitter and contemptuous while you listened to him talk of them; but when this hatred came to be expressed in action, it was of the most savage and deadly character. At Encarnacion, when the little band found themselves surrounded by the heavy masses of Minon's cavalry, the proposition, which, we believe, originated with Cassius M. Clay, was made to stand to their arms and fight it out with the Mexicans, to the last gasp, in spite of the disparity of numbers. Lieutenant Dan, who was then their guide, seconded this proposition warmly, and went about among the men, urging them "to stand up to the rack," as he called it, representing that they could hope for nothing but bad faith, resulting in cold-blooded massacre, if they surrendered to the Mexicans. He reminded them of Goliad, and the Meir surrender, and of his own experience in the last case. After showing, to his own satisfaction, that the resolution of fighting their way through was the only possible chance of safety or honorable death left them, he concluded, with the characteristic piece of savage advice, "Shoot low, boys—shoot them through their bellies, so that their groans will frighten their comrades—one groaner is worth half a dozen dummies!"

His perfect knowledge of the Mexican character, as well as his mortal hatred of them, was fully displayed in this advice. Dan knew perfectly that there would be no chance for him, for he had already been recognized as one of the Meir men by several Mexicans, whose faces he remembered well; the surrender, therefore, placed him in a desperate predicament. He knew, perfectly, that whatever faith they might keep with other prisoners, they would keep none with him, although his safety had been provided for in an express stipulation of the terms of surrender. I have never seen the mode of his escape correctly related yet, so that it is worth while to give it in his own version.

The Mexicans have a mortal hatred of the Meir prisoners, one and all—but most particularly do they detest those of them who rose at the Salado and escaped from Perote. Dan had, unfortunately, not only been prominent in both these affairs, but from the fact of speaking the language as well as a native, he had always acted as interpreter, and thus been put forward more conspicuously than any one of the other prisoners. Besides this, he had previously made himself very notorious, too, as a Ranger. All these causes combined to make his recognition general and sure at almost any point on the whole route to Mexico; and if it had not occurred immediately, there was no telling at what moment it might occur, and of course, when his body might be made the target of their cowardly hate.

He saw those men who had recognized him whispering among themselves, and from his knowledge of the Mexican character, felt sure that so soon as the commanding officers had retired and left them in charge of the guard, he would be shot from the ranks. It fortunately occurred, that when they were started, Minon and his staff was moving in the same direction down the lines of the Mexican force. Colonel Gaines rode a very swift and beautiful mare. Dan rode up to his side and whispered to him the discoveries he had made, his fears, and his determination. Gaines at once, with a generous promptness, proposed that he should take his mare to make the attempt upon, as her high-blooded metal would distance any Mexican horse with ease. This was precisely what Dan desired, and he eagerly accepted the offer. The officers had not yet been deprived of their pistols, and the holsters of Gaines remained on the saddle.

The mare was very spirited and fiery, and Dan slily roused up all her mettle by touching her with the spur. She began to pitch and plunge, and throw out her heels. This compelled the escort, or rather guard, which rode on either side of the prisoners, to open their line occasionally. Dan kept it up for some minutes, so as to remove all suspicion, and watched his chance, until he saw the guard were beginning to become careless, and regard those unruly capers rather with amusement than otherwise. Then seeing his way open as they moved slowly through the squadrons of green-coated cavalry, he suddenly reined up the mare in the midst of her capricolings, and plunging the spurs into her, she darted off like an arrow loosened from the bow, while he stooped, laying himself close along her side, after the manner of the Comanche Indians. A shower of balls was fired hurriedly after him, but without effect, as they all passed over him.

The plain to the foot of the mountains was very narrow just here; and he had observed, before he made his break, that they were opposite a road which came down a narrow valley. He made for this gap, running the gauntlet between several squadrons of cavalry, before he reached its shelter. Just as he was diving into it, he wheeled in his saddle, and amidst the whistling of balls, shook his clenched hand at them, and shouted back his defiance. This sudden escape caused great uproar and confusion among the Mexicans, and several hundred men started at full speed in the pursuit; but the gallant mare soon left them all far enough behind, as she clattered with sparkling hoofs along the deep ravine. Before the first two miles had been passed, the pursuit was out of sight in the rear.

The valley road, which he had taken at hap-hazard, without the slightest idea of where it led, now opened upon a small plain of table-land, which was occupied by a hacienda of considerable extent. As he swept by in front of the buildings, he saw a number of green-coats hastily mounting, and in another moment heard the clatter of their pursuing horses coming down the road. He looked over his shoulder and saw that it was probably a foraging party of about ten lancers. The first agony was over now, and he felt sure of the game and speed of his mare; and with his usual audacity, he determined to give the "yaller bellies" something to remember him by before he took his final leave. He accordingly reined up his mare gradually, and let them gain upon him. They thought she was failing, and raised a yell of triumph as they urged their horses to yet greater exertions.

He looked behind again, and the officer, with one of his men, was now considerably in the advance, and closing rapidly upon him. He loosened a pistol from the holster. The officer was foremost, and was already shouting to him, with many "Garachoes," to surrender, when he wheeled suddenly in his saddle and shot him dead. The lancer, who was close behind, and coming on at furious speed, attempted in vain to rein up his horse. It was too late—he was carried by the impetus of his speed within ten feet of Dan, who had by this time drawn his other pistol, with which he shot him through the head, and then galloped leisurely along, feeling sure that the remainder of his pursuers would be stopped effectually by this bloody barricade he had left across their path. He was not mistaken, for they halted there, and this was the last he saw of their green coats.

All that day long he kept the noble beast in swift motion, since at every little rancho or village he came to, it would be necessary for the fugitive to make a desperate run for it, before a pursuit could be organized. The roads were filled, too, with scouting parties of the enemy, and it required all his knowledge of their sort of tactics to enable him to dodge them. He several times very narrowly avoided rushing headlong into the very midst of these advance parties. The Mexicans are usually very noisy troops, and he would hear them talking on the march in time to dodge to one side and let them pass, for he had no fancy to try the hacienda trick over again with empty pistols, since he had nothing to load them with again. He finally threw them away as so much "make-weight," that was useless to him and embarrassing to his mare.

So he hurried on, not daring to pause a moment to rest or obtain food, until the next day, when, in a deep, wild gorge among the mountains, his game and gallant mare fell beneath him, dead! The ravenous and filthy galapotes, (turkey-buzzards,) were gouging at her fawn-like eyes before they were fairly glazed, and before her stiffened and staggering rider was out of sight. Now came the most terrible part of this wild and remarkable adventure. He was totally without food, except what little fruit of the cactus he could gather during the day while he was skulking, for he only ventured to travel at night now. This was scarcely enough to keep body and soul together; while his clothes soon became torn to pieces, and hung about his bleeding limbs like broad and tattered ribbons. He, however, still continued making his way steadfastly in the direction of General Wool's camp. At last, some of his scouts picked the poor fellow up when almost speechless with thirst and hunger;—he was yet feebly reeling along like a ghostly and haggard drunkard.

This affair very properly got him his promotion to a captaincy. But strange, perilous, and even wonderful as this escape seems, it is only one of many others quite as remarkable, by which his most eventful life has been checkered. In the Texan war with the Cherokees, which was a very bloody business while it lasted, he passed through scenes as bad, if not worse than this. Then his adventures as a Ranger are very remarkable, for of many of these I am myself personally cognizant; and of his cruel sufferings and headlong daring during the Meir imprisonment, all the country has been, to a certain degree, made aware since the publication of General Green's book.

Dan, who was my comrade in many a curious adventure, was the same Henrie of my previous narrative of the "Shot in the Eye." It is one of the drollest of his many personal affairs that I propose to relate now. I shall endeavor to give it as nearly as I can remember, in his own way, as he related it to me; though I must confess, it will be very difficult, if not impossible, to preserve the raciness of his rattle-pate and peculiar manner. It was before he joined the Meir expedition, and while yet with the Rangers, under the command of McCullough.

Dan, whose excellence as a guide was well known to the captain, was despatched by him, along with three others of the troop, on a scouting expedition, towards the head waters of the Nueces. This was in the early winter of the year before the Meir expedition, and the Mexicans were in many ways annoying and threatening the weak settlements along that river. This state of things had encouraged the Indians, as well, to make very bold descents. McCullough had on his first arrival given them both a severe lesson, upon which the marauders had taken the hint, and nothing further had been heard from either party for several months. Unwilling that his men should lie in camp at such a place as Corpus Christi, with nothing to do but drink and carouse, the prudent captain of Rangers had thought best to despatch all the most restless spirits on tours of observation in various quarters. Besides, the aspect of affairs in that part of Texas generally, had begun to seem rather forlorn, and seemed to call for unremitting vigilance.

Dan and his companions had reached the foot of the mountains in which the western branch of the Nueces takes rise, without meeting any other sort of incident than those which are common to prairie travel. Here they formed their camp, and as they had yet discovered no signs of Indians, it was concluded that they would take each his own course the next day, and after traversing as much ground as possible, return to camp and report, and if it should then appear that no sign had yet been discovered by any of them, it was agreed they should spend several days in a regular buffalo-hunting frolic, as these animals seemed to abound greatly in this region.

Accordingly they were under way quite early, each man following the bent of his own humor and fancy for the time.

Dan had been travelling in a leisurely sort of a way until noon, when he came upon a scene of such remarkable beauty that he involuntarily stopped to gaze upon it. He had, without observing it, followed up the west branch of the Nueces, until he now found himself at its very head-spring. In front of him a bold and broken mountain stood out somewhat from the chain, at the foot of which he had been riding all the morning. The front of this mountain was almost a square perpendicular, and looked as if it had been cleft from crest to foot by a bolt of thunder, and hurled from out the ranks of its peers. The huge masses of stone with which it seemed built were seamed with a sort of eccentric regularity, and evergreens were rooted along these seams. As the eye descended, these masses became more broken, and assumed a fantastic resemblance to the lines and forms of Gothic architecture in decay—while from the prairie level sprung a broken arch, one side of which was perfect in outline, and the other concealed by the over-hanging masses of evergreen shrubs. At a distance, this seemed the arched gateway of some huge cavern; but when he approached it, he found that the rock slanted in at just sufficient angle to give it, at a distance, the appearance of shadow. Instead of an enormous cavern, it proved to be only a recess or slanting niche, some twenty feet deep at the bottom—from the back part of which, a bold spring burst a little above the level of the prairie, and rushed down and out from the shadow, rejoicing over the white sand, until it sparkled in the checkered sunlight, beneath the over-hanging evergreens outside—then it coursed away toward the chain of mountains and wound about their feet. All off to the left, and beyond this remarkable mountain, seemed an interminable stretch of rolling prairies, over which, amidst clumps of cactus, were scattered herds of deer, mustangs and buffalo, in view at once.

Dan has not much poetry in him, but he could not help being both astonished and enchanted by the strange, wild loveliness of this scene. He slid from his saddle, and stood leaning against it for only a moment or two of wrapt contemplation, when the habitual instinct of watchfulness, peculiar to the Ranger, caused him to change his position, and turn his head. As he did so he perceived one of the droves of mustangs (wild horses,) moving slowly towards him. They were a long way off, and there appeared nothing peculiar about them—but it served to remind him that he had a short time before seen the unshod tracks of horses and mules moving at a gallop,—or that, though they might be nothing more than mustangs, yet the simple fact of their going at a gallop, was in itself suspicious of another fact or so—either that they were the tracks of Indian horses and mules, or of mustangs that had been chased or otherwise frightened by them; so that whatever of enchantment there may have been for him in the scene, it now gave place quickly to caution, and his head turned rapidly from side to side, with the habitual manner of the old spy.

His eye now and then fell upon the advancing drove, but not with any consciously defined suspicion. At length they disappeared slowly down a long valley, like the sway of the prairie undulations, and were out of sight so long that he had quite forgotten them, when suddenly they appeared again on this side, moving directly towards him, at a swift gallop. He bounded into his saddle as quick as thought, supposing that, may be, one or two Indians who were mustang-hunting, had lain in wait for this herd, in the deep grass of that prairie valley, and were now chasing them with the lasso. He urged his horse behind one of the many clumps of cactus around him, with the intention of laying in wait to give these dusky wild horse hunters a trial for their scalps as they went past him.

As he changed his position, the figures which were approaching became more distinctly defined against the back-ground of sky, for they were descending towards him! He saw, what sent his heart into his throat, that each animal had an Indian slung along its side, by one hand and foot, holding to either horn of the saddle! This is a common trick of theirs in approaching an enemy by day-light, on the prairies; and it is difficult of detection at a distance, by the most experienced eye, as they ride close together, and no part of the body is shown above the outline of the horse.

Dan was off in a twinkling! The tables were very suddenly turned; for instead of taking a scalp or two himself, as he had expected, it would now require the best he knew to save his own. It was well that he could trust his horse, for they had got so close to him that his escape at all must be a matter of sheer speed—he must run away from them or be run through by them. "To be or not to be," was the question now with poor Dan, while he desperately urged his good horse with quirt and spur. So soon as they saw him start, the rascals had wheeled up into their saddles again, and yelled their war-whoop like exulting devils. This was a sound which, though it came to his ears somewhat softened by the distance, was by no means calculated to diminish the energy or urgency of the calls upon the speed of his horse, which were made by Dan. He glanced furtively over his shoulder and saw that they were spreading out into the prairie with the intention of hemming him in against the mountains. He instantly perceived that his only chance was a desperate run for an elbow of the chain, which, if he could reach and turn first, he thought would secure his scalp for the present, as around it the stream became heavily timbered, and he knew they would not follow him into it for fear they might come upon his friends.

It was a tremendous race, for the Indians knew the advantage as well as he; and Dan vows that his long curly hair began to straighten and lift his cap on its ends before he reached the point, they pushed him so close and hard. By the skin of his teeth he got by before they surrounded him, and now he says his "hair fell as smooth and sleek as if a pint of bear's grease had been poured over it;" but not until he had reached up and taken *down* his cap off the stiff ends to wave as he shouted back at them in derisive triumph, and then darted beneath the shades of the friendly wood. They left him here as he expected; but as this was most evidently a dangerous neighborhood, he concluded it would be safest not to tarry here but get out of it as fast as possible, for there was no telling what new whim might take these fellows when they had spread around on his trail and found him to be alone! So away he went through the woods for five or six miles without halting.

The hurry and necessities of his flight had taken him off his course back to the rendezvous of his companions. He now first discovered this as he emerged from the timber upon the prairie again, and found himself far enough away from the course of the stream. He paused but for a moment, to collect himself and try and get back the true idea of his direction. Thinking he had it, he urged his horse into a swift run again. This was kept up for several hours, until night began to close around him, and his horse to give unmistakable indications that he must have rest before he went much further. He came at last to a small rivulet trickling along a deep, rough cut, and as he supposed, in the direction of the west branch of the Nueces. He had passed the camp far enough, he knew, but this would set him right if he followed it up when daybreak came. So he selected a small piece of meadow ground which was covered with musquit grass, and well protected from view by the great clusters of cactus which surrounded it on three sides. Here he stripped his faithful horse and turned him loose to graze, and then taking for supper a hearty draught of water, threw himself upon his blanket to sleep.

He had lost his provision wallet in the chase, and it was more than he dare venture upon to shoot game, for fear of betraying his hiding-place; and though hungry enough, he was fain this time "to go to bed supperless." He thought of home before sleep came, of course, and wished himself there most heartily, that he might attack the well-stocked pantry, the contents of which danced in most tantalizing visions before him during the whole night. This was too much a common predicament, however, to make any very strong impression upon him otherwise.

He was mounted and off very early the next morning, and was by no means delighted to perceive that his horse was considerably gaunted by the yesterday's hard work and the somewhat narrow commons of the night. However, he moved on now with something less of a hurry, as there were no indications of pursuit apparent. Following the rivulet, he soon reached the west branch, and turned up this with a brisker movement, spurred by the cheerful hope of soon rejoining his companions and finding them safe. In an hour he was in sight of the ground, and put his horse into a swift gallop in his eagerness to pass over the interval quickly. On coming up, he saw, instead of his comrades, the dead body of an Indian warrior lying across the very ashes of their camp fire, all gashed and hewn with bowie-knife cuts. All around the earth was deeply broken up, with the evidences of a desperate hand to hand struggle. The breech of a rifle, which he recognized, and a number of arrows, with a broken lance and shield, were scattered around. He felt a choking sensation and his blood ran cold at this sight.

His comrades had been surprised, no doubt, by the same party which had pursued him, but with what result it was impossible for him to tell certainly, though he had little choice but to believe and fear the worst. Amid the multitude of the tracks of unshod horses, he could distinguish the few tracks of their shod horses. There was no trace of their bodies in the hasty survey he had time to make, and it seemed very strange that this dead warrior should be left behind, so contrary to their well-known custom! He followed the trail for some time, with great caution, but could make no discovery, except a great deal of blood on the ground, until towards noon, when rising the comb of a steep ridge, he looked down into the plain below upon a large body of Indians, encamped about a mile distant.

This was a startling sight, and they perceived him at the same moment. Now he felt he would have indeed to run for his life. One glance, as he wheeled, was sufficient to show him warriors mounting the horses of his friends! He did not dread a race with the horses of the Indians so much, because his horse was more than a match for the best of theirs; but the horses of his comrades were as swift, and in every sense as good as his—now they were to be turned against him! He cursed the rashness that had induced him to follow up their trail, but this was no time to pause for regrets—he was off, down the hill, at the best speed his horse, already somewhat fagged, could raise. All depended upon getting back to the timber and losing them! He could hear their pursuing yells, distinctly, for a moment, and this was no syren's music to draw him back! He had a good mile the start, but that was no great matter, if, as he supposed, their horses were fresher than his own! He had not time now to feel any alarm, but only that there was hot work before, and he had it to attend to! His object was to get out of sight as soon as possible, for he gained a great deal by compelling them to run on his trail. He strained his horse tremendously, and succeeded, for when the sudden burst of their voices came from time to time, proving that they had reached the comb of the ridge, he looked back, and could not see it or them.

He felt a little less tight about the heart now, and had time to think something of his best course. It seemed a forlorn chance for an escape—he was over six miles from timber. He suddenly remembered that he had observed, for several days past, a heavy smoke off towards the south, and looking now in that direction, saw it filling the whole horizon with gloomy masses, which seemed to be rising but a few miles off. Observing that it was not very high, it instantly occurred to him in his extremity, for he felt sure from the action of his horse, that he would not last much longer in the hard run before them, that the safest course for him would be the most desperate, and this was to make directly for the approaching line of this fire, and take his chance of being able to force his way through it alive. With such a barrier between himself and the Indians, he was safe! Acting upon this stern and strange alternative, he urged his horse steadily towards the fire. It was not long before he met the dark advance guard of the smoke, as it rolled along the grass, and rode beneath its stifling shelter, the fire being yet a mile off.

He was now securely enough out of sight of the Indians, and springing from his horse, proceeded to prepare himself for a trial of the fiery sea. He cut his blanket into pieces, with one of which he blindfolded his horse; another he tied in a loose bag about the lower part of its head, enveloping the mouth and nostrils. He then enveloped his own face in a loose vizor of the same material. The blanket was coarse and let in air enough to barely sustain life for a short time, while it kept out the smoke. He could hear the yells of his pursuers seemingly close at hand. He was now in utter darkness, and mounting quickly again, headed his horse directly for the fire. On he went, not knowing where; the reins were tightened, and the lash and spur applied with the energy of desperation.

Hotter and hotter the air became, but on he careered, heady and blind. The fire has struck him with a roaring surge! His hair flames crisply, and the flesh of his body seems to be burning! The frantic and panting horse attempts to shy: but no, the fierceness of the agony has turned that rider's arm and will to iron!

It *cannot* shy—the poor horse! On! on! scorching through the stifling blaze! A few bounds more and the terrific surges are past! The fresh air has met him! He tore the envelope from his face and leaped from the staggering horse upon the charred hot ground. The blanket is torn away from its mouth, and the animal begins to revive quickly, though it shivers and can scarcely stand for the mortal terror! He is safe! He has accomplished an unparalleled feat!

He hears faintly above the crackling and roar of the retiring flames a howl of triumph from his pursuers, who imagine they have driven him into the fire, and that he is burnt, horse and all. He makes a feeble attempt to answer them defiantly, but can scarcely hear his own voice. Stunned, and gasping to recover the use of their almost stifled lungs, he and his horse stand, side by side, upon that blackened plain, without moving a step for more than an hour.

But the perils of the day were by no means passed. Before him, as far as the eye could reach, there was only one charred, level, smouldering waste, which had to be crossed before he could reach water, for which both himself and horse were now almost perishing. He started on at last, taking his course at random, for one seemed to his bewildered sense about as good as another. He did not ride at first, but mercifully led his poor horse, until the heat of the ground and the still smouldering stubs of grass became insufferable to his feet, and then he turned to mount. He now, for the first time, looked at the animal carefully, and to his horror, saw that nearly every hair upon its body was gone, and little but the bare skin left, and that was so badly scorched in places, as to come off at the slightest touch.

This was dreadful enough, but—water! water! water! he must have that, or they would both die. He sprang into the saddle and urged the wretched creature along with the last energies of his sinking life. In an hour he had begun to grow dizzy, and the blackened earth swam round and round, and tossed him to and fro! Now a strange noise was about him; and as the lifting waves of the earth would almost seem to leap up into his face, he would catch glimpses of huge wolves careering on them, turning up their fiery eyes to his, and howling at him with red hot open mouths and lolling tongues! Suddenly his horse rushed down a steep bank, and there was a great splashing. Water! Blessed God, water! He tumbled from his saddle into the cold delicious fluid.

In an instant his senses had returned, and he saw himself surrounded by thirty or forty prairie wolves, some of whom were swimming in the water after him, while the others sat upon the bank of the small lake, and howled their gathering cry. He struck those which were nearest with his gun barrel and beat them off, while he had time to draw his heavy knife. One of them had seized his passive horse, who, while it was endeavoring to pull him down, stood still and drank—the long eager draughts. He split the wolf's head with his knife, and soon sent the rest back out of the water, yelling with their wounds. But those upon the bank only howled the louder, and they were answered near at hand and from afar by hundreds of others, who were swiftly gathering in at the well-known call to a banquet.

He now remembered that these weird and infernal brutes always collect in large numbers, to follow in the wake of a great prairie fire, and tear the carcasses of those animals that are killed; or band together, to chase and drag down those that come through alive, but scorched, blinded and staggering, as was his poor horse. They become very savage with blood, impunity and numbers, and very few creatures which have escaped from the hungry flames can escape from their yet more ravenous jaws. The creature, at other times, is utterly contemptible for its cowardice; but he shuddered when he called to mind the dreadful stories he had heard of its deadly fierceness on such occasions as this.

"My God!" he moaned aloud: "Wasn't it bad enough for me to pass that hell of flames back yonder! and have I only escaped that to meet a fate a thousand times more hideous?"

He looked at his horse; the animal was now, too, partially refreshed, and began to be conscious of the new danger as it gazed around with staring eyeballs upon the eager and swiftly gathering crowd that howled along the bank. He snorted in affright, and lifted his head with a wildly mournful neigh, that seemed to poor Dan the most piteous sound that ever rung upon his ear before. There was some comfort though, the horse had life enough in him to make one more run for safety.

He mounted, and after having fired his rifle, with deliberate aim, into the thickest of them, charged right through at full speed. They leaped at his feet and attempted to seize his horse's legs, but the animal was too mortally frightened for them to impede his way for an instant. Through he trampled, and away across the prairie he flies, snorting with terror, and moving with as great speed as if perfectly fresh; and away, too, in pursuit, swept the yelling herd of wolves. There were more than a hundred now, and seemed increasing in numbers at every jump; for as Dan glanced his frightened eyes around, he would see them straitened out with speed and their mouths wide open, coming to join the terrible route from every direction over the prairie. He looks behind him—they were close upon his heels. The great part of them, particularly those in front, and who seemed most fierce and ravenous, were scorched nearly naked; and with the white foam flying, their long red tongues, their fiery glaring eyes, they presented the most hideous picture of unearthly terror that ever mortal lived to be chased by unless by the horrible phantasmagoria of madness!

He fired his pistols back at them, but it made no difference; they only yelled the louder, and came on the more fiercely, while five joined their long train for each one that he had killed. If his horse should fall or give out, they would both be torn to fragments in an instant! This appalling conviction caused him to give all of eye and nerve that were left him in the mortal fright to steadying and guiding his horse, for the only hope now lay in him. He soon perceived, however, that he was leaving the pack far behind, for there is little comparison between the speed of a horse and that of the prairie wolf.

He now began to feel something of hope; and as the frantic speed of his horse placed yet a greater distance between them, the unimaginable dread seemed to be lifting from his life. Now he could not hear their yells, and could barely distinguish, far in the rear, the long snake-like train yet moving on in the relentless chase, over the undulations of the bare plain. He sees timber ahead, and shouts in an ecstacy of joyful relief, for then he himself at least is safe! He can climb a tree—and in the delight of that thought, he has no time for thinking that his poor horse cannot climb trees!

The horse sees, and is inspirited, too—for to all creatures on the prairies there seems to be a vague feeling of safety in the sight of woods. But, alas, poor horse! They have reached the timber, but scarcely a hundred rods have been passed over, when the faithful creature gives out; and after a few ineffectual efforts still to obey the urging spur, can only lean against the trunk of a tree, and pant and groan with exhaustion. Dan ascends the tree, tying the lariat of his horse to one of the lower limbs. He then loaded his arms in the forlorn hope of defending him if they came up. All was still as death, but the loud panting of the exhausted animal. He ascended higher to look out for the approach of the wolves, for he had a faint hope that they had given up the chase. But, alas! his heart sinks again. There they come, the long yellowish looking train: and several large white wolves have joined them now. He knows well the tameless and pitiless ferocity of these red-eyed monsters, and feels that his true, his noble horse, must go!

Now he can hear their cry! They are in the woods. The poor horse shivers—looks back, and utters that wild and wailing neigh, as they rush upon him in a body. Dan fires down among them; but what avail is it! In a twinkling, his gallant beast is down, and has been torn to atoms! The halter of the lariat hangs empty beside the tree.

Now they lie panting around the foot of the tree, with their fiery eyes turned wistfully up at him—for the horse had been only a mouthful a piece. Whenever he makes a movement, they rise with eager yells, and leap up towards him, as if to meet his fall. Dan says, that in the utter and dreadfully hopeless desperation of his position now, a grotesque sort of humor possessed him of a sudden, and he commenced deliberately firing down at the red glaring eyeballs of the white wolves, and would roar with laughter, and fairly dance upon his ticklish perch with glee, when he saw the creature tumble over with a shrill death-cry; and then the whole pack rush on it and tear it into shreds in an instant, with gnashing cries.

He says he amused himself in this way for an hour, and made them tear to pieces every white wolf that had joined the chase. This sport delighted him so much, that he became careless, and narrowly escaped falling. He only saved himself by dropping his gun, which they seized, and almost tore its stock to pieces before they discovered it was not eatable. I saw the dents of their teeth in the barrel afterwards. Darkness was coming on, and they seemed not in the least disposed to go; and he felt that he must tumble out from the faintness of hunger and fatigue, if he was compelled to spend another hour in that tree without food. He had become entirely reckless now, and loaded up his pistols, determined, if he must fall, to bring death with him for some more of them.

Suddenly he heard a distant yelling on the prairie, like that which had sounded so dreadfully behind his flight. The wolves sprung to their feet in a body, and with pricked ears, listened. He looked out towards the prairie, and could faintly discover a large buffalo bull plunging along over the plain, surrounded by a great herd of wolves, who were tearing him at every jump. He could even hear the low bellowing of the creature's agony. Another victim! and his thirsty guardians started to join the chase. One after another they went; while those who staid behind would turn their heads to look back wistfully at him, and whine and lick their dry chaps. When the chase come in sight though, off they started in a body with savage yells. He fired his pistols after them in farewell, and killed one of the hindmost, while another, with a broken shoulder, kept on yelling with the pack.

He knew he would be safe now if he could get a fire kindled before they returned, if they did so at all. Before they were out of sight, he had reached the ground, and with trembling eagerness proceeded to light a fire with the help of his flint and steel, which every Ranger carries. He soon had a great fire blazing, and then cutting a piece from the last wolf he had killed, proceeded to roast it for food. When he had eaten, he felt so much refreshed that he could now proceed to make provision for the night's rest. He gathered a great deal of dried wood, and built a large fire in a circle about the spot he had selected to sleep upon. The wolves came back in about an hour after he had finished his arrangements for the night; but he now felt perfectly secure, for though he could see their hungry eyes shining all round the outside of the circle, and they kept up a continued howling all night long, he laid himself down and slept soundly until morning.

When he waked up, the wolves were all gone but one or two, craunching at the bones of yesterday's feast. He shot one of them with his pistol, and made a breakfast off of it. He picked up the gun, and found that though very much torn, it could still be used. He now took his course, and started to foot it into the settlements. After a week of almost incredible suffering, he got in safe, and saw nothing more of the wolves or of his comrades, who are thought to have been carried off prisoners, and afterwards murdered by the Indians on their attempting to escape.

Dan was sick of a fever for several weeks at Corpus Christi after he got in, and raved incessantly about wolves.

CHAPTER XVII.

THE DARKIE FIDDLER AND THE WOLVES.

POOR Dan Henrie's adventure with the wolves has reminded me of one or two other incidents sufficiently characteristic of the habits of that remarkable animal to be worthy of relation here, by way of interlude.

The wolf, besides being the most ubiquitous of our predatory animals, is the most active, tenacious and difficult of extirpation. It is everywhere. It fills-in the chinks of desolation. Its savage, grinning head peers through all the broken glooms of our stern wildernesses—a ghoul-like presence—hideous, gaunt and fierce! It knows no sympathies, and we give it none. Yet there is one droll incident with which my boyhood was familiar, which seems to indicate a certain susceptibility to the softer emotions—or more refined senses—at least.

In the early days of the settlement of South Kentucky, there was great trouble with the wolves. The large gray wolf of the more wooded northern and middle districts, greatly abounded in the heavy forests of the Green River Bottom, particularly in the neighborhood of Henderson, which is situated on the Ohio, not far below the mouth of Green River. The barn-yard suffered to a great extent, in the way of pigs, calves, etc., from their depredations, which frequently, in mid-winter, were even carried to the audacious extreme of attacking human beings. Indeed, it was no unusual thing for the belated footman, at such times, when they were pressed by hunger, to find himself surrounded by a herd of them in the woods. Some striking stories of hair-breadth escapes and desperate ventures, belong to this period and condition of things. No one of them ever made a stronger impression upon me than the adventure of old Dick, the fiddler.

He was "a good old good-for-nothing darkie," as the word went in the neighborhood, whose sole merit consisted in his fiddling—but, by the way!—singular as this merit was,—it in reality constituted him by far the most important "gemmen of color" within forty miles around. The fact is, nothing of any interest could occur without his presence! It was as important—skinny as it was!—as the very face of the man in the moon,—beneath whose auspices the corn-shockings, the weddings, the "break-downs" and Juba dances of the neighborhood were enacted.

Old Dick, who was the property of one of the Hendersons, from whom the town and county take their names, was esteemed by his good-natured and wealthy master as decidedly a privileged character. He had his time pretty much to himself, and no one pretended to interfere with its disposal, as his master humorously styled him a "necessary nuisance" to the neighborhood, because he kept the darkies in a good humor by his fiddle. Now Dick had most strongly developed the strongest and most marked traits of the fiddler, the world over, namely, punctiliousness and punctuality. Upon either of these points he was peculiarly irritable, nay even ferocious. With all the proverbial timidity of the "child of genius," Old Dick was yet as savage as a hyena at any improprieties of etiquette which might chance to turn up during the sable orgies over which he presided; but nothing caused him to so far forget "*the* proprieties" in his own person, as the intervention of any unusual or accidental causes of delay which prevented his being *on hand* in time! Poor Dick!—but the story I have to tell of him will explain!

On the occasion of a grand wedding festival among the colored gentry of a neighboring plantation, some six miles distant, Old Dick was, of course, expected to officiate as master of the ceremonies. It had been an unusually severe winter, and a heavy snow lay upon the ground on the eventful evening, when, having donned his "long-tailed blue," with its glittering gilt buttons, and mounted the immense shirt collar, by the aid of which the dignity of his official character was properly maintained, the ancient Apollo sallied forth, fiddle in hand, to dare the perils of the distant way alone: for the younger darkies had all gone to the frolic hours ago, with a haste and eagerness altogther unbecoming his importance.

The moon was out, and the stars twinkled merrily over head, as the spry old man trudged away over the crisp and crackling snow. The path, which was a very narrow one, led, for the greater part of the way, through the dark shadows of a heavy bottom forest, which yet remained as wild as when the Indians roamed it, and was untraversed by a wagon road for many miles.

The profound and dreary solitude of the way could not have failed to impress any one who was not either more or less than human, except under conditions of entire pre-occupation in one absorbing thought, such as now held absolutely the body and soul of the old man, in the strained tension of an anxious hurry to reach the seat of operations, in exact time. He was goaded at every step by the maddening vision of the expectant ranks of sable gentility, rolling the whites of their eyes and stamping their stocking feet upon the puncheon floor, impatient of his delay; for the truth was, that he had lingered a little too long over the polishing of those brass buttons and the setting of that plentitude of collar, and he now first became conscious of it as he had come forth beneath the moon and perceived its unexpected height above the horizon.

On he dashed with unrelaxing energy, heedless of the black shadows and hideous night-cries in the deep forest. Wolves were howling around him in every direction, but he paid no attention to sounds that were so common. However, he was soon compelled to give more heed to these animals than was by any means pleasing or expected. He had now made nearly half of his journey, and the light opening ahead through the trees showed him the "old clearing," as it was called, through which his path led. The wolves had been getting excessively noisy for the last mile; and to the undescribable horror of the old man, he could hear them gathering about him in the crackling bushes on either side, as they ran along to keep pace with his rapid steps. The woods very soon seemed to the old man to be literally alive with them, as they gathered in yelling packs from far and near.

Wolves are cautious about attacking a human being at

once, but usually require some little time to work themselves up to the point. That such was the case, now proved most lucky for poor old Dick, who began to realize the horrible danger, as a dark object would brush past his legs every few moments, with a snapping sound like the ring of a steel trap; while the yells and patter of the gathering wolves increased with terrible rapidity. Dick knew enough of the habits of the animal to be fully aware that to run would insure his instant death, as the cowardly pack would be sure to set upon him in a body on the instant of observing any such indication of fear. His only chance was to keep them at bay by preserving the utmost steadiness until he could reach the open ground before him, when he hoped they might leave him, as they do not like to attack in the open ground. He remembered, too, that an old hut still stood in the middle of the clearing, and the thought that he might reach that haven gave him some comfort.

The wolves were becoming more audacious every minute, and the poor old soul could see their green eyes glaring fiery death upon him from all the thickets around. They rushed at him more boldly one after another, snapping as they went past in closer and closer proximity to his thin legs—indeed, the frightened fiddler instinctively thrust at them with his fiddle to turn them aside. In doing so the strings were jarred, and the despairing wretch took on some hope to his shivering soul, when he observed the suddenness of the sound caused the wolves to leap aside with surprise. He instantly drew his hand across the strings with vehemence, and to his infinite relief they sprang back and aside as if he had shot amongst them. Taking immediate advantage of this lucky diversion in his favor, as he had now reached the edge of the clearing, he made a break for the hut, raking his hand across the fiddle strings at every jump, until they fairly roared again. The astonished wolves paused for a moment on the edge of the clearing with tails between their legs, looking after him; but the sight of his flying form renewed at once their savage instincts, and with a loud burst of yells, they pursued him at full speed. Alas for the unlucky fiddler, had he been caught now, it would have been all up with him, even had his fiddle continued to shriek more unearthly shrieks than that of Paganini ever gave forth. He had broken the spell by running, for had they caught him now, they would never have paused to listen, had he been an Orpheus in reality.

Luckily the old man reached the hut just as they were at his heels, and slamming the rickety door behind him, he had time to climb out on to the roof, where he was comparatively out of danger. I say comparatively, for the perch he now occupied, was too rickety to make it any thing rather than desirable, except by contrast with the immediate condition from which he had escaped.

The wolves were now furious, and thronging the interior of the hut, leaped up at him with wild yells of gnashing rage. The poor old sinner was horribly frightened, and it required the utmost activity of motion to keep his legs from being snapped by them. Wild with the agonized terror as he was, poor old Dick had managed to cling to his fiddle through it all, and remembering that it had saved him in the woods, he now, with the sheer energy of desperation, drew his bow shrieking across the strings, with a sound that rose high above all their deafening yells, while, with his feet kicking out into the air, he endeavored to avoid their steel-like fangs. An instant silence followed this sudden outburst, and Dick continued to produce such frightful spasms of sound as his hysterical condition conceived.

This outbreak kept the wolves quiet for a moment or two, but old Dick soon learned to his increased horror that even wolves are too fastidious to stand bad fiddling, for they commenced a renewal of the attack, as soon as the first surprise was over, more furiously than ever. This was too much for the poor fiddler, and most especially when the head of a great wolf was thrust up between the boards of the roof, within a few inches of where he sat. He gave himself up now for a gone darkie, and with the horrified exclamation—

"Bress God!—who dar?"

He fell to fiddling Yankee Doodle with all his might, unconsciously, as the dying swan is said to sing its own requiem in its closing moments. With the first notes of the air silence commenced; Orpheus had conquered! the brutes owned the subduing spell, and the terror-stricken fiddler, when he came to himself—astonished at the sudden cessation of hostilities—saw he was surrounded by the most attentive and certainly appreciative audience he had ever played before—for the moment there was the slightest cessation of the music, every listener sprang forward to renew the battle, and set his pipe-stem legs to flying about in the air again.

But he had now learned the spell, and so long as he continued to play with tolerable correctness, was comparatively safe. The old fiddler soon forgot his terror now in professional pride, for he was decidedly flattered by such intense appreciation; and entering fully into the spirit of the thing, played with a gusto and effect such as he thought he had never before surpassed or even equalled. Even the wedding, with its warm lights, its sweetened whiskey, was forgotten for the time in the glow of this new professional triumph.

But all pleasures have their draw-backs on this earth; and as time progressed, he began, with all his enthusiasm, to feel very natural symptoms of cold, fatigue, and even exhaustion. But it would not do—he could not stop a moment before they were at him again—and there they persistently sat, that shaggy troop of connoisseurs, fidgeting on their haunches, with lolling tongues and pricked ears, listening to their compulsory charmer, for several weary hours, until the negroes at the wedding, becoming impatient or alarmed about the old man, came out to look for him, and found him thus perched upon the roof of the tottering hut, sawing away for dear life, while he was ready to drop every instant from sheer fatigue and the freezing cold. They rescued the old man from his comfortless position, while the lingering forms of his late audience told that they most unwillingly surrendered the fruition of their unwonted feast.

CHAPTER XVIII.

SKATER CHASED BY WOLVES.

EVERYBODY has read the remarkable adventure with the wolves on the ice, related by Mr. Whitehead. The story has made so strong an impression upon me, that I cannot resist the temptation of preserving it here, along with the previous narrative, as incidental to our "Wild Scenes," entirely legitimate here. I present it with an illustration, as one of the most effective stories ever given about wolves.

During the winter of 1844, being engaged in the northern part of Maine, I had much leisure to devote to the wild sports of a new country. To none of these was I more passionately addicted than to skating. The deep and sequestered lakes of this State, frozen by the intense cold of a northern winter, present a wide field to the lovers of this pastime. Often would I bind on my skates, and glide away up the glittering river and wind each mazy streamlet that flowed beneath its fetters on toward the parent ocean, forgetting all the while time and distance in the luxurious sense of the gliding motion —thinking of nothing in the easy flight, but rather dreaming, as I looked through the transparent ice at the long weeds and cresses that nodded in the current beneath, and seemed wrestling with the wave to let them go; or I would follow the track of some fox or otter, and run my skate along the mark he had left with his dragging tail until the trail would enter the woods. Sometimes these excursions were made by moonlight; and it was on one of these occasions that I had a rencontre which even now, with kind faces around me, I cannot recall without a nervous looking-over-my-shoulder feeling.

I had left my friend's house one evening just before dusk, with the intention of skating a short distance up the noble Kennebec, which glided directly before the door. The night was beautifully clear. A peerless moon rode through an occasional fleecy cloud, and stars twinkled from the sky and from every frost-covered tree in millions. Your mind would wonder at the light that came glinting from ice, and snow-wreath, and incrusted branches, as the eye followed for miles the broad gleam of the Kennebec, that like a jeweled zone swept between the mighty forests on its banks. And yet all was still. The cold seemed to have frozen tree, and air, and water, and every living thing that moved. Even the ringing of my skates echoed back from the Moccasin Hill with a startling clearness, and the crackle of the ice as I passed over it in my course seemed to follow the tide of the river with lightning speed.

I had gone up the river nearly two miles, when coming to

a little stream which empties into the larger, I turned into it to explore its course. Fir and hemlock of a century's growth met overhead, and formed an archway radiant with frost-work. All was dark within; but I was young and fearless, and, as I peered into an unbroken forest, that reared itself on the borders of the stream, I laughed with very joyousness; my wild hurrah rang through the silent woods, and I stood listening to the echo that reverberated again and again, until all was hushed. Suddenly a sound arose—it seemed to me to come from beneath the ice; it sounded low and tremulous at first, until it ended in one wild yell. I was appalled. Never before had such a noise met my ears. I thought it more than mortal; so fierce, and amidst such an unbroken solitude, it seemed as though a fiend had blown a blast from an infernal trumpet. Presently I heard the twigs on shore crack as though from the tread of some brute animal, and the blood rushed back to my forehead with a bound that made my skin burn, and I felt relieved that I had to contend with things earthly, and not of spiritual nature—my energies returned, and I looked around me for some means of escape.

The moon shone through the opening at the mouth of the creek by which I had entered the forest, and considering this the best means of escape, I darted towards it like an arrow. 'Twas hardly a hundred yards distant, and the swallow could scarcely excel my desperate flight; yet, as I turned my head to the shore, I could see two dark objects dashing through the underbrush at a pace nearly double in speed to my own. By this great speed, and the short yells which they occasionally gave, I knew at once that these were the much dreaded gray wolves.

I had never met with these animals, but from the description given of them, I had but little pleasure in making their acquaintance. Their untameable fierceness, and the untiring strength which seems part of their nature, render them objects of dread to every benighted traveller.

> "With their long gallop, which can tire
> The deer-hound's hate, the hunter's ire,"

they pursue their prey—never straying from the track of their victim—and as the wearied hunter thinks that he has at last outstripped them, he finds that they but waited for the evening to seize their prey, and falls a prize to the tireless animals.

The bushes that skirted the shore flew past with the velocity of lightning, as I dashed on in my flight to pass the narrow opening. The outlet was nearly gained; one second more and I would be comparatively safe, when my pursuers appeared on the bank above me, which here rose to the height of ten feet. There was no time for thought, so I bent my head and dashed madly forward. The wolves sprang, but miscalculating my speed, fell behind, while their intended prey glided out upon the river.

Nature turned me towards home. The light flakes of snow spun from the iron of my skates, and I was some distance from my pursuers, when their fierce howl told me I was still their fugitive. I did not look back, I did not feel afraid, or sorry, or glad; one thought of home, of the bright faces awaiting my return, and of their tears if they never should see me, and then every energy of body and mind were exerted for escape. I was perfectly at home on the ice. Many were the days that I spent on my good skates, never thinking that at one time they would be my only means of safety. Every half minute an alternate yelp from my fierce attendants made me but too certain that they were in close pursuit. Nearer and nearer they came; I heard their feet pattering on the ice nearer still, until I could feel their breath and hear their snuffing scent. Every nerve and muscle in my frame was stretched to the utmost tension.

The trees along the shore seemed to dance in an uncertain light, and my brain turned with my own breathless speed, yet still they seemed to hiss forth their breath with a sound truly horrible, when an involuntary motion on my part, turned me out of my course. The wolves, close behind, unable to stop, and as unable to turn on the smooth ice, slipped and fell, still going on far ahead; their tongues were lolling out, their white tusks glaring from their bloody mouths, their dark, shaggy breasts were fleeced with foam, and as they passed me, their eyes glared, and they howled with fury. The thought flashed on my mind, that by this means I could avoid them, viz: by turning aside whenever they came too near; for they, by the formation of their feet, are unable to run on ice except in a straight line.

I immediately acted upon this plan. The wolves, having regained their feet, sprang directly towards me. The race was renewed for twenty yards up the stream; they were already close on my back, when I glided round and dashed directly past my pursuers. A fierce yell greeted my evolution, and the wolves, slipping upon their haunches, sailed onward, presenting a perfect picture of helplessness and baffled rage. Thus I gained nearly a hundred yards at each turning. This was repeated two or three times, every moment the animals getting more excited and baffled.

At one time, by delaying my turning too long, my sanguinary antagonists came so near that they threw the white foam over my dress as they sprang to seize me, and their teeth clashed together like the spring of a fox-trap. Had my skates failed for one instant, had I tripped on a stick, or caught my foot in a fissure of the ice, the story I am now telling would never have been told.

I thought all the chances over; I knew where they would first take hold of me if I fell; I thought how long it would be before I died, and then there would be a search for the body that would already have its tomb; for oh! how fast man's mind traces out all the dread colors of death's picture, only those who have been near the grim original can tell.

But I soon came opposite the house, and my hounds—I knew their deep voices—roused by the noise, bayed furiously from the kennels. I heard their chains rattle: how I wished they would break them! and then I should have protectors that would be peers to the fiercest denizens of the forest. The wolves taking the hint conveyed by the dogs, stopped in their mad career, and after a moment's consideration, turned and fled. I watched them until their forms disappeared over a neighboring hill, then taking off my skates, wended my way to the house, with feelings which may be better imagined than described. But even yet I never see a broad sheet of ice in the moon-shine, without thinking of that snuffing breath and those fearful things that followed me so closely down the frozen Kennebec.

CHAPTER XIX.

THE MUSTANG, OR WILD HORSE.

"Round-hoof'd, short-jointed, fetlocks shag and long,
Broad breast, full eye, small head and nostrils wide,
High crest, short ears, straight legs, and passing strong,
Thin mane, thick tail, broad buttock, tender hide—
Look what a horse should have!"

"LOOK what a horse should have!" Willie of Avon being judge! and acknowledge, gentle sportsman, that the wild, rattling, poacher scamp had as sharp an eye for the parts of the noble animal on four legs, as he exhibited in his spiritual anatomy of the animal on two. Can any of you beat that with all your modern breeding, in and out, crossings and improvements? Can even the Napoleon of the turf himself suggest an addition or subtraction to or from this masterly summary of what the "horse" should be?—not the draught-horse, the race-horse, the saddle-horse, the hunting-horse, the trotter or the pacer!—but the *nonpareil*,—uniting in himself the nearest approach to the perfection of all these!

"But," says the gent., "deuce take it! where are you going to find such a horse, now you've got him described? It's like shaking a basket of spring strawberries under the nose of a convalescing man, and then pleading the doctor on him, to tantalize us by dilating upon Shakspeare's ideal, when such an animal has long since been crossed and trained out of being!"

Very true, sir! very true! "*The horse*," with his exuberance of power and unity of splendid traits, is ruled down now into "strains" of a single characteristic,—his parts and paces determined with mathematical certainty before he is foaled. Though there is a great deal gained in convenience by this, there is more lost in the general excellence and nobility of the animal. We need to recur again occasionally to the primeval horse to throw a dash of freedom into the hard lines of our too strictly ruled strains; to find this, we shall probably always go back to the Arab on his yellow sands. While I admit this to be the true mine of the "porcelain earth" for the horse manufacture, I am astonished that our American breeders have paid so little attention to a "chip of the same grit" we have nearer home. I refer to the mustang, or wild horse of our great prairies.

A very common and natural misapprehension exists with regard to the value of the mustang, from the fact that it is only the inferior animals of a drove that are taken, as a general thing; and again, that the hunters always keep the finest themselves, and send in the trifling ones to trade off to the settlements; and it is only such as these we ever get a sight off, unless we make a trip to the Rocky Mountains or California in person! But it is a great mistake to suppose that all mustangs are like the long-headed, donkey-tempered, spindle-shanked, dwarfish creatures we see occasionally in the country.

It would be just as wise to judge the stock in our racing stables by some pot-bellied, shag-haired, scrub colt we might chance to stumble upon, picking the short grass along with the pigs in a country lane, as to form an opinion of the wild horse as he is, fetterless and proud, upon his boundless plains, from these miserable specimens. You must recollect that the best are not to be taken every day; that their liability to capture is exactly proportionate to their want of speed, under the most usual method of securing them with the lasso! For this to be done, you are aware he has to be fairly run upon by the hunter, with a start of a mile or two, sometimes; and the animal overtaken with such odds must be immensely inferior to the one in pursuit!

So far is the fact of this inferiority from being found to exist in the case of the finest of them, that I have known instances of mustangs being chased for three or four days together, all the time, night and day, with fresh horses put in every four or five hours, and yet without any sensible flagging of their speed; without their having been sufficiently pushed to prevent them from stopping occasionally to graze and drink. Their great powers of endurance will not be particularly wondered at, when you remember the history of their origin.

It will be recollected that the adventurers, who, lured by the golden romance the stories of the earliest navigators had thrown over the New World, had been induced to attach themselves to the expedition of Cortez, were cavaliers, the dissolute and spendthrift sons of the noble families of Spain, who expecting to retrieve their desperate fortunes by the realization of enormous wealth, strained the credit of their friends to the last pitch that they might equip themselves with a splendor worthy of their rank, and the glory of such an enterprise.

Those were the palmy days of Spanish power, and her nobility could command the choicest resources of the Old World; and haughty and luxurious as they were, of course nothing short of the purest and far-descended blood of Barbary and the Deserts could prance beneath their purple housings. Steeds, whose descent, could we believe the quaint old chroniclers of the time, might be traced, without a spot or blemish, back to the veritable pair who shook the big drops of the Flood from their manes, and breasted its devouring waves successfully, were the companions of the mad-cap coxcombs on their perilous voyage.

You will remember their appearance on horseback alarmed the simple natives more than even their pale faces and thunder. They considered horse and rider as one animal,—like the Centaur of the Greek, a supernatural one,—and sent them human victims for food, to propitiate their wrath. These facts all prove that there was not even a tradition of the existence of such an animal on our hemisphere at that time.

It will be recollected, finally, that led on by a remorseless avarice, which even the palace halls of the Montezuma, heaped to the ceiling with ingots of gold, could not touch, they penetrated far into the interior, in the fantastic search of mountains, whose rocks were of the precious metal without alloy; and rivers, whose beds were amethyst, and pearl, and glittering dust; and that instead of the realization of these gorgeous fancies, they met with fierce tribes amidst the crags and valleys, who cut them to pieces. But as these warlike men exhibited the same terror and astonishment at the sight of the horse, the gallant beasts, as their riders fell, were permitted by the superstitious conquerors to gallop away for a new life of freedom upon the wide savannahs below.

There were several entire parties of the cavaliers killed to a man, by these mountain hordes, all of whose horses escaped. These bounded away joyfully, with neighings, until they reached the luxuriant pasture of the plains, and then fell to work to multiply and replenish.

From this royal lineage the wild horse of both continents has undoubtedly descended. They spread gradually from the pampas of California to the bleak and sterile ridges of Canada, where starvation and the cold dwindled them down to the shaggy pine-knot of a pony, retaining still the bright, prominent eye, and devilish, indomitable spirit of their ancestry. So that you see the pedigree of the mustang is more immaculate than that of the proudest winner of a hundred fields. But, independent of these historical facts, no man who is familiar with the Arab can cast his eye over a "Cavayard" of Mexican mares, who are unadulterated mustangs, without being instantly struck by the remarkable resemblance between the two races.

You see there the same long, and rather angular outline; the same thin, wavy mane, sometimes from two to three feet in length; the same silky coat; the same round, flat hoof, the bushy fetlock, and the spur distinctly defined; the same round, straight fore-leg and short pasterns; the same gray-hound hams, and somewhat ragged hips; the same short coupling; the same fine ear, thin head, rather lengthened for symmetry; wide, elastic nostrils, and deep mouth; but foremost of all, the prominent socket; the wide-open lid, the large eye-ball, lit with a tameless, but not vicious fire, with its free play showing the broad stripe of creamy white; and when they drink, which they do but once a day, the same trick of plunging the nostrils up to the eyes in the water, and swallowing with huge gulphs.

Then mount one, and if you can stick there, you will find the analogy fully sustained. Day after day, in a long, springy gallop, it will carry you eighty or a hundred miles, for weeks together, with scarcely a perceptible diminution of spirit or vigor, and requiring nothing with all this but a long draught of cool, clear water, and the grass of the prairies.

This is the mustang as he really is; as he is to be seen in thousands multiplied, upon the ocean-like meadows of the great South-West! But such specimens as this are to be seldom seen off his native wilds, for the reason I have given above; and which must be self-evident, that he is seldom taken, and when he has been, is far too valuable to the hunter to be parted with. Mounted upon these magnificent animals, they take in hundreds the stunted, vicious little devils that have given reputation to the mustang among us!

Like human hunchbacks these creatures seem to become

splenetic, and unconquerably ill-grained, in a ratio equal their declension from the full standard of proportion and power.

The cavayards of the Rio Grande valley and California, are composed sometimes of a thousand mares and eight or ten studs, by whom the females are divided into families of from eighty to a hundred and twenty, the number a good deal regulated by their individual prowess. For wars of jealous rivalry are incessantly occurring among them, and who that is best able to protect his concubines has most of them. They sometimes have very furious battles with the wild asses of the country, from which they generally come off worst. These are most merciless ravishers; and after having frequently killed, or entirely used up the stallions, they will scatter the cavayard so that they can never be got together again.

The mares, which have all been disabled from running fast by a cruel practice on the part of their owners, of severing one of the tendons at the knee, cannot escape from these ferocious gallants, who, more inexorable than the "Old Man of the Sea" of Sindbad, will cling to them for days till their object be accomplished, through sheer exhaustion on the part of the victim. The produce of this connection

> "Who in the lusty stealth of nature take
> More composition and fierce quality—

is a clean-limbed, vigorous, powerful animal. Indeed, the mule thus bred is, immeasurably, far the most active, spirited, swift and enduring of all the long-eared genus. They are not so heavy-boned as the Kentucky mules, but they can kill two or three of them as travellers, and are really most delightful animals for the saddle; and being high before, with light heads, some of them are very handsome, and quite the average height of our saddle horses.

As our hemisphere is indebted to the priest accompanying

Cortez for the ass, as it is to the cavaliers for the horse, it affords quite a suspicious comment upon the morals of the reverend fraternity that their brute representatives should inherit such carnal propensities, and disturb the solitudes of nature even to this late day by so obstreporous displays of them!

These mules approach nearly in temper and form to the horse. I speak of the finest of them, of course, for they are very heely, and, as in the case of the mustangs, are seldom captured. You never see a drove of mustangs without a considerable proportion of mules among them; which goes to prove that the wild ass plays a consistent game with his peer, the wild stallion; and, indeed, it is no unusual thing to come across them in the spring and fall engaged in most desperate contests. The method of managing these duelloes is rather a comical one on the part of the ass.

I once had an opportunity of witnessing an "affair" of the kind, which was something after this fashion. The ass was his own trumpeter, and announced his approach from afar with the euphoneous and ear-splitting symphony for which he is so famous the world over. The ladies of the herd seemed to be thrown into great consternation by this ferociously amatory prelude, and rushed together in a trembling crowd around their rightful lord for protection. He, extricating himself and shaking his streaming mane upon the winds, with a disdainful toss of his fine crest, gallops out in front to meet his vulgar and boisterous enemy—who, with his wide jaws distended, in a very paroxysm of harmonious delivery, comes tearing on with headlong violence. The chivalrous stallion receives him with a salute from his heels that fairly rings again upon his hard shaggy limbs—this compliment, which would seem to have been sufficient to have shaken, if not overturned a stout-sized barn—has not the effect of even checking the impetus of the uncouth foe, who rushes on, his mouth still open, right at the throat of the generous steed, thus breaking through his "guard," and fastening those massive distended clamps upon his windpipe, hangs there like a bull-dog.

Then comes a sudden silence, and the frightened dames, their bodies clustered together as close as they can crowd, their heads all turned toward the combatants, stare in trembling terror at the death-struggle. Many a frantic plunge the poor horse makes—but all the lithe vigor of his polished limbs avails him nothing—now rearing erect in the desperation of his agony, he clatters his fore hoofs upon the tough shoulders of his assailant, but they make about as much impression there, as they would have done upon the trunk of a live oak. Now, with every muscle strained, and the big veins almost bursting through his delicate skin, he springs wildly forward into the air as though he would bound clear over the ugly brute; but no—with a stolid and passive sturdiness, he hangs on, until, at last, all his mighty strength expended in vain but furious strugglings, with a deep smothered groan, the noble stallion falls heavily upon his side. And now the rude conqueror condescends to quit his hold, and with his bloody jaws distended in a still louder bray of triumph, he rushes at the shivering squad of mares! And such a scatterment! Like mad, they rush off in every direction—he right upon their heels! Soon he closes with some wretched unfortunate, and then comes another frantic struggle between savage lust and fear.

The battles between the stallions though, are gallant displays of graceful and splendid action—they rear and wrestle like the athlete of olden time—their long and silky manes dishevelled—their large eye-balls suffused and red, glowing with angry fires—their pied and glossy coats stained with blood upon the milk white ground, and gleaming with the rapid play of agile limbs. Mr. Miller, our artist, who took the sketch of the scene we give, on the spot, through a glass, has presented rather, the grace and playful action of their lives, than this fierce scene.

The colors of the mustang are surpassingly rich and beautiful. They are all intense and decided. You will find them white as the driven snow, without a dark hair on their bodies; and again, black as the concentrated essence of midnight—the sunbeams

"Smoothing the ebon down of darkness till it smiled,"

at every movement of their buoyant humors; then a deep blood bay, with black mane and tail, or a rich red sorrel. Again, you find these dark colors mottled in clear relief upon the pure white. The effect is sometimes exquisite beyond description. I have seen them "spotted like a Pard," and marked in elegant rosettes like the skin of the African panther. The startling contrast of these deep colors, in graceful lines, banded and star'd, flecked and dotted, upon the snowy ground, is above the "Ken of Fancie," beautiful.

The Comanches—Nomadic tribes, who from their mountain fastness descend upon the plains below for plunder—like birds of prey stooping from their eyries, are mounted upon the finest specimens of these horses that are to be found, and with such rapidity do they move, that they will traverse hundreds of miles, carrying death and fear with them along a whole frontier, and yet retreat to their rocky holds in safety before the inhabitants can organize a pursuit.

The warriors have a great passion for these "paint horses" as they are called, and if I live to the age of Methuselah, I shall never forget the picturesque appearance of a party of twenty of them we pursued once for fifteen miles, all of whom were mounted upon fancifully mottled horses. Over the prairie and through the deep woods we scurried in that wild desperate chase—the dark gaunt savage forms on their snowy and freckled steeds, now and then to be seen ahead of us, glancing past the leafy trunks of the great trees—now in a line like a great spotted snake, arrowy gliding over the green sea of grass.

They had run their horses nearly forty miles before we got on their trail, and yet our American horses, which were perfectly fresh, were thoroughly used up before we closed with them—but "thereby hangs a tale," touching and strange, indeed—which we cannot stop here to tell.

The incident strikingly illustrates though, the wonderful powers of this animal.

The bearing of the stallions toward their families is the very ideal of chivalry—each one seems to consider himself solely responsible for the safety of those he has taken under his protection. He is always on the alert—feeding apart from them on the highest ground, his watchful survey—every moment or two scans the horizon, and if any thing suspicious is detected, off he dashes, fearless in his might and speed, and circling around the doubtful object till he has determined its character—if it be an enemy, his trumpet neigh gives warning to his dames, who have been quietly feeding all this time, to be off upon their flight! while he, with proud curvetings, follows on as if half determined not to fly at all, "sometimes he trots as though he told his steps," facing back towards his pursuer, while

> "His nostrils drink the air, and forth again,
> As from a furnace, vapors doth he send."

And when a long look and the nearer approach of the enemy has satisfied his curiosity, wheeling again, he flies with surpassing speed and louder neighing after his retreating herd—while

> "Through his mane and tail the high wind sighs,
> Fanning the hairs, who wave like feathered wings."

It is a very common thing, when the hunters with the lasso dash in among the herd, for these gallant fellows to injure them or their horses seriously, by kicking and biting them. The hunters seldom venture upon the experiment of lassoing them, for the moment an old stallion feels the lasso upon his neck he will rush at the man and tear him from his seat. I knew an instance in which a Mexican was maimed for life. Some of these stallions are very famous for their incredible swiftness, beauty and endurance. The hunters know their color, their fine parts and haunts as well as they know the features of the Pilot Knobs.

You all remember Kendall's fine description of the "white steed of the prairies," so remarkable for his pace that no hunter had ever yet been able to make him break it! I had often heard of the same animal from them, and what is a curious coincidence, all the white mustangs I have ever seen are natural pacers.

There is another animal even more magnificent than these, frequenting the plains west of San Antonia. I had a good opportunity of seeing this fellow, and was one of a party that chased him for several days, in the effort to run him down that we might "pen" him, the only method of hunting them which is ever successful in securing one of the splendid creatures. But we must defer the story for another time.

The code in these herds is a very imperious one. Rivalry is not submitted to from any quarter. As soon as the stud colts begin to "feel themselves" they are most unceremoniously banished by the old patriarch. They then lead a solitary life for several years, until feeling confident in their strength, they dash into the nearest herd, and if they should prove able, whip off the leader and take possession of his seraglio.

In passing those prairies diversified like old English parks with a cluster of timber here, and a huge moss-hung live-oak there, I have frequently been amused by the disconsolate air of one of these expatriated horses, standing "solitary and alone" beneath the shade, his head drooping, evidently brooding over bitter memories, and ruminating dire revenge. The hunters always have a laugh at the sight of such a fellow.

But the point I wish particularly to direct the attention of our breeders to. is the importance of crossing the mares upon our big-boned American stock. A great many facts have come under my observation which would prove this to be an exceedingly interesting field of inquiry. The experiment has already been tried upon the western frontier of Texas, and it is perfectly astonishing what a splendid animal is produced by the cross of even a very coarse American stud, so he has size, upon these high-blooded and fiery little mares. A single cross makes the best saddle horse, take him altogether, I have ever met with, and we have some pretty passible hacks in Kentucky! It could hardly well be otherwise, when we look at the pure descent of these mares!

Yet apart from these considerations of utility, if a herd of buffalo be the grandest and most formidable of our prairie sights, certainly a drove of mustangs must be accounted the most magnificently beautiful. No imagination can compass the exceeding grace and airy freedom of the arched and silken-tossing chaos, as it sways to and fro, glistening in beamy mail beneath the sun, while sportively unconscious of observation. How grandly they plunge, curvette and wrestle, wheel like trained columns, charge, scatter and form again in the swift change of magic convolutions, shifting like cloud shadows eddied on an April breeze along the grass, as swift, if not as fleeting!

So they appear from the distance, at which they can alone be viewed, as in our sketch. Sometimes I have come upon them suddenly amidst the motts of timber; when the momentary, but nearer view, would disclose the mottled variety of their coats to which I have referred; but most usually they are seen in swift battalions, scurrying across the plains, and stopping for a moment, on the last undulation, for a parting look at the intruder, cluster with flying hair against the sky, and are gone!

CHAPTER XX.

A BIRD'S-EYE VIEW OF THE SPECLATER.

Turn we now to the northward, for our "Wild Scenes" have lingered long upon the green and waving Plains that shimmer in the breezy sunshine of the mellow South. We have felt the slumbering electricity in its treacherous air jar us through smiles, and amidst its fierce extremes of beauty and of terror, realized something of the wild unexpectedness of action peculiar to life amidst the latent power of such fierce elements, as there "do mostly congregate."

The "Hunter-Naturalist"—like an invisible Presence—has walked with us amidst these scenes, "informing the

Spirit" of them all with this most gossip and desultory mood in which our volume was at first conceived.

A summer's journey of sporting adventure towards the North, dating at a much later period in my life than those previously given as personal, included a sojourn amongst that linked and wonderful cluster of Lakes, extending from Hamilton county, in the west of New York, north to Lake Champlain and the St. Lawrence. Something of the "Wild Scenes" and characteristic incidents amidst the haughty solitudes of those rugged hemlock-bristled Ariondacks, and their chaste, cold, glistening Lakes, I must give in a fragmentary way.

I had reached Lake Pleasant in Hamilton county, the semi-civilized outpost of the wilderness interior of "Sporting Grounds," through the ordinary tribulations of jolting, fatigue, mud, rain, etc., in company with an English friend, a placid "son of the angle," in the strict Waltonian sense, but altogether an unaccustomed hunter of wilderness game.

Lake Pleasant, upon the outlet end of which we were temporarily located in a rude board hovel, dignified as "mine inn!"—was overlooked at the opposite by an abrupt mountain—one of the Ariondacks—named from the Indian name, the Speclater. The inlet came in at its foot, and from the steep top, a bird's-eye view could be obtained of the whole scene of our future operations. After a night's rest, we made a day of it to clamber the huge rocky sides of this ancient sentinel that from its bald crest we should look forth, that our eyes might be "made aware."

I wanted to convey some idea of what we saw, but I find that though very nice in theory the practice is difficult. I could only think, as we ascended, in the words of one who spake of old—"Get thee up into the top of Pisgah, and lift thine eyes westward, and northward, and southward, and eastward, behold it with thine own eyes!" And, verily, when we reached the top of Mount Speclater did we lift our eyes and behold the promised land of sportsmen—the Canaan, not of milk and honey, by a long jump—but of the *feræ naturæ*—"a whole yearth full 'er God-a-mighty's wild varmints!" as a sublimity-struck Connecticut Pedlar ejaculated from the same point of view! Of a truth it was a wonderful sight—looking down at your feet, then off to the South, and then to the North-west, upon this wild chaos of savage-looking hills, lit up by the scattered shine of thirty-six Lakes, which, within the space of about the same number of miles in length, look like bright patches which had fallen in benediction out of a summer's sky into these sullen glooms!

There they go, far away beneath us—those younger ranks of pine-haired Titans, that make the blue line of the Ariondack! See them stretch their misty arms to one another, rank upon rank, to form these cordons of impregnable defence about those shadowy basins, up from which the silver sheen of many a grotesque form of Lake is thrown into our dazzled eyes.

What a sight is this, within twenty-four hours of New York, with its smoke, and din, and crush!

Hurrah! to think that these bright sheets are gleaming down through their still blue depths with shoals of the magnificent salmon trout, with their dark marbled backs and lustrous mottled sides, and that every silver thread of river, rivulet and inlet binding them together, glitters upon its ripples or within its shaded pools to the arrowy leap of that crimson flecked keystrel of the streams, the brook trout!

Hurrah! hurrah! to think, too, that these unbroken forests which still wear the solemn look of Earth's Primeval births, yet shelter within their difficult fastnesses, her earliest children. That the huge moose which came before the red man, yet rouses the sluggish echoes with its hoarse bellowings. That the red deer whistles and snorts to the boding howl of the tireless gray wolf; and the brown bear, like a clumsy boxer, cuffs the screaming panther away from its newly slain feast!

The Indian is gone, but yet his ancient foes and victims have flourished apace, and may usurp their inheritance.

Hurrah! hurrah! Arkwright and Fulton have not yet conquered the free earth of God in this direction—and bound *all* its limbs in chains!

"The undevout astronomer is mad"—and the devout sportsman may be forgiven, if at such a sight he, too, grow mad and should fall to capering, and become something of a heathen in his glee, shouting as I did.

"Take my cap, Jupiter, and thank thee!" Against such uncanonical sins I hereby formally warn all other faithful sons of Nimrod, who may be "taken aback" under similar circumstances.

As to the propriety of capering and throwing up one's cap on the top of a mountain, I must in meekness confess to its being "*highly* improper"—"unworthy the dignity," etc.—but bless our soul, who could help it? Not any genuine sportsman, I am sure, whether he be "Venator," "Piscator," or "Anceps!"—or all combined as—"I flatter myself!"—ahem!

No, it was not in human nature—or more *inclusively*, sportsman's nature—to look down upon a scene so gloriously fresh—so impregnably savage—hemmed in with its blue-topped barriers forever!—without feeling rich—rich as the discoverer of some new gold-bearing island of the tropic sea of dreams—richer far than one of England's proud lords when he waved his hand towards his fenced and great domain; for this, too, was mine—was ours—was all mankind's—was GOD'S, as the executor for ALL!

And what if I were guilty of some saltant absurdities? There were no game law iniquities upon my shoulders to weigh down my heels!—all this was *free*, and the fatness thereof was mine for the winning—mine to be struggled for manfully with my brother—mine to be pouched, carried off and eaten, if my right hand retained its cunning! Even my placid friend, Piscator, felt within him the movings of a mild exultation, as he stretched forth his hands above it in calm blessing, and peacefully smiled!

Here and there the white mist-clouds lay along the hill-sides above them—seeming to form high up against the purpled green the ærial double of the lakes—and there, no doubt, the swift-winged swallows—though we couldn't see them—dived through the fleecy waves like brook-trout, and the fish-hawk swooped *like* the ravenous salmon—if they didn't *at* them below!

Of this we had much more palpable evidence, for we saw many of them rise, beating their wings with exulting screams as they went circling up and up, bearing a three to a five pounder in their talons. Fat pickings for fish-hawks, any how, in these thirty odd lakes! How I envied the rascals, and wished to hear the war-cry of a bald eagle, and see him come down from the clouds above, hurled swiftly, like the bolt he once bore, upon resistless wings, to strike the gluttons and make them drop their struggling prey, and then to see the conquering robber pause and dive with a roar of plumes down the still air and snatch the glistening spoil before it reached the wave again.

These are the quick, fierce battles of the air-kings that we sometimes see from such a perch!

But let us count our riches over, and name their names and places that we may know them.

Sheer down from our pinnacle on the northern side lies Lake Pleasant—a great white opal, with an emerald in the centre. This is

The captain jewel of the carcanet,"

and old earth wears it proudly for its beauty, and its name

is most happily named. Its shape is somewhat irregular, and its length is four miles, with an average breadth of two miles, and a depth of sixty feet. At the opposite extremity is the narrow but deep outlet which forms the Sockendog River, after passing through Cungamunck Bay, a few miles farther on, and then strikes off to the north-east, a bold and boisterous mountain stream, clattering among the hills until it looses itself in the great Hudson, as its western branch.

The shores of Lake Pleasant have quite a cultivated aspect —this is of course comparative. A number of beautiful grazing farms are opened to view around its rolling shores down to the water's edge. They are very rudely cultivated yet, but they might be made surpassingly lovely some day.

At the N. W. extremity of Lake Pleasant is the inlet of Round Lake, which is about half a mile in length. Round Lake! Gloomy, wild and picturesque Round Lake! twin sister of Lake Pleasant, "but grander and more rude than she!"—rimmed, like a Titan's brimming drinking cup, with low rocks, all around and above them the unbroken forest slanting up to blue-topped hills. How deep, austere and solemn its repose.

What a shadow beside the sunny loveliness of its contrasted sister! It is three miles both ways, and deeper than Lake Pleasant. There is no sign of cultivation upon its savage shores except at the outlet. It has several inlets, which go glimmering faintly through the narrow valleys towards the north-west. They connect it still with smaller lakes, Echo Lake, Lake Sound, and—O! euphonious accord!—*Mud* Lake!

When a few miles to the west another chain commences with Long Lake, which is two miles and a half in length by a half in width. This connects with Fly Lake, which is smaller still, and this with Falls Lake, about the same size, which outlets into Piseco, eleven miles west. This is a famous lake, and is about seven miles long and twelve wide. Through its outlet, West River, it is one of the feeders of Sockendog River, which forms the west branch of the Hudson.

This, too, is a lovely lake, partaking of many of the features of Lake Pleasant. There is some rude presence of civilization on the north end and eastern side, where a few farms and a small village are to be seen along the smoothly undulating shore. The country opens level to the south-east, but on the north-west the Panther mountain beatles over it protectingly stern.

This lake has been made renowned among sportsmen by the feats of the noted Piseco Club—a fraternal band who went thither once a year upon a devout pilgrimage to offer up a sacrificial hecatomb of fish bones and buck's horns to the manes of their hirsute progenitor, Ham! After very nearly exhausting its waters and shores, they have deserted them, and are now threatening some one of the wilder lakes we see towards the north-west. Here, when we talk of exhausting Piseco, we must be understood as when talking of the progress of civilization—in a comparative sense—for be it understood—these six devout pilgrims regarded *one hundred pounds a day* as the small expression of their fervid religious zeal; and the beautiful lake fell into discredit with them so soon as it refused to render up this slight diurnal tribute. Sportsmen of less zeal still find it a charming resort.

Now look away to the north-west, and you can count along the line of vision, until it is lost in the dim serrated line of the Blue Ariondack, twenty-five wild, lovely lakes, upon whose virgin solitudes no Piseco Club has ever intruded with its exhausting zeal. Look closely now, and you will be able to trace the threads of three of the finest trout streams in America. They form the eastern branch of the Hudson!

Here we are perched above and in the centre of the head

springs of that majestic river, and can almost trace even the attenuated rills to their junction, and we can see, too, in the blue mountains, the dividing ridge between its waters and the clear, gelid flood of the St. Lawrence!

A glorious perch, is it not?

First: six miles N. W. we can see Jessup's River. This is the nearest stream abounding with speckled trout, and where sport at *this season* is sure to be abundant. To "the Bridge" and to "the Indian Clearing" everybody must go *first* "to feel the joy that *anglers* feel."

This last place has been rendered immortal by the extraordinary feat of our friend Porter, of the *Spirit of the Times*. We do not venture to give the number of pounds within a given time—he is "tall" enough and his shoulders are broad enough to bear the responsibility—but we can bear witness, from our high and responsible position, in the presence of all these solemn-looking hills and lakes, that our "experience" at the Indian Clearing entirely bears him out in the assertion of prodigies to be wrought there.

Then comes Whittaker Lake—thereby hangs a tale! Then comes the two Dug Mountain Lakes and Mason Lake—these are all small.

Now comes Louis Lake—the next most famous to Piseco, and affording now better fishing and hunting. It is twelve miles from the Speclater, and is the favorite resort of those who come for a short stay and ready sport. This is one of the most beautiful of the lakes—its outlet forms a junction with Jessup's River in a few miles, and is thence called Indian River to its junction with the east branch of the Hudson.

But I have not space for more particular enumeration. I must pass to the curious Trinity of the Cedar Lakes, which empty, too, into the Hudson by Moose River—better fishing even than the Jessup's River—and here we are at Racquett's Lake, which is in this direction almost the *ultima thule* and

El Dorado of the sportsman combined. It is fourteen by seven miles, average, broken into two great basins, connected by a narrow strait. It is the largest and most savagely picturesque of the lakes, and most abounding in game of every sort.

Trout of both kinds are so abundant in the great basins and the numerous inlets, that the sport soon becomes fatiguing. It has twenty-four islands, of from one hundred acres to ten feet. On the west side is the inlet of a singular chain of small lakes, eight in number, all of which abound in both varieties of trout, and the accompanying fish, suckers, chubs, shiners, blue cats, sun perch, etc. This remarkable chain extends about fourteen miles north and east of the lakes, is deep, clear and ice cold. On the east side of Racket Lake is the inlet of Blue Mountain Lake, which is cold—almost to freezing point—and like a solid crystal set upon a snowbank of blanched sand.

You can see, as you hang suspended in mid-air here in your boat, the shoals of trout go by in twenty feet water! Think of that! Then comes Long Lake again—this time in earnest—for it is twenty miles long, with an outlet towards Lake Champlain. Here is the difficult paradise of sportsmen; and from Louis Lake, north, the moose becomes more abundant, with its attendant train of smaller game, and the distance, all told, from our perch on Speclater Mountain to Long Lake, is only *sixty miles!* These are the principal points of attraction within the range of our utmost vision which I have here noted; though now we can perceive that even yet there are more than thirty-six lakes, the names and distances of which I have not space to notice in this bird's-eye view.

But verily, this view of this our exceeding riches, in a land so rude and unpromising in the mouth of fame, and it may be together with the rareness of the air, has sharpened our appetite for testing again the flavor of the good things therein contained. Yea, our placid friend, Piscator, stroketh his stomach as his anticipative eyes are turned towards yonder humble looking house. Let us descend. What have we here, our tidy hostess? Fresh green peas—a salmon trout—a delicate steak of venison—strawberries, currants, cream! O, ye gods on high Olympus! Shade of Epicurus! Let us fall to!

The blessing of Piscator was somewhat curiously commentated—"Thank thee for thy manifold mercies, good Lord: Amen. Verily a good wife is a jewel unto her husband!" Amen! we responded.

CHAPTER XXI.

TROLLING IN JUNE.

"TROLLING," anywhere over good water, has its merits, but "trolling" over Lake Pleasant and Round Lake, of a sultry, pulseless summer's day, after the season has gone by, has its romance; and it is concerning this striking feature thereof, that I propose now to write.

"Patience is a virture of the serene gods," say the meek brothers of the angle; but I say their godships never subjected that sublimest attribute to the test of trolling one of the last days of June anywhere in Hamilton county; neither do I believe Old Nick ever thought of that merciful dispensation in favor of Job, or we should have heard a different story. It passeth all comprehension—not "—— still imagination in bottomless conceit—" could——! But I anticipate!

I was extremely ambitious of salmon trout—or "lakers," as they call them; and must confess that my inner visuals were so preoccupied by the glistening image of a twenty-pounder dancing in the air before them, while preparing to come here, that it never once occurred to me to inquire whether I should be in season or out of season for them. As for my friend Piscator, his contented fancy had never soared above a brook-trout of three pounds; and when he heard the stories of these huge fellows, his large eyes would grow rounder, and lambent with a liquid inspiration at the thought.

With what an eager smile, betwixt wonder and awe, he would listen, while he toiled at his delicate tackle, renewing its parts and strengthening its joints in preparation for the momentous struggle! We impatiently questioned our oracle, George Holland, as to the chances of success in trolling; but George, like all other oracles, was both prudent and mystical. He saw that we were determined that it *should* be in season, whether or no; that we *would* take some salmon trout, "bite or no bite;" and therefore he waived answering our questions directly, but told of his success *four weeks ago;* said the day was not very fine for 'em—but we might *try*, and if they *did* bite, we would probably take some! Encouraging, very! and the sly twinkle in the fellow's eye, still more so! But we hadn't come two hundred miles to be discouraged, and we went.

My friend had new-rigged his tackle with the painstaking skill of true science—while I, who pretend to no knowledge of the niceties of art, had left mine to the experience of George. The "shiners" were taken for bait with a dip net at the outlet, and then in a light boat we launched upon the lake. We were two in a boat—which is contrary to all precedent, as laid down in the Journal of Lake Piseco Trout Club, which has been appended to Wiley & Putnam's elegant edition of Walton and Cotton. There it is described *ex cathedra*, as follows—

The trolling is done by rod and reel, each fisherman using two at the same time; the reels are improved by having a bearing upon them instead of a catch, so that the rod may be laid down with the line extended without running out, unless struck by a fish or some other obstruction. When a fish seizes the bait the oarsman quits his oars, the other is handed to him, and he reels up the line to prevent its falling upon the bottom, or the fish, from entanglement.

This, of course, implies one fisherman to a boat—but with such an oarsman as ours, we found there was not the slightest danger of entanglement, with one at each end, while the oarsman was left free to use the gaff without any risk of unsteadying the boat too much by giving him two things to do at a time. Our tackle, however, agreed precisely with their formula, which we give.

The tackle is of the most delicate kind; a leader of from six to nine feet of single gut, with snell having five hooks, arranged with two at the end placed back to back, two more one inch above, and a fifth, or slip hook, one inch above, which passes through and secures the upper and lower jaw of the minnow, which serves for bait; one of the middle hooks is placed in the back of the bait, and one of the lower hooks in the tail. These hooks are so small that they will scarcely allow the barrel of a quill to rest in them.

Thus far we were "conformists;" and George, after a few strokes of the oars, paused, and taking a shiner from the bucket in which they swam, placed one upon each of our lines. The operation is a very nice one—as the object is to retain the fish in the position of swimming, and keep it alive, too, as long as possible, by closing its jaws with the slip hook, which prevents it from drowning; the two other hooks on the same side are so carefully placed under the back fin and through the tail, that I have seen them swim briskly off after an hour's trolling. George then cast them off, and struck out for the deep water with powerful strokes which made the boat fairly leap again.

The shores of Lake Pleasant on this side slope beautifully over a fair sand bottom for several hundred yards to the deep water. Before we reached this dark transparency, our lines had been reeled off to over a hundred and fifty feet, and were trailing a few feet below the surface, far in our rear. Our oarsman then altered his stroke to a slow and noiseless dip, which scarcely rippled the calm surface. Now a "strike," if we were to get one at all, might be expected—and with this skillful rowing, our wake closed far enough this side the bait to leave it floating in calm water, where the trout might see the flash of the shiner's side gleam slant down the cold depths of the "spring-holes" where they lay.

There we sat, stem and stern, Piscator and I, holding our poles erect, like statues, petrified by our own eagerness, while the angry sun looked down in sweltering wrath upon our simplicity. Not a breeze came with its blessing to turn aside his curse—not a cloud went up to the sky to shelter us with brooding wings. The pitiless lake held up its burnished shield—still as the death of winter—to hurl the sun's keen arrows, yellow with heat, full in our faces. Round and round Lake Pleasant (infernal mockery of name!) went the slow boat, until the silence of its glide became torture to me, for I longed to hear the ring of ripples and the cool splash of oars. How I began to curse the skill of our patient boatman. As we wheeled slowly past the island it looked like heaven, with the dark, cool shadows of its towering pines. How I longed to have said my prayers more regularly, that I might be permitted to lie down beneath them—and caught myself murmuring rapidly over and over, with my childhood's intonation of piety—*i. e.* through the nose—"And now I lay me down to sleep," &c.

But I couldn't catch up! Not a bite yet. That would have been some comfort! I moaned as I tossed my basting limbs to and fro.

"Curse all salmon-trout! would that the bull-frogs and mud-cats had ye in the spawn—hope ye may all be toasted alive upon the trident of the god of waters—ye illusory imps—ye speckled whelps, hag-born—may it be the fate of each of ye to be frozen stiff and be made into runners to some furred Kamskatkan's dog-drawn sled!—but pshaw!—there's no outlet that way; curse 'em anyhow! Phew, O scizzors!"

George—*loquitur*—"Gentlemen, think we'd better go into Round Lake—the water's colder and deeper there, we'll have a better chance?"

Ego—"Yes! in the name of mercy go anywhere—where its cold—into Round Lake or Nova Zembla. Wish Round Lake, Lake Pleasant and all the rest of your lakes were boiling in the cauldron of Hecla, and I was sitting on an iceberg to witness it—how I would rejoice to see the bleached salmon tossed up on the bubbles!"

Piscator—solemnly—"but then we should eat them without the glory of capturing them alive. Unless I had felt them play upon my tackle I should have no stomach for their blanched sides. It is a wish unworthy a true brother of the angle!"

Ego—"Piscator, when you die, the Zodiac will be the richer, for you will surely be translated into the sign of the fish!—to join the patriarchs who have gone before—Walton, and Cotton, Mr. Secretary Bibb—when he does go! A breeze! a breeze! my kingdom for a breeze! George, let us away to Round Lake—this bad cannot be made worse!"

We pass into the narrow inlet, and the boat glides briskly among the parched water lilies, the drooping flags and long bowed grass. A half mile of its winding way, and we are shot, with a long sweep of oars, into Round Lake. "Beautiful! beautiful!"—I exclaimed aloud—"What a scene of fairie."

Piscator—"Verily, it seems promising for trout here, at last, George. They are known to bite on this deep water such days as this?"

Ego—"No, unfortunate Piscator—you may rest assured never! They would scald their noses if they came near enough the surface to strike, even here."

George—with a sly evasion—"It requires a breeze, sir, for them to bite most any time!"

Piscator—"Here goes with another shiner—breeze or no breeze, we must have a trout for dinner! Would that I had my hook of flies!"

Ego—"Piscator, thou unbelieving Thomas! What would'st thou do with flies here?"

"Piscator—We of the brotherhood know them to work miracles, and therefore believe in their efficacy."

Ego—with a gasp and a sigh of exhaustion—"I see! Ah, Piscator! Piscator! The ruling passion strong in death!"

"George—Looking behind him—"A breeze! There comes a breeze, gentlemen!"

"Thank the good gods," and I almost overset the boat as I lifted up my forehead eagerly to catch the first cool brush of its coming wing.

"Now for a trout," chuckled Piscator, with glistening eyes.

Ah, it comes at last—so cool—so balmily delicious—driving the white-topped wavelets before it—on! on with it came the black shadow of that angel-ridden cloud to shelter us. I could have shouted for my joy—aye, lifted up my exulting soul in pæans, as cloud after cloud came drifting on their white plumes over us, with a legion of airy ministers which had come to our relief; but that my eyes fell upon the warm face of Piscator, shining with perspiration and expanded into a smile of pleasing expectancy as he watched the vibrations of his line. I was amazed into dumbness. I gazed upon the devotee in "a mute astound," when lo! a heavy jerk—a lurch and a shout, "you've got him!" from George, made me aware that a fish had struck. "Reel him in!" said George, as I hastily let go the line. "Reel him in," he has line enough." I reeled away, while Piscator, too generous to show his disappointment, did the like with his, watching at the same time with benevolent interest for my success.

It was a pause of breathless interest, as I reeled rapidly up for a few moments. "Curse it, George," I exclaimed petulantly, "I feel nothing—the fellow has broken away." He was watching my line—"No! no! reel on—you have him, you'll feel him directly." Reel! reel! reel! and now a few faint surges which bent the rod slightly. There! the flash of his gleaming side darts up the blue wave! now he has waked up! Tug! splash! whiz—there he goes bounding clear out of water on the taut line! Steady! steady! George is ready with the gaff. Now he rises again—there, he has it! Floundering over our feet lays a beautiful two-pound laker!

"No great shakes after all, Master George—but ah! what a lovely creature it is. Here, let me look at him well before his glorious colors fade. See his long gracefully tapering body; see the dark greenish purple of his richly marbled back, how it lightens quickly down his side, like silver burnished bronze; and then those rows of spots so regularly placed along it—the two outside of yellow, like gold drops, that down the middle of small carbuncles! There! there! the splendors are fading already!"

Beautiful dweller of the dark blue waters, farewell until we meet again at the dinner table! Ah, Piscator! Piscator! my hapless friend! you perceive the jealous Deities of the lake have visited an austere judgment upon you in permitting to me alone the "*spoila opima*" of the excursion, can you not perceive the reason?

Piscator—"To rebuke your want of faith and wishes on their behalf this day, I suppose!"

Ego—"Infatuated! can you not feel that it has been to punish your presumption in wishing you had flies—when George, our oracle and their High Priest, had already revealed to you that they would only take living shiners, and were not to be fooled by mimic monsters of wool and feathers! you shamefully discredited their sagacity thereby!"

Piscator—with suspended nostrils and lightning in his eye—"Pshaw, nonsense! I shall take a trout greater than five of thine before we reach yonder shore!"

Ego—compassionately—"Vain man!"

Again we glided off, across and about, around and around

we went for a weary time the same noiseless way—when suddenly our curse came again, and I remembered—

> "Down dropt the breeze, the sails dropt down,
> 'Twas sad as sad could be."

And then:

> "All in a hot and copper sky,
> The bloody sun, at noon," &c. &c.

I verily shuddered as I felt the hot stagnation settle upon my forehead and my lungs. I looked appealingly to Piscator. What? Horror!—the despairing wretch!—the disappointment and all has been too much for him! With head thrown back, and eyes rolling wildly towards the zenith—his large manly throat bared, he held—the brandy flask to his lips!—the forgotten brandy flask! and then my time came. I imbibed from it contemplatively and laid it aside solemnly. I had rested the end of my rod in the gunwale of the boat, and did not take it up again. I laid myself reposefully in the bow. The vanity of all sublunary things—but most that of trolling for lakers out of season, had been made apparent to me. I looked up to the clouds—above us they had vanished, and all was "a hot and copper sky:" as if to the spell of some strange wizard of the North, their careering legions had been called down and rested toward the pole upon the mountain tops—still!—still as if they paused in the terror of a weird necromancy, which held them frozen in its dreadful will. They were strangely piled, and strewn, and marshalled. I never saw such clouds before—the forms were all of white, with a dark distinct outline. I became strangely elated and laughed out wildly, and then muttered—

"Aye, yonder is the pageant of our lives—the substance whereof our realities are made, and yet how strange it seems, how it has become so palpable. Look at it closely; you will see there

> 'The shadows of all forms that think and live
> Till Death unite them, and they part no more;
> Dreams and the light imaginings of men,
> And all that faith creates of love, desires
> Terrible, strange, sublime and beauteous shapes.'

Every thing there, Piscator! Even to that white throne, heaped up like a reflex of the frowning Speclater; and there on the cloudy Olympus I can see particular deities of Lake Pleasant and Round Lake. It must be confessed, that though their 'brows are awful,' their tails look somewhat 'fishy!' See! there is a veritable representative of the salmon trout whom you have this day insulted! He kneels with a graceful bend of his pedestal fin, and with open mouth is complaining to their Godships concerning you. See how they wag their misty heads and scowl the feathery bolts of their ire down at you! Tremble, presumptuous Piscator!'

Piscator—laughing dolorously—"Aye! aye! my Pithian! Pass him the flask, George!"

Ego—with a grandiose wave of the arm—"No, sir! no more brandy. My inspiration is *there*–

> ——————— All the gods
> Are there, and all the powers of nameless worlds;
> Vast sceptred phantoms; heroes, men and beasts;
> And Demogorgon, a tremendous gloom;
> And he, the supreme Tyrant on his throne
> Of burning gold.'

Blind worm—(I should call you angle-worm, Piscator)—can you not see them? Look, I say!—there is the Northern Bear, distinct, upreared upon his mighty hinder parts, and boxing with his frosty paws the small and feathery curled effigy of a French poodle, which assails him from above with snarling jaws!"

Piscator—"Bah! you are becoming a political prophet. Do you see John Bull there?"

Ego—indignantly—"Where are your eyes? Do you not

see him on this side below the bear, tumbling down the white cliffs of Albion, from which he has just been brought by one stroke of those white gelid paws—with hoofs in air, and upward mouth wide-stretched with bellowings? (Piscator is an Englishman!) Eyeless Angle-worm! can you not see?"

Piscator—placidly—"No, no! I have no eyes for your mad visions!"

Ego—with furious emphasis—"Mad, are they?

> ————'Call at will
> Thine own ghost or the ghost of Jupiter,
> Hades, or Typhon, or what mightier gods—hey!'"

A tremendous lurch! Boat nearly turned over! My rod almost bent double! as the boat is wheeled violently from its course, and we all thrown as violently upon our sides, for in the wake a huge trout leaped from the water, and when he falls back the boat rights, and we all look foolish.

George, vehemently—"There, you've lost him!"

Piscator, indignantly—"There! if you had held your rod in your hand, instead of ranting nonsense on your back you wouldn't have lost that twelve-pounder!"

Ego—faintly—"But he didn't bite at a fly, or at the hook of a fly fisher!"

Moral—never troll lake trout after the first of June.

CHAPTER XXII.

A NIGHT HUNT UP THE CUNGAMUNCK.

ALTHOUGH the most inveterate of veteran fly-fishers, Piscator had, even in our short survey of these wild sporting grounds, become thoroughly aroused to a sense of "higher things" than brook trout, and not in the least discouraged at the signal failures of the first flights of his ambition at the great lake trout, he now breathed quicker, with a yet more eager emulation for nobler quarry still! In short, as our guide, George, said—"He's down on the deer up Cungamunck!"

The reader is no doubt familiar with the mode of hunting

deer "by torch-light," which has been so often described—but I have some doubts about his being so with that of hunting them "by candle-light," which, I believe, is peculiar to the Lake country. This hunt must take place during the warm months, when flies are most abundant. Indeed, it is as much to escape from their persecutions as to browse upon certain varieties of water-plants, which then make their appearance along the edges of the marshes, streams, and lakes, that the deer come into the water to feed, and thus afford an opportunity for this evening sport.

Yes, the "dander" of my placid associate, Piscator, "is riz!" He vows in his mild, but not the less significant manner, that nothing short of a "ten prong buck" will satisfy him, and so proceeds in a severe and ominous silence with his preparation.

The beautiful "double-barrel"—which had heretofore been guilty of nothing more serious than wood-cock and ducks—was to be unscrewed, taken apart, and cleaned to the last degree of scrupulous nicety, in preparation for the more important work on hand. Then, with mathematical precision, it was duly charged, and then, with a flask in each pocket—for *two* kinds of ammunition are indispensable on such occasions! and a well-filled cigar case, he is ready! And he casts his eyes about—something is wanting! Yes! yes! the "India rubber overall." For Piscator, like all true brothers of the angle that I have yet met, has a peculiar horror of risking the wetting his skin.

I have, after much study, accounted satisfactorily for this phenomenon, by the philosophical conclusion, that they are haunted by the constant apprehension of transmigration into the corporate forms of the trout, to which they are so devoted. I had even ventured to hint as much to Piscator, but the nervous dread with which he evidently avoided the subject, caused me to forbear, in courtesy, pressing it farther! Being a zealous disciple of Priesnitz, I have no fear of cold water before my eyes; and therefore my equipment in this respect was considerably simplified, though I must confess to you I had an ever-present terror of the flies, which was quite an offset to Piscator's transmigration, and cost me quite as much preparation to guard against.

I knew that the oil of pennyroyal was a specific against their attacks; but aside from my aversion to the use of so disagreeable an article, I had forgotten it, so that the only resource left me, had been to buy a green veil at Northfield, and cutting a hole in the centre large enough for the crown of my broad brimmed leghorn to pass through, I had the ends taken up and a "puckering string" run around them, so that they could be drawn close about my neck—thus securely surrounding my face with a net which would defy even "black gnats." Thus, with rifle (which is my favorite weapon) in hand, and my personal dividend of *ammunition* in pocket, I, too, considered myself equipped for the night hunt.

Piscator was characteristically disregardful of "the flies," and laughed quite as much at my precautions against them as I had done at his against getting wet. He said, somewhat pedantically, that "Patience was a more magnanimous divinity than Prudence, seeing that the one was always irritable, distrustful, and guarding herself against the wisdom of the Higher Powers, while the other was content in calm humility to abide the evil the Gods might send along with the good!"

Whereto I replied—"The Gods do not send black gnats, Piscator; for I have sufficient proof in their color that they are hatched in Acheron, and are loosed upon earth by the Evil Deities to make good men swear against Jupiter—therefore, I guard against the crime rather than provoke it—while you impiously shield your shoulders against the rain, which is confessedly the chiefest benediction of the covering heavens."

Piscator did not reply, but somewhat petulantly tossed his India rubber overall upon his shoulders, and calling our guide, tramped away, followed by me, towards the boat at the outlet. There we found every thing needful already in the boat. The additions to its ordinary equipment were very few and simple. A stout pine stick had been let into an auger hole through a board which had been placed across the bow. This stood some four feet high; and upon the top of it was placed a triangular shaped box, open at the wide end, and which was intended to hold the lighted candles. Then there was a low seat, which was intended for the marksman, who sat forward, just behind the staff and box-lantern; then we had a paddle, which was to be used when we reached the scene of operations, where the ordinary oars were to be laid aside.

Now we embarked, and set off down the narrow but deep outlet. It here takes the name of Sockendog river, and its course towards the southeast is through a wide valley, between two chains of hills. The water spreads over the surface of this valley in reality, though it is so overgrown by the "mash" of tall grass, flags and water-lilies, that the real channel seems like a dark shining ribbon laid along a rippled and rustling waste of green. Soon we reached Cungamunck Bay, which spreads a quarter of a mile in width, with the hills rising abruptly on the east. It is a pretty sheet of water, covered with the white and yellow flowers of the lily. Sockendog plunges on through a gorge by the foot of the hills, while we turn towards the north-west, pushing through the grass and lilies for the thread-like channel of the Cungamunck river, which comes winding down from out a forest of wild hills.

Now the valley narrows rapidly, and the hills stand marshalled on either hand in close dark lines. The sun is yet over an hour high, and its yellow glitter is broken upon our faces through the firs and pines which bristle on the ridges. We are gliding with a "stilly creeping" glide, beneath their long shadows and up the tortuous vistas of this curious stream, which comes creeping slowly down through the grass like a great snake out of its lair of night, with here and there the golden morning glistening on its scales.

It was a strange, lonely scene, and a dream-like hush was over it, so that we could hear our hearts beat above the soft lapsing of the deeply winnowed oars. It seemed so wild, and was so still here, that no other sounds should intrude but the splash of the plunging bull-frog, the rustling ripple of the wading deer among the flags, and the musically shrill metallic warble of the black-winged scarlet tanager, from out the deep shadows of the hill-side forest of old pines and hemlock. Now is the time when the deer begin to come down from the hills to feed upon the tender grasses and water plants that grow in the bed and along the edges of the stream; and we may expect any moment, when we make the short turns, which, although the stream is deep, are often hardly long enough for the boat to lie in, or wide enough for the oars, to see a tawny head uplifted in the startle, and reaching out from the long grass over the channel to gaze at our coming with pricked ears.

Piscator and I drew lots for the first shot at starting, and I won, so that I had the forward seat, and with rifle at "present," I sat in statue-like and breathless expectation as we made each turn, and came upon a new and always wilder and more lovely picture of green islets, deep receding coves, where the trout leaped like quick gleams of moonlight over the white lilies—or small meadows waving to and fro, in live contrast with the gray and solemn-looking boulders of granite which are piled up behind them, with the matted and snake-like roots of the ancient pines above, twisted and twined along their edges. I was so lulled and enchanted by the constantly varying beauty and the presiding repose of these scenes, that, with all the eager instincts of the sportsman rampant in my veins, I could not help hoping, at moments, that no deer would make its appearance, and thus compel me to mar this harmonious calm. Nor did it happen so, for, contrary to our expectation, not one showed itself to tempt me, although it was three miles up to where this stream outlets in Elm Lake.

It was in the last half mile of our approach to this and around its mashy shores, that we looked for the sport of the night to begin in earnest; and any that might have occurred on the way would have been incidental, and could therefore be well dispensed with for the higher and more placid enjoyment of the scene. As we approached the Lake the stream became more shallow, and we were compelled at last to get out and let our guide drag the boat up the ripples. The sun was now setting, and at the first place where the low water thus compelled us to land for a few moments, we were suddenly introduced to that most inconceivable torment, the black gnat!

As the shades of evening advance, these gnats, which at first hover near the surface of the water, rise slowly on the strata of miasmatic air. Wishing to examine some object on the sand-bar more closely, I stooped, when instantly, as if an infinitesimal shower of red-hot sand or fine vitriol drops had been dashed into my face and eyes, I felt them—blistering against neck and bosom, up sleeves and pants, they at once invested me in a maddening reality of the fabled terrors of the shirt of Nessus! No imagination is sufficiently vivid to conceive the intensity of that keen-poisoned, stinging nettle-rash with which we found ourselves suddenly assailed by this invisible torturer from Acheron, rising to meet us on its thick, pestilent airs. I did not know what it meant at first, and, blinded with the pain, rushed with the instinct of the cold water man, to plunge my face in the stream for relief. This was, fortunately, the best thing I could have done; and I now gasped out, "George! George! what is it!" "The gnats, sir! the gnats—you had better put on your veil!"

I did so as quickly as possible; and when I turned, there

stood Piscator, with a wild look of endurance, earnestly fighting away at his invisible torturers with a leafy bough which he had plucked; his warm face glowed again with the malignant ardor of their stings, and he stopped at intervals in the fierce battle to rub his goaded limbs, and fairly danced in the restless shifting of his feet. Suffering as I was, or rather, had been, I could not help laughing at the comical sight. But he did not regard me, and coolly proceeded to stuff the legs of his pants down his boot-tops, to protect himself from their assaults in that quarter; and then turning up his coat collar, tied his handkerchief about his ears, and soon, with recovered equinimaty, came smiling to his seat in the boat, while the bough played yet faster about his face. I could but wonder at the man. I watched him in utter amaze; puzzled whether most to admire the thickness of his skin or the immovability of his temper. As soon as the boat was in motion they left us, for they were drifted behind on air-currents in our wake.

We were soon at the wider mash meadows, which indicated our approach to the outlet of Elm Lake, and here was the ground where the night hunt was to commence. Darkness had not not yet settled down, and until it came our lights would be of no avail; so the oars were hid, and the boat run through the mash to shore, and there we were to stand until it became dark enough to light the candles!

We stood underneath the bordering pines, and as soon as we became stationary—heavens and earth! the dusky air thickened with the black and venomous swarms of mosquitos, flies and gnats, and the hungry diapason of their blistering music was fairly roared into our ears! No herd of famished wolves was ever so desperately ravenous as this fierce multitude *seemed* to be—for as I was fully protected by my veil, I could afford to be philosophical in my observations on the suffering of the two outside unfortunates.

George was very loquacious, and having provided himself

with a thick bough, kept that in motion with his words; for he seemed to have a desperate sort of feeling that he must këep up our courage and his own by talking, or else we would be compelled to give in! He amused us in this trying interval with many stories of his bold adventuring through these northern snows (a fortunate contrast!) in hunting the dangerous moose. While Piscator puffed his segar—patiently fought in open battle his myriad foes, and smiled appreciatingly through his torture as the stories sped. How I admired the superhuman heroism of the man!

I could not help enjoying the forlorn and melancholy efforts of the guide to be merry in his suffering. But the night settled rapidly, though it brought no alleviation of the plague of flies, which on warm evenings most abound after sunset for some hours. Now George stepped cautiously to the stern of the boat, and taking the candles from the box, proceeded to light them and place them in the triangular box on the staff at the bow. Then with great care we noiselessly took our seats, and he paddled the boat with surprising stillness up the outlet. Mine was the foremost seat—as allotted—and though the light above shone powerfully upon the shrubs and grass in front of us on the side of the channel, yet not one ray of it fell upon me! So with a far-thrown light before us, we glided in darkness up the channel, seeing every blade of grass as we advanced, while we were ourselves unseen! But the sky had now clouded, and the white mist began to curl up before us, and we only saw the rank grass and elder bushes in advance as it lifted at intervals.

We glided through the white-wreathed silence for awhile, with the mash plants and grass showing through the gloom on one side, and the tall shrubs on the other, when suddenly there is a splashing to our right—the boat stops—splash! splash! splash! off they go with a loud whistle as they plunge away—two deer are gone! They had been frightened by the incessant movement of our hands in striking off the clinging flies!

George curses strong and deep, "sotto voce," and we move on into the lake without a word from us. Now we are gliding along its marshy shore, and the only sound we make is that caused by the low grating of the bottom of our boat against the heavy leaves of the water-lilies, which cover the whole surface as far as we can see, but that is not far. The heavy mist-wreaths still curl up around us and arching to our light, roll and spread their whitened volumes murkily. The slow boat ploughs through these fantastic shapes as if it labored with their weight; but now and then an eddy of the mountain wind lifts them, whirling in broken masses, and reveals the dark shadows of the forest on the shore, with the shining flags that push up among the bordering lilies. The night is becoming chill, and we have crept into every cove and winding strait among the inlets along the shore, and still the same slow-rising vapor twists and rolls in huge white phantoms, bushing past us; and, lifting in solemn sweep upon the winds, the jaws of darkness open over the broad water, as if on that side the abyss of black infinity were yawning to engulph us. No deer yet, for they seem to have been all startled by our first misadventure; we should have seen a dozen eyes shine our light before this! We are cold as cold can be, for much time has now passed, and chilled, too, by the disappointment. Now we shoot into a narrow cove between two islands. The long grass and shrubs on either side nearly meet above our heads, we must move with still greater caution lest we brush them.

Now the narrow way widens again somewhat, and we go winding on, while our advance light dawns with a strange gleam beneath the curling vapor upon the dense wall of leafy stems on either side, and we seem urging up, among ghastly clouds, the glistening steep of night. It is a wild, unearthly scene; we shudder with chilly awe, for the vast weight of midnight has crushed the world, the wide and mighty world, into that little circle of light with its wizard shapes, thronging above and around us—all else is void—nothing! nothing!

Ha! close to my hand a little summer duck comes swimming. That looks as if there were an outer world—a something beyond this wizzard chaos! See it comes close in our charmed circle—it cannot get away. Its great black eyes shine still, as if it were in a dream of dazzled splendors, it does not see us, it moves as the sleep walker moves, round and round, yet not away. There, I had nearly caught it with my hand, but it glided like a beam-eyed shadow from beneath my grasp. It seems as ghostly as all else here.

Hark! a splashing plunge in the deep marsh to our right, that sounds like earth—like a reality!

"Hist!" says George, in a whisper, "rise up! rise softly, he stands there—over the bushes—see his eyes!"

"Steady, George." I rise as carefully as my stiffened limbs would permit, and now the mist-wreaths on an eddy of the night-wind rise with me. Slowly! slowly! See the antlered head above the cover and the shining eyes. A shrill, loud whistle—I fire as he bounds—a heavy plunge—a struggle in the tossing covert and all is still!

"Youv'e got him! you got him that time, sir!" shouted George, and the sound of his human voice broke the spell that was upon me, as of a heavy vision, and with a long breath of suppressed excitement, I plunge after him to assist in dragging our prey to the boat. It was a fine buck, and I had shot him between the eyes. Ah, that was a moment of cruel exultation, but I will not tell you how I triumphed at the blank looks of poor Piscator, when, as he took his seat now in front, we discovered that the lights were nearly exhausted, and that there would be little chance for him to get a shot at all! The candles soon gave out, and we got lost upon the lake, where our bewildered guide continued to row up and down until nearly daylight, through the pitchy darkness; at last he found a landing by accident, and, nearly frozen, we made our way to the house of a hunter, whose kind hospitality gave rest to our weary and chilled frames.

CHAPTER XXIII.

TROUTING ON JESSUP'S RIVER.

We could not remain quiet long at a time, for my restless friend had not yet had a fair trial of the "flies" at trout. After all, laugh at Piscator's violent passion for it as I may, the sport which lasts longest, is the most abundant, the most admired, and most practised by the frequenters of the Lake country, is that of taking the speckled or brook trout with the rod!

The larger lakes afford good trolling grounds, when resorted to in the right season; but the trolling season, which begins in March, is too early for the majority of anglers, who cannot leave their spring business for mere sport. But when summer comes, business is over; then the rejoicing anglers, like children broke loose from school, scatter abroad over the mountainous places of the land, literally gasping with panting bosoms for fresh air.

To such it makes little difference, when they reach here, to find that the fishing-grounds for trout are not close at hand, but that they must go yet farther from five to thirty miles, among the rough wild hills, to fresher streams, amidst valleys deeper than these. It seems strange, to be sure, and very provoking to them, if they go without a proper knowledge of the season—to find that these wide clear sheets, with all their inlets and outlets, are but so much dead water to them—affording no sport after the tenth of June, worth notice. But they are soon over this, for the mountain breezes are very inspiriting; and with expanding chests they look towards the blue ridges with emulation, and brace themselves up to meet the rude exigencies of a "tramp" and "shanteeing out" for a few days, amidst storm or sunshine, as the evening heavens may send!

"The Bridge" at Jessup's River, is well known to sportsmen, and to this point we made our first fly-fishing expedition. The eyes of Piscator glistened at the thought, and early was he busied with almost hasty fingers through an hour of ardent preparation amongst his varied and complicated tackle. Now was *his* time for triumph! In all the ruder sports in which we had heretofore been engaged, I, assisted by mere chance, had been most successful—but now the infallible certainty of skill and science were to be demonstrated in himself, and the orthodoxy of flies vindicated to my unsophistic sense.

The preparations are simple, and were early completed. The tidy housewife soon had ready the huge loaves of fresh nice bread—the can of yellow butter, and other minor appliances of a feast in the woods—the main condiments and dishes of which we were expected to supply from our own sharpened appetites and skill. Then the cooking apparatus, which was primitive enough to suit the taste of an ascetic, as it consisted in a single frying pan. Then the blankets, with the guns, ammunition, rods, &c.

These were all disposed in the wagon of our host, which stood ready at the door. It was a rough affair, with stiff wooden springs, like all those of the country, and suited to the mountainous roads they are intended to traverse, rather than for civilized ideas of comfort. We, however, bounded into the low-backed seat; and if it had been cushioned to suit royalty, we could not have been more secure than we were of luxurious comfort—a fanciful illusion which it took but little time, however, to dissipate in an astound, as we found ourselves rumbling, pitching, and jolting over a road even worse than that which brought us first to the lake. It seemed to me that nothing but the surprising docility of the pretty span of glossy black ponies which drew us, could have saved us, strong wagon and all, from a sudden return to our original atoms. I soon got tired of this, and sprang out with my gun, determined to foot it ahead, in the hope of seeing a partridge or red squirrel.

The wagon, with its thundering rumble, was soon left behind, and for several miles I tramped on alone through the oppressive stillness of those old spruce and hemlock forests, which line the road upon the hill-side and down steep shaded valleys. It was then I observed the extraordinary stillness, which I found characterized the woods there, in whatever direction I had penetrated.

I wondered for some time what was the cause, and what it was I missed so much, until I discovered the almost total absence of the different varieties of squirrel. Then I understood at once.

These creatures are the great enliveners of forest scenery, and we unconsciously as much expect to hear them rattling over the dry leaves—their rustling leap from bough to bough—the pattering of nuts they are unhusking over head—their saucy chattering and defiant bark—or to see their graceful forms leap across the path—dart up and around the standing trunks or along the dead logs, as we do, to see the trees themselves, or hear the winds murmur through their leaves. Every where, except in the tropics, they are ever-present and more essential to the complete characteristics of forest scenery, than even the birds themselves. This is particularly the case at the north, where the varieties of the birds are neither so abundantly musical or large as in the Middle States. I never saw woods before through which you might walk all day, from day to day, for weeks, and most probably not see or hear the sound of a single squirrel.

I had spent much time in the woods, and had not been able to reconcile myself to this strange want, which impressed me, even before I heard the cause, with something like a funeral desolation—with the shadow of a feeling like that which we would have in walking through the echoing streets of a plague-depopulated city. I was greatly surprised when I found how analogous the case really was. On inquiring among the old hunters, I heard from them the reason.

In the first place, the chickaree, or common red squirrel, is the only one, except the little chip squirrel, they have there at all as a resident variety—for although the gray squirrel has occasionally made its appearance for a little while, the black martin, which is very abundant, is said to enter its hole and destroy it, before it has time to breed much, while the hole of the chickaree is too small for it to gain admittance. Well, about twenty years ago, the country was literally overrun one summer by a plague of red squirrels, curiously enough, too, accompanied by great numbers of the little deer mouse or jumping mouse. The two united, destroyed nearly the whole of the standing crops of grain, and swarmed over the outhouses and even the dwelling-houses themselves, and along the fences by the roadside, and indeed through the woods every where.

The people were alarmed by the apprehension of great loss, and even a partial famine, when suddenly the curse was swept away in a most singular manner. The squirrels all at once began to act strangely; they were observed to drag themselves slowly along the ground across the roads, so that the people could crush them with their heels. Those on the fences would mope and stagger along the rails, or falling off, would be seen in dozens hanging by one claw, until they dropped dead to the ground. They could be killed by hundreds, with a small stick, and the very air became impure with the stench of their dead bodies. On examination, it was found they were literally covered over their whole bodies witn warty and vermillion-colored pustules, which looked very foul and angry. The mice were visited in the same way, and nearly all, if not *all*, died off; since, for several years after, not a creature of either kind was to be seen, and to this day they have remained remarkably scarce.

This story seemed very strange to me, but one day I shot a young red squirrel, the first I had killed since I came—for lack of opportunity—and I found it covered by this same warty disease, which had been described as causing their extermination so long ago. The pustules were quite small upon it, and not so thickly placed as in the time of the plague, when they were as large as a pea of good size, and there was not the space of a pin's head any where between them! This accounts for their not having increased more rapidly—since the fact shows that the disease continues to linger with them, preventing, as I suppose, their arriving at maturity, in the majority of cases.

But I have gone a good way aside from my theme to narrate these curious facts, and must get back to the 'Bridge' again, at which we arrived about the middle of the afternoon. There we found an old field just across the bridge. It was called Wilcox's Clearing, and like all such places I had seen in this fine grazing region, was still well sodded down in Timothy, blue grass, and clover. Our luggage having been deposited in the shantee, which consisted nearly of boards torn from the old house, which were leaned against the sides of two forks, placed a few feet apart, we set off at once for the Falls, a short distance above. This was merely an initial trial, to obtain enough for dinner, and find the prognostics of the next day's sport in feeling the manner of the fish.

At the Falls the river is only about fifteen feet wide, though its average width is from twenty-five to thirty. The water tumbles over a ledge of about ten feet, at the bottom of which is a fine hole, while on the surface sheets of foam are whirled round and round upon the tormented eddies—for the stream has considerable volume and power.

We stepped cautiously along the ledge, Piscator ahead, and holding his precious flies ready for a cast, which was most artistically made, not without a glance of triumphing pity at poor me, who was preparing to do the same with the humble angle-worm. The 'flies' fall—I see the glance of half a dozen golden sides darting at them—but, by this time, my own cast is made, and I am fully occupied with the struggles of a fine trout.

What a thrilling sensation it is!—the bite of the first trout!—renewed each season, too, in all the strength of novelty, when you, perhaps, for the fiftieth time after the weary interval otherwise employed, feel again the electric shock of its pull, communicated through your arm to all your frame—the heart bounds as gladly, and the eyes gleam in as wild an ecstacy of delight, for the moment, as on your boyhood's first capture. But the 'black flies' swarmed by this time with such a wounding, maddening buzz into my eyes, nostrils and mouth, behind my ears, and up my sleeves, that no mortal enthusiasm could stand it any longer.

"Here, George, in heaven's name take my rod! My veil! —where is it? I have forgotten it!"

"No, here it is—I thought of it!" and he drew it from his bosom. How I blessed the fellow! It was on and adjusted in an instant—and then I had time to draw a long breath and look around me.

"Hey! seven trout. What, did I catch all those in this little while?" I exclaimed, in a surprise not very complimentary to Piscator's 'flies.'

"I caught one of 'em!" growled he—while he perseveringly whipped the foam with his flies. I turned towards him, and through my green veil his forlorn, despairing face looked jaundiced. I was moved to pity.

"Try the worms, good Piscator—here they are. This is not the right time of day for them to take the flies in this river, I judge!"

He was soothed, and eagerly improving the door of escape thus opened to him, took off the flies and used worms with immediate and brilliant success, which brought back the placid smile to his face, and he would now and then as calmly brush away the distracting swarm of flies from his face, as if they had been mere innocent motes. He had only taken the one with his flies at the first instant of his cast—and afterward, not a single trout would rise to them. But later that evening came a temporary triumph for Piscator. The hole at the Falls was soon exhausted, and we moved on down to glean the ripples. It was nearly sundown, and here the pertinacious Piscator determined to try the flies again. He cast with three, and instantly struck *two* half-pound trout, which, after a spirited play, he safely landed. Never did I see so proud a look of exulting triumph as that which glowed upon his as he bade me "look there!" when he landed them.

"Very fine, Piscator! a capital feat! but I fear it was an accident! You will not get any more that way!"

"We shall see, sir!" said he proudly, and commenced whipping the water again, but to no avail, while I continued throwing them out with great rapidity.

I carefully abstained from watching him, for I had no desire to spoil his evening sport by taunting him, to continue his experiment. I soon observed him throwing out the fish with great spirit again. I merely shouted to him across the stream—"The angle-worm, once more, Piscator?"

"Yes!" with a laugh.

As the sun went down, the black gnats began to make themselves felt in their smarting and infinitesimal myriads, and we forthwith beat a hasty retreat to the shantee. These creatures, which are the most diabolical pests that ever haunted the air and water-side, are, I think, identical with the sand fly in Texas—where it is the terror of all low, sandy, bottom lands, and valleys below the sea range. It follows the black fly, which is about half the size and a good deal the shape of the common house fly. About an hour after its appearance in the afternoon, and its coming is considered the universal signal for retreat from the fishing grounds, as no heroism, not even that of Piscator, could long withstand their assaults.

We had taken about ten pounds of trout; and the first procedure, after reaching the camp, was to build a 'smudge,' or smoke-fire, to drive away these abominable gnats, which fortunately, take flight with the first whiff of smoke—and the next was to prepare the fish for dinner, though not till *all* had been carefully dressed by the guide, and placed in the cold current of the little spring stream near, that they might keep sound.

Now came the rousing fire, and soon some splendid trout were piled upon dishes of fresh pealed elm bark before us. They were very skillfully cooked, and O, ye deluded Epicureans! let me tell ye! ye know not, on your rich and massive plate, the true flavor of this rare morsel for the Gods to smack their lips at, that I took up in my fingers from the bark dish—no, the ripe, high color of the flesh—the sweet, melting, luscious, glorious titillation of the palate by which I was exalted there in that rude shantee, to the highest heaven of the sense, you cannot know! The exquisite aroma has passed away before it reaches you, fading with the splendid colors of the skin, and ye cannot catch it! Not all your wealth can transport it in the season, delicious as we had it. You can get them so in the winter, when it is cold enough to freeze them instantly on coming from the water, but not otherwise.

The feast being over, then to recline back upon the fresh couch of soft spruce boughs, and with a cigar in mouth, watch the gathering 'night-shades' brooding lower and more low upon the thick wild forest in front—far into the depths of which the leaping flames of our crackling fire go, darting now and then with a revealing tongue of quick light—and listening to the owl make hoarse answer to the wolf afar off

—to think of wild passages in a life of adventure years ago amidst surroundings such as this; with the additional spice of peril from savage and treacherous foes, and then, as the hushed life subsides into a stiller mood, see the faces of loved ones come to you through the darkness, with a smile from out your distant home, and while it sinks sweetly on your heart, subside into happy and dream-peopled slumber! "This! this is *bliss!*" the bliss of the shantee to the wearied sportsman! a bliss unattainable to the sluggish and jaded gourmand of the city!

We were on foot with the sun next morning, and after another feast, which we appreciated with unpalled appetites, we set off for some deep spring holes nearly a mile above the Falls. The morning set cloudy, and rain fell piteously for several hours. During this time we had reached the neighborhood of the holes, after an abominably rough scramble along the mountain side; and here George set to work to construct a raft of the decayed spruce which stood around. This completed, it was launched with great labor into the stream; and as the day was beginning to clear off, Piscator so far conquered his horror of getting wet, as to agree to start. We pulled noiselessly up to the spring hole, and found it very deep, and quite large for the general size of the stream.

The instant my hook was in the water, a fine trout was hung, and even Piscator, who still persevered with the flies, was successful the *first cast*, as usual. But as no further notice was taken of the flies by the trout, and I continued to pull out the noble fellows as fast as I could throw my hook in, he changed very quickly again to the worm. The sport was now magnificent, and all the time, one line or the other was singing through the deep water to the struggles of a trout, and often both at the same time. We found the raft very convenient, for having no landing net, while they were playing vigorously, we would take them on a spring upward through the water, and by a quick movement, adding to their impetus, would land them on the raft. We took several of that most splendidly beautiful of all trout, the "red bellied"—for their bellies are as if of burnished gold, heated to a red heat, while the spots upon their sides fairly glitter, while their fins are black, bordered with white.

The moment they were hooked, we could see their sides flash up from the depths of the hole like the gleam of an angry blaze, and they shot like fiery meteors through the air as they leaped from it. We moved on slowly down the stream with our raft, after they ceased to bite here, and took from one to two and four pounds from every hole we passed, until I became weary of the sport, and even Piscator confessed himself for once to have had enough of trout fishing. The time had come for our return home, and now the interminable rain set in again more violently than ever, and our guide, who had fifty pounds of trout upon his shoulder, shrank from clambering back over the mountain with such a burden, and we landed on the opposite side of the river, to return by a new and longer though more level route.

Of all the dismal and exhausting walks ever taken, this seemed to me the most so. A violent west wind had set in, dashing on its cold current the colder rain into our faces. We were chilled and wet in an instant after starting. Much of the way led through a deep tangle of elder and raspberry bushes, which were as high as our heads, and bent with the burden of icy rain drops. So this gave us a double bath. We managed—or, our guide did for us!—to get lost in the bargain; had five miles to tramp through the thick pine woods, plunging through swamps, and stumbling into deep holes, over roots, dead trees, and rocks. There was one comfort before us, at least, the prospect that we should find our host waiting for us at the bridge with the wagon.

On we staggered bravely—splash! splash! drip! drip! Above us, under, and on every side, the gelid rain! As is an incessant shower bath, far more exhausting than a protracted plunge—so was this wading through wet bushes beneath the pitiless pelting rain. I am sure that it abstracted a greater amount of vital heat and strength from us than wading the same length of time in cold water would have done. At least I never remember to have been more utterly exhausted than when we reached the bridge, and found, to our great joy, the wagon in waiting.

Fortunately, our host had been prudent enough to bring blankets with him, and wrapping our shivering bodies in these, we hurried off on our return. It was no use going to our shantee for comfort—the fire was out, and the rain had set in for a week to come, and it was a poor affair at best. Though it was a break-neck road, I urged him with chattering teeth, to drive faster; but the immovable Piscator quietly suggested that I should "take it easy!" I stared at the man, for I was excessively nervous and irritable, politely wishing him in a warmer place with his philosophy. He only laughed, and as that made me still more angry, I was soon nearly warmed up again.

Strange as the remedy may seem to those who are not familiar with the miracles of bathing, I took forthwith a bath of very cold water on reaching home. This warmed me instantly and thoroughly, and then the flesh brush and dry clothes completed the magical process of immediate transfer from the arctic to the tropics, which my sensations underwent, without the aid of fire or sun.

I never felt more delightfully than I did when I sat down to a fine dinner that evening in the old Tavern, and very much of this pleasurable feeling of entire comfort I attributed to the prompt use of the cold bath. I have mentioned Piscator's hydrophobia, so far as the external application of cold water was concerned, and the fact, that when we met at table, he appeared, in spite of his philosophy, far from refreshed or cheerful, I could not help attributing it to his neglect of this precaution. Poor Piscator, with all his puisance in 'flies,' his appetite for that delicious trout dinner failed him.

CHAPTER XXIV.

ANECDOTES OF MOOSE AND DEER HUNTING AMONG THE NORTHERN LAKES.

I HAVE already furnished a description of two modes of hunting deer, practised in the lake country; one by driving them into the lake, the other, by candle light on the marsh. These are methods almost peculiar to this Ariondack region, while there are several more which they practice there, in common with many other parts, such as driving on the "run-ways"—still-hunting, and hunting on the "crust" with snow-shoes.

Deer are so surprisingly abundant, that it is worth while

to know something of the how, the wherefore and the when of all these methods—for nothing is more certain than that you can get this game, and an abundance of it, if you only go at the right time, and seek it in the right way.

The two favorite methods of taking deer are running them into the lake, and hunting them on the crust—the first for summer and fall, the other for winter, of course.

The proper time for the first method is about the beginning of September—when the down is off their horns, and they are getting into the "blue coat." That is—the season may be said to be then commenced, for, of course, the deer are improving every day. In three weeks more they will be "seal fat," and will take to the water almost as soon as you start them. This sport continues until the lakes freeze over, when hunting on the crust takes its place.

Driving on the run-ways is not much practiced here, for the run-ways are so numerous that it requires a large company to man them all, which must be done in most instances to insure sport, since it is next to impossible to tell through which of them all the deer will pass a second time.

But as I could at any time start a deer within half a mile of where I then quartered, at a rude farm house near a small lake, and that within the hour, too, by the help of the old hound, Ring, it is not to be wondered at that I have several times succeeded, with all the uncertainty, in getting a deer on the run-way. None but a native, with his fly-proof skin, can ever do much at "still hunting" here, so long as the warm weather lasts,—for as the whole success of this hunt depends upon your preserving the most perfect and statue-like stillness, it requires a test of heroism which I could never bring myself up to meet. It is easy enough to find where the deer are, and even to catch a glimpse of them or hear them as they run off, but your hands must be going so incessantly, for the protection of your excoriated face and neck, that the wary and keen-sighted creatures are almost sure to see you first, and then you only get whistled at by them for your pains!

So that, after trying every other mode of summer and fall hunting, you are compelled to fall back upon the lakes at last. Round Lake and Pleasant used to be famous for this hunt, but they have fallen greatly into disrepute now; though it is still very easy any warm morning to drive a deer into this end of Lake Pleasant, as I have found by repeated experiments.

However, there are other lakes at hand where the sport is much more exciting and sure. Whittaker Lake is now more resorted to, and that, too, with more surprising success, than any other nearer than Louis Lake. It always has been, and must continue, so long as there are any deer in the country, to be the favorite place of refuge for them, on account of its peculiar conformation. Its two islands, and the many narrow coves for which it is peculiar, offer many facilities for ready escape, by losing the dogs. In this hunt there should generally be at least two boats on the lake. This is particularly necessary at Whittaker, where there were formerly two boats. To give some idea of the method of conducting this hunt, practiced by the natives here, each of whom is a good oarsman of course, I will give an outline of what three men accomplished in a single day's hunt.

Three is the proper number to act without mutual embarrassment, two to man the boats and one to "put out" the dogs. This party had two dogs, one of which was remarkably sagacious and well trained. They shanteed on the shore the over night, and the dogs were put out by sunrise in the morning.

The two boatmen, or rather one in a boat and the other in a small canoe, took position; the boat hid in the grass of the marsh at one end, and the canoe under the alders at the point of one of the islands. In a very short time a large buck came splashing through the marsh in a terrible panic, and nearly ran over the man in the boat, who shot him before he reached the deep water. The dogs were then put out again, and before ten o'clock they brought another deer down to the water—but this fellow skulked, swam across a narrow cove, and made off again. He did not return to this lake, which is very unusual, but made off to another, Elm Lake, three miles distant. The dogs were not reclaimed until noon. After feeding and a short rest, they were put out for a third race, and in a little while drove in a third deer, which struck out for the widest part of the lake.

Both hunters started in pursuit; the oarsman cut it off from land, and the boatsman, who was furnished with a long, forked stick, across the prongs of which a slip-noose of rope was tied, now came up by the side of the swimming deer, and threw the rope over its head. It plunged very violently, but in spite of its struggles he pushed its head under water with the assistance of the fork, and soon drowned it. This was a fine doe.

The dogs were again put out, and after a long race brought in a yearling spike buck. It came to the water twice, but as it had the wind of the two hunters, both times it turned and went out. It came at last on the opposite side, and struck right out for the open water. The canoe man did not succeed in cutting it off this time, and it reached one of the islands. The boatman shot at it as it was going out, and missed.

They then took a position on each side to prevent its escape, while "Old Sound," who had reached the shore, and comprehended in a moment how matters were, swam to the island and soon routed the little buck, which now attempted to reach the second island. The man in the canoe cut it off this time, and darting up alongside of it as it swam, seized it by its short horns, and drawing its head back, cut its throat.

But the boatman in the meantime had his hands full as

well. He had not time to load his gun or see what became of the young buck, for the other dog had brought down an enormous old buck, which took water at the same time near him. He lay still and let it swim out some distance, and then gave chase. He was soon up with him in wide water, and attempted to throw the noose over its horns. The buck showed fight, and striking up, suddenly knocked the stick from his grasp. Then, with stiffened bristles, and a hoarse low of wrath, it raised itself in the water, and planted its fore-feet on the side of the boat.

The man was too old a hunter to be much alarmed, though the deer seemed determined to turn the boat over or get in. The gun was empty, as we have said, but these men always throw a stout club of heavy green wood into the bottom of the boat to provide against contingencies such as these; indeed, they frequently take nothing else with them, as this is usually sufficient to kill any deer. A rapping blow across the head with this club caused the buck to drop back into the water, with his courage considerably cooled.

However, it soon renewed the fight, and as it caught most of the blows aimed at its head upon its immense horns, the man found he had both a tough and a dangerous job before him. The deer, in the meantime, was making gradually for the shore, and the hunter saw that it would effect its escape at last, if he continued to fight—so he directed all his efforts to turning it off from shore, shouting at the same time to his comrade for help. He was nearly worn out with fatigue, and had received several severe blows from the horns of the deer, when his friend came to his assistance and shot it through the head.

It was now nearly dark, and with four deer as the result of one day's sport, they returned perfectly satisfied, as well as worn out, to their shantee for the night. This day's work, though an unusually successful one, will stand in its modes and incidents, for a pretty fair epitome of the sport of "driving deer into the lake!" The Piseco Club boast of having noosed a buck and taken him a prisoner to shore, and tied him up to a tree. But this is a feat very easy of accomplishment, so far as noosing the deer is concerned; though, I suppose, no one else would fancy the troublesome and useless job of getting the animal out of the water alive.

The boatman often takes the deer by the tail, and makes it draw the boat; and I know of instances where the perilous feat of seizing a buck by the horns, and holding its head under water until drowned, has been performed. But such feats as this last are as rare as they are unwise. The most amusing instance I have heard, though, of these attempts to capture a grown animal, is furnished in that which was made by a party of sagacious hunters in this neighborhood, a winter ago, to take an old bull moose alive with ropes. As this leaves the feat of the Piseco Club far in the shade, I am tempted to give it.

Some lucky hunter had lately succeeded in capturing a couple of moose alive, and had sold them to a menagerie company for a round sum. This set all the hunters in a furor to capture live moose. The yard of a famous large bull having been discovered by a half-breed Indian hunter, he was accompanied by several of the hunters about Lake Pleasant, on a grand turn-out to make the attempt upon this fellow. The snow was very deep, and the moose was soon brought to a stand by the men on their snow-shoes. When they came up, they found he had backed himself into a strong position, with the roots of a torn-up tree in his rear, on one side, and a great shelving rock on the other. He was an enormous fellow, and they proceeded to make their demonstrations with most respectful caution.

One of the party ascended the trunk of the inclining tree from his rear, and climbing thence on to the shelving rock above, from, as he supposed, a very safe elevation, succeeded in throwing a rope-noose over one of its spreading antlers.

Another adventurer, more daring than the first, took up a position on the trunk of a fallen tree, almost touching the flanks of the animal with his feet, and reaching over dropped a second rope upon its horns, and was proceeding triumphantly to give it a turn around the trunk, thinking they had it all safe now. The creature shook its head, and making a sudden plunge forward, jerked the men headforemost from both rocky shelf and log, snapping their nooses. They fell against the hinder parts of the moose; but as those in front, seeing their danger, made a great clamor at the moment, the animal did not notice them; though, as it retreated back to its strong position, it trampled upon their prostrate forms with its hind feet. The fellows yelled to them to shoot, but as they had irritated the moose in front, it made a dash at them again, and they crawled out considerably bruised. Not discouraged by any means, as yet, another of the party succeeded in getting hold of the end of the broken rope, and this was immediately secured to a limb of the fallen tree once more.

They now thought they were certain to triumph, as they roped its horns more securely than before, and proceeded to throw slip-nooses among its feet, in the hope that it might step into them, and that they would then be able to throw it. It was very wary of the ropes. They thus caught one foot only, after worrying the whole day with the creature, and getting several of the party even more severely hurt. But when the hunter who had this rope, and who was standing directly in front of the infuriated animal, attempted to jerk the foot from under it, it made one tremendous surge at him, snapped the rope about its horns, and tossed him into the air some ten feet on its broad, snow-shoveling antlers—while the second hero of the ropes on the log had his legs jerked from under him, and fell as the first had fallen. There was a frightened scattering of the whole party this time in earnest, while the moose, with bristling sulkiness, retreated again to its old position. The bruised and crippled hunter who had been thus summarily tossed, seized his gun, limped up close to the moose, and shot it dead in his rage, just as if he had any right to have expected any other treatment for his folly.

This party was thoroughly satisfied with their single experiment, and have very safely promised their anxious mothers and sweethearts, never to make another such.

But crust hunting is by far the most destructive method of pursuing the deer known in this region. The deer form "yards" on the bleak northern sides of the mountains, and these are sometimes five or six miles in extent, and containing a great number of deer. They have deep roads or paths leading in every direction, through the snow, and will never leave these unless forced by the dog to do so. The deer seldom runs far, but stops to fight until the hunter comes up and kills it with his rifle, and sometimes with a club or axe.

There is a well authenticated instance in illustration, that I will relate. My guide has been a famous hunter in his day. When he was about sixteen his father lived upon a high hill, in sight of my shantee. In a valley half a mile from the hut, he had a small sugar camp. One bright morning, early in March, when a slight snow had fallen over night, upon the old crust, which was thin and melted through in places, Clark, who was a stout youth, started to the sugar camp to clean and set the troughs, as it promised to be a fine day for the sap to run. He said he would be back in time for breakfast, and followed by a noble hound, he was soon out of sight.

The family waited and waited in vain for his return, until noon, when his father, overcome by uneasiness, started in pursuit of the boy—for knowing that he had no kind of weapon, not even a pocket-knife, with him, he could not but fear that some accident had happened. He met him returning, panting up the hill.

"Why, Clark! what in the name of wonder has been keeping you all the morning?"

"I got myself into business, and had it to attend to; I've been killing deer!"

"Killing deer? What, did you gouge their eyes out? you'r got nothing about you to kill deer with."

"But I found a spruce knot that answered!"

The boy then went on to relate how he had found the tracks of four deer that had come into the sugar camp. The dog pursued them. It should be explained that the spring thaw had commenced, and the snow was nearly melted down, except under the shade of the deep woods, where it was as deep as ever, and the crust so thin that the deer went through easily. So soon as they came to the deep snow the dog stopped one. The boy followed along, and where the snow had thawed he found an old spruce log of great size, which had fallen into decay and left the knots of the limbs, which run back clear into the heart, round as ever and heavy almost as iron. Clark snatched up one of these, and when he came in sight the dog immediately seized the deer and dragged it down on the snow. Clark came up with his knot-club and knocked it on the head. They then followed on again, and in a short time came up with another, which was served in the same way, and a third also.

The fourth got to the Cungamunck river, and plunged into a small hole through the ice. The dog would follow on the ice as it swam round and round, and watching an opportunity, seize the deer by the nose, and pulling back with all his might, endeavor to drag it out. The deer would place its fore feet against the ice and resist this proceeding, until Clark came up at last, and for fear his dog might be dragged in and get under the icė, he ended the pulling match by knocking the deer on the head.

This was a pretty fair morning's work for a youth without arms of any kind, but those nature had given him. This same dog, "Old Sound," met with a great many adventures in his day. One of these is worth relating. His master, with two other men, were out deer hunting in snow shoes, and on the side of Dug Mountain the dog started three deer. They followed on, and soon killed two of them; the other, a fine young three-year old buck, showed himself to be, as the old man said, "the cunningest deer I ever see'd!" There is a tremendous ledge on the side of this mountain, which gives it its name, for it is bare of earth and almost perpendicular, and looks as if it had been "dug" down the face.

The deer was in full view, and commenced climbing up along the edge of this ledge to escape from the dog, who, when he came up, in vain essayed the same feat. After falling back several times, in the effort to follow the deer, the sagacious creature gave it up, and followed along the foot of the ledge to the other side. The deer looked as if he must fall from its airy perch every instant, and they expected to see it dashed to pieces; but it descended in safety, to be met by the dog on the other side. There the chase was renewed until the old man knew, by the manner of his bark, that the dog had brought it to bay. The three hunters now endeavored to outstrip each other in getting to the deer; but the others, not being accustomed to snow shoes, got theirs entangled, in their hurry, and fell. The old man came up in sight of the deer alone.

He had followed the tracks in the snow, and to his great surprise had not heard the dog bark for some time. There stood the deer in the snow, bolt upright, with its feet gathered up under it, and with bristles raised as if for a spring, but it remained perfectly still, eyeing the approaching hunter.

"There's the deer," he said to himself, "but where's my dog? I can't see him any where!" But the first thing to be done was to shoot the deer—which he did. The animal fell over in the snow, and to his great astonishment, the dog bounded up from beneath its feet, shaking the snow from his hair.

Old Sound looked rather humiliated, and seating himself a little distance off, gazed upon his dying conqueror in demure silence. "The cunningest deer" having been baffled in an extraordinary effort to get rid of its noisy foe, had adopted the curious expedient of first beating him down in the snow with its fore-paws, and then deliberately standing on his prostrate body. Deer do some ugly things of this kind occasionally. One of the neighboring hunters, who was passing through the woods on the crust, without any weapon but his pocket-knife, came upon three deer, one of which was an immense buck.

The buck eyed the man as he came up, until he was within a few yards of him, and then made right at him with his hair turned the wrong way. He knocked the man down in the snow, and commenced very deliberately stamping him to death. He kept it up until the man lay still, and then he would step off a little distance and turn to look at his victim. If the man moved, he would plunge upon him again and give him another pounding, until he was content to lie still. This game had been repeated several times; and the man, whose strength was fast going, felt that he would soon be killed if he could not get out of this scrape in some way—for even if he laid still the deer showed no disposition to leave him, and he must freeze to death soon in his cold bed. He now for the first time bethought him of his knife, and at the expense of another pounding, got his hand into the pocket.

The deer stood off a little distance watching him; but when he had secured the knife, and managed to work it open with one hand, he made a movement by kicking up the snow with his feet. The buck was on him in an instant, as usual, and the man, urged now to despair, rose upon his elbow, and making three or four savage cuts upwards with his knife, succeeded in reaching the vitals of the buck who staggered off a few paces and fell dead upon the snow with all its entrails let out. The man got home with great difficulty and was laid up for some time after with his hurts. This was a lesson he never forgot, and always took a gun with him afterwards when he went into the woods on a crust.

Piscator and I having determined on a trip to the famous Whittaker Lake, we set off on a fine morning before sunrise, and on foot, accompanied by two guides and as many dogs, well trained to this lake hunting. The morning proved to be especially warm, and one of the guides most expressively characterized it, as we passed up the southern side of a long hill—

"I swow! but it's a yaller day!" was gasped out by the fellow.

I laughed heartily, and thought that might "pass." The little oxen performed miracles in dragging the sled with our boat on it through the inconceivably rugged and tangled woods, to the lake. The two guides went ahead to open the way. We reached the margin between twelve and one. When I reached the gap of the forest, which gave us an outlook over the lake—for I was some little distance ahead—imagine my astonishment at seeing four or five deer leisurely feeding on the edge of the water, on the opposite shore. My first hasty impulse was to fire my rifle at them, they seemed so close; but then I remembered, and was at the same time reminded by the guide who followed, that the lake was nearly half a mile wide. The deer had not observed or heard us, since we had approached as quietly as possible.

I stood and watched for some time the graceful and unconscious creatures leisurely cropping the lily leaves and buds that lay upon the surface of the calm lake. What a shame it seemed that we had thus come to disturb and rouse, with a bloody reveille, this happy quiet. They seemed, in their hill-girt home, to be utterly ignorant of man's harshness in the world, and the old buck tossed his antlered head, as proudly as if he were sole monarch of these wilds. They were in view, feeding and sporting along the water of the edge for a full half hour.

It would have been a lesson for those "budge doctors of the stoic fur," of whom my friend Piscator is an emulous disciple, to have witnessed the elate and eager longing of the smile which radiated from his face while he gazed upon this tranquil scene. His double-barrel quivered in his grasp with the excitement, and his round, red lips looked watery. With such a sight before us, you may rest assured there was no time lost in dispatching our "bite" of a dinner, preparatory for work. The boat was now quickly launched, and the moment it touched the water, loud and unearthly cries, deafening and sonorous, rose from every part of the lake. I looked around in astonishment, and the eyes of Piscator sought mine with something of a wild flaring in them, but the guides smiled.

"Them's the loons!" said George.

Two or three of them now swam out from the point of the nearest island, and curiously approached us. I saw at once that it was the loon, or northern diver; one of the most beautifully marked of all the water-fowl. They properly resented our intrusion upon their lovely and secluded breeding-places, of which they evidently had not been conscious until the splash of launching our boat upon their favorite element conveyed to them, through some mysterious medium of sympathy, the warning of our dangerous approaches. Their cry is strangely human, and yet inhuman; too, and there is a wild and mournful quaver in it, such as I have always observed to be peculiar to birds which frequent desolate and solitary places. There is a strange and harmonious fitness in this which never struck me so forcibly at any other time, as during our stay at this lonely place.

Louden, the "yaller-day" man, who was to put out the

dogs to drive the deer, was first taken across the lake with his two dogs, and landed. George, who was now beginning to develope new traits, which we afterwards found rather characteristic of the professional guide among the lakes, then brought back the boat for us. There were two islands in the lake, a mile and a half long, and we were to stand upon the larger one. At least, so Master George insisted. He, in the boat, alone, was to undertake to drive the accomodating deer that might swim into the lake, along up to us, to be shot. A delectable plan, truly! We were to stand, like two innocents, on the island, to enjoy the sport of seeing our guide chase and capture all the deer that came in. I instantly perceived that this was one of the knavish tricks of the guide, who, having in some such way laid the troublesome sportsman on the shelf, quietly monopolizes all the fun to himself. I now began to obtain some insight into this same Master George, in whom I fondly hoped I had found that paragon—an honest guide. I would not stand this impudent trick, of course, since I paid the fellow for ministering to *my* amusement, not his own. The pretence was, that the boat, with two in it, would be too much freighted for the swift rowing necessary for overtaking the deer. And good, easy Piscator, eager as he was to retrieve his lost ground, and immortalize himself in the world of his own self-content, by killing the first deer, would insist that George must be right, as it was his business to know better than we.

I insisted that he did not know better, and that it was sheer knavery in him, and so indignantly urged it, that Piscator was persuaded at last; and as I surrendered the first chance to him —he was to take his seat first in the boat I now left them, and took my stand on the other end of the island. Soon all was perfect silence again, broken only at intervals by the clarion-like whoop of the troubled loons I watched two of them, which, as I lay upon the moss, could see me only indistinctly, and urged by their strong curiosity, swam back and forth, each time coming slowly nearer me, until they were so close that I could see the shine of their dark eyes, and the white rings about their necks.

Soon the dogs open musically on, far up on the deep-wooded side of Dug Mountain. It is a short and spirited race, and while I lie abstractedly tracing the reverberations of their voices among the mountains—a splash! My heart leaps. There! The deer has taken water at the southern end of the lake. See, he swims already! It's a noble fellow! Ha! he is not coming for the open water! We shan't get him! He swims across that narrow cove—now he's out! See him shake the drops from his tawny hair, as he walks deliberately into the woods again!

There come the dogs! Old Turk, with his face half white and black, stands upon the shore an instant, snuffing over the water. In he plunges! What a bold and rapid swimmer! He swims out into the lake towards us. The trick has told—he has lost the deer. George puts out in the boat to meet him. He takes him in and rows towards where the buck went out. He has nearly reached the shore—the dog stands with his fore paws on the edge of the boat, snuffing the air. There! he plunges—he has caught the scent again, and away he goes, with eager yells, on the track.

He is off, and Master George does not return to us with the boat. The rascal is out of our reach, and is determined now, in spite of me, to carry out his purpose. Knowing that he can invent some excuse which will satisfy Piscator, I swallow my anger; for this is his chance, and if he chooses to lose it, well and good. In half an hour the deer is back, takes the water on the other side of the lake, and makes for the second island. Master George is off, and pulling with his best might and skill to cut the deer off from the shore. He has started too soon; the deer has seen him, and turns. They both disappear behind the point of the island.

The audacious rascal! One of us should have been in that

boat. The deer will be lost, for the gun he has is worthless. In a moment we hear the gun, and then all is silent for nearly half an hour. He has probably shot the deer. A pretty business this! We paying this impudent fellow to take the deer from under our very noses. I was greatly enraged, and it was well he did not make his appearance soon. But the other dog has started now. A noisy and exciting chase to and fro along the shore woods. After awhile, who should make his appearance but Master George again, shouting at the top of his voice, as he turned a point of the island, with some small object swimming in the water before him—

"Here's your deer! Here's your deer!"

"The devil it is!" I exclaimed, for I had now rejoined Piscator. "That's no deer. It looks more like a rabbit or musk-rat."

"Come along down shore and shoot it; its a fawn," shouted our redoubtable boatman.

"Why, you rascal, I don't want to hurt that little creature! Take it alive!" I shouted.

The fellow felt he had his peace to make, and accordingly did his best to take the fawn alive. In his efforts to accomplish this, a most ludicrous and amusing scene occurred. The dog Turk, who had lost the trail of his deer at the water, then joined in the chase after the fawn, and now came swimming boldly out after it. George had seized the active little creature by the hind feet, and was endeavoring to drag it into the boat. He had nearly succeeded, when Turk leaped half way out of the water and upon the back of the bleating fawn. George must release his hold to fight off the dog, and now the struggle commenced. The fierce and headstrong Turk, as in duty bound, is determined to kill the game, and George that he shall not. While these two are struggling, the poor little fawn would make some headway, then George would be compelled to take up his oars. The boat would shoot alongside again, and he would seize it by the ears or tail to have the same scene over again, for Turk was on hand to drag it back into the water, when he had lifted it partly out. George became furious at last, and his half-frantic, half-despairing screams of—

"You Turk! Get away, Turk! Begone Turk!" mingled with the bleating of the fawn and the angry barking of the dog, and the splash and sputtering of the watery strife, produced a combination of sounds and scene so irresistibly comic, that I sunk to the very earth with peal upon peal of unrestrainable and almost hysterical laughter; for I enjoyed so immensely the agony of George, that I had no time to think of that of the poor little fawn.

At last this ludicrous contest came to a crisis. The fawn had all this time been making for the shore, and now it had struck shallow water, and was about to make its escape, when George seized his gun and shot it through the head. I had rather the blood of this little spotted thing had been on his conscience than mine, and to do him justice, he seemed very sorry for it afterwards. It turned out that the fellow had missed the deer after all, and let it escape. I now peremptorily put a stop to that favorite joke of his—going alone—and as Piscator had lost his chance, went into the boat myself. I was still angry, but I had not the heart to abuse him after affording me so hearty a laugh.

It was late, but the dogs made another start, and after a short race, a fine young buck entered the water, and instead of swimming, attempted, as the others had, to skulk along the shore. We knew he was lying down, for we should have seen his whole body, had he been standing up in the shallow marsh. We watched in silence to see what the next maneuvre would be when the dog came up, when suddenly a gun exploded from the woods on shore, the deer rose, and with a long bound, made for the shore. It was out of our rifle range, but I could not resist the inclination, and sent a ball after him as he went into the bush. It was the presuming guide who put out the dogs. He did not see us as we lay concealed in the grass, and had fired at the deer. The dogs came up, we put them on the track, and they went off splendidly.

It was not more than a minute, and we all three stood in open view upon a log, upon which we had run the boat, when the deer came in again at precisely the same place. We stood still as if suddenly congealed—I with my rod half-driven home; it came cautiously into the water at first, but did not seem to have noticed us, as is always the case if you are perfectly motionless. At last it struck across the lake; we waited until it was too far from shore to turn back.—"Now!" I sprang into the boat, which George pushed off at the same moment, and we darted through the water. We soon closed upon the deer, which commenced bleating as we approached, and it saw that capture was sure—but yonder came the dogs swimming out to us. We must make quick work of it.

"Shoot!"

I fired a ball into its head, and as it was going down, George seized it by its hind legs, and drew it into the boat. The weather now becoming unfavorable for the continuation of our sport, we concluded to break up our shantee the next day, and dismissing our worthless guide, we pushed on some six miles further, through the mountains to the north, to Louis Lake, where we purposed spending a week in hunting and fishing at the shantee of "Old Sturge." His two boys, who were fifteen and sixteen years old, officiating as our guides.

This is the most picturesque and loveliest of all the lakes; and here we had abundant sport. The boys were extraordinary specimens of the Wild Turkey breed of natural-born hunters, and proved to be admirable guides. These youths had been in the habit of walking since their early childhood the most incredible distances, in these wild mountains, and entirely alone. They were equally at home every where, as much so as the wild deer they hunted.

Old Sturge himself is a 'case' for any country. He will walk forty miles a day with as little trouble as a dandy would feel it to be promenading from the Astor to the Broadway hotel; and 'Sturge' will have the advantage in that, though he only carries a pack on his shoulders of sixty or eighty pounds dead weight, the dandy is burdened with an unappreciable quantity of live brass. He goes in and out to his favorite Lake twice a day, something as if it were "only cross the way." He is a helter-skelter, harum-scarum, good-natured, headlong fellow, who is forever blundering into the most ludicrous scrapes with wild animals, and yet has manhood enough to come out right end up usually.

He always has a number of traps set near the Lake. He was coming in one morning with one or two old hunters, and passing by a trap on the way, found a large bear caught by the hind-leg. Without waiting to shoot the creature, or indeed thinking at all of it, he rushed upon it with his knife to cut its throat. Bruin of course met him with the hug fraternal, and then commenced between them a desperate struggle. His comrades were too much paralyzed with laughter to come to his help, and before he succeeded in despatching the bear with his knife, his clothing had all been stripped off, and himself badly torn and bruised.

Nobody on the face of the earth but 'Old Sturge,' would ever have dreamed of doing such a stupidly reckless thing; but this is only one out of many such madcap capers. However, he is pioneering a settlement to Louis Lake most effectively, by taking there a large family of children—most of them boys, and as hardy as young partridges. He intends to keep a corner of the shantee for sportsmen, who prefer Louis Lake, and the tough, wiry old fellow will hold himself in readiness to carry them astride his shoulders—if they desire it—thirty miles further into the wilderness.

There is an amusing story told of Old Sturge's first interview with a moose, which is worth giving before we dismiss him. It was soon after he came to the country from 'down east,' and when he was somewhat green upon the subject of 'wild varmints' in general.

Some one had shown him how to set his traps at Louis Lake, and one morning when he went to visit them, rifle in hand, he saw a huge black beast lying in the place of one of his traps. He said he thought it was the Old Harry himself, with a bundle of pitchforks, and iron-wooden shovels on his head—but though mortally frightened, and very much disposed to run back home, he concluded finally, that to save his manhood he must take a shot at it any how. It had not seen him, and he was quite close, so he blazed away. Whether he shut his eyes or not, he does not know, but the creature paid no attention to him, and did not even turn its head.

Finding himself alive after this desperate venture, he took courage, hid behind a tree, and loaded again. He fired again with the same result. He began now to think that it surely bore a charmed life, and said that when he looked along the barrel at it, it grew as large as a meeting house, and that when in spite of his fear he aimed right at the middle of this great pile, the ball would go clear through, and it would close up again. He says he got madder and madder, and worse and worse scared every time he shot, until he supposed he had been at it an hour or two, when, as his last load was fired, the great black beast got up and gave one tremendous bound. He heard his steel trap fall clashing back against the stones, and it was gone.

After he had sufficiently recovered from his trepidation, he went up to the trap, and found there, between its saw-like teeth, the veritable 'split hoof,' for which the old gentleman he took it for is so famous! He swears to this day that there was a strong smell of sulphur in the woods, which remained for weeks afterwards.

He came into the settlement in a great fright with the hoof, but the old hunters looked wise and solemn, shaking their heads. Sturge, poor fellow, could get no consolation out of them. When winter came, he went with a party to hunt moose, and when in the yard, they came upon a huge bull moose, Sturge was for making tracks as fast as his snow shoes would let him, yelling—

"That's him! there he is again!"—but the hunters stopped him with roars of laughter, and let him shoot at the bull until he brought it down, when he satisfied himself that it had not the 'forked tail,' and therefore was not the genuine Old Harry! But this was when Sturge was young and verdant, and his mistake after all was no more remarkable than many others that have been made at the susceptible age. He has killed many moose since, but always has to fire a great many shots at them—for he says that somehow, since that time, they "*will* look so big he can't see his sights!"

CHAPTER XXV.

HUNTING ELEPHANTS IN SOUTH AFRICA.

BUT the "Hunter-Naturalist" is not confined to the "wild scenes" of our young continent. There yet remain upon the oldest continent of the Old World "Realms of Ancient Solitude" as vast, as savage, as difficult of penetration; where action as wild, and passions as uncontrolled as those we have been witnessing and depicting, find "verge and room enough."

The same audacious spirit of inquiry and passionate abandon of taste, which has characterized the half-scientific, half-Nomadic explorer here, has carried, in some stage of development, the "Hunter-Naturalist" in whatever direction the empire-measuring eye of Britain has been turned, forward as the "surveyor," in advance of *chain and staff*, to explore, of his own free will, and report of his own free fancy, concerning the prospective riches of these remote lands.

Thus a new class of adventurers has grown up under the far-seeing policy, first of the Honorable East India Company, and afterwards, perforce of example, under the general military administration of British colonial affairs, which aspires at once to combine all characteristics of the Boones and Audubons of our history. The stories of tiger hunting on elephants by officers of the British army, which have for so long constituted the staple of savage romance in that direction, as to render their details now superlatively stale, have yet had their effect in developing this new British type, though it be but a secondary one; yet the lawless magnificence of action and association which had rendered the character of Pioneer and Hunter-Naturalist nearly synonomous in renown here, had still more to do with this result in affording the most extraordinary and illustrious instances of individual heroism the world ever saw. Men became emulous of this personal glory, with which the association of single names with the conquest of empires, first with mere handfulls of followers, as with Cortez and Pizarro, and afterwards through all unexpected disparities of numbers, down to the solitary man, as with Boone, had been made so familiar since the discovery of the New World. If there were no new worlds to discover, there were at least new regions to explore; if there were no more Perus or Mexicos to conquer, there were great herds of peaceful elephants browsing the unpenetrated forests of the vast interior of Africa, in the hunt of which energies as restless and irrepressible could be expended. Thus the pacific and curious traveller, such as Bruce, or "more merchant-like," as Marco Paulo and Sir John Mandeville, has given place to such Nimrods on parole as Major W. Cornwallis Harris, R. Gorden Cummings, etc., of the British army in South Africa, who have lately made themselves illustrious as having gone forth—if not literally

"——— With a pine
For a spear, 'gainst the mammoth,"

at least practically, with their short rifles against

"——— foaming behemoth."

The adventures of these men open a new and very curious, as well as striking chapter of "Wild Scenes and Wild Hunters" in the old world. Each tells his own story with the characteristic extravagance of the adventurer; but this consists more in expression than fact. They are both inspired with the genuine spirit of the "Hunter-Naturalist," and in their eager emulation of securing "trophies" of specimens, have done much to illustrate the Natural History of an immense and wholly unknown country. Of the two, Harris has ten years the precedence in the field; and to say the least, there is a somewhat suspicious resemblance between many of the incidents in Cummings' book and his on the "Sports of South Africa." This coincidence, however natural, from the fact that much the same ground has been gone over by both, is yet strong enough to show that Cummings has taken Harris for his master and model. As a proper introduction to these "Wild Scenes," I shall give from Cummings a general sketch of the habits of the elephant.

Before proceeding further with my narrative, it may here be interesting to make a few remarks on the African elephant and his habits. The elephant is widely diffused through the vast forests, and is met with in herds of various numbers. The male is very much larger than the female, consequently much more difficult to kill. He is provided with two enormous tusks. These are long, tapering, and beautifully arched; their length averages from six to eight feet, and they weigh from sixty to a hundred pounds each. In the vicinity of the equator the elephants attain to a greater size than to the southward; and I am in the possession of a pair of tusks of the African bull elephant, the larger of which measures ten feet nine inches in length, and weighs one hundred and seventy-three pounds. The females, unlike Asiatic elephants in this respect, are likewise provided with tusks. The price which the largest ivory fetches in the English market is from £28 to £32 per hundred and twelve pounds. Old bull elephants are found singly or in pairs, or consorting together in small herds, varying from six to twenty individuals. The younger bulls remain for many years in the company of their mothers, and these are met together in large herds of from twenty to a hundred individuals. The food of the elephant consists of the branches, leaves and roots of trees, and also of a variety of bulbs, of the situation of which he is advised by his exquisite sense of smell. To obtain these he turns up the ground with his tusks, and whole acres may be seen thus plowed up. Elephants consume an immense quantity of food, and pass the greater part of the day and night in feeding. Like the whale in the ocean, the elephant on land is acquainted with, and roams over, wide and extensive tracts. He is extemely particular in always frequenting the freshest and most verdant districts of the forest; and when one district is parched and barren, he will forsake it for years, and wander to great distances in quest of better pasture.

The elephant entertains an extraordinary horror of man, and a child can put a hundred of them to flight by passing at a quarter of a mile to windward; and when thus disturbed, they go a long way before they halt. It is surprising how soon these sagacious animals are aware of the presence of a hunter in their domains. When one troop has been attacked, all the other elephants frequenting the district are aware of the fact within two or three days, when they all forsake it, and migrate to distant parts, leaving the hunter no alternative but to inspan his wagons and remove to fresh ground. This constitutes one of the greatest difficulties which a skillful elephant-hunter encounters. Even in the most remote parts, which may be reckoned the head-quarters of the elephant, it is only occasionally, and with inconceivable toil and hardship, that the eye of the hunter is cheered by the sight of one. Owing to habits peculiar to himself, the elephant is more inaccessible, and much more rarely seen, than any other game quadruped, excepting certain rare antelopes. They choose for their resort the most lonely and secluded depths of the forest, generally at a very great distance from the rivers and fountains at which they drink. In dry and warm weather they visit these waters nightly, but in cool and cloudy weather they drink only once every third or fourth day. About sundown the elephant leaves his distant mid-day haunt, and commences his march toward the fountain, which is probably from twelve to twenty miles distant. This he generally reaches between the hours of nine and midnight, when, having slaked his thirst and cooled his body by spouting large volumes of water over his back with his trunk, he resumes the path to his forest solitudes. Having reached a secluded spot, I have remarked that full-grown bulls lie down on their broadsides, about the hour of midnight, and sleep for a few hours. The spot which they usually select is an ant-hill, and they lie around it with their backs resting against it; these hills formed by the white ants, are from thirty to forty feet in diameter at their base. The mark of the under tusk is always deeply imprinted in the ground, proving that they lie upon their sides. I never remarked that females had thus lain down, and it is only in the more secluded districts that the bulls adopt this practice; for I observed that, in districts where the elephants were liable to frequent disturbance, they took repose standing on their legs beneath some shady tree. Having slept, they then proceed to feed extensively. Spreading out from one another, and proceeding in a zigzag course, they smash and destroy all the finest trees in the forest which happen to lie in their course. The number of goodly trees which a herd of bull elephants will thus destroy is utterly incredible. They are extremely capricious, and on coming to a group of five or six trees, they break down not unfrequently the whole of them, when, having perhaps tasted one or two small branches, they pass on and continue their wanton work of destruction. I have repeatedly ridden through forests where the trees thus broken lay so thick across one another that it was almost impossible to ride through the district, and it is in situations such as these that attacking the elephant is attended with most danger. During the night they will feed in open plains and thinly-wooded districts, but as day dawns they retire to the densest covers within reach, which nine times in ten are composed of the impracticable wait-a-bit thorns, and here they remain drawn up in a compact herd during the heat of the day. In remote districts, however, and in cool weather, I have known herds to continue pasturing throughout the whole day.

The appearance of the wild elephant is inconceivably majestic and imposing. His gigantic height and colossal bulk, so greatly surpassing all other quadrupeds, combined with his sagacious disposition and peculiar habits, impart to him an interest in the eyes of the hunter which no other animal can call forth. The pace of the elephant, when undisturbed, is a bold, free, sweeping step; and from the peculiar spongy formation of his foot, his tread is extremely light and inaudible, and all his movements are attended with a peculiar gentleness and grace. This, however, only applies to the elephant when roaming undisturbed in his jungle; for, when roused by the hunter, he proves the most dangerous enemy, and far more difficult to conquer than any other beast of the chase.

Harris has given a most graphic description of the imposing scene of his first introduction to the South African Elephants. Here it is in his own picturesque style.

Early in the afternoon the Hottentots returned with the oxen, and we proceeded without loss of time to the eastward, following the course of the mountains through very high grass, and passing between two conical hills of singular appearance, which stood like sentinels on either hand; after crossing six inconsiderable streams, we with some difficulty gained the vicinity of a remarkable abrupt opening in the range, which through a telescope appeared to afford a practicable road to the northward. Both our wagons stuck fast in the Saut river, and were with difficulty extricated by the united efforts of the teams. The heat was intense, not a breath stirred; the heavy black clouds fast collecting bade us prepare for a deluge. We therefore formed the camp in an elevated and sheltered position, under the lee of a high stone enclosure, which only required the entrance to be closed with bushes to make a secure pound for the cattle. Scarcely were these arrangements completed, when a stream of liquid fire ran along the ground, and a deafening thunder-clap exploding close above us, was instantly followed by a torrent of rain which "came dancing down to the earth," not in drops, but in continuous streams, and with indescribable violence, during the greater part of the night; the thunder now receding and rumbling less and less distinctly, but more incessantly, among the distant mountains—now pealing in echoes over the distant hills, and now returning to burst with redoubled violence over our heads.

> ———————— "Far along,
> From peak to peak, the rattling crags among,
> Leapt the wild thunder, not from one lone cloud,
> But every mountain soon had found a tongue."

The horses and oxen were presently standing knee-deep in water; our followers remained sitting all night in the baggage wagon, which, being better covered, fortunately resisted the pitiless storm. Sleep, however, was out of the question, the earth actually threatening to give way under us, the lightning being so painfully vivid that we were glad to hide our heads under the pillow.

Those only who have witnessed the setting in of the south-west monsoon in India, are capable of understanding the awful tempest I have attempted to describe. About an hour before dawn its fury began to abate, and at sunrise it was perfectly fine, but the rivers were quite impassable. I proceeded with some of the Hottentots to reconnoitre the pass, but found that it was impassable for wagons, being nothing more than a narrow channel flanked by perpendicular crags, between which the Saut river rushes on its way to join the Singkling, making a number of abrupt windings through a most impracticable country, intersected by a succession of rocky declivities. From the highest peak we saw several herds of buffaloes, and whilst descending came upon the tracks of a huge elephant that had passed about an hour before. This being the largest foot-print we had seen, I had the curiosity to measure it, in order to ascertain the animal's height—twice the circumference of an elephant's foot being, it is notorious, the exact height at the shoulder. It yielded a product of about twelve feet, which, notwithstanding the traditions that have been handed down, I believe to be the maximum height attained by the African elephant.

We followed the trail across the Saut river, which had now considerably subsided, and finding that it proceeded eastward along the mountain chain, returned to our encampment for horses and ammunition.

Leaving the wagon to proceed to a spot agreed upon, we again took the field about ten o'clock, and pursued the track indefatigably for eight miles over a country presenting every variety of feature. At one time we crossed bare stony ridges, at another threaded the intricacies of shaggy but dilapidated forests; now struggling through high fields of waving grass, and again emerged into open downs. At length we arrived among extensive groups of grassy hillocks, covered with loose stones, interspersed with streams, and occasional patches of forest, in which the recent ravages of elephants were surprising. Here, to our inexpressible gratification, we descried a large herd of those long-sought animals, lazily browsing at the head of a distant valley, our attention having been first directed to it by the strong and not to be mistaken effluvia with which the wind was impregnated. Never having before seen the elephant in his native jungles, we gazed at the sight before us with intense and indescribable interest. Our feelings on the occasion even extended to our followers. As for Andries, he became so agitated that he could scarcely articulate. With open eyes and quivering lips he at length stuttered forth—

"*Dar stand de olifant!*"

Mohanycom and Lingap were immediately dispatched to drive the herd back into the valley, up which we rode slowly and without noise, against the wind; and arriving within one hundred and fifty yards unperceived, we made our horses fast, and took up a commanding position in an old stone kraal. The shouting of the savages, who now appeared on the height, rattling their shields, caused the animals to move unsuspiciously towards us, and even within ten yards of our ambush. The group consisted of nine, all females, with large tusks. We selected the finest, and with perfect deliberation, fired a volley of five balls into her. She stumbled, but recovering herself, uttered a shrill note of lamentation, when the whole party threw their trunks above their heads, and instantly clambered up the adjacent hill with incredible celerity, their huge fan-like ears flapping in the ratio of their speed. We instantly mounted our horses, the sharp loose stones not suiting the feet of the wounded lady, soon closed with her. Streaming with blood, and infuriated with rage, she turned upon us with uplifted trunk, and it was not until after repeated discharges, that a ball took effect in her brain, and threw her lifeless upon the earth, which resounded with the fall.

Turning our attention from the exciting scene we have described, we found that a second valley had opened before us, surrounded by bare strong hills, and traversed by a thinly wooded ravine. Here a grand and magnificent panorama was before us, which beggars all description. The whole face of the landscape was actually covered with wild elephants. There could not have been fewer than three hundred within the scope of our vision. Every height and green knoll was dotted over with groups of them, whilst the bottom of the glen exhibited a dense and sable living mass—their colossal forms being at one moment partially concealed by the trees, which they were disfiguring with great strength; and at others seen majestically emerging into the open glades, bearing in their trunks the branches of trees, with which they indolently protected themselves from the flies. The back-ground was filled by a limited peep of the blue mountainous range, which here assumed a remarkably precipitous character, and completed a picture at once soul-stirring and sublime!

Our approach being still against the wind, was unobserved, and created little alarm, until the herd that we had left behind suddenly showed itself, recklessly thundering down the hill to join the main body, and passing so close to us that we could not refrain from firing a broadside into one of them, which, however, bravely withstood it. We secured our horses on the summit of a stony ridge, and then stationing ourselves at an opportune place on a ledge overlooking the wooded defile, sent Andries to maneuvre, so that as many of the elephants as possible could pass before us in order of review, that we might ascertain by a close inspection whether there was not a male amongst them. Filing sluggishly along, they occasionally halted beneath an umbrageous tree, within fifteen yards of us, lazily fanning themselves with their ample ears, blowing away the flies with their trunks, and uttering the feeble and peculiar cry so peculiar to Indian elephants. They all proved to be ladies, and most of them mothers, followed by their little old-fashioned calves, each trudging close to the heels of her dam, and mimicking all her motions. Thus situated, we might have killed any number we pleased, their heads being frequently turned towards us in such a position, and so close, that a single ball in the brain would have sufficed for each; but whilst we were yet hesitating, a bullet suddenly whizzed past Richardson's ear, and put the whole herd to immediate flight. We had barely time to recede behind a tree, before a party of about twenty, with several little ones in their wake, were upon us, striding at their utmost speed, and trumpeting loudly with uplifted heads. I rested my rifle against the tree, and firing behind the shoulder of the leader, she dropped instantly. Another large detachment being close behind us at the same moment, we were compelled to retreat, dodging from tree to tree, stumbling amongst sharp stones, and ever coming upon fresh parties of the enemy. This scene of ludicrous confusion did not long continue, and soon approaching the prostrate lady, we put an end to her struggles by a shot in the forehead. Andries now came up in high good humor at his achievements, and in the most bravado manner, discharged his piece into the dead carcass, under the pretence that the animal was shamming. His object evidently was to confound the shots, for, thrusting his middle finger into the orifice made by my two-ounce ball, he with the most modest assurance declared himself the author of the deed, being pleased altogether to overlook the fact of the mortal shot having entered the elephant on the side opposite to that on which he was stationed, and that his own ball, whether designedly or not, had all but expended my worthy and esteemed fellow-traveller.

On our way to the camp, of the exact position of which we were uncertain, in consequence of the late inundation, we passed three other large herds of elephants. One of these standing directly in the route, we attacked it, and pursued the fugitive about a mile over loose stones. Much has been said of the attachment of elephants to their young, but neither on this, nor on any subsequent occasion, did we perceive them evince the smallest concern for their safety. On the contrary, they left them to shift for themselves, and Mohanycom and Lingap, who were behind us, assagaied one, the tail of which they brought in. We slew another old female as we ascended the brow of an eminence, and at the same moment perceived our wagons within a few hundred yards of the spot. The whole herd dashed through the camp, causing indescribable consternation amongst cattle and followers, but fortunately no accident occurred; and after the fatiguing day's work we had undergone, we were not sorry to find ourselves at home.

Watery clouds hung about the sun as he set heavily behind the mountains. Loud peals of crashing thunder rent the air, and ere it was yet dark, we had a repetition of yesterday's storm; the river roaring past us with frightful fury; troops of elephants, flying from the scene of slaughter, passed close to our wagons during the darkness, their wild voices echoing amongst the mountains, and sounding like trumpets above the tempest. It was impossible to keep the fires burning; and the oxen and sheep were alarmed to such a degree that they broke from the kraal, and sought safety in the wilderness. Tired as I was, the excitement I had undergone banished sleep from my eyes. I ruminated on the spirit-stirring events of the day, and burned with impatience to renew them. Heedless of the withering blast that howled without, I felt that my most sanguine expectations had been realized, and that we had already been amply repaid for the difficulties, privations and dangers that we had encountered in our toilsome journey towards this fairy-land of sport.

It was still raining heavily when the day gloomily dawned. The mountain torrents having overflowed their banks, the valley in which we were encamped had become a continuous pool of water, and those of our followers who had slung their hammocks beneath the wagons, were partially submerged. High-roads had been ploughed through the mire by the passage of elephants, and whole acres of grass, by which we had been surrounded the preceding evening, had been completely trampled down. Soon after sunrise it cleared up, and the cattle having been recovered, we armed a party with hatchets, and proceeded on foot to cut out the teeth of the slain elephants; but walking was exceedingly toilsome, and our feet sinking to the ankles in black mud, were extricated with inconceivable difficulty. Taking advantage of our situation, an irritated rhinoceros sallied from behind an old stone wall; and the damp causing three of the balls to miss fire, he was actually amongst us, when my ball fortunately pierced his eye, and he fell dead at our feet.

Not an elephant was to be seen on the ground that was yesterday teeming with them; but on reaching the glen, which had been the scene of our exploits during the early part of the action, a calf about three feet and a half high, walked forth from a bush, and saluted us with mournful piping notes. We had observed the unhappy little wretch hovering about its mother after she fell, and having probably been unable to overtake the herd, it had passed a dreary night in the wood. Entwining its little proboscis about our legs, the sagacious creature, after demonstrating its delight at our arrival by a thousand ungainly antics, accompanied the party to the body of its dam, which, swollen to an enormous size, was surrounded by an inquest of vultures. Seated in gaunt array, with their shoulders shrugged, these loathesome fowls were waiting its decomposition with forced resignation; the tough hide having defied all the efforts of their beaks, with which the eyes and softer parts had been vigorously assailed. The conduct of the quaint little calf now became quite affecting, and elicited the sympathy of every one. It ran round its mother's corpse with touching demonstrations of grief, piping sorrowfully, and vainly attempted to raise her with its tiny trunk. I confess that I had felt compunctions in committing the murder the day before, and now half resolved never to assist in another; for in addition to the moving behavior of the young elephant, I had been unable to divest myself of the idea that I was firing at my old favorite, Mowla-Bukhsh, from whose gallant back I had vanquished so many of my feline foes in Guzerat —an impression which, however ridiculous it must appear, detracted considerably from the satisfaction I experienced.

The operation of hewing out three pairs of tusks occupied several hours, their roots, embedded in massy sockets, spreading over the greater portion of the face. My Indian friends will marvel when they hear of tusks being extricated from the jaws of a female elephant—but with very few exceptions, all that we saw had these accessories, measuring from three to four feet in length. I have already stated my belief that the maximum height of the African male is twelve feet; that of the female averages eight and a half—the enormous magnitude of the ears, which not only cover the whole of the shoulder, but overlap each other on the neck, to the complete exclusion of the *mahout*, or driver, constituting another striking feature of difference between the two species. The forehead is remarkably large and prominent, and consists of two walls or tables, between which, a wide cellular space intervening, a ball, hardened with tin or quicksilver, readily penetrates to the brain, and proves instantaneously fatal.

The barbarous tribes that people Southern Africa, have never dreamed of the possibility of rendering this lordly quadruped serviceable in a domestic capacity; and even amongst the colonists, there exists an unaccountable superstition that his subjugation is not to be accomplished. His capture, however, may readily be achieved; and as he appears to possess all the aptitude of his Asiatic relative, the only difficulty that presents itself, is the general absence, within our territories, of sufficient food for his support. Were he once domesticated and arrayed against the beasts of the forest, Africa would realize the very *beau ideal* of magnificent sport. It is also worthy of remark, that no attempt has ever been made on the part of the colonists to naturalize another most useful animal, the camel, although the soil, climate, and productions appear alike to favor its introduction.

All this is plain sailing, and something we common mortals can comprehend, foreign and unusual as its picturings and details are; but it is nothing comparatively with what Mr. Cummings has to tell of different modes of hunting the elephant, as practised by himself higher up in the extraordinary valley of the Limpopo. Hear him for his story—

On the 17th of September I resolved to leave the fountain of Seboono, as it was much disturbed, and to proceed with a few Bakalahari to a small yet famous water about six miles to the south-east. We accordingly saddled up and held thither. On reaching this fountain, which is called by the natives "Paapaa," I found the numerous foot-paths leading to it covered, as I had anticipated, with fresh spoor of elephant and rhinoceros. I then at once proceeded to study the best spot on which to make our shooting-hole for the night. It would be impossible to prevent some of the game from getting our wind, for the foot-paths led to it from every side. The prevailing wind was from the east, so I pitched upon the south-west corner of the fountain. The water was not more than twenty yards long and ten broad. The west side was bounded by tufous rock, which rose abruptly from the water about five feet high. The top of this rock was level with the surrounding vley, and here all the elephants drank, as if suspicious of treading on the muddy margin on the other three sides of the fountain. I made our shooting-box within six or eight yards of the water, constructing it in a circular form, of bushes packed together so as to form a hedge about three feet high. On the top of the hedge I placed heavy dead old branches of trees, so as to form a fine clear rest for our rifles; these clean old branches were all lashed firmly together with strips of thorn bark. All being completed, I took the Bakalahari and our steeds to a shady tree, about a quarter of a mile to leeward of the fountain, where we formed a kraall, and off-saddled. This day was particularly adapted to bring game to the water, the sun being extremely powerful, and a hot, dry wind prevailing all the afternoon. I told Carey that we were certain of having a good night's sport, and I was right, fer we undoubtedly had about the finest night's sport and the most wonderful that was ever enjoyed by man.

A little before the sun went down, leaving our kraal, we held to the fountain, having with us our heavy-metaled rifles, karosses and two Bakalahari. We also had two small guns, my double-barreled Westley Richards and Carey's single-barreled gun. As we approached the fountain, a stately bull giraffe stood before us; the heat of the day had brought him thither, but he feared to go in and drink; on observing us, he walked slowly away. Two jackals were next detected. Guinea-fowl, partridges, two or three sorts of pigeon and turtle-dove, and small birds in countless thousands, were pouring in to drink from every airt, as we walked up to our hiding-place and lay down. In a few minutes the sun was under; but the moon was strong and high (it being within three nights of the full), and the sky was clear, with scarcely a cloud. Very soon a step was heard approaching from the east: it was a presuming black rhinoceros. He came up within ten yards of the hiding-hole, and, observing us with his sharp, prying eye, at once came slowly forward for a nearer inspection. I then shouted to him; but this he did not heed in the slightest. I then sprang up and waved my large kaross, shouting at the same time. This, however, only seemed to amuse Borèlé, for he stood within four yards of us, with his horn threatening our momentary destruction, nor would he wheel about until I threw a log of wood at him. Black rhinoceroses are very difficult to scare when they do not get the wind; the best way to do so is to hit them with a stone—that is, in the event of the sportsman not wishing to fire off his gun.

Soon after Borèlé departed, four old bull elephants drew

near from the south. They were coming right on for the spot where we lay, and they seemed very likely to walk over the top of us. We therefore placed our two big rifles in position, and awaited their forward movement with intense interest. On they came, with slow and stately step, until within twenty yards of us, when the leading elephant took it into his head to pass to leeward. We let him come on until he got our wind; he was then within ten yards of the muzzles of our heavy-metaled rifles; on winding us, he tossed his trunk aloft, and we instantly fired together. I caught him somewhere about the heart, and my big six-pound rifle burst in Carey's hands, very nearly killing us both. The elephant, on being fired at, wheeled about, and retreated to the forest at top speed. I now directed "Stick-in-the-mud" to make use of his single-barreled twelve to the pound in the event of more elephants coming up; and thanking my stars that the old Dutch rifle had not sent us both to the land of the leal, I sat down and watched the dark masses of trees that cut the sky on every side, in the hope of seeing a mass as high and wide come towering forward into the open space that surrounded the fountain.

Nor did I watch long in vain, for very soon three princely bull elephants appeared exactly where the first came on, and holding exactly the same course. They approached just as the first had done. When the leading elephant came within ten yards of us, he got our wind and tossed up his trunk, and was wheeling round to retreat, when we fired together, and sent our bullets somewhere about his heart. He ran two hundred yards and then stood, being evidently dying. His comrades halted likewise, but one of them, the finest of the three, almost immediately turned his head once more to the fountain, and very slowly and warily came on. We now heard the wounded elephant utter the cry of death, and fall heavily on the earth. Carey, whose ears were damaged by the bursting of the big rifle, did not catch this sound, but swore that the elephant which now so stealthily approached the water was the one at which we had fired.

It was interesting to observe this grand old bull approach the fountain: he seemed to mistrust the very earth on which he stood, and smelt and examined with his trunk every yard of the ground before he trod on it, and sometimes stood five minutes on one spot without moving. At length, having gone round three sides of the fountain, and being apparently satisfied as to the correctness of everything, he stepped boldly forward on to the rock on the west, and, walking up within six or seven yards of the muzzles of our rifles, turned his broadside, and, lowering his trunk into the water, drew up a volume of water, which he threw over his back and shoulders to cool his person. This operation he repeated two or three times, after which he commenced drinking, by drawing the water into his trunk and then pouring it into his mouth. I determined to break his leg if possible; so, covering the limb about level with the lower line of his body, I fired, Carey firing for his heart. I made a lucky shot; and as the elephant turned and attempted to make away, his leg broke with a loud crack, and he stood upon his three sound ones. At once disabled and utterly incapable of escaping, he stood statue-like beside the fountain, within a few yards of where he had got the shot, and only occasionally made an attempt at locomotion.

The patch of my rifle fired at this elephant's comrade had ignited a large ball of dry old dung, about eight yards to leeward of our kraal, and, fanned by the breeze, it was now burning away very brightly, the sparks flying in the wind. Presently, on looking about me, I beheld two bull elephants approaching by the self-same foot-path which the others had held. The first of these was a half-grown bull, the last was an out-and-out old fellow with enormous tusks. They came on as the first had done, but seemed inclined to pass to windward of us. The young bull, however, observed the fire; he at once walked up to it, and, smelling at it with his trunk, seemed extremely amused, and in a gamboling humor threw his trunk about, as if not knowing what to think of it. The larger bull now came up and exposed a fine broadside; we took him behind the shoulder and fired together; on receiving the shots, he wheeled about and held west with drooping ears, evidently mortally wounded.

Some time after this I detected an enormous old bull elephant approaching from the west. If we lay still where we were, he must in a few minutes get our wind, so we jumped up and ran forward out of his line of march. Here a borèlé opposed our further progress, and we had to stone him out of our way. The elephant came on, and presently got the wind of where we had been lying. This at once seemed to awake his suspicions, for he stood still among the trees, stretching his trunk from side to side to catch the scent, and doubtful whether he should advance or retreat. We then ran toward him, and stalked in within forty yards of where he stood, and, taking up a position behind a bush, awaited his forward movement. The elephant came slowly forward, and I thought would pass to windward of us, when he suddenly altered his course, and walked boldly forward right for where we stood. He came on until within seven or eight yards, when I coughed loudly to turn him. He tossed up his trunk and turned quickly round to fly; as he turned, however, we fired together, when the elephant uttered a shrill cry of distress, and crashed away, evidently hard hit. When this bull was standing before us, we both remarked that he was the finest we had seen that night: his tusks were extremely long, thick, and very unusually wide set.

We now returned to the fountain, and once more lay down to watch. Rhinoceroses, both black and white, were parading around us all night in every direction. We had lain but a short time when I detected a single old bull elephant approaching from the south by the same path which all the others had held. This elephant must have been very thirsty, for he came boldly on without any hesitation, and, keeping to windward, walked past within about eight yards of us. We fired at the same moment; the elephant wheeled about, and, after running a hundred yards, reduced his pace to a slow walk. I clapped Carey on the shoulder, and said, "We have him." I had hardly uttered the words when he fell over on his side; he rose, however, again to his feet. At this moment the same presuming borèlé who had troubled us in the early part of the night came up to us again, and, declining as before to depart by gentle hints, I thought it a fitting moment to put an end to his intrusion, and accordingly gave him a ball behind the shoulder. On receiving it, he galloped off in tremendous consternation, and passed close under the dying elephant, who at the moment fell dead with a heavy crash, and broke one of his hind legs under him in the fall.

About an hour after two more elephants came towering on from the east. When they came up they stood for a long time motionless within forty yards of the water; and at length the finer of the two, which was a very first-rate old bull, and carrying immense tusks, walked boldly forward, and, passing round the north side of the fountain, commenced drinking on the rock, just as the crippled bull had done. We both fired together, holding for his heart; the bullets must have gone nearly through him, for we had double charges of powder in our weapons. On receiving the shots he dropped a volume of water from his trunk, and, tossing it aloft, uttered a loud cry and made off, steering north; but before he was out of our sight he reduced his pace to a slow walk, and I could quite plainly hear, by the loud, painful breathing through his trunk, that he was mortally wounded; but whether the natives were too lazy to seek him, or having found him would not tell me, I know not, but I never got him. We shot another bull elephant shortly after this; he, too, uttered a shrill cry, and went off holding the same course the last one did; that was, however, all that I ever saw of him.

Eight elephants killed and four 'bagged' were the 'trophies of this extraordinary night's sport, beside the 'borèlé' and other 'small fry'—enough, surely, to have appeased the appetite for slaughter of the veritable Nimrod of old himself—but there follows a variation upon this comparatively tame sport.

The next night I put in practice a novel experiment I had long entertained—that of hunting elephants by moonlight with dogs and horses, as in the day, being very much annoyed at wounding and losing in the last week no less than ten first-rate old bull elephants. I communicated my idea to 'Stick-in-the-mud,' and we hastily proceeded to saddle my steed. I led my dogs, eight in number, through the forest to leeward of where a bull who had come to the fountain to drink had gone in, and when I saw that they had got his wind I slipped them. They dashed forward and next minute I followed the baying of the dogs, and the crash and the trumpet of the elephant. He rushed away at first without halting, and held right for the mountains to the south-west. When, however, he found that his speed did not avail, and that he could not get away from his pursuers, he began to turn and dodge about in the thickest of the cover, occasionally making charges after the dogs. I followed on as best I could, shouting with all my might to encourage my good hounds. These, hearing their master's voice beside them, stuck well by the elephant, and fought him better than in the day. I gave him my first two shots from the saddle; after which, I rode close up to him, and, running in on foot, gave him some deadly shots at distances of from fifteen to twenty yards.

The elephant very soon evinced signs of distress, and ceased to make away from us. Taking up positions in the densest parts of the cover, he caught up the red dust with his trunk, and throwing it over his head and back, endeavored to conceal himself in a cloud. This was a fine opportunity to pour in my deadly shafts, and I took care to avail myself of it. When he had received about twelve shots, he walked slowly forward in a dying state, the blood streaming from his trunk. I rode close up to him, and gave him a sharp right and left from the saddle: he turned and walked a few yards, then suddenly came down with tremendous violence on his vast stern, pitching his head and trunk aloft to a prodigious height, and, falling heavily over on his side, expired. This was an extremely large and handsome elephant, decidedly the finest bull I had shot this year. Afraid of taking cold or rheumatism, for I was in a most profuse perspiration, I hastened back to my fireside, having first secured all the dogs in their couples. Here I divested myself of my leather trowsers, shooting-belt, and veldt-schoens, and, stretched on my kaross, I took tea, and wondered at the facility with which I had captured this mighty elephant.

Feeling fatigued, I intended to lie down and rest till morning. Just, however, as I was arranging my saddles for a pillow, I beheld another first-rate old bull elephant advancing up the vley from the south. I at once resolved that he, too, should run the gauntlet with the dogs. In immense haste, therefore, I once more pulled on my old leathers, and buckled on my shooting-belt, and ran down into the rank long grass beside the fountain to meet him, armed with the large two-grooved rifle, having directed Carey and Piet to come slowly up with the dogs and my horse and gun as soon as they were ready. The elephant came on, and stood drinking within thirty yards of me. When I saw Carey coming on with the dogs and steed, I fired, but my rifle hung fire. The shot, however, gave the dogs good courage, and they fought well. The elephant took away at a rapid pace toward the other fountain where the Bechuanas lay, and at first led me through very bad wait-a-bit thorn cover, which once or twice nearly swept me out of the saddle. Presently he inclined to the west, and got into better country; I then rode close up to him, and bowled him over with four shots.

With one more glimpse of the cool extravagance characteristic of the Professional Hunter, and of which Cummings has prided himself upon giving us so many specimens, we take our leave of elephant hunting in South Africa. The following is most refreshing.

On the 31st I held south-east in quest of elephants, with a large party of the natives. Our course lay through an open part of the forest, where I beheld a troop of springboks and two ostriches, the first I had seen for a long time. We held for Towannie, a strong fountain in the gravelly bed of a periodical river: here two herds of cow elephants had drunk on the preceding evening, but I declined to follow them; and presently, at a muddy fountain a little in advance, we took up the spoor of an enormous bull, which had wallowed in the mud, and then plastered the sides of several of the adjacent veteran-looking trees. We followed the spoor through level forest in an easterly direction, when the leading party overran the spoor, and casts were made for its recovery. Presently I detected an excited native beckoning violently a little to my left, and, cantering up to him, he said that he had seen the elephant. He led me through the forest a few hundred yards, when, clearing a wait-a-bit, I came full in view of the tallest and largest bull elephant I had ever seen. He stood broadside to me, at upward of one hundred yards, and his attention at the moment was occupied with the dogs, which, unaware of his proximity, were rushing past him, while the old fellow seemed to gaze at their unwonted appearance with surprise.

Halting my horse, I fired at his shoulder, and secured him with a single shot. The ball caught him high upon the shoulder-blade, rendering him instantly dead lame; and before the echo of the bullet could reach my ear, I plainly saw that the elephant was mine. The dogs now came up and barked around him, but finding himself incapacitated, the old fellow seemed determined to take it easy, and, limping slowly to a neighboring tree, he remained stationary, eyeing his pursuers with a resigned and philosophic air.

I resolved to devote a short time to the contemplation of this noble elephant before I should lay him low; accordingly, having off-saddled the horses beneath a shady tree which was to be my quarters for the night and ensuing day, I quickly kindled a fire and put on the kettle, and in a very few minutes my coffee was prepared. There I sat in my forest home, coolly sipping my coffee, with one of the finest elephants in Africa awaiting my pleasure beside a neighboring tree.

It was, indeed, a striking scene; and as I gazed upon the stupendous veteran of the forest, I thought of the red deer which I loved to follow in my native land, and felt that, though the Fates had driven me to follow a more daring and arduous avocation in a distant land, it was a good exchange which I had made, for I was now a chief over boundless forests, which yielded unspeakably more noble and exciting sport.

Having admired the elephant for a considerable time, I resolved to make experiments for vulnerable points, and, approaching very near, I fired several bullets at different parts of his enormous skull. These did not seem to affect him in the slightest; he only acknowledged the shots by a "salaam-like" movement of his trunk, with the point of which he gently touched the wound with a striking and peculiar action. Surprised and shocked to find that I was only tormenting and prolonging the sufferings of the noble beast, which bore his trials with such dignified composure, I resolved to finish the proceeding with all possible dispatch; accordingly, I opened fire upon him from the left side, aiming behind the shoulder; but even there it was long before my bullets seemed to take effect. I first fired six shots with the two-grooved, which must have eventually proved mortal, but as yet he evinced no visible distress; after which I fired three shots at the same part with the Dutch six-pounder. Large tears now trickled from his eyes, which he slowly shut and opened; his colossal frame quivered convulsively, and, falling on his side, he expired. The tusks of this elephant were beautifully arched, and were the heaviest I had yet met with, averaging ninety pounds weight apiece.

All this is cool—very! It is picturesque, not to say theatrical! Mr. Cummings, at this rate, might be educated into a good American Borderer, and some day "come up to the scratch" in a *duello*, hand-to-claw with a Grisly Bear, after having exchanged the compliments of the morning with him beneath the cold shadows of the Rocky Mountain peaks!

CHAPTER XXVI.

THE GIRAFFE.

I HAVE before hinted at the degree in which Cummings has made Harris his model, in his new book, "Five Years in South Africa." I therefore propose to give, one after the other, the account each has furnished of his first interview with the giraffe. They are different, yet alike in many curious particulars; and as their facts are equally interesting, it is pleasing to compare the impressions of these two notorious, if not remarkable examples of the Hunter-Naturalist, from nearly the same point of view. I give Cummings the advantage of presenting his first.

This day was to me rather a memorable one, as the first on which I saw and slew the lofty, graceful-looking giraffe or camelopard, with which, during many years of my life, I had longed to form an acquaintance.

These gigantic and exquisitely beautiful animals, which are admirably formed by nature to adorn the fair forests that clothe the boundless plains of the interior, are widely distributed throughout the interior of Southern Africa, but are nowhere to be met with in great numbers. In countries unmolested by the intrusive foot of man, the giraffe is found generally in herds varying from twelve to sixteen; but I have not unfrequently met with herds containing thirty individuals, and on one occasion I counted forty together; this, however, was owing to chance, and about sixteen may be reckoned as the average number of a herd.

These herds are composed of giraffes of various sizes, from the young giraffe of nine or ten feet in height, to the dark, chestnut-colored old bull of the herd, whose exalted head towers above his companions, generally attaining to a height of upwards of eighteen feet. The females are of lower stature and more delicately formed than the males, their height averaging from sixteen to seventeen feet.

Some writers have discovered ugliness and a want of grace in the giraffe, but I consider that he is one of the most strikingly beautiful animals in creation; and when a herd of them is seen scattered through a grove of the picturesque parasol-topped acacias which adorn their native plains, and on whose uppermost shoots they are enabled to browse by the colossal height with which nature has so admirably endowed them, he must indeed be slow of conception who fails to discover both grace and dignity in all their movements.

There can be no doubt that every animal is seen to the greatest advantage in the haunts which nature destined him to adorn; and among the various living creatures which beautify this fair creation, I have often traced a remarkable resemblance between the animal and the general appearance of the locality in which it is found. This I remarked at an early period of my life, when entomology occupied a part of my attention. No person following this interesting pursuit can fail to observe the extraordinary likeness which insects bear to the various abodes in which they are met with. Thus, among the long, green grass, we find a variety of long, green insects, whose legs and antennæ so resemble the shoots emanating from the stalks of the grass that it requires a practiced eye to distinguish them. Throughout sandy districts, varieties of insects are met with of a color similar to the sand which they inhabit.

Among the green leaves of the various trees of the forest innumerable leaf-colored insects are to found; while, closely adhering to the rough, gray bark of these forest-trees, we observe beautifully-colored gray-looking moths of various patterns, yet altogether so resembling the bark as to be invisible to the passing observer.

In like manner, among quadrupeds I have traced a corresponding analogy; for, even in the case of the stupendous elephant, the ashy color of his hide so corresponds with the gray, thorny jungles which he frequents throughout the day, that a person unaccustomed to hunting elephants, standing on a commanding situation, might look down upon a herd and fail to detect their presence.

And further, in the case of the giraffe, which is invariably met with among venerable forests, where innumerable blasted and weather-beaten trunks and stems occur, I have repeatedly been in doubt as to the presence of a troop of them until I had recourse to my spy-glass; and on referring the case to my savage attendants, I have known even their optics to fail, at one time even mistaking these dilapidated trunks for camelopards, and again confounding real camelopards with these aged veterans of the forest.

Although we had now been travelling many days through the country of the giraffe, and had marched through forests in which their spoor was abundant, our eyes had not yet been gifted with a sight of "Tootla" himself; it was therefore with indescribable pleasure that, on the evening of the 11th, I beheld a troop of these interesting animals.

Our breakfast being finished, I resumed my journey through an endless gray forest of cameel-dorn and other trees, the country slightly undulating, and grass abundant. A little before the sun went down my driver remarked to me, "I was just going to say, sir, that that old tree was a camelopard." On looking where he pointed, I saw that the old tree was indeed a camelopard; and, on casting my eyes a little to the right, I beheld a troop of them standing looking at us, their heads actually towering above the trees of the forest. It was imprudent to commence a chase at such a late hour, especially in a country of so level a character, where the chances were against my being able to regain my wagons that night. I, however, resolved to chance everything; and directing my men to catch and saddle Colesburg, I proceeded in haste to buckle on my shooting-belt and spurs, and in two minutes I was in the saddle. The giraffes stood looking at the wagons until I was within sixty yards of them, when, galloping round a thick bushy tree, under cover of which I had ridden, I suddenly beheld a sight the most astounding that a sportsman's eye can encounter. Before me stood a troop of ten colossal giraffes, the majority of which were from seventeen to eighteen feet high. On beholding me they at once made off, twisting their long tails over their backs, making a loud, switching noise with them, and cantered along at an easy pace, which, however, obliged Colesburg to put his best foot foremost to keep up with them.

The sensations which I felt on this occasion were different from anything that I had before experienced, during a long sporting career. My senses were so absorbed by the wondrous and beautiful sight before me, that I rode along like one entranced, and I felt inclined to disbelieve that I was hunting living things of this world. The ground was firm and favorable for riding. At every stride I gained upon the giraffes, and after a short burst at a swinging gallop I was in the middle of them, and turned the finest cow out of the herd. On finding herself driven from her comrades and hotly pursued, she increased her pace, and cantered along with tremendous strides, clearing an amazing extent of ground at every bound; while her neck and breast coming in contact with the dead old branches of the trees, were continually strewing them in my path. In a few minutes I was riding within five feet of her stern, and, firing at a gallop, I sent a bullet into her back. Increasing my pace, I next rode alongside, and, placing the muzzle of my rifle within a few feet of her, I fired my second shot behind the shoulder;

the ball, however, seemed to have little effect. I then placed myself directly in front, when she came to a walk. Dismounting, I hastily loaded both barrels, putting in double charges of powder. Before this was accomplished she was off at a canter. In a short time I brought her to a stand in the dry bed of a water-course, where I fired at fifteen yards, aiming where I thought the heart lay, upon which she again made off. Having loaded, I followed, and had very nearly lost her; she had turned abruptly to the left, and was far out of sight among the trees. Once more I brought her to a stand, and dismounted from my horse. There we stood together alone in the wild wood. I gazed in wonder at her extreme beauty, while her soft, dark eye, with its silky fringe, looked down imploringly at me, and I really felt a pang of sorrow in this moment of triumph for the blood I was shedding. Pointing my rifle toward the skies, I sent a bullet through her neck. On receiving it, she reared high on her hind legs, and fell backward with a heavy crash, making the earth shake around her. A thick stream of dark blood spouted out from the wound, her colossal limbs quivered for a moment, and she expired.

I had little time to contemplate the prize I had won. Night was fast setting in, and it was very questionable if I should succeed in regaining my wagons; so, having cut off the tail of the giraffe, which was adorned with a bushy tuft of flowing black hair, I took "one last fond look," and rode hard for the spoor of the wagons, which I succeeded in reaching just as it was dark.

No pen nor words can convey to a sportsman what it is to ride in the midst of a troop of gigantic giraffes: it must be experienced to be understood. They emitted a powerful perfume, which in the chase came hot in my face, reminding me of the smell of a hive of heather honey in September. The greater part of this chase led through bushes of the wait-a-bit thorn of the most virulent description, which covered my legs and arms with blood long before I had killed the giraffe. I rode as usual in the kilt, with my arms bare to my shoulder. It was Chapelpark of Badenoch's old gray kilt, but in this chase it received a death blow which it never afterwards recovered.

Now comes Harris's story—and between them we shall get a pretty clear idea of the sensation of killing the first giraffe. He says:

To the sportsman, the most thrilling passage in my adventures is now to be recounted. In my own breast, it awakens a renewal of past impressions, more lively than any written description can render intelligible; and far abler pens than mine, dipped in more glowing tints, would still fall short of the reality, and leave much to be supplied by the imagination. Three hundred gigantic elephants, browsing in majestic tranquillity amidst the wild magnificence of an African landscape, and a wide stretching plain, darkened, far as the eye can reach, with a moving phalanx of gnoos and quaggas, whose numbers literally baffle computation, are sights but rarely to be witnessed; but who amongst our brother Nimrods shall hear of riding familiarly by the side of a troop of colossal giraffes, and not feel his spirit stirred within him? He that would behold so marvellous a sight must leave the haunts of man, and dive, as we did, into pathless wilds, traversed only by the brute creation—into wide wastes, where the grim lion prowls, monarch of all he surveys, and where the gaunt hyæna and wild dog fearlessly pursue their prey.

Many days had now elapsed since we had even seen the camelopard—and then only in small numbers, and under the most unfavorable circumstances. The blood coursed through my veins like quicksilver; therefore, as on the morning of the 19th, from the back of *Breslar*, my most trusty steed, with a firm wooded plain before me, I counted thirty-two of these animals, industriously stretching their peacock necks to crop the tiny leaves which fluttered above their heads, in a mimosa grove that beautified the scenery. They were within a hundred yards of me, but having previously determined to try the *boarding* system, I reserved my fire. Although I had taken the field expressly to look for giraffes, and had put four of the Hottentots on horseback, all excepting Piet had as usual slipped off unperceived in pursuit of a troop of koodoos. Our stealthy approach was soon opposed by an ill-tempered rhinoceros, which, with her ugly calf, stood directly in the path; and the twinkling of her bright little eyes, accompanied by a restless rolling of the body, giving earnest of her intention to charge, I directed Piet to salute her with a broadside, at the same moment putting spurs to my horse. At the report of the gun, and the sudden clattering of hoofs, away bounded the giraffes in grotesque confusion, clearing the ground by a succession of frog-like hops, and soon leaving me far in the rear. Twice were their towering forms concealed from view by a park of trees, which we entered almost at the same instant; and twice, on emerging from the labyrinth, did I perceive them tilting over an eminence immeasurably in advance. A white turban, that I wore round my hunting cap, being dragged off by a projecting bough, was instantly charged by three rhinoceroses; and looking over my shoulder, I could see them long afterwards fagging themselves to overtake me. In the course of five minutes, the fugitives arrived at a small river, the treacherous sands of which receiving their long legs, their flight was greatly retarded; and after floundering to the opposite side, and scrambling to the top of the bank, I perceived that their race was run. Patting the streaming neck of my good steed, I urged him again to his utmost, and instantly found myself by the side of the herd. The stately bull, being readily distinguishable from the rest by his dark chestnut robe, and superior stature, I applied the muzzle of my rifle behind his dappled shoulder, with the right hand, and drew both triggers; but he still continued to shuffle along, and being afraid of losing him, should I dismount, among the extensive mimosa groves, with which the landscape was now obscured, I sat in my saddle, loading and firing behind the elbow, and then placing myself across his path, until, the tears trickling from his full brilliant eye, his lofty frame began to totter, and at the seventeenth discharge from the deadly grooved bore, bowing his graceful head from the skies, his proud form was prostrate in the dust. Never shall I forget the tingling excitement of that moment! Alone, in the wild wood, I hurraed with bursting exultation, and unsaddling my steed, sank exhausted beside the noble prize I had won.

When I leisurely contemplated the massive frame before me, seeming as though it had been cast in a mould of brass, and protected by a hide of an inch and a half in thickness, it was no longer matter of astonishment, that a bullet discharged from a distance of eighty or ninety yards, should have been attended with little effect upon such amazing strength. The extreme height from the crown of the elegantly moulded head to the hoof of this magnificent animal, was eighteen feet; the whole being equally divided into neck, body, and leg. Two hours were passed in completing a drawing; and Piet still not making his appearance, I cut off the tail, which exceeded five feet in length, and was measurelessly the most estimable trophy I had gained; but proceeding to saddle my horse, which I had left quietly grazing by the side of a running brook, my chagrin may be conceived, when I discovered that he had taken advantage of my occupation to free himself from his halter, and abscond. Being ten miles from the wagons, and in a perfectly strange country, I felt convinced that the only chance of recovering my pet, was by following the trail, whilst doing which with infinite difficulty, the ground scarcely deigning to receive a foot-print, I had the satisfaction of meeting Piet and Mohanycom, who had fortunately seen and recaptured the truant.

Returning to the giraffe, we all feasted heartily upon the flesh, which, although highly scented at this season with the rank mokaala blossoms, was far from despicable; and after losing our way in consequence of the twin-like resemblance of two scarped hills, we regained the wagons after sunset.

The spell was now broken, and the secret of cameleopard hunting discovered. The next day Richardson and myself killed three; one a female, slipping upon muddy ground, and falling with great violence, before she had been wounded, a shot in the head dispatched her as she lay. From this time we could reckon confidently upon two out of each troop that we were fortunate enough to find, always approaching as near as possible, in order to insure a good start, galloping into the middle of them, *boarding* the largest, and riding with him until he fell. The rapidity with which these awkwardly formed animals can move, is beyond all things surprising, our best horses being unable to close with them under two miles. Their gallop is a succession of jumping strides, the fore and hind leg on the same side moving together instead of diagonally, as in most other quadrupeds, the former being kept close together, and the latter so wide apart, that in riding by the animal's side, the hoof may be seen striking on the outside of the horse, momentarily threatening to overthrow him. Their motion, altogether, reminded me rather of the pitching of a ship, or rolling of a rocking-horse, than of any thing living; and the remarkable gait is rendered still more automaton-like, by the switching, at regular intervals, of the long black tail, which is invariably curled above the back, and by the corresponding action of the neck, swinging as it does, like a pendulum, and literally imparting to the animal the appearance of a huge piece of machinery in motion. Naturally gentle, timid and peaceable, the unfortunate giraffe has no means of protecting itself but with its heels; but even when hemmed into a corner, it seldom resorted to this mode of defence. I have before noticed the courage evinced by our horses, in the pursuit of game. Even when brought into actual contact with these almost unearthly quadrupeds, they evinced no symptom of alarm, a circumstance which may possibly be traced to their meagre diet.

The colossal height, and apparent disproportions of this extraordinary animal, long classed it with the unicorn and the sphynx of the ancients, and induced a belief that it belonged rather to the group of chimeras with which the regions of imagination are tenanted, than existed amongst the actual works of nature. Of its form and habits, no very precise notions were obtained until within the last forty years; and even now, the extant delineations are far from the truth, having been taken from crippled prisoners instead of from specimens free in their native deserts. The giraffe is by no means a common animal, even at its headquarters. We seldom found them without having followed the trail, and never saw more than five-and-thirty in a day. A traveller whom I met in the Cape Colony, assured me, before I visited the interior, that he had himself counted eight hundred giraffes in a single day; and during his travels, had ridden down *hundreds*. On my return, however, after a little cross-examination, the number destroyed dwindled gradually down to *one;* which solitary individual appeared, upon further investigation, to have been been taken in a pitfall! The senses of sight, hearing and smell, are acute and delicate; the eyes, which are soft and gentle, eclipsing those of the oft-sung gazelle of the East, and being so constructed that, without turning the head, the animal can see both before and behind it at the same time. On the forehead there is a remarkable prominence; and the tongue has the power of mobility increased to an extraordinary degree, accompanied with the faculty of extension, which enables it, in miniature, to perform the office of the elephant's proboscis. The lofty maned neck, possessing only seven joints, appears to move on a pivot, instead of being flexible like that of the swan or peacock, to which, from its length, it has been likened.

The giraffe utters no cry whatever. Both sexes have horns, covered with hair, and are similarly marked with an angular and somewhat symmetrical pattern. The male increases in depth of color according to the age, and in some specimens is nearly black; but the female is smaller in stature, and of a lighter color, approaching to yellow. Although very extensive, the range of its *habitat* is exclusively confined to those regions in which the species of mimosa termed mokaala, or *kameel-doorn*, is abundant, the leaves, shoots, and blossoms of that tree being its ordinary food.

On the 22d, being encamped on the banks of a small stream, a cameleopard was killed by a lion, whilst in the act of drinking, at no great distance from the wagons. It was a noisy affair, but an inspection of the scene on which it occurred, proved that the giant strength of the victim had been paralyzed in an instant. Authors have asserted that the king of beasts is sometimes carried fifteen or twenty miles, "riding proudly" on the back of the giraffe; but notwithstanding the amazing and acknowledged power of this superb animal, I am greatly disposed to question his ability to maintain so long a race under such merciless jockeyship!

Sensations very well described—capitally, indeed!—only it is surprising how much alike "First Giraffe Hunts" must be, since such a remarkable coincidence of feeling experienced, and of the action described, should have occurred in these two thus, performed by different persons, at an interval of ten years. The fact of their being so much alike, may console those of us in this prosy real world who may chance to be emulous of a Giraffe Hunt.

CHAPTER XXVII.

SOUTH AFRICAN LIONS.

Now for the lordly King of Beasts! As these wild African Hunters found him, the grandeur of his ancestral name is not a little heightened. There are some pictures of this South African monarch of the wastes furnished as well by the daring missionaries of the Christian Church in this direction, which are quite as striking as those given by the professional Hunters themselves. These we shall give after first taking the general sketch of the habits of the animal furnished by Cumming.

The night of the 19th was to me rather a memorable one, as being the first on which I had the satisfaction of hearing the deep-toned thunder of the lion's roar. Although there was no one near to inform me by what beast the haughty and impressive sounds which echoed through the wilderness were produced, I had little difficulty in divining. There was no mistake about it; and on hearing it I at once knew, as well as if accustomed to the sound from my infancy, that the appalling roar which was uttered within half a mile of me was no other than that of the mighty and terrible king of beasts. Although the dignified and truly monarchical appearance of the lion has long rendered him famous among his fellow quadrupeds, and his appearance and habits have often been described by abler pens than mine, nevertheless I consider that a few remarks, resulting from my own personal experience, formed by a tolerably long acquaintance with them both by day and by night, may not prove uninteresting to the reader. There is something so noble and imposing in the presence of the lion, when seen walking with dignified self-possession, free and undaunted, on his native soil, that no description can convey an adequate idea of his striking appearance. The lion is exquisitely formed by nature for the predatory habits which he is destined to pursue. Combining in comparatively small compass the qualities of power and agility, he is enabled, by means of the tremendous machinery with which nature has gifted him, easily to overcome and destroy almost every beast of the forest, however superior to him in weight and stature.

Though considerably under four feet in height, he has little difficulty in dashing to the ground and overcoming the lofty and apparently powerful giraffe, whose head towers above the trees of the forest, and whose skin is nearly an inch in thickness. The lion is the constant attendant of the vast herds of buffaloes which frequent the interminable forests of the interior; and a full-grown one, so long as his teeth are unbroken, generally proves a match for an old bull buffalo, which in size and strength greatly surpasses the most powerful breed of English cattle: the lion also preys on all the larger varieties of the antelopes, and on both varieties of the gnu. The zebra, which is met with in large herds throughout the interior, is also a favorite object of his pursuit.

Lions do not refuse, as has been asserted, to feast upon the venison that they have not killed themselves. I have repeatedly discovered lions of all ages which had taken possession of, and were feasting upon, the carcasses of various game quadrupeds which had fallen before my rifle. The lion is very generally diffused throughout the secluded parts of Southern Africa. He is, however, nowhere met with in great abundance, it being very rare to find more than three, or even two, families of lions frequenting the same district and drinking at the same fountain. When a greater number were met with, I remarked it was owing to long-protracted droughts, which, by drying nearly all the fountains, had compelled the game of various districts to crowd the remaining springs, and the lions, according to their custom, followed in the wake. It is a common thing to come upon a full-grown lion and lioness associating with three or four large ones nearly full-grown; at other times, full-grown males will be found associating and hunting together in a happy state of friendship; two, three, and four full-grown male lions may thus be discovered consorting together.

The male lion is adorned with a long, rank, shaggy mane, which in some instances almost sweeps the ground. The color of these manes varies, some being very dark, and others of a golden yellow. This appearance has given rise to a prevailing opinion among the Boers that there are two distinct varieties of lions, which they distinguish by the respective names of "Schwart fore life" and "Chiel fore life;" this idea, however, is erroneons. The color of the lion's mane is generally influenced by his age. He attains his mane in the third year of his existence. I have remarked that at first it is of a yellowish color; in the prime of life it is blackest, and when he has numbered many years, but still is in the full enjoyment of his power, it assumes a yellowish-gray, pepper-and-salt sort of color. These old fellows are cunning and dangerous, and most to be dreaded. The females are utterly destitute of a mane, being covered with a short, thick, glossy coat of tawny hair. The manes and coats of lions frequenting open-lying districts utterly destitute of trees, such as the borders of the great Kalahari desert, are more rank and handsome than those inhabiting forest districts.

One of the most striking things connected with the lion is his voice, which is extremely grand and peculiarly striking. It consists at times of a low, deep moaning, repeated five or six times, ending in faintly audible sighs; at other times he startles the forest with loud, deep-toned, solemn roars, repeated five or six times in quick succession, each increasing in loudness to the third or fourth, when his voice dies away in five or six low, muffled sounds, very much resembling distant thunder. At times, and not unfrequently, a troop may be heard roaring in concert, one assuming the lead, and two, three, or four more regularly taking up their parts, like persons singing a catch. Like our Scottish stags at the rutting season, they roar loudest in cold, frosty nights; but on no occasions are their voices to be heard in such perfection, or so intensely powerful, as when two or three strange troops of lions approach a fountain to drink at the same time. When this occurs, every member of each troop sounds a bold roar of defiance at the opposite parties; and when one roars, all roar together, and each seems to vie with his comrade in the intensity and power of his voice. The power and grandeur of these nocturnal forest concerts is inconceivably striking and pleasing to the hunter's ear. The effect, I may remark, is greatly enhanced when the hearer happens to be situated in the depths of the forest, at the dead hour of midnight, unaccompanied by any attendant, and ensconced within twenty yards of the fountain which the surrounding troops of lions are approaching. Such has been my situation many scores of times; and though I am allowed to have a tolerable good taste for music, I consider the catches with which I was then regaled as the sweetest and most natural I ever heard.

As a general rule, lions roar during the night; their sighing moans commencing as the shades of evening envelop the forest, and continuing at intervals throughout the night. In distant and secluded regions, however, I have constantly heard them roaring loudly as late as nine and ten o'clock on a bright sunny morning. In hazy and rainy weather they are to be heard at every hour in the day, but their roar is subdued. It often happens that when two strange male lions meet at a fountain a terrific combat ensues, which not unfrequently ends in the death of one of them. The habits of the lion are strictly nocturnal; during the day he lies concealed beneath the shade of some low, bushy tree or wide-spreading bush, either in the level forest or on the mountain side. He is also partial to lofty reeds, or fields of long, yellow grass, such as occur in low-lying vleys. From these haunts he sallies forth when the sun goes down, and commences his nightly prowl. When he is successful in his beat and has secured his prey, he does not roar much that night, only uttering occasionally a few low moans; that is, provided no intruders approach him, otherwise the case would be very different.

Lions are ever most active, daring and presuming in dark and stormy nights, and consequently, on such occasions, the traveller ought more particularly to be on his guard. I remarked a fact connected with the lion's hour of drinking peculiar to themselves; they seemed unwilling to visit the fountains with good moonlight. Thus, when the moon rose early, the lions deferred their hour of watering until late in the morning; and when the moon rose late, they drank at a very early hour in the night. By this acute system many a grisly lion saved his bacon, and is now luxuriating in the forest of South Africa, which had otherwise fallen by the barrels of my "Westley Richards." Owing to the tawny color of the coat with which nature has robed him, he is perfectly invisible in the dark; and although I have often heard them loudly lapping the water under my very nose, not twenty yards from me, I could not possibly make out so much as the outline of their forms. When a thirsty lion comes to water, he stretches out his massive arms, lies down on his breast to drink, and makes a loud, lapping noise in drinking not to be mistaken. He continues lapping up the water for a long while, and four or five times during the proceeding he pauses for half a minute as if to take breath. One thing conspicuous about them is their eyes, which, in a dark night, glow like two balls of fire. The female is more fierce and active than the male, as a general rule. Lionesses which have never had young are much more dangerous than those which have. At no time is the lion so much to be dreaded as when his partner has got small young ones. At that season he knows no fear, and, in the coolest and most intrepid manner, he will face a thousand men. A remarkable instance of this kind came under my own observation, which confirmed the reports I had before heard from the natives. One day, when out elephant-hunting in the territory of the "Baseleka," accompanied by two hundred and fifty men, I was astonished suddenly to behold a majestic lion slowly and steadily advancing toward us with a dignified step and undaunted bearing, the most noble and imposing that can be conceived. Lashing his tail from side to side, and growling haughtily, his terribly expressive eye resolutely fixed upon us, and displaying a show of ivory well calculated to inspire terror among the timid "Bechuanas," he approached. A headlong flight of the two hundred and fifty men was the immediate result; and, in the confusion of the moment, four couples of my dogs, which they had been leading, were allowed to escape in their couples. These instantly faced the lion, who, finding that by his bold bearing he had succeeded in putting his enemies to flight, now became solicitous for the safety of his little family, with which the lioness was retreating in the back-ground. Facing about, he followed after them with a haughty and independent step, growling fiercely at the dogs which trotted along on either side of him. Three troops of elephants having been discovered a few minutes previous to this, upon which I was marching for the attack, I, with the most heartfelt reluctance, reserved my fire. On running down the hill side to endeavor to recall my dogs, I observed, for the first time, the retreating lioness with four cubs. About twenty minutes afterwards two noble elephants repaid my forbearance.

Among Indian Nimrods, a certain class of royal tigers

is dignified with the appellation of "man-eaters." These are tigers which, having once tasted human flesh, show a predilection for the same, and such characters are very naturally famed and dreaded among the natives. Elderly gentlemen of similar tastes and habits are occasionally met with among the lions in the interior of South Africa, and the danger of such neighbors may be easily imagined. I account for lions first acquiring this taste in the following manner: the Bechuana tribes of the far interior do not bury their dead, but unceremoniously carry them forth, and leave them lying exposed in the forest or on the plain, a prey to the lion and hyæna, or the jackal and vulture; and I can readily imagine that a lion, having thus once tasted human flesh, would have little hesitation, when opportunity presented itself, of springing upon and carrying off the unwary traveller or "Bechuana" inhabiting his country. Be this as it may, man-eaters occur; and on my fourth hunting expedition, a horrible tragedy was acted one dark night in my little lonely camp by one of these formidable characters, which deprived me, in the far wilderness, of my most valuable servant. In winding up these few observations on the lion, which I trust will not have been tiresome to the reader, I may remark that lion-hunting, under any circumstances, is decidedly a dangerous pursuit. It may nevertheless be followed, to a certain extent, with comparative safety by those who have naturally a turn for that sort of thing. A recklessness of death, perfect coolness and self-possession, an acquaintance with the disposition and manners of lions, and a tolerable knowledge of the use of the rifle, are indispensable to him who would shine in the overpoweringly exciting pastime of hunting this justly celebrated king of beasts.

It would be a pity, if, amidst his other lauded characteristics, the lion should not be quite as remarkable for manners as magnanimity. Moffat, the daring agent of the London Missionary Society in South Africa, who for twenty-three years was exposed to all the perils of general resident, and travelling supervision, of the Society operations in that wild region, has given many striking and memorable anecdotes of the lion, which are worth comparison with the rabidly egotistical narratives of Cumming, &c. We quote one, in his own language, of the authenticity of which there can be no reasonable doubt—at least it stands upon quite as broad a basis of authenticity as any thing in that species of literature.

Conversing with the party one evening, when sitting around the fire, on the conduct of children to their parents, I observed that they were as bad as lions. "They are worse," replied Africaner. This he illustrated from the well-known characteristics of the king of beasts; or, more properly, king of the beasts of prey. Much has been written about African lions, but the half has not been told. The following trait in their character may not be intrusive, or partaking of the marvelous, with which the tales of some travellers are said to abound. I give it as received from men of God, and men who had been experienced Nimrods, too. The old lion, when in company with his children as the natives call them, though they are nearly as big as himself; or, when numbers together happen to come upon game, the oldest or ablest creeps to the object, while the others crouch on the grass; if he be successful, which he generally is, he retires from his victim, and lies down to breathe and rest, for perhaps a quarter of an hour; in the meantime, the others draw around, and lie down at a respectful distance. When the chief one has got his rest, he commences at the abdomen and breast, and after making havoc with the tit-bits of the carcass, he will take a second rest, none of the others presuming to move. Having made a second gorge, he retires, the others watching his motions, rush on the remainder, and it is soon devoured. At other times, if a young lion seizes the prey, and an old one happens to come up, the younger retires till the elder has dined. This was what Africaner called better manners than those of the Namaquas.

Here are others as droll from the same source:—

Passing along a vale, we came to a spot where the lion appeared to have been exercising himself in the way of leaping. As the natives are very expert in tracing the maneuvres of animals by their foot-marks, it was soon discovered that a large lion had crept towards a short black stump, very like the human form; when within about a dozen yards, it bounded on its supposed prey, when, to his mortification, he fell a foot or two short of it. According to the testimony of a native who had been watching his motions, and who joined us soon after, the lion lay for some time steadfastly eyeing its supposed meal. It then arose, smelt the object, and returned to the spot from which he commenced his first leap, and leaped four several times, till at last he placed his paw on the imagined prize. On another occasion, when Africaner and an attendant were passing near the end of a hill, from which jutted out a smooth rock of ten or twelve feet high, he observed a number of zebras pressing round it, obliged to keep the path, beyond which it was precipitous. A lion was seen creeping up towards the path, to intercept the large stallion, which is always in the rear to defend or warn the troop. The lion missed his mark, and while the zebra rushed round the point, the lion knew well, if he could mount the rock at one leap, the next would be on the zebra's back, it being obliged to turn towards the hill. He fell short, with only his head over the stone, looking at the galloping zebra switching his tail in the air. He then tried a second and a third leap, till he succeeded. In the meantime two more lions came up, and seemed to roar and talk away about something, while the old lion led them round the rock, and round it again; then he made another grand leap, to show them what he and they must do next time. Africaner added, with the most perfect gravity, "They evidently talked to each other, but though loud enough, I could not understand a word they said; and, fearing lest we should be the next objects of their skill, we crept away and left them in council."

This is a fine story, and I do not regard it with near the suspicion with which I do those vaunting ones of personal adventure to which I have referred. I do not at all doubt the sagacious measuring of strength with distance by the lion. How else could certainty be secured in the next experiment—though the self-educating processes of the young lion are plainly indicated. Another story of more tragic character is given.

The following fact will show the fearful dangers to which solitary travellers are sometimes exposed. A man belonging to Mr. Schmelen's congregation, at Bethany, returning homewards from a visit to his friends, took a circuitous course in order to pass a small fountain, or rather pool, where he hoped to kill an antelope, to carry home to his family. The sun had risen to some height by the time he reached the spot, and seeing no game, he laid his gun down on a shelving low rock, the back part of which was covered over with a species of dwarf thorn-bushes. He went to the water, took a hearty drink, and returned to the rock, smoked his pipe, and being a little tired, fell asleep. In a short time the heat reflected from the rock awoke him, and opening his eyes, he saw a large lion crouching before him, with its eyes glaring in his face, and within little more than a yard of his feet. He sat motionless for some minutes, till he had recovered his presence of mind, then eyeing his gun, moved his hand slowly towards it; the lion seeing him, raised its head, and gave a tremendous roar; he made another and another attempt, but the gun being far beyond his reach, he gave it up, as the lion seemed well aware of his object, and was enraged whenever he attempted to move his hand. His situation now became painful in the extreme; the rock on which he sat became so hot that he could scarcely bear his naked feet to touch it, and kept moving them, alternately placing one above the other. The day passed, and the night also, but the lion never moved from the spot; the sun rose again, and its intense heat soon rendered his feet past feeling. At noon the lion rose and walked to the water, only a few yards distant, looking behind as it went, lest the man should move, and seeing him stretch out his hand to take his gun, turned in a rage, and was on the point of springing upon him. The animal went to the water, drank, and returning, lay down again at the edge of the rock. Another night passed; the man, in describing it, said, he knew not whether he slept, but if he did, it must have been with his eyes open, for he always saw the lion at his feet. Next day, in the forenoon, the animal went again to the water, and while there, he listened to some noise apparently from an opposite quarter, and disappeared in the bushes. The man now made another effort, and seized his gun; but on attempting to rise, he fell, his ankles being without power. With his gun in his hand, he crept towards the water, and drank; but looking at his feet, he saw, as he expressed it, his "toes roasted," and the skin torn off with the grass. There he sat a few moments, expecting the lion's return, when he was resolved to send the contents of the gun through its head; but as it did not appear, tying his gun to his back, the poor man made the best of his way on his hands and knees, to the nearest path, hoping some solitary individual might pass. He could go no farther, when, providentially, a person came up, who took him to a place of safety, from whence he obtained help, though he lost his toes, and was a cripple for life.

The preceding lion stories, selected from many more, will serve for the present to illustrate something of the character of that noble, but dangerous creature.

Here is another from Moffat, of quite as curious though rather of the opposite and a more grotesque nature.

As to his being afraid of the human eye, I shall touch on that subject in another part of my work, when I describe those which have tasted human flesh, for which they ever afterwards retain an uncommon relish. With all their boldness, they are sometimes arrant cowards. On one occasion, I remember a man who, coming unexpectedly on a lion, fainted. The lion raised himself to look over the bushes, and seeing no one, seemed to suspect a plot, and scampered off with his tail between his legs. It is but justice to add, that the man was no less cowardly; for, on awaking from his swoon, and looking this way and that, he imagined the object of his terror was still there, and taking to his heels, he made towards the wagon. I have known Bushmen, and even women, drive the lion away from the prey he has just seized, by beating their clubs on dry hides, and shouting; nevertheless, by day, and especially by night, he is an object of terror.

Here is yet another, from a Missionary of South Africa, which is analogous. It is from a narrative of a visit to the Mauritius and South Africa, by James Backhouse.

A Bushman residing near the Orange river, in the direction of Hardcastle Kloof, was hunting with some companions, and observing a considerable number of vultures soaring in the air, he concluded that some animal had been accidentally killed, of which he might possibly obtain a share; he therefore left his companions and repaired to the spot, where he found a hartebeest lying, off which he drove a number of these birds. On doing this, a lion, which he supposed had killed the hartebeest and satisfied its hunger, came from behind a neighboring bush and growled at him.

Petrified with fear, the Bushman stood perfectly still. The lion walked round him, so close as to brush him with its tail, uttering at the same time a low growl; it went to a short distance and sat down, looking at the Bushman, who kept his eye upon it and drew back a few paces; but when he drew back the lion advanced, he therefore stood quite still till the lion retired a little and lay down. The Bushman seized the opportunity, picked up a few straws of dried grass and began to try to strike a light; but as soon as the lion heard the tapping of the flint and steel, it rose again and walked around the Bushman, brushing him as before; again the Bushman was still, and again the lion retired. The Bushman once more plied his flint and steel, and again the lion advanced from his retreat. At this moment the Bushman succeeded in obtaining a light, but such was his terror that, forgetting himself, he continued blowing at it till it scorched his face. The lion made a stand when he saw the flame, and as this increased when the burning grass was dropped into a dry bush, the lion fled. The Bushman, who had been thus detained from noon to sunset, lost no time, when the lion was sufficiently far gone, in also making his retreat; he said he had never run so fast before, and when he reached his companions he was pale and sick with fright.

These missionary stories most strikingly illustrate that mysterious power over "the beasts of the field" which is undoubtedly exercised by all beings, even though they be degraded Hottentots, who chance to bear the "upturned countenance" which was stamped upon the human race as a "sign of dominion." Cumming gives a still more extraordinary relation of an incident of the same class which happened to himself. Although this has generally been set down as an apocryphal anecdote, yet I am, from my own experience of animals, if not for many other reasons, disposed to believe it a real incident, and therefore give it as he tells it literally.

Ruyter came towards me, and I ran forward to obtain a view beyond a slight rise in the ground to see whither the lioness had gone. In so doing I came suddenly upon them, within about seventy yards; they were standing looking back at Ruyter. I then very rashly commenced making a rapid stalk in upon them, and fired at the nearest, having only one shot in my rifle. The ball told loudly, and the lioness at which I had fired wheeled right round, and came on lashing her tail, showing her teeth, and making that horrid, murderous deep growl which an angry lion generally utters. At the same moment, her comrade, who seemed better to know that she was in the presence of man, made a hasty retreat into the reeds. The instant the lioness came on, I stood up to my full height, holding my rifle, and my arms extended, and high above my head. This checked her in her course; but on looking round and missing her comrade, and observing Ruyter slowly advancing, she was still more exasperated, and, fancying that she was being surrounded, she made another forward movement, growling terribly. This was a moment of great danger, I felt that my only chance of safety was extreme steadiness; so, standing motionless as a rock, with my eyes firmly fixed upon her, I called out in a clear, commanding voice, "Holloa! old girl, what's the hurry? take it easy; holloa! holloa!" She instantly once more halted, and seemed perplexed, looking round for her comrade. I then thought it prudent to beat a retreat, which I very slowly did, talking to the lioness all the time. She seemed undecided as to her future movements, and was gazing after me and snuffing the ground when I last beheld her.

But here we have another adventure of his with a lioness, too, in which he does not prove altogether so successful in "running his face" upon the roused lady of the wastes.

Suddenly I observed a number of vultures seated on the plain about a quarter of a mile ahead of us, and close beside them stood a huge lioness, consuming a blesbok which she had killed. She was assisted in her repast by about a dozen jackals, which were feasting along with her in the most friendly and confidential manner. Directing my followers' attention to the spot, I remarked, "I see the lion;" to which they replied, "Whar? whar? Yah! Almagtag! dat is he;" and instantly reining in their steeds and wheeling about, they pressed their heels to their horses' sides, and were preparing to betake themselves to flight. I asked them what they were going to do. To which they answered, "We have not yet placed caps on our rifles." This was true; but while this short conversation was passing, the lioness had observed us. Raising her full, round face, she overhauled us for a few seconds, and then set off at a smart canter towards a range of mountains some miles to the northward; the whole troop of jackals also started off in another direction; there was, therefore, no time to think of caps. The first move was to bring her to bay, and not a second was to be lost. Spurring my good and lively steed, and shouting to my men to follow, I flew across the plain, and, being fortunately mounted on Colesburg, the flower of my stud, I gained upon her at every stride. This was to me a joyful moment, and I at once made up my mind that she or I must die.

The lioness having had a long start of me, we went over a considerable extent of ground before I came up with her. She was a large, full-grown beast, and the bare and level nature of the plain added to her imposing appearance. Finding that I gained upon her, she reduced her pace from a canter to a trot, carrying her tail stuck out behind her, and slewed a little to one side. I shouted loudly to her to halt, as I wished to speak with her, upon which she suddenly pulled up, and sat on her haunches like a dog, with her back towards me, not even deigning to look round. She then appeared to say to herself, "Does this fellow know who he is after?" Having thus sat for half a minute, as if involved in thought, she sprang to her feet, and, facing about, stood looking at me for a few seconds, moving her tail slowly from side to side, showing her teeth, and growling fiercely. She next made a short run forward, making a loud, rumbling noise like thunder. This she did to intimidate me; but, finding that I did not flinch an inch nor seem to heed her hostile demonstrations, she quietly stretched out her massive arms, and lay down on the grass. My Hottentots now coming up, we all three dismounted, and, drawing our rifles from their holsters, we looked to see if the powder was up in the nipples, and put on our caps. While this was doing the lioness sat up, and showed evident symptoms of uneasiness. She looked first at us, and then behind her, as if to see if the coast were clear; after which she made a short run towards us, uttering her deep-drawn, murderous growls. Having secured the three horses to one another by their rheims, we led them on as if we intended to pass her, in the hope of obtaining a broadside. But this she carefully avoided to expose, presenting only her full front. I had given Stofolus my Moore rifle, with orders to shoot her if she should spring upon me, but on no account to fire before me. Kleinboy was to stand ready to hand me my Purdey rifle, in case the two-grooved Dixon should not prove sufficient. My men as yet had been steady, but they were in a precious stew, their faces having assumed a ghastly paleness, and I had a painful feeling that I could place no reliance on them.

Now, then, for it, neck or nothing! She is within sixty yards of us, and she keeps advancing. We turned the horses' tails to her. I knelt on one side, and, taking a steady aim at her breast, let fly. The ball cracked loudly on her tawny hide, and crippled her in the shoulder, upon which she charged with an appalling roar, and in the twinkling of an eye she was in the midst of us. At this moment Stofolus's rifle exploded in his hand, and Kleinboy, whom I had ordered to stand ready by me, danced about like a duck in a gale of wind. The lioness sprang upon Colesburg, and fearfully lacerated his ribs and haunches with her horrid teeth and claws; the worst wound was on his haunch, which exhibited a sickening, yawning gash, more than twelve inches long, almost laying bare the very bone. I was very cool and steady, and did not feel in the least degree nervous, having fortunately great confidence in my own shooting; but I must confess, when the whole affair was over, I felt that it was a very awful situation, and attended with extreme peril, as I had no friend with me on whom I could rely.

When the lioness sprang on Colesburg, I stood out from the horses, ready with my second barrel for the first chance she should give me of a clear shot. This she quickly did; for, seemingly satisfied with the revenge she had now taken, she quitted Colesburg, and, slewing her tail to one side, trotted sulkily past within a few paces of me, taking one step to the left. I pitched my rifle to my shoulder, and in another second the lioness was stretched on the plain a lifeless corpse. In the struggles of death she half turned on her back, and stretched her neck and fore arms convulsively, when she fell back to her former position; her mighty arms hung powerless by her side, her lower jaw fell, blood streamed from her mouth, and she expired. At the moment I fired my second shot, Stofolus, who hardly knew whether he was alive or dead, allowed the three horses to escape. These galloped frantically across the plain, on which he and Kleinboy instantly started after them, leaving me standing alone and unarmed within a few paces of the lioness, which they, from their anxiety to be out of the way, evidently considered quite capable of doing further mischief.

Such is ever the case with these worthies, and with nearly all the natives of South Africa. No reliance can be placed on them. They will to a certainty forsake their master in the most dastardly manner in the hour of peril, and leave him in the lurch. A stranger, however, hearing these fellows recounting their own gallant adventures, when sitting in the evening along with their comrades round a blazing fire, or under the influence of their adored "Cape smoke" or native brandy, might fancy them to be the bravest of the brave. Having skinned the lioness and cut off her head, we placed her trophies upon Beauty and held for camp. Before we had proceeded a hundred yards from the carcass, upwards of sixty vultures, whom the lioness had often fed, were feasting on her remains.

These tawny ladies appear to have a temper of their own, in common with the sex generally; indeed, it appears to be the united testimony of travellers, that the lioness is most apt to be aggressively dangerous when she has cubs; while the attacks of the lion are only to be greatly dreaded when wounded, while he stands on the defensive. Harris, however, exhibits the monarch in one of those grand and terrible outbursts of apparently causeless wrath, to which he, in common with the elephant and all the larger beasts, seem to be subject, both in their native wilds and in confinement. Here is his story.

Peeping out, however, to ascertain if there was any prospect of its clearing up, we perceived three lions squatted within a hundred yards, in the open plain, attentively watching the oxen. Our rifles were hastily seized, but the dampness of the atmosphere prevented their exploding. One after another, too, the Hottentots sprang out of the pack wagon, and snapped their guns at the unwelcome intruders, as they trotted sulkily away, and took up their position on a stony eminence at no great distance. Fresh caps and priming were applied, and a broadside was followed by the instantaneous demise of the largest, whose cranium was perforated by two bullets at the same instant. Swinging their tails over their backs, the two survivors took warning by the fate of their companion, and dashed into the thicket with a roar. In another half hour the voice of *Leo* was again heard at the foot of the mountains, about a quarter of a mile from the camp; and from the wagon top we could perceive a savage monster rampant, with his tail hoisted and whirling in a circle, charging furiously along the base of the range, and in desperate wrath, making towards John April, who was tending the sheep. Every one instinctively grasped his weapon, and rushed to the rescue, calling loudly to warn the expected victim of his danger. Without taking the smallest notice of him, however, the infuriated monster dashed past, roaring and lashing his sides, until concealed in the mist. Those who have seen the savage monarch of the forest, in crippled captivity only, immured in a cage barely double his own length, with his sinews relaxed by confinement, have seen but the shadow of that animal which "clears the desert with his rolling eye."

This is by far the noblest picture of the king of brutes in all the magnificence of his freedom, and terror of his might and wrath, that I remember in the whole range of this species of literature. The simple grandeur of the recital is in most unfavorable contrast with a rather sputtering attempt, on the part of Cumming, to "do up the sublime," in his description of a rencontre with the dreaded "man-eater lion," which carried off one of his men at night from the midst of his camp, and was next day slain by him. There is such huge overstraining of epithetical horrors on the part of the narrator of an event, sufficiently hideous in itself, that I decline inserting it here—but shall quote instead from the gallant Missionary, Moffat, a much more modest and comprehensible account of an incident something parallel, which will at least convey a most clear idea of what the appetite of a lion is, as well as something of the dangers from them to be encountered by the traveller in South Africa.

Having put my wagon in order, taken a driver, and a little boy as leader of the oxen, and two Barolongs, who were going to the same place, I left the station, my wife and family, for an absence of two or three months. Our journey lay over a wild and dreary country, inhabited by Balalas only, and but a sprinkling of these. On the night of the third day's journey, having halted at a pool, (Khokhole), we listened, on the lonely plain, for the sound of an inhabitant, but all was silent. We could discover no lights, and, amid the darkness, were unable to trace footmarks to the pool. We let loose our wearied oxen to drink and graze, but as we were ignorant of the character of the company with which we might have to spend the night, we took a firebrand, and examined the edges of the pool to see, from the imprints, what animals were in the habit of drinking there, and, with terror, discovered many spoors of lions. We immediately collected the oxen, and brought them to the wagon, to which we fastened them with the strongest thongs we had, having discovered in their appearance something rather wild, indicating that either from scent or sight, they knew danger was near. The two Barolongs had brought a young cow with them, and though I recommended their making her fast also, they very humorously replied that she was too wise to leave the wagon and oxen, even though a lion should be scented. We took a little supper, which was followed by our evening hymn, and prayer. I had retired only a few minutes to my wagon to prepare for the night, when the whole of the oxen started to their feet.

A lion had seized the cow only a few steps from their tails, and dragged it to the distance of thirty or forty yards, where we distinctly heard it tearing the animal, and breaking the bones, while its bellowings were most pitiful. When these were over, I seized my gun, but as it was too dark to see any object at half the distance, I aimed at the spot where the devouring jaws of the lion were heard. I fired again and again, to which he replied with tremendous roars, at the same time making a rush towards the wagon, so as exceedingly to terrify the oxen. The two Barolongs engaged to take firebrands, advance a few yards, and throw them at him, so as to afford me a degree of light, that I might take aim, the place being bushy. They had scarcely discharged them from their hands, when the flame went out, and the enraged animal rushed towards them with such swiftness, that I had barely time to turn the gun and fire between the men and the lion, and providentially the ball struck the ground immediately under his head, as we found by examination the following morning. From this surprise he returned, growling dreadfully. The men darted through some thorn-bushes with countenances indicative of the utmost terror. It was now the opinion of all that we had better let him alone if he did not molest us.

Having but a scanty supply of wood to keep up a fire, one man crept among the bushes on one side of the pool, while I proceeded for the same purpose on the other side. I had not gone far, when, looking upward to the edge of the small basin, I discerned between me and the sky four animals, whose attention appeared to be directed to me, by the noise I made in breaking a dry stick. On closer inspection, I found that the large, round, hairy-headed visiters were lions; and retreated on my hands and feet towards the other side of the pool, when coming to my wagon-driver, to inform him of our danger, I found him looking, with no little alarm, in an opposite direction, and with good reason, as no fewer than two lions, with a cub, were eyeing us both, apparently as uncertain about us as we were distrustful of them. They appeared, as they always do in the dark, twice the usual size. We thankfully decamped to the wagon, and sat down to keep alive our scanty fire, while we listened to the lion tearing and devouring his prey. When any of the other hungry lions dared to approach, he would pursue them for some paces, with a horrible howl, which made our poor oxen tremble, and produced any thing but agreeable sensations in ourselves. We had reason for alarm, lest any of the six lions we saw, fearless of our small fire, might rush in among us. The two Barolongs were grudging the lion his fat meal, and would now and then break the silence with a deep sigh, and expressions of regret that such a vagabond lion should have such a feast on their cow, which they anticipated would have afforded them many a draught of luscious milk. Before the day dawned, having deposited nearly the whole of the carcass in his stomach, he collected the head, back bone, parts of the legs, the paunch, which he emptied of its contents, and the two clubs which had been thrown at him, and walked off, leaving nothing but some fragments of bones, and one of my balls, which had hit the carcass instead of himself.

When it was light we examined the spot, and found, from the foot-marks, that the lion was a large one, and had devoured the cow himself. I had some difficulty in believing this, but was fully convinced by the Barolongs pointing out to me that the foot-marks of the other lions had not come within thirty yards of the spot, two jackals only had approached to lick up any little leavings. The men pursued the spoor to find the fragments, where the lion had deposited them, while he retired to a thicket to sleep during the day. I had often heard how much a large, hungry lion would eat, but nothing less than a demonstration would have convinced me that it was possible for him to have eaten all the flesh of a good heifer, and many of the bones, for scarcely a rib was left, and even some of the marrow bones were broke as if with a hammer.

After this, I think the curiosity of few would carry them so far as to desire to test the appetite of a hungry South African lion under any circumstances, where "proxy" could not conveniently be substituted as in this case, with the poor cow. Here I will take leave of the South African lion with the remark, that with all the grandeur of his roarings, his strength, and his appetite, he is on the whole a most pusillanimous sneak; and in consistent ferocity, is not near so much to be dreaded, or so formidable, indeed, as our Grisly Bear, which is not only fully his equal in strength, but surpasses him in courage altogether.

CHAPTER XXVIII.

THE RHINOCEROS AND HIPPOPOTAMUS.

Our African adventurers plume themselves evidently upon having out-Heroded the Herods of all previous Romance of Hunting—in having capped the climax of dashing extravagance, by combatting both behemoth and the unicorn in their own meadows and beneath forests as hoar as their renown. It certainly constitutes a very striking element of true romance—this picture of two young men penetrating the most ancient solitudes of earth, to battle, single-handed, with these sole representatives of monsters before the Flood, whose huge remains now fill the generations with such awe!

Verily the rifle has brought us back to the antediluvian prowess of that period, concerning which it is recorded, as I have before remarked,—"and there were giants in those days!"

Cumming, in his off-hand way, thus introduces us to the unicorn.

Of the rhinoceros there are four varieties in South Africa, distinguished by the Bechuanas by the names of the borèlé, or black rhinoceros, the keitloa, or two-horned black rhinoceros, the muchocho, or common white rhinoceros, and the kobaoba, or long-horned white rhinoceros. Both varieties of the black rhinoceros are extremely fierce and dangerous, and rush headlong and unprovoked at any object which attracts their attention. They never attain much fat, and their flesh is tough, and not much esteemed by the Bechuanas. Their food consists almost entirely of the thorny branches of the wait-a-bit thorns. Their horns are much shorter than those of the other varieties, seldom exceeding eighteen inches in length. They are finely polished with constant rubbing against the trees. The skull is remarkably formed, its most striking feature being the tremendous thick ossification in which it ends above the nostrils. It is on this mass that the horn is supported. The horns are not connected with the skull, being attached merely by the skin, and they may thus be separated from the head by means of a sharp knife. They are hard and perfectly solid throughout, and are a fine material for various articles, such as drinking-cups, mallets for rifles, handles for turner's tools, &c. &c. The horn is capable of a very high polish. The eyes of the rhinoceros are small and sparkling, and do not readily observe the hunter, provided he keeps to leeward of them. The skin is extremely thick, and only to be penetrated by bullets hardened with solder. During the day the rhinoceros will be found lying asleep or standing indolently in some retired part of the forest, or under the base of the mountains, sheltered from the power of the sun by some friendly grove of umbrella-topped mimosas. In the evening they commence their nightly ramble, and wander over a great extent of country. They usually visit the fountains between the hours of nine and twelve o'clock at night, and it is on these occasions that they may be most successfully hunted, and with the least danger. The black rhinoceros is subject to paroxysms of unprovoked fury, often ploughing up the ground for several yards with its horn, and assaulting large bushes in the most violent manner. On these bushes they work for hours with their horns, at the same time snorting and blowing loudly, nor do they leave them in general until they have broken them into pieces. The rhinoceros is supposed by many, and by myself among the rest, to be the animal alluded to by Job, chap. xxxix., verses 10 and 11, where it is written, "Canst thou bind the unicorn with his band in the furrow? or will he harrow the valleys after thee? Wilt thou trust him because his strength is great? or wilt thou leave thy labor to him?" evidently alluding to an animal possessed of great strength and of untameable disposition, for both of which the rhinoceros is remarkable. All the four varieties delight to roll and wallow in mud, with which their rugged hides are generally incrusted. Both varieties of the black rhinoceros are much smaller and more active than the white, and are so swift that a horse with a rider on his back can rarely overtake them. The two varieties of the white rhinoceros are so similar in habits, that the description of one will serve for both, the principal difference consisting in the length and set of the anterior horn; that of the muchocho averaging from two to three feet in length, and pointing backwards, while the horn of the kobaoba often exceeds four feet in length, and inclines forward from the nose at an angle of forty-five degrees. The posterior horn of either species seldom exceeds six or seven inches in length. The kobaoba is the rarer of the two, and it is found very far in the interior, chiefly to the eastward of the Limpopo. Its horns are very valuable for loading rods, supplying a substance at once suitable for a sporting implement and excellent for the purpose. Both these varieties of rhinoceros attain an enormous size, being the animals next in magnitude to the elephant. They feed solely on grass, carry much fat, and their flesh is excellent, being preferable to beef. They are of a much milder and more inoffensive disposition than the black rhinoceros, rarely charging their pursuer. Their speed is very inferior to that of the other varieties, and a person well mounted can overtake and shoot them. The head of these is a foot longer than that of the borèlé. They generally carry their heads low, whereas the borèlé, when disturbed, carries his very high, which imparts to him a saucy and independent air. Unlike the elephants, they never associate in herds, but are met with singly or in pairs. In districts where they are abundant, from three to six may be found in company, and I once saw upward of a dozen congregated together on some young grass, but such an occurrence is rare.

Here, too, is his first introduction to the unicorn.

Shortly after this I found myself on the banks of the stream beside which my wagons were outspanned. Following along its margin, I presently beheld a bull of the borèlé, or black rhinoceros, standing within a hundred yards of me. Dismounting from my horse, I secured him to a tree, and then stalked within twenty yards of the huge beast, under cover of a large, strong bush. Borèlé, hearing me advance, came on to see what it was, and suddenly protruded his horny nose within twenty yards of me. Knowing well that a front shot would not prove deadly, I sprang to my feet and ran behind the bush. Upon this the villain charged, blowing loudly, and chased me round the bush. Had his activity been equal to his ugliness, my wanderings would have terminated here, but by my superior agility I had the advantage in the turn. After standing a short time, eyeing me through the bush, he got a whiff of my wind, which at once alarmed him. Uttering a blowing noise, and erecting his insignificant yet saucy-looking tail, he wheeled about, leaving me master of the field, when I sent a bullet through his ribs, to teach him manners.

But the most extraordinary fact connected with the history of the rhinoceros comes under the observation of Cumming immediately after this incident. It is thus introduced:—

On the forenoon of the 23d a native came and informed me that he had discovered a white rhinoceros lying asleep in a thick cover to the south. I accordingly accompanied him to the spot, and commenced stalking in upon the vast muchocho. He was lying asleep beneath a shady tree, and his appearance reminded me of an enormous hog, which in shape he slightly resembles. He kept constantly flapping his ears, which they invariably do when sleeping. Before I could reach the proper distance to fire, several "rhinoceros birds," by which he was attended, warned him of his impending danger by sticking their bills into his ear, and uttering their harsh, grating cry. Thus aroused, he suddenly sprang to his feet and crashed away through the jungle at a rapid trot, and I saw no more of him.

These rhinoceros birds are constant attendants upon the hippopotamus and the four varieties of rhinoceros, their object being to feed upon the ticks and other parisitic insects that swarm upon these animals. They are of a grayish color, and are nearly as large as a common thrush; their voice is very similar to that of the mistletoe thrush. Many a time have these ever-watchful birds disappointed me in my stalk, and tempted me to invoke an anathema upon their devoted heads. They are the best friends the rhinoceros has, and rarely fail to awaken him even in his soundest nap. "Chukuroo" perfectly understands their warning, and, springing to his feet, he generally first looks about him in every direction, after which he invariably makes off. I have often hunted a rhinoceros on horseback, which led me a chase of many miles, and required a number of shots before he fell, during which chase several of these birds remained by the rhinoceros to the last. They reminded me of mariners on the deck of some bark sailing on the ocean, for they perched along his back and sides; and as each of my bullets told on the shoulder of the rhinoceros, they ascended about six feet into the air, uttering their harsh cry of alarm, and then resumed their position. It sometimes happened that the lower branches of trees, under which the rhinoceros passed, swept them from their living deck, but they always recovered their former station; they also adhere to the rhinoceros during the night. I have often shot these animals at midnight, when drinking at the fountains, and the birds, imagining they were asleep, remained with them till morning, and on my approaching, before taking flight, they exerted them selves to their utmost to awaken Chukuroo from his deep sleep.

This account of the bird guardians of the rhinoceros, though apparently extravagant, is not without many correspondencies throughout the natural world. We have among us a familiar instance in the habits of the cow-pen bird. Audubon says, concerning it:

This species derives its name from the circumstance of its frequenting cow-pens. In this respect it greatly resembles the European starling. Like that bird it follows the cattle in the fields, often alights on their backs, and may be seen diligently searching for worms and larvæ among their dung. In spring, the cattle in many parts of the United States are much infested with intestinal worms, which they pass in great quantities, and on these the cow-bird frequently makes a delicious repast.

Of the abundance of the rhinoceros in the upper part of

the valley of the Limpopo, Harris gives us the following graphic sketch:

The country now literally presented the appearance of a menagerie; the host of rhinoceroses in particular that daily exhibited themselves, almost exceeding belief. Whilst the camp was being formed, an ugly head might be seen protruded from every bush, and the possession of the ground was often stoutly disputed. In the field, these animals lost no opportunity of making themselves obnoxious—frequently charging at my elbow, when in the act of drawing the trigger at some object—and pursuing our horses with indefatigable and ludicrous industry, carrrying their noses close to the ground, moving with a mincing gait, which ill-beseemed so ungainly and ponderous a quadruped, and uttering the while, a sound between a grunt and a smothered whistle. In removing the horn with an axe, the brain was discovered seated in a cavity below it, at the very extremity of the snout—a phenomenon in the idiosyncracy of this animal, which may in some measure account for its want of intelligence and piggish obstinacy, as well as for the extraordinary acuteness of smell with which it is endowed. Irrascible beyond all other quadrupeds, the African rhinoceros appears subject even to unprovoked paroxysms of reckless fury; but the sphere of vision is so exceedingly limited, that its attacks, though sudden and impetuous, are easily eluded, and a shot behind the shoulder, discharged from the distance of twenty or thirty yards, generally proves fatal.

On our way from the wagons to a hill, not half a mile distant, we counted no less than twenty-two of the white species of rhinoceros, and were compelled in self-defence to slaughter four. On another occasion, I was besieged in a bush by three at once, and had no little difficulty in beating off the assailants.

But we will dismiss this fierce, grotesque, and ridiculous animal, with the following striking remark from Moffat, which exhibits its prodigious strength in a more formidable light than any thing else we have yet heard of it. He says, speaking of the black rhinoceros:

They fear no enemy but man, and are fearless of him when wounded and pursued. The lion flies before them like a cat; the mohohu, the largest species, has been known even to kill the elephant, by thrusting his horn into his ribs.

But Harris's account of behemoth is too graphic to be omitted or amended. Here it is:

Of all the mammalia, whose portraits, drawn from ill-stuffed specimens, have been foisted upon the world, the *Behemoth* has perhaps been the most ludicrously misrepresented. I sought in vain for the colossal head—for those cavern-like jaws, garnished with elephantine tusks—or those ponderous feet with which "the formidable and ferocious quadruped" is wont "to trample down whole fields of corn during a single night." Defenceless and inoffensive, his shapeless carcass is but feebly supported upon short and disproportioned legs, and his belly almost trailing upon the ground, he may not inaptly be likened to an overgrown "prize pig." The color is pinkish brown, clouded and freckled with a darker tint. Of many that we shot, the largest measured less than five feet at the shoulder; and the reality falling so lamentably short of the monstrous conception I had formed, the "river horse" or "sea cow," was the first, and indeed the only South African quadruped in which I felt disappointed.

Our next movement brought us to the source of the Oori or Limpopo—the gareep of Moselekatse's dominions. Led by many fine streams from the Cashan range, this enchanting river springs into existence as if by magic; and rolling its deep and tranquil waters between tiers of weeping willows, through a passage in the mountain barrier, takes its course to the northward. Here we enjoyed the novel diversion of hippopotamus shooting, that animal abounding in the Limpopo; and dividing the empire with its amphibious neighbor, the crocodile. Throughout the night, the unwieldy monsters might be heard snorting and blowing during their aquatic gambols, and we not unfrequently detected them in the act of sallying from their reed-grown coverts to graze by light of the moon; never, however, venturing to any distance from the river, the strong-hold to which they betake themselves on the smallest alarm. Occasionally during the day they were to be seen basking on the shore amid oose and mud, but shots were more constantly to be had at their uncouth heads when protruded from the water to draw breath, and if killed, the body rose to the surface. Vulnerable only behind the ear, however, or in the eye, which is placed in a prominence so as to resemble the garret window in a dutch house, they require the perfection of rifle practice, and after a few shots, become exceedingly shy, exhibiting the snout only, and as instantly withdrawing it. The flesh is delicious, resembling pork in flavor, and abounding in fat, which in the colony is deservedly esteemed the greatest of delicacies. The hide is upward of an inch and a half in thickness, and being scarcely flexible may be drawn from the ribs in strips, like the planks from a ship's side. Of these are manufactured a superior description of *jambok*, the elastic whip already noticed as being an indispensable piece of furniture to every boor proceeding on a journey. Our followers encumbered the wagons with a large investment of them, and of the canine teeth, the ivory of which is extremely profitable.

It is truly surprising how completely a little cool common sense will sometimes strip a favorite marvel of all prodigious attributes. The thing was never more completely done than by Harris in this instance. Being a clever artist himself, he took sketches of the animal on the spot; which fully confirm his words, if they were not equally strengthened by other travellers in the same region. But Mr. Cumming, however, has chosen to dissent from him after a fashion so peculiarly his own, that I cannot, among other reasons, resist giving it for the contrast between the mental habitudes of the two men it affords. While Harris is simply content with giving a clear and effective delineation of what he sees, Cumming is so egregiously beset with the mania for the pro-di-gi-ous and for the amplification of his own deeds, that it is evident if he had chanced to have seriously encountered "rats" during his "five years in South Africa," they would have been nothing short of mammoth rats — or colossal at the very least. He had come upon a herd of fourteen hippopotami, several of which he had already wounded and lost, having made his first shot at one which temporarily escaped. He says of it—

The one I had first shot was now resting with half her body above water on a sand-bank in the Limpopo. From this resting-place I started her with one shot in the shoulder and another in the side of the head; this last shot set her in motion once more, and she commenced struggling in the water in the most extraordinary manner, disappearing for a few seconds, and then coming up like a great whale, setting the whole river in an uproar. Presently she took away down the stream, holding to the other side; but, again returning, I finished her with a shot in the middle of the forehead. This proved a most magnificent specimen of the female of the wondrous hippopotamus, an animal with which I was extremely surprised and delighted. She far surpassed the brightest conceptions I had formed of her, being a larger, a more lively, and in every way a more interesting animal that certain writers had led me to expect.

The "certain writers" alluded to so significantly, must include our friend Harris, who so clearly differs with the enthusiastic elephant-hunter in his admiring appreciation of the sprightly graces of the sea-cow. It is always a pity when doctors disagree, but it rather seems like adding insult to injury on the part of Cumming, when he first steals from his master Harris, and then snubs him.

CHAPTER XXIX.

BUFFALO AND ANTELOPES OF SOUTH AFRICA.

After treating of Behemoth, I suppose buffalo and antelopes must be classed as small game, although the Buffalo is represented as a larger animal than our Bison, and the Eland, which is classed as an antelope, "not unfrequently attains the height of nineteen hands, and weighing two thousand pounds!" Tolerable specimens these of small game for any country! but we have to admit that all things are comparative, and where the giraffe of nineteen feet is the standard in height and the elephant of bulk, the processes *in dimuendo* must necessarily be slow.

This South African is undoubtedly the true Buffalo, and is in some respects individually a more formidable animal than that known by the same name upon our plains. Harris speaks of a specimen of the African buffalo slain by him, standing sixteen hands and a half at the shoulder; his ponderous horns, measuring four feet from tip to tip, liko a mass of rock, overshadowing his small, sinister, gray eyes, imparting a cunning gloom and vindictive expression to its head, which was of such weight that *one* powerful man could with difficulty lift it into the wagon; Cumming, however, surpasses him, as usual, since it required the utmost strength of *two* men to lift the head of a similar monster he slew! He says—

I ordered the Bechuanas to release the dogs; and spurring Colesberg, which I rode for the first time since the affair with the lioness, I gave chase. The buffaloes crossed the valley in front of me, and made for a succession of dense thickets in the hills to the northward. As they crossed the valley, by riding hard I obtained a broadside shot at the last bull, and fired both barrels into him. He, however, continued his course, but I presently separated him, along with two other bulls, from the troop. My rifle being a two-grooved, which is hard to load, I was unable to do so on horseback, and followed with it empty, in the hope of bringing them to bay. In passing through a grove of thorny trees I lost sight of the wounded buffalo; he had turned short and doubled back, a common practice with them when wounded. After following the other two at a hard gallop for about two miles, I was riding within five yards of their huge broad sterns. They exhaled a strong bovine smell, which came hot in my face. I expected every minute that they would come to bay, and give me time to load; but this they did not seem disposed to do. At length, finding I had the speed of them, I increased my pace; and going ahead, I placed myself right before the finest bull, thus expecting to force him to stand at bay; upon which he instantly charged me with a low roar, very similar to the voice of a lion. Colesberg neatly avoided the charge, and the bull resumed his northward course. We now entered on rocky ground, and the forest became more dense as we proceeded. The buffaloes were evidently making for some strong retreat. I, however, managed with much difficulty to hold them in view, following, as best I could, through thorny thickets. Isaac rode some hundreds yards behind, and kept shouting to me to drop the pursuit, or I should be killed. At last the buffaloes suddenly pulled up, and stood at bay in a thicket within twenty yards of me. Springing from my horse, I hastily loaded my two-grooved rifle, which I had scarcely completed when Isaac rode up and inquired what had become of the buffaloes, little dreaming that they were standing within twenty yards of him. I answered by pointing my rifle across his horse's nose, and letting fly sharp right and left at the two buffaloes. A headlong charge, accompanied by a muffled roar, was the result. In an instant I was round a clump of tangled thorn trees; but Isaac, by the violence of his efforts to get his horse in motion, lost his balance, and at the same instant, his girths giving way, himself, his saddle, and big Dutch rifle, all came to the ground together, with a heavy crash, right in the path of the infuriated buffaloes. Two of the dogs, which had fortunately that moment joined us, met them in their charge, and, by diverting their attention, probably saved Isaac from instant destruction. The buffaloes now took up another position in an adjoining thicket. They were both badly wounded, blotches and pools of blood marking the ground where they had stood. The dogs rendered me assistance by taking up their attention, and in a few minutes these two noble bulls breathed their last beneath the shade of a mimosa grove. Each of them, in dying, repeatedly uttered a very striking, low, deep moan. This I subsequently ascertained the buffalo invariably utters when in the act of expiring.

On going up to them, I was astonished to behold their size and powerful appearance. Their horns reminded me of the rugged trunk of an oak tree. Each horn was upward of a foot in breadth at the base, and together they effectually protected the skull with a massive and impenetrable shield. The horns, descending, and spreading out horizontally, completely overshadowed the animal's eyes, imparting to him a look the most ferocious and sinister that can be imagined.

This conveys to us a striking picture of the power and prowess of the individual animal, but; although these gentlemen are, with perhaps pardonable exaggeration, constantly using the term "vast," in reference to the herds of buffalo encountered by them in these regions, yet I am compelled to classify this use of a word so significant along with that they uniformly make of *forest*, which after all means in reality, according to their own showing, nothing more than what we term "bushy woodlands"—being groves of mimosa bushes or shrubs, eighteen or nineteen feet in height, on the *tops* of which the giraffe is represented as browsing. It sounds about as droll to a backwoodsman's ears to hear these shrubs called forest trees, as it would to hear a herd of three thousand buffaloes called "vast," when armies of hundreds of thousands, or even millions, are by no means considered either extraordinary or unusual on our plains. Things are comparative in more ways than one; and although the African buffalo may stand higher on its legs than our bison, the bulk is certainly not greater. And as for the petty herds in which it moves, expressing anything of that indescribable grandeur with which the American animal is poured along in countless shaggy legions over trembling plains, the very idea of comparison is like that of a mill-tail to Niagara; or the dangers of shooting cowardly lions, helpless sea-cows, peaceful elephants and harmless giraffes, amidst the stupid, poorly armed, half-monkey tribes of Africa, accompanied by huge wains, lumbered with the luxuries of wines, cigars, tea, coffee and bread,—with the perils to be faced by the wild border hunter of America!

Mounted on his mustang, with the occasional luxury of a pack mule and coffee and sugar for the first week out, the Borderer will traverse thousands of miles alone, armed with rifle and knife, through desert regions, scoured by the fiercest, most cruel, the best mounted Nomads in the world, whom he must baffle wile with wile and force by force—will meet, single-handed, the terrible Grisly Bear that knows no panic, and cannot be turned aside when roused, even by fire—or cross, unscathed, the thundering track of myriad Bisons; and think himself very lucky, if, at the end of a year or two, after having eaten up his saddle skirts and made soup of his moccasins some half dozen times—he gets back to a trading post or settlement, and can obtain a taste once more of a "corn dodger," and a little "bald-face" or "old rye!"

These are what we call *Hunters* in America, and such are the comparative conditions of suffering and *danger* in the life here and in South Africa! yet Harris, on his return from his South African Expedition, with great simplicity, enumerates it among his other hardships, that he had lived for four or five months upon *nothing* but the monotonous round of tea, coffee, brandy, bread and meat!!!!

Our Hunters and Hunter-Naturalists do not withal consider themselves heroes by any means—and would laugh at you for the supposition; such things are too much matters of course with them. Yet I do not the less respect the manly and dashing achievements of these British South African adventurers, nor hesitate to deny to them in their fine zeal for "specimens," the true and hardy spirit of the Hunter-Naturalist. I would insist, nevertheless, upon having it understood, as before hinted, that some things are comparative as well as others. With one more short picture from Harris, I am done with the buffalo. He says—while on the Limpopo—

Wild buffaloes, too, might often be seen from the wagons. Riding up a narrow defile, flanked by steep banks, I one morning found myself suddenly confronted with the van of a vast troop of these formidable animals, which were ascending from the opposite side—their malevolent gray eyes scowling beneath a threatening brow. Unable to turn, they must have charged over me, had my horse not contrived to scramble up the bank; from the top of which I fired both barrels into the leader, a ponderous bull, whose appearance stamped him father of the herd. Falling on his knees, the patriarch was instantly trampled under foot by his followers as they charged, bellowing, in close squadrons down the declivity, with the fury of a passing whirlwind, and making the woods re-echo to the clatter of their hoofs.

But the only South African animal which at all approximates in its habits the prodigious migratory movements of our bison, is a beautiful antelope of the smaller species, alled by the Dutch Boers the Springbok. Cumming thus describes his first sight of the migrations of the springbok—

A person anxious to kill many springboks might have bagged thirty or forty that morning. I never, in all my subsequent career, fell in with so dense a herd of antelopes, nor found them allow me to ride so near them. Having inspanned, we proceeded with the wagons to take up the fallen game. Vast and surprising as was the herd of springboks which I had that morning witnessed, it was infinitely supassed by what I beheld on the march from my vley to old Sweir's camp; for, on our clearing the low range of hills through which the springboks had been pouring, I beheld the boundless plains, and even the hill sides which stretched away on every side of me, thickly covered, not with "herds," but with "one vast herd" of springboks; far as the eye could strain the landscape was alive with them, until they softened down into a red mass of living creatures.

To endeavor to form any idea of the amount of antelopes which I that day beheld, were vain; but I have, nevertheless, no hesitation in stating that some hundreds of thousands of springboks were that morning within the compass of my vision. Old Sweirs acknowledged that it was a very fair "trek-bokken," but observed that it was not many when compared with what he had seen. "You, this morning," he remarked, "behold only one flat covered with springboks, but I give you my word that I have ridden a long day's journey over a succession of flats covered with them, as far as I could see, as thick as sheep standing in a fold."

My limits press upon me so, that, with regret, I take leave of the antelopes, the most brilliant and interesting of the groups of African game, with a parting glimpse of the magnificent riches of the great valley of the Limpopo, in strange, grotesque and lovely forms.

Here may be seen the graceful pallah, shy and capricious, with knotted and excentrically inflected horns of extraordinary proportions; the rare and majestic water-buck, which is never found at a distance from rivers, in which he delights to plunge; the sluggish roan antelope of the elevated downs and ridges, charging viciously, when unable to continue its flight, with its heavy build and size equaling that of a large horse. Here too, is found the majestic koo-doo, with its brilliant colors of lively French gray, approaching to blue; with transverse white bands over the back and loins;

The grotesque and awkward gnoo wheels and prances in every direction, his shaggy and bearded head arched between slender and muscular legs; his long, white tail streaming to the wind; his wild, sinister eyes flashing fire, and his frequent snort, like the roar of a lion. The sassayby, with his crescent horns, drooping hind quarters and brilliant colors, purple and violet, and the hartebeest of bright orange, and legs excentrically marked; the splendid oryx, with its sweeping tail, reversed mane, shaggy breast and straight, slender horns; the beautiful zebra, with the more faintly banded quagga, and the riet-buck of the sedge-grown rivulets; the prodigious eland, fat always like a prize ox, and nearly as large; and most glorious of all, the swift and rare sable antelope, with its scimetar-shaped horns and snowy breast, flying along the mountain ridges.

These are but a few of the twenty different varieties of the antelope, in which this veritable Paradise of the Feræ Naturæ abounds, and most of those here enumerated are frequently in view in one landscape, which will yet be diversified by the presence of the larger beasts we have spoken of before. Verily is the life of the Hunter-Naturalist filled with "Wild Scenes!"

www.ingramcontent.com/pod-product-compliance
Lightning Source LLC
LaVergne TN
LVHW021106110826
845150LV00001B/182